KRISHNAMURTI

THE YEARS
OF
AWAKENING

Other Volumes in the Krishnamurti Biography
by Mary Lutyens
From Avon Books

KRISHNAMURTI: THE OPEN DOOR
KRISHNAMURTI: THE YEARS OF FULFILLMENT

by J. Krishnamurti

TALKS AND DIALOGUES

KRISHNAMURTI

THE YEARS
OF
AWAKENING

MARY LUTYENS

AVON BOOKS ◆ NEW YORK

AVON BOOKS
A division of
The Hearst Corporation
105 Madison Avenue
New York, New York 10016

Copyright © 1975 by Mary Lutyens
Published by arrangement with Farrar, Straus and Giroux, Inc.
Library of Congress Catalog Card Number: 75-17840
ISBN: 0-380-71113-3

First Avon Books Trade Printing: February 1991
First Avon Books Mass Market Printing: September 1976

AVON TRADEMARK REG. U.S. PAT. OFF. AND IN OTHER COUNTRIES, MARCA REGISTRADA,
HECHO EN U.S.A.

Printed in the U.S.A.

OPM   10 9 8 7 6 5 4 3 2 1

Contents

Foreword

This account of the first thirty-eight years of Krishna-murti's life has been written at his suggestion and with all the help he has been able to give me. Nevertheless I have been left free to tell his story in my own way; no one has looked over my shoulder and neither Krishnamurti nor anyone close to him has asked, or been asked, to approve the text. It is a very personal account, recording his strange uprbringing and the many phases he went through in growing to maturity—his difficulties, doubts, unhappiness, personal relationships and spiritual awakening, which was followed by years of intense physical suffering. Above all, it shows the circumstances of the unfolding of Krishnamurti's teaching and demonstrates his extraordinary achievement in freeing himself from the many hands that clutched at him in an endeavor to force him into the role of traditional Messiah.

Krishnamurti first asked Mr. B. Shiva Rao, who was for many years a member of the Indian Parliament and who has known him longer than anyone else alive, to write this book. Mr. Shiva Rao undertook the assignment and collected and arranged a great deal of documentation. Serious eye trouble, however, prevented him from creating a book out of his material. I then agreed to write it, and Mr. Shiva Rao, who has been a close friend of mine for fifty years, most generously handed over to me all his documentation. Hardly a month has gone by for the past two years when he has not sent me from India answers to the many questions with which I have plied him. I cannot believe that two authors have ever had a happier collaboration.

My qualifications for taking on the work are that I have known Krishnamurti since 1911, when I was three, that from 1922 to 1929 I shared many of the experiences here recounted and that for the last three of those years I played a part in his life. Although for many years thereafter I saw very little of him, absence has never diminished our friendship.

This book is no doubt a more intimate record than Mr. Shiva Rao would have written, though we have always been in agreement as to how to tell Krishnamurti's story —to let it unfold itself as far as possible in the words of the chief characters. As it is a very strange story, at times an almost incredible one, its genuine flavor would, we felt, be lost were it to be told as straight narrative, With the presentation of contemporary letters and documents the reader will now be in possession of all the facts. This method has the special advantage of not allowing personal friendship to intrude or distort. I appear in the story as one of the many characters, and what that character thought and felt is taken from diaries written at the time.

Mr. Shiva Rao and I also agreed that after 1933, when Krishnamurti's own teaching came into flower, the book could not be written in the same way, for since then his life has been chiefly in his work. It is not the intention in this volume to paraphrase or interpret his present teaching. I can only draw the reader's attention to his many books published since 1954, by Gollancz in England and Harper & Row in America.

My regret is that there is no scope here to portray the quality that Mrs. Besant must undoubtedly have possessed to inspire as she did such devotion in thousands of people all over the world. Loyalty was perhaps her most outstanding characteristic and it was a clash of loyalties that darkened the last years of her life and makes her appear here more as a dupe than as a force in her own right. Krishnamurti's love for her, which comes out so clearly in his letters, must be the best tribute to her at that time in her life when she had relinquished her own psychic powers and come to rely on the powers of others whom she trusted. As for the integrity of C. W. Leadbeater, the person she trusted most in all occult matters, I have not been able to make up my mind, although in 1925 I spent nine months in his community in Sydney in daily contact with him. I then believed implicitly in his clairvoyance; I do not *dis*believe in it today. An extraordinary man, a man of charm and magnetism and with an apparent sincerity it was hard to doubt, to me he remains an enigma.

Adepts or Masters, and such highly evolved spiritual en-
tities as the Bodhisattva, the Lord Maitreya, the Ma-
chachohan and others, are found in all religious cultures
where Hinduism and Buddhism have spread. The mean-
ings given to them and the particular functions attributed
to them vary from one culture to another. In the present
work their names have the meaning bestowed on them by
Theosophists. The visual descriptions of these beings,
however, and the wholesale creation of Initiates and lower
grade pupils on the Path of Discipleship, belong to that
era when C. W. Leadbeater had the greatest occult influence on the Theosophical Society. I should make it clear
that the Theosophy on which Krishnamurti was brought
up was this "Leadbeater Theosophy" which is, I understand, very largely discredited by Theosophists today, although there is still an Esoteric Section of the Society.

In not mentioning by name all Krishnamurti's many
friends who worked for him so devotedly during the
period covered by this book no slight is intended. I have
felt obliged to confine myself to naming those about whom
he wrote in his letters or who had some influence on the
course of his development.

Birth and Childhood

Jiddu Krishnamurti was born on May 11, 1895, in the small hilltown of Madanapalle about a hundred and fifty miles north of Madras. As the eighth child who happened to be born a boy he was, in accordance with Hindu orthodoxy, called after Sri Krishna who had himself been an eighth child. The Jiddu family were Telugu-speaking Brahmins, a Brahmin being the highest caste. Krishnamurti's great-grandfather had held a responsible position under the East India Company and been an eminent Sanskrit scholar; his grandfather had also been a very learned man and a Civil Servant, while his father, Jiddu Narianiah, after graduating from Madras University, became an official in the Revenue Department of the British administration, rising by the end of his career to the position of Tashildar (rent collector) and District Magistrate. The family were not, therefore, poor by Indian standards.

Narianiah had married his second cousin, Jiddu Sanjeevamma, who bore him eleven children, only six of whom survived childhood. It seems to have been a very happy marriage. Narianiah described his wife as having a very beautiful melodious voice and liking to sing to him. Indian life in those days was primitive and the caste system rigidly adhered to. An open drain to carry all water used for household purposes ran beside the house where Krishnamurti was born; it was cleaned by the sweepers, the "untouchables," who belonged to no caste at all. The sweepers were not allowed into the house except to collect sewage, and, in a Brahmin household, no food would be prepared, cooked or served by a non-Brahmin; moreover, in South India the cook would invariably be a South Indian Brahmin since the South Indians were such strict vegetarians that even the eating of eggs was forbidden by their caste rules. There was nothing to prevent a poor Brahmin from taking a domestic job in a Brahmin household, though he

would not, of course, undertake any of the tasks performed by the sweepers or lower castes. The castes did not
intermarry and no one could change his caste except in a
future life. Europeans were on a par with "untouchables."
Sanjeevamma would throw the food away if so much as
the shadow of a European fell across it, and if an Englishman entered the house on official business, the rooms he
had been in were scoured and the children put into clean
clothes. Such was the environment into which Krishnamurti was born.

Sanjeevamma had a premonition that this eighth child
of hers was to be in some way remarkable and she insisted
that the baby should be born in the *puja* room on the
ground floor, a special room set aside for prayers in orthodox Hindu households. Narianiah gave way to her whim
although the *puja* room was not normally entered at night
after food or in the morning before washing.

Only a cousin with experience as a midwife was present
at the birth which, unlike Sanjeevamma's other con-
finements, was quick and easy. Narianiah sat in the next
room with his watch in his hand. At half past midnight the
door of the *puju* room was opened a crack for the cousin
to whisper "Sirasodayam," meaning in Sanskrit "the head
is visible." This for Hindus is the precise moment of birth,
essential for astrological calculations. As in Hindu astrol-
ogy the day is reckoned from 4 a.m. to 4 a.m., Krishna
was born on May 11, whereas by Western reckoning he
would have been born at 12:30 a.m. on the 12th.

The baby's horoscope was cast next day by Kumara
Shrowtulu, one of the most renowned astrologers of that
region. He was able to assure Narianiah that his son was
to be a very great man indeed. For many years it seemed
most unlikely that this prediction would be fulfilled.
Whenever the astrologer met Narianiah he would ask,
"What of the boy Krishna?" Narianiah's reply was evidently never very hopeful for the astrologer would again
assure the disappointed father, "Wait. I have told you the
truth; he will be somebody very wonderful and great."

In November 1896 Narianiah was transferred to
Cudappah, a much larger town and one of the worst in
the district for malaria. The following year, a very bad
famine year, the two-year-old Krishna had malaria so
badly that for some days he was not expected to live and,
although Narianiah was transferred again in 1900 to the

healthier town of Kadiri, Krishna was for many years at-
tacked by periodic bouts of the fever, and he also suffered
a great deal from nose bleeding.

At Kadiri, when he was six, Krishna, like all Brahmin
boys at the start of their education, went through the
sacred thread ceremony, or *Upanyanam*. This ceremony
marks their entrance into *Brahmacharya*, meaning that
they take on the responsibilities of Brahminhood, for every
Brahmin boy is born a priest. Narianiah described this important occasion:

It is our custom to make it a family festival, and
friends and relations were invited to dinner. When all
the people were assembled, the boy was bathed and
clothed in everything new—very rich clothes are used
if the parents can afford them. Krishna was brought
in and placed upon my knee, while on my stretched
hand I supported a silver tray strewn with grains of
rice. His mother, sitting beside me, then took the in-
dex finger of the boy's right hand, and with it traced
in the rice the sacred word, AUM, which in its Sanskrit rendering, consists of a single letter, the letter
which is, in sound, the first letter of the alphabet in
Sanskrit and in all the vernaculars. Then my ring was
taken from my finger, and placed between the child's
finger and thumb, and my wife, holding the little
hand, again traced the sacred word in Telugu characters with the ring. Then again without the ring, the
same letter was traced three times. After this, mantrams were recited by the officiating priest, who
blessed the boy, that he might be spiritually and intellectually endowed. Then, taking Krishna with us, my
wife and I drove to the Narasimhaswami temple to
worship and pray for the future success of our son.
From there we drove to the nearest Indian school,
where Krishna was handed over to the teacher, who,
in sand, performed the same ceremony of tracing the
sacred word. Meanwhile, many of the friends of the
schoolchildren had gathered in the room, and we dis-
tributed among them such good things as might serve
as a treat to the pupils. So we started our son in his
educational career according to the ancient Brahmin
custom.

Krishna's little brother, Nityananda, just three years younger, would run after him when he went to school, longing to go too. Nitya was as sharp as Krishna was vague and dreamy; nevertheless there was a very close bond between these brothers. Krishna would often return home from school at Kadiri without a pencil, slate or book, having given them to some poorer boy. In the mornings beggars would come to the house when it was the custom to pour a certain quantity of unboiled rice into each outstretched hand. Krishna's mother would send him out to distribute the rice and he would come back for more, saying that he had poured it all into the first man's bag. In the evening when Narianiah sat with his friends on the veranda after returning from the office, beggars would come again for cooked food. This time the servants would try to drive them away but Krishna ran inside to fetch food for them, and when Sanjeevamma made a special treat of sweetmeats for the children, Krishna would take only part of his share and give the rest to his brothers; all the same Nitya would ask for more which Krishna never failed to give him.

Every evening while they were at Kadiri, Krishna and Nitya would accompany their mother to the large Narasimhaswami temple, celebrated for its sanctity. Krishna always showed a religious vein. He also, surprisingly, had a mechanical turn of mind. One day, when his father was away, he took his father's clock to pieces and refused to go to school or even to eat until he had put it together again. These two rather contradictory strains in his nature, as well as his generosity, have persisted throughout his life.

Narianiah's frequent transfers as well as Krishna's bouts of fever interrupted the boy's schooling (for one whole year he was unable to go to school at all), so that in lessons he fell far behind other boys of his age. Moreover, he hated book learning and was so dreamy as to appear at times mentally retarded. Nevertheless he was keenly observant when his interest was aroused. He would stand for long stretches at a time watching trees and clouds, or squat on the ground gazing at plants and insects. This close observation of nature is another characteristic that he has retained.

In 1903 the family, after three quick transfers, were back at malaria-ridden Cudappah where the following

year Krishna's eldest sister died. Narianiah recorded that
his wife "was heartbroken at our daughter's death, a girl
of only twenty years, highly spiritual, who cared for nothing that the world could give her." It was soon after her
death that Krishna showed for the first time that he was
clairvoyant. In a memoir of his childhood, written when
he was eighteen, he says that his mother "was to a certain
extent psychic" and would often see her dead daughter:

> They talked together and there was a special place
> in the garden to which my sister used to come. My
> mother always knew when my sister was there and
> sometimes took me with her to the place, and would
> ask me whether I saw my sister too. At first I laughed
> at the question, but she asked me to look again and
> then sometimes I saw my sister. Afterwards I could
> always see my sister. I must confess I was very much
> afraid, because I had seen her dead and her body
> burnt. I generally rushed to my mother's side and she
> told me there was no reason to be afraid. I was the
> only member of my family, except my mother, to see
> these visions, though all believed in them. My mother
> was able to see the auras of people, and I also some-
> times saw them.

In December 1905, when Krishna was ten and a half
and the family were still at Cudappah, the worst blow of
all fell on them—Sanjeevamma herself died. Krishna
wrote in this same memoir:

> The happiest memories of my childhood center
> round my dear mother who gave us all the loving
> care for which Indian mothers are well known. I can-
> not say I was particularly happy at school, for the
> teachers were not very kind and gave me lessons that
> were too hard for me. I enjoyed games as long as
> they were not too rough, as I had very delicate
> health. My mother's death in 1905 deprived my
> brothers and myself of the one who loved and cared
> for us most, and my father was too much occupied to
> pay much attention to us ... there was really nobody
> to look after us. In connection with my mother's
> death, I may mention that I frequently saw her after
> she died. I remember once following my mother's

form as it went upstairs. I stretched out my hand and seemed to catch hold of her dress, but she vanished as soon as she reached the top of the stairs. Until a short time ago, I used to hear my mother following me as I went to school. I remember this particularly because I heard the sound of bangles which Indian women wear on their wrists. At first I would look back half frightened, and I saw the vague form of her dress and part of her face. This happened almost always when I went out of the house.

Narianiah confirmed that Krishna saw his dead mother:

We are in the habit of putting on a leaf, a portion of the food prepared for the household, and placing it near the spot where the deceased was lying, and we did so accordingly in the case of my wife. Between 9 and 10 a.m. of the third day, Krishna was going to have his bath. He went into the bathroom, and had only poured a few lotas of water over his head, when he came running out, unclothed [though wearing a loin cloth] and dripping wet. The house in which I lived at Cudappah was a long, narrow house, the rooms running one at the back of the other like the compartments of a train. As Krishna passed me running from the bathroom, I caught his hand and asked him what was the matter. The boy said his mother had been in the bathroom with him, and as she came out he accompanied her to see what she was going to do. I then said: "Don't you remember that your mother was carried to the burning ground?" "Yes," he said, "I remember, but I want to see where she is going now." I let him go and followed him. He went to the third room and stopped. Here was the place where my wife's saris used to be stretched for drying overnight. Krishna stood intently gazing at something, and I asked him what was going on. He said, "My mother is removing her wet clothes, and putting on dry ones." He then went into the next room, and sat down near the leaf on which the food was placed. I stood by him some minutes, and he said his mother was eating. By and by he arose and went towards the stairs, and still I followed him. He stopped half-way up, and said he couldn't see her any more. Then we sat down together and I questioned him as to how she looked, and whether she spoke to him. He said she looked just as usual, and had not spoken to him.

After his wife's death Narianiah took a few months' leave and returned to Madanapalle for the sake of the children's health; when he resumed service again he was able to remain there until his retirement. Krishna and Nitya were both admitted on January 17, 1907, to the High School at Madanapalle which they attended until January 1909.

About two miles from their house was a lonely hill with a temple on the top and Krishna liked to go up there every day after school. None of the other boys wanted to accompany him, as it was a stiff climb over stony ground, but he would often insist on taking Nitya with him. He also liked taking his friends on picnics. As his father was now a District Magistrate, a position of some importance, Krishna's brothers considered it beneath their dignity to carry the food to the picnic spot; Krishna, who had no such feelings of self-importance, would take the food from the servants and carry it himself.

Narianiah, though an orthodox Brahmin, had been a member of the Theosophical Society since 1881 (Theosophy embraces all religions) and Sanjeevamma had evidently been sympathetic to his ideas, for Krishna recalled that as he was kept so much at home with fever during childhood while his brothers were at school, he often went into her *puja* room about noon when she would be performing her daily ceremonies, and she would then talk to him about Mrs. Annie Besant, one of the leaders of Theosophy who was greatly beloved in India because of the work she had done for Indian education. He also remembered that as well as pictures of the Hindu deities on the walls, there was a photograph of Mrs. Besant in Indian dress sitting cross-legged on a *chowki* covered with a tiger skin.

When Narianiah retired at the end of 1907 at the age of fifty-two on a pension of only Rs. 112 a month, half his former salary, he wrote to Mrs. Besant, who was now President of the Theosophical Society, to offer his "wholehearted and full time service" in any capacity in exchange for free accommodation for himself and his sons in the Compound of the international Headquarters of the Society at Adyar near Madras. He told Mrs. Besant that while in Government service he had been in charge of 800 square miles containing 160 villages, and felt he would be able to manage a fairly large estate. He pointed out that he was a widower with four sons, varying in age from fifteen to five, and that as his only daughter was married there was no one but himself to look after the boys. It was Krishna's eldest brother, Sivaram, who was fifteen. The boy of five, Sadanand, five years younger than Nitya, was mentally deficient.

Mrs. Besant turned down his offer on the grounds that there was no school at Adyar nearer than three miles; this would involve the expense of sending the children there in a pony cart, and, anyway, boys would be a disturbing influence in the Compound. Narianiah, undaunted, appealed to her three more times in the next few months. By good luck one of the secretaries of the Society felt in need of an assistant at the end of 1908 and suggested Narianiah for the post. After meeting him at the Theosophical Convention in December, Mrs. Besant at last agreed to accept his services, and on January 23, 1909, he moved to Adyar with his four sons and a nephew. Sivaram joined the Presidency College in Madras in preparation for a medical career, while Krishna, Nitya and their cousin went to the Pennathur Subramanian High School at Mylapore, walking the three miles there and back every day. Little Sadanand was neither physically nor mentally well enough to go to school at all.

As there was no house available inside the Compound, the family lived just outside it in a dilapidated cottage with no indoor sanitation. Narianiah's sister, who had quarrelled with her husband, came to stay with them at first to do the cooking and housekeeping, but she seems to have been a slovenly woman and a very bad cook. The boys arrived at Adyar in shocking physical condition. Great credit should be given to Narianiah for his persistence, for if he had not succeeded in getting to Adyar it is very doubtful whether any of his sons would have reached maturity.

2

The Leadbeater Scandal

At the time Narianiah went to live at Adyar, the Theosophical Society estate already comprised some 260 acres on the south side of the wide Adyar river, just south of Madras, with a mile of river frontage and half a mile of private beach. The Headquarters building, standing on the bank of the river and consisting of library, Convention hall, shrine-room, offices, guest rooms and suites of rooms for the leaders of the Society, is virtually unchanged today. A path leading from it direct to the sea still passes through a coconut grove, and then under the arches of Adyar's famous banyan tree, the second largest in India, to come out at the wide stretch of sandy beach where the river flows into the Bay of Bengal. In the perfect winter climate there can be few places in the world more beautiful than Adyar.

The Headquarters building was once a modest Anglo-Indian house called Huddlestone's Gardens flanked by two octagonal pavilions. This, together with twenty-seven acres of land, was bought for £600 in 1882 by the first President of the Society, Colonel Olcott. Gradually, adjoining properties were acquired, new houses built and old ones re-built to accommodate the growing number of Theosophical residents and visitors. These houses and properties, together with a printing press, communal Hindu kitchen and a small farm, were incorporated into one great compound. Huddlestone's Gardens itself has been so altered and enlarged that nothing can be discerned of the original house but the two pavilions.

After Mrs. Besant became President in 1907, members of the Society were encouraged to build themselves houses to occupy whenever they visited Adyar, on the understanding that in their absence she could dispose of the accommodation as she chose, and that on their deaths the buildings became the property of the Society.

The Theosophical Society had been founded in America in 1875 by Colonel Henry Steel Olcott, a veteran of the Civil War who was interested in spiritualism and mesmerism, and Madame Helena Petrovna Blavatsky, the notorious Russian, considered by her enemies to be a complete fraud, and worshipped by her adherents as a seer and miracle-worker whose occult powers derived from the highest spiritual source. The Society had three objects: 1. To form a nucleus of the Universal Brotherhood of Humanity without distinction of race, creed, sex, caste or color; 2. To encourage the study of Comparative Religion, Philosophy and Science; 3. To investigate the unexplained laws of nature and the powers latent in man. The headquarters of the Society was moved in 1882 from America to the more spiritual climate of India, and from there Theosophy rapidly spread throughout the world.

Olcott, who was forty-three when the Society was founded, was its President, but it was Madame Blavatsky, a year older, who was the inspiration for its Eastern or esoteric heart, culled from the ancient wisdom of several religions—virtually a society within the Society, the great difference being that whereas members of the public were encouraged to join the outer organization, only Theosophists of two years' standing could apply for membership of the Esoteric Section and were not accepted unless they had done some work for the Society. (Narianiah was a member of the E.S., as it was called, and it was as assistant to the Recording Secretary of the E.S. that he had been allowed to come to Adyar.)

Inherent in this inner teaching was a belief in evolution through a series of lives to ultimate perfection, when the ego, the soul, is released from the wheel of karma, that inexorable law by which it reaps what it sows both of good and evil from life to life. At a certain stage in evolution, the ego is ready to enter on the Path of Discipleship which will lead eventually to Adepthood and membership of the Great White Brotherhood of perfect beings who govern and direct the world. A few of these Adepts (Masters or Mahatmas as they were called) voluntarily chose to remain in human form in order to help the evolution of those just entering on the Path. The two Masters who had taken the Theosophical Society under their special protection, the Master Morya and the Master Kuthumi, lived in Tibet. They still retained the bodies of their last incarnation, though being untouched by sorrow or care they had lived to a very great age and appeared always in the prime of life. These bodies, however, were too sensitive to withstand the impact of living in the everyday world.

The Master Kuthumi wore the body of a Kashmiri Brahmin and was as fair complexioned as any European, with blue eyes, brown hair and beard, whereas the Master Morya, his close friend and companion, a magnificent horseman, was a Rajput king in a dark handsome Indian body with black hair and flashing black eyes. Madame Blavatsky, before she founded the Theosophical Society, had lived for some time in a monastery in Nepal and claimed to have met these Masters frequently in their human forms. But it was not necessary to go physically to Tibet to see them; they could be visited on the astral plane by their earthly pupils, or materialize themselves in their etheric forms to those privileged enough to see them, passing through locked doors like ghosts. Colonel Olcott, after meeting Madame Blavatsky, developed his psychic powers and thereafter he, like his colleague, was sometimes visited by the Masters as well as meeting them frequently on the astral plane in their Tibetan homes.

Above the Masters came a hierarchy of glorious beings, one of whom is inseparable from any account of Krishnamurti's early life. This was the Lord Maitreya, the World Teacher—the Christ in the West, the Bodhisattva in the East, not to be confused with the Buddha who, according to Theosophists, was a still higher entity. The Lord Maitreya, they maintained, had twice taken possession of a human body in order to bring to the world a new teaching at a period of dire need—first that of Sri Krishna in the fourth century B.C. and then that of Jesus. The time would soon be ripe when the Lord Maitreya would once again take posssesion of a human vehicle and give a new religion to the world. In the meantime, he too lived in the Himalayas, in a house with a wonderful garden, quite close to the Masters Morya and Kuthumi, in a body of the Keltic race with red-gold hair and beard, and violet eyes. The human body he would choose when the time came would have to be sufficiently sensitive for him to be able to function through it, yet not so sensitive as the body he used in Tibet which could not have survived for long in the noise and stress of a town.

As early as 1889 Madame Blavatsky had told a group

of Theosophical students that the real purpose of establishing the Society was to prepare humanity for the reception of the World Teacher when he appeared again on earth, and this was repeated more publicly by Mrs. Besant in 1896, five years after Madame Blavatsky's death. Theosophists also believed that each time a great religious teacher appeared it was to usher in a new sub-race. This time it was to be the sixth sub-race of the fifth root-race that was to develop in Australia. (Later the cradle of this sub-race was changed to California.) In 1909, at a public lecture in Chicago on her favorite theme "The Coming Race and the Coming Teacher," Mrs. Besant announced: "We look for Him to come in the Western world this time—not in the East as did Christ two thousand years ago." Indeed the Western vehicle had already been chosen in the person of a very good-looking and intelligent boy of thirteen, Hubert van Hook, son of Dr. Weller van Hook of Chicago, the General Secretary of the Theosophical Society in the United States. This boy had been picked out by Mrs. Besant's closest colleague, C. W. Leadbeater, while on a lecture tour of America a few years before, and brought to Europe for a time where Mrs. Besant had met him; when she saw him again in Chicago in 1909 she too was so struck by him that she prevailed on his mother to leave her husband and bring the boy to Europe and India for special training for his marvellous destiny. Meanwhile, unknown to Mrs. Besant, Leadbeater had already chosen another vehicle for the Lord Maitreya, and Hubert was soon to be dropped.

Charles Webster Leadbeater, C.W.L. as he was often called, had been born in the same year as Mrs. Besant, 1847, but had come to Theosophy five years sooner. Little is known of his early life except that as a boy he went to Brazil, where his father was a railway contractor, and led a life of adventure in the course of which his father died and his younger brother Gerald was murdered in 1862 by bandits. After returning to England he entered Oxford University but soon had to leave when in 1866 the bank failed in which all the family money was invested. Nevertheless he managed to take Holy Orders in 1878 and became curate of St. Mary's, Bramshott, in Hampshire. His inborn interest in occultism was stimulated by the books of A. P. Sinnett, particularly *The Occult World*, one of the leaders of Theosophy in England, and in 1883 he joined the Society. A year later he was introduced by Sinnett to Madame Blavatsky and immediately asked to become her pupil. When she accepted him he gave up the church, became a vegetarian, severed all ties with England and followed her to India. He claimed that she entirely changed his character in seven weeks. A very shy man, one of the first tasks she set him as a challenge during the voyage to India was to carry a full chamber pot along the main passenger deck in broad daylight. He declared that never again did he care what anybody thought of him, a true statement so far as one can judge.

Leadbeater remained in the far East, first at Adyar and then in Ceylon, for the next five years. At Adyar he developed his psychic powers, and in Ceylon, having become a Buddhist on his first arrival in the East, he taught in a school for poor Buddhist boys founded by Colonel Olcott under the aegis of the T.S. In 1887 Mr. Sinnett, who still considered Leadbeater to be his protégé, asked him to return to England to tutor his son and another boy, George Arundale, the nephew and adopted son of Miss Francesca Arundale, one of the many rich ladies who were attracted to Theosophy. George Arundale was to play a considerable part in Krishna's early life.

Leadbeater agreed to Sinnett's request on condition that he might bring with him to be educated in England one of his Singalese pupils, C. Jinarajadasa, whom he believed to be a reincarnation of his murdered brother. The year before Leadbeater's return to England Mrs. Besant had been converted to Theosophy when she was asked to review for the *Pall Mall Gazette* the two massive volumes of Madame Blavatsky's *The Secret Doctrine*; she afterwards met the author and, like Leadbeater, fell instantly under her spell. In 1890 Mrs. Besant and Leadbeater were brought together for the first time at a Theosophical meeting in London, and after the death of Madame Blavatsky the following year, he became the greatest human influence in Mrs. Besant's life.

Annie Besant, née Wood, had already had a tempestuous career by the time she was converted to Theosophy. Married at twenty to a Church of England clergyman, Frank Besant, brother of Sir Walter Besant, she separated from him six years later, in 1873, although it meant parting with her son; having ceased to believe in the divinity of Christ, her conscience would not allow her to take the Sacrament.

In 1876 her daughter was also legally taken from her after a long court battle in which she conducted her own defense.[1] Thereafter she continued to fight uncompromisingly for the causes she espoused and the vindication of principles she considered vital: freedom of thought and expression, women's rights, Fabian socialism, birth control, and workers' rights in the early days of the Trade Union movement. Before her conversion to Theosophy, Charles Bradlaugh, Dr. E. B. Aveling and Bernard Shaw had been her closest friends and associates, and the first two probably her lovers. (Leadbeater's resemblance to Shaw was most striking, especially in old age). Annie Besant must have been very beautiful as a young woman and all through her life she retained extraordinary charm. From the beginning of her career, both before and after her conversion, she was a prolific writer and a very powerful orator. India, where she first went in 1893, became her spiritual home; thereafter for the next forty years until her death she devoted her amazing energy and talents to India's service and to the spreading of Theosophy throughout the world. But India's freedom and progress were even dearer to her than Theosophy, and in every sphere—educational, social, religious and political—she worked for India's welfare. Courage, staying power and loyalty were her greatest qualities.

Courage, energy and magnetism were also outstanding characteristics of Leadbeater, but just as Mrs. Besant outstripped him in causes other than Theosophical so he outshone her in psychic power. In 1895 in England they had made occult investigations together into the cosmos, the beginnings of mankind, chemistry and the constitution of the elements, as well as frequently visiting the Masters together in their astral bodies. (The Master Morya was Mrs. Besant's guru, the Master Kuthumi Leadbeater's.) They found also that they were able to "see" into the past lives of some of their devoted disciples as well as into their own, and when they found how often they themselves and their friends had been in close relationships in past incarnations, they began to make charts of these past lives. It was in those years before the turn of the century that Mrs. Besant's psychic powers were at their height. Gradually she allowed them to wane as her Indian work, to which

---

[1] Both children returned to her when they came of age and both became Theosophists. After the separation she changed the pronunciation of her name from Bezánt to Běsant.

she believed she had been directed by her Master, absorbed her more and more until she came to rely almost exclusively on Leadbeater for occult communications. Although she continued to lecture in Europe and America, India became her home and she always spent the winter months there.

Leadbetter, having built up for himself a great reputation in the Society as writer, speaker, clairvoyant, and as teacher—particularly of small groups of boys—went on two long lecture tours of America and Canada between 1900 and 1904, and then on to Sydney in 1905, taking with him one of his favorite English pupils and acquiring new ones in America. The scandal in which the whole Society was soon to be embroiled could not have come as much of a surprise to him. Mrs. Besant herself had been hearing rumors for some time of immoral practices which she had indignantly denied. As far back as his curacy days there had been talk about him and some of the boys in the church choir, and it was said that Mr. Sinnett had removed his son from his care. However, none of this gossip was substantiated. Then in 1906, after Leadbeater's return to England, the fourteen-year-old son of the Corresponding Secreatry of the Esoteric Section in Chicago, whom Leadbeater had taken with him to San Francisco on the first lecture tour, confessed to his parents the reason for the antipathy he had conceived for his mentor, to whom he had at first been greatly devoted—Leadbeater had encouraged him in the habit of masturbation. Almost simultaneously the son of another Theosophical official in Chicago charged Leadbeater with the same offense without apparently there being any collusion between the two boys. Then a typewritten, unsigned, undated, cipher-letter was produced; it had been picked up by a suspicious cleaner on the floor of a flat in Toronto in which Leadbeater had stayed with the second boy and was said to have been written by Leadbeater. The code was simple and when broken revealed one passage of such obscenity, for those days, that the letter could not by law be printed in England. When decoded the offending passage read: "Glad sensation is so pleasant. Thousand kisses darling."

When Mrs. Besant in India heard all this she wrote to Leadbeater in great distress. He denied writing the incriminating letter though confessed unashamedly to having advocated masturbation as a prophylactic in certain cases, as a far lesser evil than either consorting with prostitutes or guilty obsession with erotic thoughts. He promised, however, never again to encourage the practice within the Theosophical Society, not because he did not believe in it but for Mrs. Besant's sake. She was satisfied and declared to his detractors that the letter was a forgery.

The matter was not allowed to rest there—understandably at a time when not only was homosexuality abhorrent to the general public but when it was still widely held that masturbation led to madness. A commission was appointed by the Executive Committee of the American Section of the Society and sent to London to place the matter before Colonel Olcott, the President, who had no alternative but to ask Leadbeater to appear before the Council of the British Section to answer the charges. Leadbeater was most willing to attend but before the meeting at the Grosvenor Hotel on May 16, 1906, he handed in his resignation in order, as he told Olcott, to save the Society from embarrassment. After the meeting Olcott was pressed by the Council to expel him but finally it was agreed to accept his resignation so as to avoid publicity.

It came as a terrible shock to Mrs. Besant, who had not gone to England for the hearing, to learn that Leadbeater under cross-examination had admitted that in the cases of other boys, as well as of the two under consideration, he had not only advocated the regular practice of masturbation but might have given a certain amount of "indicative action," and that he might also have advised the same practice to certain boys before the development of their sexual urges. (This last admission he denied when he saw the shorthand report and attributed it to a faulty transcription.) After an initial impulse on Mrs. Besant's part to resign from the Society out of loyalty to him, she temporarily turned against him and even began to doubt their occult experiences together. She went so far as to send out a circular to the Secretaries of the Esoteric Section throughout the world condemning his conduct and stating that she and Leadbeater had been "glamourized" for years into believing they had seen the Masters, glamour being a most pejorative word in the sense in which she used it. Mrs. Besant and Leadbeater had advanced far along the Path of Discipleship by this time, having taken each step together in the presence of the Masters, and they were now high Initiates. One of the first requirements for Initiation was absolute sexual purity; Mrs. Besant was, therefore, in a most unhappy predicament: if Leadbeater was impure he could not be an Initiate, yet if he were not an Initiate her visions of standing with him before the Masters must have been delusions.

The Theosophical Society was split over the Leadbeater scandal; the only person who remained perfectly cool and unrepentant throughout was Leadbeater himself, although after twenty-two years of working for the Society his livelihood as well as his reputation had been taken from him. In a letter of June 30, 1906, before Mrs. Besant had definitely turned against him, he tried to explain to her his point of view more precisely:

My dear Annie . . . My opinion in the matter which many think so wrong was formed long before Theosophical days. . . . There is a natural function in the man, not in itself shameful (unless indulged at another person's expense) any more than eating or drinking . . . the accumulation takes place, and discharges itself at intervals—usually a fortnight or so, but in some cases much oftener, the mind in the latter part of each interval being constantly oppressed by the matter. The idea was to take in hand before the age when it grew so strong as to be practically uncontrollable, and to set the habit of the regular, but smaller artificial discharges, with no thoughts at all in between. . . . The interval usually suggested was a week, though in some cases half that period was allowed for a time. The recommendation was always to lengthen the interval so far as was compatible with the avoidance of thoughts or desire on the subject. Of course, you will understand that this sexual side of life was not made prominent, but was taken only as one point among a large number of directions for the regulation of life. . . . So when boys came under my care I mentioned this matter to them among other things, always trying to avoid all sorts of false shame, and to make the whole appear as natural and simple as possible, though, of course, not a matter to be spoken of to others. . . . With very much love I am as ever, Yours most affectionately C. W. Leadbeater.

Six months later, after she had repudiated him, he
wrote:

> . . . you will do me justice to remember that I have
> never said a single word connecting the advice which
> I have given with any yoga practice, or claiming for
> it anything more occult than the design to keep sen-
> sual thoughts under control, and to avoid co-habita-
> tion with women. I fear that you have been somewhat
> misled here. . . . It was never my custom to arouse
> such feelings [of sex] before they existed; as I said
> to you in a previous letter, I never spoke of matters
> until I had seen certain preliminary symptoms. . . . I
> have not the very least wish to persuade you to adopt
> these opinions, but I should be thankful if I could dis-
> abuse your mind of the idea that we were decieved
> when we stood together in the presence of the Mas-
> ters, because that idea is not only in itself a mistake
> to my thinking but is causing many people to doubt
> our testimony to their existence, which is sad.

Mrs. Besant could not bear to remain estranged from
Leadbeater for long, and although she did not yet have the
power to reinstate him, her faith in him revived completely so that by February 1907 he was able to write to
her, "I cannot tell you how glad I am that the veil is at
last lifted, and the idea of glamour banished from your
mind."

After his resignation Leadbeater lived quietly for almost
three years, either in the country in England or in Jersey
with occasional visits to Europe. Although he could do no
public work for Theosophy he continued to teach privately and was helped financially by contributions from
the many friends he had retained in the Society. Most of
the boys and young men who had been in his charge
vouched for his absolute purity. Among them was Jinarajadasa, the boy he had brought with him from the school
in Ceylon in 1889. After taking a degree at Cambridge in
Sanskrit and Philology, Raja, as he was usually called, had
become a valuable lecturer for Theosophy, and while touring America soon after the scandal he so vigorously defend-
ed his old tutor that Colonel Olcott expelled him from
the Society for causing dissension. Other faithful friends in
America were the van Hooks. Mrs. van Hook showed her

confidence in Leadbeater by bringing Hubert to stay with
him near Dresden in the summer of 1907. It was then that
Mrs. Besant met Hubert for the first time. Hubert was
only eleven then. It would be two years before Mrs.
Besant was to urge his mother to take him to India to be
trained as the vehicle for the World Teacher. Mrs. Besant
and Leadbeater did more occult investigations while they
were at Dresden and looked into the past lives of more of
their friends, including Hubert's.

Meanwhile Colonel Olcott had died at Adyar in February 1907. Mrs. Besant was his natural successor as
President; not only did he wish it but he had been visited
several times on his deathbed by the Masters and instructed by them to appoint her as such. Their presence was
witnessed both by Mrs. Besant and Mrs. Marie Russak, a
rich American widow and Theosophist who had taken
charge of the Colonel when his health failed during his
last voyage from America to India. The Masters also assured the Colonel that Mrs. Besant had not been a victim
of "glamour" and that he, Olcott, had been too hard on
Leadbeater, whereupon the young man, now anxious to
reconcile Leadbeater with the Society, dictated to him a
letter of apology, though begging him to give up his advice
to boys which the Masters considered wrong because it
"offended the standard of ideas of the majority of the Society," but hinting at the same time that his help in the
work would soon be needed again.

Nevertheless, because the Society realized that once
Mrs. Besant became President, Leadbeater's reinstatement
was bound to follow, she had to fight for the succession,
particularly in America where the feeling against Leadbeater was most virulent, so it was not until June 1907
that she was elected, but then with a huge majority. Sure
enough, after a succsesful campaign on his behalf, Leadbeater was readmitted into the Society at the end of 1908
and asked to return to Adyar, though he was never again
to hold any official position in the Society. Jinarajadasa
was then also brought back into the fold.

Mrs. Besant needed Leadbeater's help badly at Adyar,
where she was now to stay longer than anywhere else during the year, but no doubt she also wished to keep an eye
on him in spite of his promise never again to advocate his
controversial teaching within the Society. At the Annual
Theosophical Convention in December, before his arrival,

she publicly referred to him as a martyr who had been wronged both by herself and by the Society, adding the assurance that never again should a shadow come between her and her brother Initiate.

3

The Discovery

Leadbeater arrived in Adyar on February 10, 1909, less than three weeks after Narianiah had settled there with Krishna and his brothers. Mrs. Besant left Adyar for other parts of India soon after Leadbeater's arrival; she returned on April 9 and was off again to Europe on the 22nd.

Leadbeater went back to live in the same pavilion, called the Octagon Bungalow or the River Bungalow, as he had occupied when he first went to Adyar with Madame Blavatsky in 1884. Consisting of two rooms with a veranda running round them, it is part of the original house and still stands on the east side of the Headquarters building. Although Leadbeater was almost sixty-two he was as active and ebullient as ever. His chief work was to be in dealing with the huge correspondence that came from all over the world. He had brought with him as secretary a young Dutchman, Johann van Manen, who lived in the room adjoining the Octagon Bungalow; he was also glad to have the help of a young Englishman, Ernest Wood, who knew shorthand and had already been for three months at Adyar working on the official monthly publication, the *Theosophist*. Wood lived in what was called the Quadrangle, the cheapest place to stay on the estate—some old outbuildings converted into twenty-one minimally furnished cells. In the room next to Wood lived a young Indian, Subrahmanyam Aiyar, who was a great friend of Narianiah. Wood had met Krishna and Nitya, and both he and Subrahmanyam were helping the boys with their homework.

It had become a habit for van Manen and Wood to break off work for an hour in the evenings to go down to the beach to bathe with a party of friends, including Subrahmanyam. Krishna and Nitya, with some of the other children who lived just outside the Compound, would also go down to the beach to paddle and watch the swimmers. One evening Leadbeater went with his young assistants to bathe and on returning to the bungalow told Wood that one of the boys on the beach had the most wonderful aura he had ever seen, without a particle of selfishness in it. Wood expressed great surprise on being told that this boy was Krishna, for having helped him with this homework he considered him to be particularly dim-witted. Leadbeater, unshaken, predicted that one day the boy would become a spiritual teacher and a great orator. "How great? As great as Mrs. Besant?" Wood asked. "Much greater," Leadbeater replied. The exact date of Leadbeater's first meeting with Krishna is uncertain but as Mrs. Besant left Adyar on April 22 without, apparently, hearing anything about it, the meeting probably did not take place until after her departure.

It could not have been Krishna's outward appearance that struck Leadbeater, for apart from his wonderful eyes, he was not at all prepossessing at that time. He was under-nourished, scrawny and dirty; his ribs showed through his skin and he had a persistent cough; his teeth were crooked and he wore his hair in the customary Brahmin fashion of South India, shaved in front to the crown and falling to below his knees in a pigtail at the back; moreover his vacant expression gave him an almost moronic look. People who had known him before he was "discovered" by Leadbeater said there was little difference between him and his youngest brother, Sadanand. Moreover, according to Wood, he was so extremely weak physically that his father declared more than once that he was bound to die.

Shortly after meeting Krishna for the first time, Leadbeater revealed to Wood that the boy was to be the vehicle for the Lord Maitreya "unless something went wrong" and that he, Leadbeater, had been directed to help train him for that purpose.

In June another young Englishman arrived at Adyar, Richard Balfour Clarke, a former engineer who hoped to find some kind of work in the Theosophical center and was quickly drawn into Leadbeater's entourage. Leadbeater repeated to him what he had already told Wood— that Krishna had a most extraordinary aura, and so to a lesser extent had his brother Nitya. Leadbeater also told Clarke that the Master Kuthumi had informed him, "There is a purpose for that family to be here, and both those boys will undergo training which you will hear more about later."

On the day Dick Clarke arrived, the residents of Adyar were present at Nitya's *Upanyanam*. (Nitya was just eleven so his *Upanyanam* took place much later than was customary. His mother's death may have been the reason for this.) Leadbeater was watching Krishna very carefully all through the ceremony and shortly afterwards he asked Narianiah if he would bring his remarkable son to his bungalow one day when there was no school. Narianiah did so. Leadbeater placed Krishna beside him on the sofa, rested his hand on the boy's head and began to describe his former life. Thereafter on Saturdays and Sundays the visits and narration of past lives continued, the lives being written down by Narianiah who was, at first, always present. Later on they were taken down by Wood in short-hand.

Krishna himself recalled:

When I first went over to his room I was much afraid, for most Indian boys are afraid of Europeans. I do not know why it is that such fear is created, but apart from the difference in color which is no doubt one of the causes, there was, when I was a boy, much political agitation and our imaginations were much stirred by the gossip about us. I must also confess that the Europeans in India are by no means generally kind to us and I used to see many acts of cruelty which made me still more bitter. It was a surprise to us, therefore, to find how different was the Englishman who was also a Theosophist.

Krishna at the time Leadbeater discovered him knew very little English so that communication between him and his new friend was at first practically non-existent, quite apart from the boy's shyness and timidity. It was equally difficult for Krishna to communicate at school where the lessons were conducted in either English or Tamil, of which he knew as little as English. So stupid did he appear at school that the teacher was constantly sending him out of the classroom and would forget all about him until he called some other boy stupid, whereupon Krishna would be remembered and brought back. He was caned almost every day for being unable to learn his lessons. Half his

time at school was spent in tears on the veranda; when the
teacher failed to call him back he might have remained on
the veranda all night if bright little Nitya had not taken
his hand and led him home.

Leadbeater did not tell Mrs. Besant at once about his
new discovery; it was not until September 2 that he wrote
expressing to her his consternation at the overcrowded and
insanitary conditions of the "hovel" in which Narianiah
was living, with a pariah village close up against it at the
back. There was no water closet, and the family all slept
on the floor without mosquito nets. Leadbeater suggested
that they should be moved into a house in the Compound,
a hundred yards from the Headquarters building, which
was standing empty though in need of some repair. He
added that Narianiah's children were very quiet and well
behaved and would cause no trouble; he and van Manen
were teaching them to swim and had helped "the elder"
with English composition and reading so he had "come to
know a little of them." He went on to say that he had
used "one of the boys" as a case to investigate past lives
and had found him to have a past of very great importance—"a better set of lives even than Hubert though I
think not as sensational." He was sure, he continued, that
the boy was not there by accident:

> I should not be at all surprised to find that the fa-
> ther had been brought here chiefly on account of that
> boy; and that was another reason why I was shocked
> to see the family so vilely housed, for it seems to me
> that if we are to have the karma of assisting even in-
> directly in the bringing up of one whom the Master
> has used in the past and is waiting to use again, we
> may at least give him the chance to grow up de-
> cently!

The name given to the boy throughout his successive
lives was Alcyone, pronounced with a hard c. Leadbeater
wrote enthusiastically to Mrs. Besant about his investigations into these lives which were now occupying nearly all
his time, and sent her batches of them to read while she
was still abroad; but it was not until October 6 that he informed her: "Alcyone is at present a boy of 13½, named
Krishnamurti, the son of your E.S. Assistant sec. Narianiah." Krishna was in fact fourteen and a half but for

some years Leadbeater and everyone else believed him to have been born in 1896, for his horoscope did not come to light until later.

By November, Leadbeater had investigated twenty lives and had worked out another ten by the following year. These thirty *Lives of Alcyone* began to appear in the *Theosophist* in April 1910 under the title "Rents in the Veil of Time." They ranged from 22,662 B.C. to A.D. 624, each one with a larger *dramatis personae*. Alcyone was a female in eleven of them. Mrs. Besant appeared in them throughout under the pseudonym of Heracles, Leadbeater as Sirius, Nitya as Mizar, Krishna's mother as Omega and his father as Antares; Hubert van Hook was Orion. Many other people were brought into the "Lives" under a pseudonym and this gave rise to a great deal of heart-burning and snobbery when once they were published. "Are you in the Lives?" became the question most constantly asked by one Theosophist of another, and, if so, "How closely related have you been to Alcyone?"

Shiva Rao, who had been a very young master at the preparatory school attached to the Central Hindu College at Benares and who went to Adyar to help Leadbeater write out the charts comprising some two hundred characters, all related to each other throughout thirty incarnations, believed then, and still believes, in Leadbeater's clairvoyant powers.

The tabulation of the various lives with the many thousands of details of the family connections revealed to me the meticulous care that must have characterized the clairvoyant investigations [Shiva Rao has recently stated]. Of positive evidence of their genuineness obviously there could be none: but the ability to trace with comparatively few errors the family ties of such a large group of souls through life after life amidst a maze of details struck me as so far beyond anyone's mental resources, however prodigious might be his memory, as to rule out invention. Every few days I came across a discrepancy and made a note of it. When I had three or four of such instances, I would bring them to Leadbeater's notice. He would then close his eyes for some minutes and say, "You are right; substitute B for A, Y for X etc."

The revisions suggested by him I found later fitted precisely into the scheme.

The identity of Alcyone must have been revealed to Mrs. Besant by someone at Adyar before Leadbeater told her, for she was writing to the latter from Paris on October 8, "Krishnamurti is evidently brought to Adyar to be helped, and we must do our best for him and the Master will tell you what he wishes done."

By this time Mrs. van Hook and Hubert were on their way to Adyar, full of expectations, encouraged by Mrs. Besant when she had seen them earlier in the year in Chicago, that Hubert was to be trained as the vehicle for the Lord Maitreya.

If Alcyone and Mizar [Nitya] could share some lessons with Hubert it would be good [Mrs. Besant wrote to Leadbeater from Geneva in the middle of October], and they are likely to be attracted to each other, knowing their relations in the past, and being under the care of same Master [Kuthumi, Leadbeater's own Master]. Whatever He wishes must obviously be done, and we cannot let other opinion interfere. You can count on me to do any service I can.

It is doubtful whether she realized as yet that Hubert had been supplanted.

What the Master directed Leadbeater to do was far-reaching. As Leadbeater told Dick Clarke:

We have a very difficult job to do; we have to take these two boys out of an orthodox environment, change their diet, teach them physical exercise and Western methods of bathing. We have to take them away from school where they are being beaten by a master who ought to be selling bootlaces instead of being a teacher. There will be a lot of opposition to all this and yet it has to be done.

"All this," of course, would have been much easier to accomplish if Leadbeater could have removed the boys at once from under their father's roof, but as he wrote to Mrs. Besant on October 14, "I am endeavoring to steer a rather cautious course; of course I must carry out the in-

structions given to me [by the Master] but after all that
has happened within the last few years, I must not take
too prominent an interest in boys of 13! When you are
here I shall be bolder." He added that Narianiah was to
move into the house in the Compound as soon as it was
"cleaned and repainted."

A particularly brutal caning of both boys in the middle
of October which had "very much disturbed their astral
bodies" gave Leadbeater an excuse to persuade Narianiah
to remove them from school altogether. Narianiah was
very hesitant at first because without a Government school
education it would be impossible for them to get jobs in
any of the professions or in the Civil Service; Leadbeater,
however, half promised that Mrs. Besant would interest
herself in their welfare and perhaps even arrange for them
to be educated in England; in the meantime, pending Mrs.
Besant's return to Adyar, he and his friends would see that
the boys lacked nothing in the way of teaching. Narianiah
accepted this temporary solution, and Dick Clarke,
Subrahmanyam Aiyar, Ernest Wood and Don Fabrizio
Ruspoli (a former lieutenant in the Italian navy married
to an Englishwoman, who had relinquished his career
when he became a Theosophist) gave them regular lessons
in the Octagon Bungalow while Leadbeater himself taught
them history when he had the time. But English was the
subject most emphasized, for it was very much hoped that
Krishna would be able to talk to Mrs. Besant when she returned to Adyar at the end of November.

Dick Clarke also had the task of grooming the boys;
they were de-loused—there were lice even in their eye-
brows; their hair was allowed to grow in front and was cut
to shoulder length; the dentist fitted Krishna with a plate
which Clarke had to tighten every day; but it seems to
have been Leadbeater who supervised their washing, making sure they did not neglect to wash between their legs.
He deplored the ceremonial Hindu way of bathing by
merely pouring water over the body while still wearing a
loin cloth; but this European manner of washing was, later
on, to cause a great deal of trouble.

In training his boys, one of Leadbeater's chief concerns
was to eliminate fear in them. Krishna recounted that
once, when Leadbeater was teaching him to swim, he
avoided through timidity a particularly deep and frighten-
ing hole. He was not aware that this had been observed

until later in the evening Leadbeater said, "And now we will go down to the sea again and find that hole," and the boys were marched back to the beach. But even Leadbeater was exasperated at times by Krishna's apparent stupidity. Often during his lessons the boy would stand by the open window with his mouth open looking at nothing in particular. Over and over again he was told to shut his mouth; this he did but the next moment it fell open again. At last one day Leadbeater became so irritated that he slapped the boy on the chin. That, declared Krishna, ended their relationship; his mouth remained closed but he never felt the same about Leadbeater again.

Although still sleeping in their father's "hovel" and having their two main meals with him, the boys spent the rest of their time with Leadbeater, heavily chaperoned by their many tutors. A daily routine was laid down for them: they got up at five, performed orthodox Brahminical ablutions in cold water at the side of a well, did their morning meditation and then went to the Octagon Bungalow for hot milk served by a caste servant to comply with orthodox feeling. They would then gather round Leadbeater for a short talk on "higher things," after which they would take some form of outdoor exercise and return to the bungalow for warm baths, clean clothes and the day's lessons.

Mrs. van Hook and Hubert had arrived by the middle of November. Mrs van Hook took an immediate liking to the two Indian boys and began teaching them with Hubert, who was a year younger than Krishna but much taller and infinitely more advanced intellectually. Mrs. Russak, who had been with Colonel Olcott at the end and witnessed the Masters' visits to him, came with the van Hooks. Mrs. Russak had built a two-storied house for herself at Adyar beside the river between the Headquarters building and the Octagon Bungalow. The van Hooks went to live in the lower floor of this house while Mrs. Russak occupied the upper, which was connected by a bridge with Headquarters.

In the efforts of all concerned to teach Krishna English, his spiritual progress had not, of course, been neglected. Leadbeater reported to Mrs. Besant that on the night of August 1 he had taken the two boys in their astral bodies while they were asleep to the house of Master Kuthumi who had put them both on probation as his pupils. Discipleship under a Master was in two stages—probation (for a period that might extend to seven years) and acceptance, when the pupil was drawn into such close unity with his Master that the Master could no longer expel him from his consciousness. These two first steps on the Path of Discipleship were in preparation for the first Initiation which brought the pupil into membership of the Great White Brotherhood, though still at quite a lowly level, for four more initiations must follow until the attainment of Adepthood. Leadbeater and Mrs. Besant had passed their fourth Initiation together at the time she became President in 1907. Leadbeater's martyrdom in 1906 had been necessary, they believed, for this fourth great step. Only one more step lay between them and perfection.

The qualifications for even the first Initiation seemed almost beyond human achievement—perfect physical health, absolute mental and physical purity, unselfishness of purpose, universal charity, compassion for all animate things, truthfulness and courage in any emergency, and a calm indifference to, but a just appreciation of, everything that constituted the transitory world.

In the five months between Krishna's being taken on probation and his acceptance, Leadbeater took him every night in his astral form to the Master's house for fifteen minutes' instruction, at the end of which the Master would summarize his talk into a few simple sentences for Krishna to remember. The next morning in the Octagon Bungalow Krishna would struggle to write down what he remembered of the Master's words. Both Dick Clarke and Mrs. Russak vouched for the fact that these notes were written down by Krishna himself with great laboriousness, that the words were his own or, rather, what he had managed to "bring through" and remember of the Master's words, and that the only outside help he had received was with his spelling and punctuation. These notes were afterwards turned into a little book, *At the Feet of the Master*, which has been translated into twenty-seven languages, run into some forty editions, and is still in print.

4

First Initiation

On November 27, 1909, Mrs. Besant at last arrived back
at Adyar after her seven months' tour, and her first meeting with Krishna took place. He and Nitya were among
the large party who went to the Madras station to meet
her. Krishna, his hair now grown and wearing clean white
garments, was given a garland of roses to throw over her.
The train was delayed by an accident on the line. Krishna
afterwards described her arrival:

> ... some of us were bare-footed and that part of the
> platform unprotected by the roof became very hot.
> My feet grew so uncomfortable that, after dancing
> about for some time, I took refuge on Don Fabri-
> zio Ruspoli's feet. . . . At last she arrived and every-
> body pressed towards the railway carriage from
> which she stepped down. There was such a rush that
> I could hardly see anything of her at all and was only
> just able to get near enough to her to throw the gar-
> land over her and salute her in our Indian way. Then
> other people came up and [I] doubt [if] she noticed
> me at all. Finally Mrs. Besant and Mr. Leadbeater
> went off in the motor car while Don Fabrizio
> Ruspoli, Mr. Clarke, Nitya and myself followed them
> in Sir Subramanian's carriage.[1] After reaching Adyar
> we went back to Mr. Leadbeater's bungalow and
> waited there a long time while he was talking with
> Mrs. Besant in the main building. At last we heard
> the peculiar coo-ee by which Mr. Leadbetter often
> called us. He was standing on the Shrine Room
> verandah which looks down upon his bungalow, and

[1] Sir Subramania Aiyar, Vice-President of the T.S. 1907-11 and a
former judge of the High Court of Madras. Krishna was correct in
writing Sir Subramanian, for that is how it would have been pronounced without his family name. Aiyar was often spelt Iyer.

he told my brother and myself that Mrs. Besant
wished to see us. We both felt very nervous as we
went upstairs for although we were very eager to
meet her, we had heard how great she was. Mr. Leadbeater went into her room with us, and we found her
standing in the middle of the room. Mr. Leadbeater
said: 'Here is Krishna with his brother.' As is the
custom with us towards those for whom we have
great reverence, we both prostrated ourselves at her
feet. She lifted us up and embraced us. I do not
remember what she said to us, as I was still very nervous, although full of a great happiness. We did not
stop very long as there was to be a meeting of T.S.
members as usual in the big drawing room on the
same floor. As we were going in we met my father
and Mrs. Besant said to him: 'I suppose this will be
the first of the private T.S. meetings that your sons
have attended. I hope you approve of their coming.'
He replied that he was very glad. I sat at her feet facing the people who were gathered there, and I was
very nervous.

During the three weeks Mrs. Besant remained in Adyar
before going up to Benares (as Banaras was called until
1947) for the annual Theosophical Convention,[1] the boys
went every day to see her in her room, and on December
5 she admitted them to the Esoteric Section. Soon after
her departure Leadbeater "brought through" messages
from the Master to say that the boys' father must be made
to realize that his sons no longer belonged to him but to
the world; that it must be conveyed to him "clearly and
unmistakably" not to interfere in any way with regard to
their food or to any other detail of their lives; for the next
few years it was the Master's wish that they should be
"kept entirely apart from other boys and should associate
only with those who were under Theosophical influence."
Before Mrs. Besant left for Benares on December 14
she had arranged that in her absence the boys should sleep

[1] The annual Convention of the T.S. was held on alternate years
at Adyar or Benares. Benares was the center of the Indian Section
and Adyar the international center. Before she became President,
Mrs. Besant had lived chiefly at Benares where she had her own
rented house, Shanti Kunja. In 1912 this house was bought by subscription for Mrs. Besant's and Krishna's lifetime.

in her room as Narianiah's new house was not yet ready. Narianiah was happy to comply with this arrangement because it was her wish. So now Leadbeater had the boys exactly where he wanted them, right away from their father's sphere of influence. Mrs. Besant's room and balcony were to be kept strictly private; only Mrs. Russak was allowed to go into the room to clean it so that no other female influence should contaminate it. Ten days after Mrs. Besant's departure Krishna wrote his first letter to her. It was in his own writing, which was being closely modelled on Leadbeater's:

Dec. 24th 1909

My Dear Mother,

Will you let me call you mother when I write to you? I have no other mother now to love, and I feel as if you were our mother because you have been so kind to us. We both thank you so much for taking us away from home and letting us sleep in your room; we are so happy there, but we would rather have you here, even if we had to sleep at home. They are so kind to us, they have given us beautiful bicycles, and I have learnt to ride mine, and I go out on it each day. I have ridden 31½ miles, and I shall add some more this evening. I have seen you sometimes in the shrine-room, and I often feel you at night and see your light. I send very much love.

Your loving son
Krishna

Dick Clarke and Ruspoli always accompanied them on these bicycle rides, and sometimes Leadbeater as well. In the early mornings they would bicycle across the Elphinstone Bridge and along the whole length of the Madras Marina towards Fort St. George. On December 30, ten days after getting the bicycles, Leadbeater was able to report to Mrs. Besant that Krishna's cyclometer now stood at 143 miles and that he was a rapid and fearless rider, deciding promptly in a crisis. Shortly afterwards they bicycled to Chingleput, sixty-six miles there and back.

As well as bicycling and swimming, an old water tank just behind the Octagon Bungalow had been filled in to make a tennis court. Krishna thought it "very wonderful to see how well Mr. Leadbeater played in spite of his

being over sixty years of age. I think he was more active
than any of us and played a very steady game."

Apart from Nitya, Hubert seems to have been the only
boy Krishna was allowed to see, though even Hubert was
not allowed to touch his bicycle or his tennis racquet or
anything else belonging to him. This must have distressed
Krishna since to give and to share were so much a part of
his nature. Hubert was probably jealous of Krishna, and
Leadbeater would have seen this in his aura. Leadbeater
believed that inanimate objects could be magnetized for
good or evil; therefore a bad emanation from Hubert
could be transferred to Krishna's racquet or bicycle and
thence to Krishna himself. Mrs. van Hook evidently accepted Hubert's inferior position with a very good grace
and so, it seemed, did Dr. van Hook back in Chicago.
Ironically, the doctor had done more than anyone else in
America to bring about Leadbeater's readmission into the
Society.

Leadbeater now prevailed on Narianiah to allow the
boys to eat at the "Dharmashala," a new kitchen-dining-
room built specially for Mrs. Besant and a few privileged
friends, where the food, cooked and served by Brahmins,
was better and less highly spiced than at home. Leadbeater
was also preparing for the boys a room in the Headquarters building for them to move into when Mrs. Besant returned to Adyar. He had no intention of allowing them to
go back to their father even when the new house was
ready for occupation. He might have allowed Nitya to go
back but Krishna refused to be parted from this little
brother on whom he depended so much.

There was frequent friction between Narianiah and
Leadbeater, who had no patience with orthodox Hindu
sentiments and put down to selfishness the father's natural
reluctance to allow his sons to be removed altogether from
his influence. Leadbeater was quite ruthless; he was coarse
in many ways, rude—especially to women, though never
to Mrs. Besant—and had no hesitation in swearing. He
had doubtless learnt from Madame Blavatsky that such behavior was not inconsistent with holiness, she herself
being an extremely coarse woman much given to swearing.
There was never a natural affinity between Leadbeater and
Krishna, who was so gentle and whose Brahmin fastidious-
ness was often shocked by this hearty Englishman, just as
Leadbeater was shocked by orthodox Hindu practices.

Mrs. Besant was far more tactful in her handling of
Narianiah. He had gone to Benares for the Convention
and she talked very seriously to him, impressing on him
that all the Masters' instructions for the boys, as relayed
by Leadbeater, must be carried out, including a new order
that had just come through: the boys were only to be
away for an hour for the traditional ceremony on the anniversary of their mother's death on January 7; they were
not to miss their milk on that day nor their meal at the
"Dharmashala," and this was the last time they would be
permitted to take part in any such ceremony. Narianiah,
who had a great reverence for Mrs. Besant, was happy to
carry out her wishes and returned to Adyar in a very
friendly mood. In the end the boys did not attend the ceremony at all because by the time they got there it was all
over.

Leadbeater telegraphed to Mrs. Besant on December 31
to tell her that that night the Master Kuthumi had intimated that he was going to accept Krishna as his pupil
and to ask her to make sure she attended the ceremony at
the Master's house in her astral body. Leadbeater also
wrote to her on the 31st, "This is the shortest probation of
which I have heard—only five months." The astrologer, G.
E. Sutcliffe, had written an article for the *Theosophist*
foretelling a very unusual conjunction of stars and planets
on January 11, 1910, which, Sutcliffe believed, presaged
the birth of the Christ on that day. "If it were but a little
later," Leadbeater wrote in this same letter of December
31, "might it not be the *second* birth of the body which
the Christ will take? But I suppose it is too soon to hope
for that yet. Still, things are moving with such marvellous
rapidity that nothing seems too good to be true." Krishna
added a postscript to this letter: "It seems almost as
though it [his acceptance] could not be true, but He is so
good. Please be there, dear Mother. I send very much love
to you. Krishna."

In answer to Leadbeater's telegram Mrs. Besant told
him in a letter of January 1, 1910, about the memories
she had brought back the night before and asked him to
confirm whether they had been correct and whether it was
true that "Surya" (the Lord Maitreya's pseudonym in the
"Lives") had given Krishna into her and Leadbeater's
charge. Leadbeater replied, "It is true that the Lord Maitreya solemnly gave him into our charge on behalf of the

Brotherhood. Krishna was deeply impressed and has been different ever since."

Krishna himself gave Mrs. Besant his own version of what had happened, though he was apparently unaware of the part the Lord Maitreya had played:

> It was very beautiful. When we went to our Master's house, we found Him and Master Morya and Master Djwal Kul[1] all standing talking, and They spoke very kindly. We all prostrated ourselves, and the Master drew me to His knee, and asked me whether I would forget myself entirely and never have a selfish thought, but think only how to help the world; and I said indeed I would, and I wanted only to be like Him some day. Then he kissed me and passed His hand over me, and I seemed to be somehow part of Him, and I felt quite different and very very happy, and I have had that feeling ever since. Then They all three blessed me and we came away.

On January 3 Mrs. Besant was writing again to Leadbeater: "I am very happy about Krishna and am sorry I am of so little use, though I am doing the little I can. But I am happy that he is in such strong and loving hands as yours. I should not be surprised if the initiation follows very quickly, perhaps on the 11th."

Five days later came a dramatic exchange of telegrams. Leadbeater to Mrs. Besant in Benares: "Initiation ordered for eleventh. Surya in person will officiate. Ordered afterwards visit Shamballa.[2] Involves thirty-six hours seclusion." The reply came back: "Close Shrine and my verandah locking stairs door for time required. Use my room, my secretary's and Mrs. Lübke's[3] as needed. You hold my authority for everything."

[1] This Master was still wearing the Tibetan body in which he had obtained Adepthood only a few years before and which showed some signs of aging. He lived in a cabin he had built with his own hands, close to the Master Morya whose pupil he had been.

[2] An oasis in the Gobi Desert where lived the King of the occult hierarchy, the Sanat Kumara of Hindu scripture.

[3] Mrs. Helen Lübke, an elderly lady who worked in the library at Adyar from 1908–11. Her room, which had originally been Madame Blavatsky's, was next to Mrs. Besant's drawing-room. Leadbeater did not approve of her. He had written to Mrs. Besant on December 15, 1909, ". . . it absolutely will not do to have such a depleting creature as Mrs. Lubke permeating the atmosphere where they sleep."

From the Monday evening of January 10 until the morning of the 12th Leadbeater and Krishna were shut up in Mrs. Besant's bedroom. Mrs. Lübke had already been turned out and her room cleaned and white-washed, for this was the room that Leadbeater was preparing for Krishna and Nitya; the shrine-room was locked (there was a separate staircase by which the residents could get to the shrine-room for their meditation); Ruspoli slept outside the shrine-room to see that the early morning visitors did not "bang their lanterns too vigorously"; and Nitya or Dick Clarke kept a constant vigil outside Mrs. Besant's door. Clarke recorded that Leadbeater and Krishna "remained away from their bodies during the best part of two nights and a day, coming back very occasionally and then only partially, though sufficiently to absorb nourishment (mostly warm milk) which we administered at their bedsides." Krishna lay on Mrs. Besant's bed and Leadbeater on the floor.

According to Leadbeater in a letter to Mrs. Besant of January 12, Krishna woke on the Tuesday morning (the 11th) crying out, "I remember! I remember!" Leadbeater asked him to tell him all he remembered and these memories were written down

correcting his tenses where they were wrong, and supplying a word here and there when he could not express himself, but carefully *not* adding anything from my own knowledge, or in any way modifying his expressions. All that about the strength of the sea and the smile like the sunlight is word for word as he said it, and it seems quite an inspiration for a boy of thirteen writing in a foreign language. His intention was to write all this out by hand but it would have taken him two days, and he was so tired that Mrs. Russak offered to type it for him from my notes. But it is entirely his choice of words, not hers. . . . He does not mention that after our return from the great audience last night to the Master's house, the Master admitted him to Sonship [signifying an even closer relationship between Master and pupil], and accepted Nitya "because of his overflowing love and his unselfish devotion to My son Krishna" as He said. So we have every great cause for rejoicing all round.

He is tired with the strain of it all, but very well

and radiantly happy. The father behaved capitally,
embraced him affectionately, prostrated himself before me, rejoiced exceedingly and generally acted
quite like a human being. I told only very few what
was to happen, but somehow it seems to have leaked
out, and I think almost everyone here knows. So far
as I have heard they all take it in the right way, and
are very happy over it, but I have not had time to see
any of them yet.

Below is Krishna's account of his Initiation addressed to
Mrs. Besant:

January 12th, 1910.

When I left my body the first night, I went at once
to the Master's house and found Him there with the
Master Morya and the Master Djwal Kul. The Master talked to me very kindly for a long time, and
told me all about the Initiation, and what I should
have to do. Then we all went together to the house of
the Lord Maitreya, where I had been once before,
and there we found many of the Masters—the Venetian Master, the Master Jesus, the Master the Count,
the Master Serapis, the Master Hilarion[1] and the two
Masters Morya and K.H. [Kuthumi]. The Lord Maitreya sat in the middle, and the others stood round
Him in a semicircle like this [diagram].

Then the Master [Kuthumi] took my right hand,
and the Master Djwal Kul my left, and they led me
in front of the Lord Maitreya, you and Uncle [Lead-
beater] standing close behind me. The Lord smiled at
me, but He said to the Master:—

"Who is this that you thus bring before me?" And
the Master answered:

"This is a candidate who seeks admission to the
Great Brotherhood." Then the Lord asked:—

[1] A Greek, marvellously handsome, and younger than the other
Adepts. The Venetian Master, so called because he had been born
in Venice, was, however, the handsomest of them all. Master the
Count was Prince Ragozci, the Comte de St. Germain, an aristocrat
who lived in his family castle in Hungary. The Master Serapis was
also Greek by birth, although his work had been done in Egypt.
Jesus, whose body the Lord Maitreya had last used, was now a
Master living among the Druses of Mount Lebanon in a Syrian
body.

"Do you vouch for him as worthy of admission?"
The Master replied:—

"I do." The Lord continued:—

"Will you undertake to guide his steps along the
Path which he desires to enter?" And the Master answered:—

"I will." Then the Lord asked:—

"Our rule requires that two of the higher Brethren
shall vouch for every candidate; is any higher Brother
prepared to support his application?"

The Master Djwal Kul said:—

"I am prepared to do so." Then the Lord said:—

"The body of the candidate is very young. If he
should be admitted, are any members of the Brotherhood who still live in the outer world ready to take
charge of him and to help him on his upward way?"
Then you and uncle came forward and bowed and
said:—

"We are ready to take charge of him." The Lord
continued:—

"Are your hearts full of love for him, so that such
guidance will be easy?" and you both replied:—

"They are full of love, brought over from many
lives in the past."

Then the Lord spoke to me for the first time:—

"Do you on your part love these two Brethren, so
that you will gladly submit yourself to their
guidance?" And of course, I answered:—

"Indeed I do love them with all my heart."

He asked:—

"You desire then to join the Brotherhood which exists from eternity unto eternity?" And I said:—

"I wish to join when I am fit to do so."

He asked:—

"Do you know the object of this Brotherhood?" I
replied:—

"To do the work of the Logos [the trinity that gov-
erns our Solar System] by helping the world."

Then he replied:—

"Will you pledge yourself to devote all your life
and all your strength henceforth to this work, forgetting yourself absolutely for the good of the world,
making your life all love, even as He is all love?"

And I answered:—

"I will, with the Master's help." He continued:—

"Do you promise to keep secret those things which you are told to keep secret?" And I said:—

"I do promise." Then He showed me many astral objects and I had to tell Him what they were. I had to distinguish between the astral bodies of a living man and a dead man, between a real person and a thought-image of a person, and between an imitation Master and a real one. Then He showed me many cases, and asked how I would help in each, and I answered as well as I could. Then He showed me an image of my worst enemy [his school-master?], a cruel man whom I had hated, because he had often tortured my younger brother and me; and He said:—

"Will you help even this creature, if he needs your help?" But there can be no hatred in the Master's presence, so I replied:—

"Surely I will." At the end He smiled and said that the answers were very satisfactory, and then He asked all the other Masters:—

"Do all present agree to the reception of this candidate into our company?" And all said that They did.

Then the Lord turned away from me and called towards Shamballa:—

"Do I this, O Lord of Life and Light, in Thy Name and for Thee?" And at once the great Silver Star flashed out over His head, and on each side of it in the air there stood a figure—one of Lord Gautama Buddha and the other the Mahachohan.[1] And the Lord Maitreya turned and called me by the true name of the Ego and laid His hand upon my head and said:—

"In the name of the One Initiator, whose Star shines above us, I receive you into the Brotherhood of Eternal Life; see to it that you are a worthy and useful member of it. You are now safe forever, for

[1] The Mahachohan, the Buddha and the Manu were the three aspects of the Logos who had reached the grades of Initiation which gave them consciousness on the planes of nature beyond the field of humanity's evolution. Though performing different functions, they were of equal status and came immediately below the King of the World in the occult hierarchy.

you have entered upon the stream; may you soon attain the further shore!"

Then He gave me the Key of Knowledge and showed me how I might always and anywhere recognize any member of the Great White Brotherhood when I met Him; but these things, He said, I must not repeat.

Then He spoke to my two sponsors and asked them to take charge of the necessary buddhic experiences. Then all the Masters, one by one, touched my head and spoke kindly to me and congratulated me, and the Lord Maitreya gave me His blessing. Then the Star disappeared and we all came away, and I awoke feeling wonderfully happy and safe.

I very soon went to sleep again, and all that day I was away from my body, being taught about the buddhic plane, and how to form a buddhic body and a mayavirupa [a materialized astral body]. But I do not remember that very clearly in this brain; because it has come down through several planes.

The next night I was taken to see the King, and that was the most wonderful experience of all for He is a boy not much older than I am, but the handsomest I have ever seen, all shining and glorious, and when He smiles it is like sunlight. He is strong like the sea, so that nothing could stand against Him for a moment, and yet He is nothing but love, so that I could not be in the least afraid of Him. And the Silver Star that we have seen is just part of Him—not sent there, for He is there and everywhere all the time, but just somehow made so that we can see it. But when we do not see it, He is there just the same. He told me that I had done well in the past, and in the future I should do still better; and if my work should be difficult I must never forget His presence, for His strength would be always behind me, and His Star would shine over me. Then He raised His hand in blessing and we came away. There were three other Shining Ones who stood behind Him, but I did not look at Them, for I could not take my eyes from Him. On the way there and back I saw enormous ruins and a great bridge, different from any other that I have ever seen; but I was thinking so much of Him, that I did not notice them very much.

Mrs. Besant "brought back" her own memories of the ceremony without any prompting from Leadbeater, for she was writing to him on January 12:

> I went over—but of course you know at five [a.m. on the 11th], and stayed till 6.15. So it is definitely fixed that the Lord Maitreya takes this dear child's body. It seems a very heavy responsibility to have to guard and help it, so as to fit it for Him, as He said, and I feel rather overwhelmed, but we are together in it and your wisdom will illuminate. I feel we have accepted and pledged our lives to a very solemn task. And then Shamballa—in the presence of the King. How much I should like to talk it over with you. The dear boy looked so beautiful, like a picture of the child Christ, with his large solemn eyes, full of love and trust. Does he remember it all?

Mrs. Besant was going even further than Leadbeater in stating that it was "definitely fixed" that the Lord Maitreya was to take Krishna's body.

She wrote to Krishna himself in answer to his account of the Initiation, and he replied on January 23: ". . . in this new life everybody is so kind—the Lord Maitreya and all the Masters, and the members who work for Them at Adyar; all are quite different from the people that I used to know, so that it is a different world for me. Even my father is different now, and everything is beautiful. I hope I may be good enough for it all."

Mrs. Besant must have felt a little conscience-stricken about Hubert, because she was writing to Leadbeater on January 25, "We cannot, of course, expect as much from Hubert as from dear Krishna, the preceding lives have differed so much. Then, of course, it is difficult for the American body to be as self-effacing and as docile as the Indian. But as he was thought of as possible for the Lord Maitreya's indwelling, we may work for him with much hope, do you not think?" Hubert, who had been put on probation before he arrived at Adyar, was not accepted until December 1912.

Shortly before her return to Adyar in February Mrs. Besant asked Leadbeater, "Charles dear, why do you undervalue yourself and over-value me so much always, I am sure you do far more for the dear boys than I do. You al-

ways think too little of yourself, and do not realise one bit
what you are, and it was you who found the boys and res-
cued them." No doubt he had intimated how badly her
presence was needed at Adyar.

First Teaching

The truth was that relations between Narianiah and Leadbeater could never remain friendly for long. Although Narianiah had been delighted by Krishna's Initiation he was now making serious trouble. Naturally he knew of Leadbeater's past history and, as he disliked and distrusted him, he was very ready to listen to tales brought to him by Mrs. Besant's servant Lakshman. Lakshman had been deeply shocked when on entering Mrs. Besant's bathroom one day he had found Krishna naked, while Leadbeater, wearing only a shirt half way down his thighs, was washing the boy's hair. Nakedness was an outrage to Hindu orthodoxy and a breaking of caste rules. Lakshman also claimed that he had seen Krishna naked in Leadbeater's presence in the Octagon Bungalow.

These tales were passed on to Mrs. Besant who felt there was only one thing to do, to get Narianiah to transfer to her the legal guardianship of the boys. Early in March, therefore, after her return to Adyar, she asked Sir Subramania Aiyar, the Vice-President of the Society, to draw up a document to be endorsed by Narianiah expressing gratitude to her for all her care of, and solicitude for, the boys and conferring on her the full rights of a guardian. The only condition inserted in the draft was that in the event of her death the document would cease to have validity and the custody of the minors would revert to their father. Narianiah signed this document on March 6 without, apparently, any unwillingness. All he wanted, it seemed, was to remove the boys from the proximity of Leadbeater. Mrs. Besant, knowing that Leadbeater was still to be their true guardian, very wisely decided to remain in India for the whole of that year, 1910, and keep the boys close to her as far as possible in order to avoid any more gossip. The boys had moved into Mrs. Lübke's room next to hers, which had been divided in half and an-

43

other bathroom added. Krishna and Nitya occupied the
eastern half and Dick Clarke the other half. Although at
the same time Leadbeater moved from the Octagon Bungalow to sleep at Headquarters, his room was as far away
as possible from theirs and he continued to use the Octagon Bungalow as an office and a schoolroom for the
boys.

The boys lived a life of quiet routine after Mrs. Besant's
return. Krishna recorded, "Our mother gave us an hour's
reading lesson every morning. We read together Rudyard
Kipling's *Jungle Book* and I enjoyed it very much. *Cap-
tains Courageous, The Scarlet Pimpernel, I will Repay*
and some Shakespeare plays." The early morning bicycle
rides continued, Leadbeater continuing to note the miles
registered on Krishna's cyclometer, and there was tennis
and swimming in the evenings.

But as soon as Mrs. Besant left Adyar in April for a
short visit to Benares Narianiah became troublesome
again. "He seems to have had a fit of insanity," Leadbeater reported to her on April 18. Leadbeater was able to
assure her, however, of the Master's understanding of this
in the Master's own words:

> "The work you are doing for me is of such impor-
> tance that you cannot hope that it will escape the at-
> tention of the darker powers, and the nominal father
> by his anger and jealousy offers them a convenient in-
> strument. I regretfully reiterate . . . the less he sees of
> the boys for the next few years the better. He must
> kindly but firmly be made to understand that he must
> no more interfere with them in any way whatever
> than with their brother Hubert. . . . I approve the
> careful arrangements you have made with regard to
> bathing, eating and sleeping; when any change is
> needed I will myself tell you."

A few months later the Master was further instructing
Leadbeater:

> "They [the boys] have lived long in hell; try to
> show them something of Paradise. I want them to
> have everything the opposite of those previous condi-
> tions. Instead of hostility, distrust, misery, squalor, ir-
> regularity, carelessness and foulness, I want them

surrounded by an atmosphere of love and happiness, confidence, regularity, perfect physical cleanliness and mental purity. . . . Keep them as far as you can within your aura and Annie's, so that they may be protected from all evil and carnal thoughts. . . . I want you to civilize them; to teach them to use spoons and forks, nail brushes and toothbrushes, to sit at ease upon chairs instead of crouching on the ground, to sleep rationally on a bed, not in a corner like a dog. Long hours of sleep are specially necessary, but take care they do not sleep in the pyjamas that are responsible for so much evil in your civilization. Underclothes must always be of silk, linen or cloth and no wool or flannel must touch the skin. No undue tightness must be permitted anywhere, and the shape of the foot must on no account be spoiled. Keep their heads always cool, and whenever possible uncovered. His [Krishna's] body must be developed to be straight and strong, agile and muscular, with soldierly carriage, deep chest and great lung power. The most scrupulous cleanliness under all conditions is of primary importance."

It was Leadbeater's insistence on this "scrupulous cleanliness," particularly on the European custom of bathing naked and washing between the legs, that caused so much unpleasant gossip at Adyar. Leadbeater doubtless showed Krishna how to wash in this way but both Krishna and Nitya always maintained that there had never been the slightest hint of immorality.[1]

At the end of September 1910, Mrs. Besant took the boys with her when she went to Benares and they stayed in her house, Shanti Kunja, in the fifteen-acre Theosophical estate, close to the Central Hindu College which she had founded in 1898 and which was perhaps of all her achievements the one she was most proud of. The boys had already met some of the teachers at the Central Hindu

[1] Hubert later swore to Mrs. Besant that Leadbeater had "misused" him, but as he was extremely vindictive by that time his testimony, though unshaken, was perhaps not altogether reliable. Hubert put up with life at Adyar for five years. He afterwards went to Christ Church, Oxford, and then to Northwestern University, Illinois. He married and became an attorney in Chicago. (*The Last Four Lives of Annie Besant* by A. H. Nethercote, p. 193n., Hart-Davis, 1961.)

College when they had come to Adyar for a holiday in May, but now a deep attachment was to develop between Krishna and the Principal of the College, George Arundale (Fides in *The Lives of Alcyone*), a large, dark, good-looking man of thirty-two, whom Leadbeater had formerly tutored in England and who had come to Benares in 1903 after taking an honors degree at Cambridge in Moral Science. Krishna also became very friendly with the English professor at the College, A. E. Wodehouse, elder brother of P. G. Wodehouse, who had been professor of English at Elphinstone College, Bombay, before becoming interested in Theosophy and moving to Benares at Mrs. Besant's request. Wodehouse had won the Newdigate Prize for poetry when he was at Corpus Christi College, Oxford, as well as the Chancellor's Essay Prize. (A book of his poems was published after the first war.)

As well as Arundale, Krishna picked out four other members of Mrs. Besant's closest followers, known as the Yellow Shawl Group because they wore yellow silk shawls at their meetings, to whom he felt particularly attracted and whom he considered full of spiritual promise. He asked Mrs. Besant if he might teach these five men the qualifications for discipleship as they had been taught to him the year before by the Master between his probation and acceptance. Mrs. Besant was delighted, and in reporting his request to Leadbeater she added, "It is so good to see him opening out, bless him." She was glad to receive Leadbeater's letter of approval, saying in her answer to it: "I rather feel that in things of this sort it is best to let him follow his own heart and impulse, and that those will guide him right. . . . He is developing very rapidly, and shows no trace of shyness or timidity, but a pretty and gracious dignity," and the next day she wrote again, "Krishna's English under stress of talking, is much improved, and he fathers George [Arundale] quite quaintly."

Krishna himself wrote to Leadbeater to ask him to send the notes he, Krishna, had made, based on the Master Kuthumi's instruction.

I arranged his notes as well as I could [Leadbeater stated later], and typed them all out. Then it seemed to me that as they were mainly the Master's words I had better make sure that there was no mistake in recording them. Therefore I took the typewritten copy which I had made to the Master Kuthumi, and asked Him to be so kind as to read it over. He read it, altered a word or two here and there, added some connecting and explanatory notes and a few other sentences which I remember having heard Him speak. Then he said: "Yes, that seems correct; that will do"; but He added: "Let us show it to the Lord Maitreya." And so we went together, He taking the book, and it was shown to the World-Teacher Himself, who read it and approved. It was He who said: "You should make a nice little book of this to introduce Alcyone to the world." We had not meant to introduce him to the world; we had not considered it desirable that a mass of thought should be concentrated on a boy of thirteen, who still had his education before him. But in the occult world we do what we are told, and so this book was put into the printer's hand the following morning.

Before Leadbeater's typescript of the notes arrived, Mrs. Besant, accompanied by Krishna and Nitya, Mrs. van Hook and Hubert, had been on a short tour to Lahore and Delhi. It was the first time the Indian boys had been north and they complained so bitterly of the cold that Mrs. Besant had wadded silk coats made for them, assuring Leadbeater "there is no perspiration in this weather and no fear of smell." She must have received a letter from Leadbeater about the typescript while she was away, for on October 23 she was writing to him excitedly from Delhi: "We are so delighted about the approval of the Master and the Lord Maitreya of the first literary effort of Alcyone. We must print and bind it very prettily—his first gift to the world. Is it to be "Alcyone" or Krishnamurti? We will do it as soon as I return."[1] She added that Krishna's manners were now "quite perfect, dignified and sweet, with no trace of shyness."

Whether *At the Feet of the Master* was written by

---

[1] The author was "Alcyone." The first edition of the book, published in December, was bound in blue cloth with an impress in gold on the cover of the Path leading to an Egyptian gateway. The latest photograph of Alcyone was the frontispiece. Twelve copies bound in blue leather were also issued. All the proceeds from the book went, at Krishna's request, to Mrs. Besant.

Krishna has always been a debatable point. Mrs. Besant seems to have had no doubt as to its authenticity, though Krishna himself stated in his Foreword: "These are not my words; they are the words of the Master who taught me." As his original notes, which he almost certainly wrote himself, have not survived there is no way of telling to what extent Leadbeater revised them. Anyway, the typescript had reached Benares by the time Krishna returned there at the end of October and he began to teach from it the four qualifications for discipleship—Discrimination, Desirelessness, Good Conduct and Love. As the five members of his special group were all so much older than he was (as well as Arundale they included I. N. Gurtu, headmaster of the boy's preparatory school attached to the College), his instruction was naturally likened to Christ teaching the Elders in the Temple. His special group, which grew gradually in numbers, became an inner core of the Yellow Shawl Group. It was known as the Purple Order from its insignia—a purple shawl, a purple sash embroidered in gold and inscribed J.K., worn over the shoulder, and a silver badge on a purple ribbon. Krishna was its Head and Mrs. Besant and Leadbeater its Protectors.

But lessons and exercise were not neglected. Every afternoon there were strenuous tennis matches, Krishna and George taking on Hubert and Wodehouse and nearly always winning. Krishna was also given a camera at Benares which he loved. He became an extremely patient and painstaking photographer.

Wodehouse wrote about him at this time:

> What struck us particularly was his naturalness . . . of any kind of side or affectation there was not a trace. He was still of a retiring nature, modest and deferential to his elders and courteous to all. To those whom he liked, moreover, he showed a kind of eager affection, which was singularly attractive. Of his "occult" position he seemed to be entirely unconscious. He never alluded to it—never, for a single moment, allowed the slightest hint of it to get into his speech or manner. . . . Another quality was a serene unselfishness. He seemed to be not the least preoccupied with himself. . . . We were no blind devotees, prepared to see in him nothing but perfection. We

were older people, educationalists, and with some experience of youth. Had there been a trace in him of conceit or affection, or any posing as the "holy child," or of priggish self-consciousness, we would undoubtedly have given an adverse verdict.

Krishna has never lost his beautiful manners due to an innate consideration for others, and in spite of all the adulation he has received since he was fourteen he has remained modest and self-effacing.

Leadbeater was evidently pressing now for Krishna to continue his education in England, for Mrs. Besant wrote to him on November 3 quite sharply for once: "We need not settle anything about England until after my return. We can talk it all over then and see if Master will advise. If it be possible to avoid the disturbance of study and expense involved, it will be much better." There is no written record of the Master's advice on this point but as Mrs. Besant returned with the boys to Adyar at the end of November, Leadbeater would have conveyed to her verbally the Master's instructions: the boys were to be in England in less than six months' time.

On January 11 of the following year, 1911, on the anniversary of Krishna's Initiation, George Arundale, in Benares, formed yet another organization, the Order of the Rising Sun, the purpose of which was to draw together those in India who believed in the near coming of a great spiritual teacher, to help prepare public opinion to receive him and to create an atmosphere of welcome and reverence. A few months later the idea was enthusiastically taken up by Mrs. Besant and Leadbeater and under the new name of the Order of the Star in the East turned into an international organization. Officers were appointed for each country consisting of a National Representative and an Organizing Secretary. Mrs. Besant and Leadbeater were made Protectors of the new Order of which Krishna was the Head, Arundale Private Secretary to the Head, and Wodehouse Organizing Secretary. There were to be no rules or subscriptions; each member was to receive a certificate of membership and to be allowed to wear the badge of the Order, a silver five-pointed star in the form of a brooch, pendant or pin. National Representatives and other high officials might wear gold stars. A quarterly magazine, printed at Adyar and called the *Herald of the Star*, with

Krishna as its nominal editor, was also started; the first number appeared in January 1911.

Some of the older members of the Theosophical Society questioned Mrs. Besant's right to establish such an organisation for a specific purpose outside the three objects of the Society, but Mrs. Besant reminded her critics of the fact that Madame Blavatsky had "regarded it as the mission of the T.S. to prepare the world for the coming of the next great Teacher, though she put that event perhaps half a century later than I do."

The Society at this time had only about sixteen thousand active members throughout the world. Theosophists divided themselves into Lodges according to locality or special activities; every town was at liberty to form its own Lodge, and cities or big towns might have several Lodges—thus the sixteen thousand members were divided into over six hundred Lodges. This system had its dangers in that it made it easier for factions to break away and become independent of Adyar. Such a rift had occurred in America a few years before, and now the establishment of the Order of the Star in the East resulted in a more serious schism, Rudolph Steiner in Germany being one of the important members to break away, taking most of the German Lodges with him to form his own Anthroposophical Society. The T.S., however, recovered from this blow and continued to grow; by 1920 there were 36,350 members and by 1928 it had reached its peak with a membership of 45,000.

6

In England

After a tour in Burma in January–February 1911, Mrs. Besant left Adyar on March 22 with Krishna and Nitya en route for England. In Benares on the way to Bombay, European clothes were bought for the boys and a doctor performed the task of sewing up the large holes in the lobes of their ears which, as in all Hindu children, had been pierced when they were very young. Leadbeater had insisted that Krishna's "body could not be handed over with these holes." The local anaesthetic used by the doctor had little effect apparently. Mrs. Besant was very upset by the operation which hurt Krishna more than it hurt Nitya and took longer. She held the boys' hands all the time and tried, unsuccessfully, to transfer the pain to herself.

Accompanied by George Arundale, who had taken some months' leave from the Central Hindo College to become the boys' tutor, they sailed from Bombay on April 22 on the S.S. *Mantua*. Mrs. Besant reported in the first of her weekly letters to Leadbeater that although the boys found their new shoes very constricting they were managing their English clothes well and that Nitya could dress himself all but his tie. Krishna was delighted because the captain, Captain Normand, who had known Mrs. Besant for twenty years, had allowed him "to see something of the workings of the ship, particularly the 'Marconi apparatus.'" They left the ship at Brindisi and went by train to Calais via Turin on account of sea-sickness, from which Mrs. Besant suffered acutely all her life. Krishna and Nitya also proved to be very bad sailors.

There was, of course, tremendous excitement among English Theosophists when Mrs. Besant arrived in London. *The Lives of Alcyone* had been appearing in the *Theosophist* for the past year and it was known that Mrs. Besant was bringing with her "Alcyone" himself, nor was there any secret about the marvellous role he was destined to

51

play. A great crowd, therefore, was waiting to meet her and her wards when they arrived at Charing Cross Station on May 5. Among those gathered on the platform was the thirty-six-year-old Lady Emily Lutyens, wife of the architect Edwin Lutyens, who had recently been converted to Theosophy on reading some of Mrs. Besant's books. In her enthusiasm she had already started a new Theosophical Lodge devoted to the practical application of Theosophy to social problems.

Lady Emily has recorded her first impression of "Alcyone": "I had eyes for none but Krishna, an odd figure, with long black hair falling almost to his shoulders and enormous dark eyes which had a vacant look in them. He was dressed in a Norfolk jacket. Mrs. Besant piloted him along the platform, anxious to keep the crowd from pressing on him." As Lady Emily left the station she found one of the members of the T.S. in an almost fainting condition; she was somewhat psychic and had been overcome by the glory of Krishna's aura.

Mrs. Besant and the boys went to stay at 82 Drayton Gardens, South Kensington, with her closest friends, the widow of Jacob Bright and her unmarried daughter Esther.[1] Mrs. Besant's first meeting in London was held on May 8 at the Theosophical Headquarters in Bond Street; she announced the formation of the Order of the Star in the East and said that all who wished to enroll as members should give their names to George Arundale. Lady Emily was one of the first to do so, and a few days later Mrs. Besant asked her to become National Representative of the Order for England.

Two other recent converts, who had been brought into the Society by Lady Emily, were Miss Mary Dodge, an extremely rich and equally generous American lady, crippled with arthritis, and her great friend Muriel, Countess De La Warr, who lived with her at Warwick House, St. James's. Miss Dodge put a car at Mrs. Besant's disposal while she was in England.[2]

[1] Jacob Bright, M.P., P.C. (1821–99), was the younger brother of John Bright. 82 Drayton Gardens now belongs to the Society of Authors. It had a larger garden then with a few big trees in it.

[2] Lady Emily had met Miss Dodge through her husband, whose client she had been. Lady De La Warr (pronounced Ware) was a daughter of Earl Brassey. She had married Earl De La Warr in 1891 and obtained a divorce in 1902. Lady Emily was a daughter

Krishna and Nitya remained in Europe for four months, during which time Krishna, as well as Mrs. Besant, sent regular reports of their activities to Leadbeater at Adyar. A program of study under Arundale, with exercise and some amusements thrown in, was arranged for them, never forgetting the importance of a nourishing diet and ten hours sleep a night. It had evidently been decided by this time that they should go to Oxford, for Mrs. Besant wrote that they need not take Latin for Responsions. For the time being they were studying arithmetic, algebra up to simple equations, Sanskrit, essay writing and Shakespeare. For exercise they took riding lessons, went to Sandow's famous gymnasium in St. James's Street and played croquet in the back garden of Mrs. Bright's house, where they stayed the whole time they were in London. Mrs. Besant gave them two "very fine boats" to sail on the Round Pond in Kensington Gardens, and Arundale gave Krishna a model steam engine which he loved. Nevertheless they found the noise of London very trying, and their boots, loose as they were, so tired their feet that they were reluctant to walk. Nitya, who was then the more clothes-conscious of the two, begged to be allowed to wear trousers as knickerbockers were "rather young." He was also given a jacket like one he had seen and coveted on an Eton boy. Mrs. Besant took Nitya, who was almost blind in the left eye, to what she considered to be the best oculist in London, Mr. Treacher Collins, who said that nothing could be done for him: "The retina was injured either before or at birth and fibrous tissue had formed over the injury." Nitya's partial blindness was not noticeable except as a very slight squint.

What Krishna enjoyed most were the theatres they were taken to. In the course of their stay in London they went to see *The Prisoner of Zenda*, *The Scarlet Pimpernel*, *Julius Caesar* with Herbert Tree as Antony, *Macbeth*, *The Only Way*, *Baby Mine*, *Hope*, George Grossmith in *Peggy*, *Kismet*, *A Royal Divorce* and Kinemacolour at the Scala. The Oxford and Cambridge and Eton and Harrow cricket matches at Lords were also very much enjoyed as well as Madame Tussaud's, the Military Tournament, Trooping the Colour and fireworks at the White City, whereas the

---

of the 1st Earl of Lytton who had been Viceroy of India. She had married in 1897. Her connection with India appealed to Mrs. Besant.

Zoo, St. Paul's (two visits) and Kew Gardens hurt their feet, and the "electric tube" they did not like at all.

Lady Emily managed to get seats for them in the Admiralty stand for the Coronation procession of George V on June 22 and took them herself together with the two eldest of her five children, Barbara, who was three months younger than Nitya, and Robert, aged eleven.[1] Lady Emily described the occasion:

> There was no means of finding our car afterwards owing to the crowds, so we had to walk back to my house in Bloomsbury Square. At that time walking was an agony to the two boys, who had never worn shoes before coming to Europe. It was also something of a torture to Krishna, with his shy and retiring nature, to be obliged to face crowds, especially as his long hair, with European clothes, always provoked such comments as "Get yer air cut." The reason for this peculiar style of hairdressing was that traditionally the Buddha, when as Prince Siddartha he had left home to seek enlightenment, had cut off his long locks to the shoulders with his sword. It was decided by those in charge of Krishna, probably at the Master's orders, that as he was to be a future Buddha (on Mercury, some millions of years hence) he should already adopt the Buddhist coiffure. They do not seem to have considered the feelings of the shy boy subjected to such a penance. As we walked away from the Admiralty through the dense crowds, constant jeers were hurled at poor Krishna. There was one notable exception: as we passed through Seven Dials one woman standing at her door exclaimed as we passed, "God bless his beautiful face!"

Lessons were not so important that they prevented Mrs. Besant from taking the boys with her to various places in England and Scotland when she went to hold Theosophical meetings and enroll members in the Order of the Star. They went first to Oxford for two nights where Lady Emily, who went with them, remembered them at a

---

[1] Mrs. Besant wrote to Leadbeater of Robert Lutyens that he was a delightful small boy whom Krishna liked, and added that he was a great-grandson of Bulwer Lytton. This would have impressed Leadbeater who regarded Bulwer Lytton as a great occultist. Leadbeater maintained that only an Initiate could have written *Zanoni*.

garden party on a bitterly cold May day—"two shivering little Indian boys" looking so forlorn and cold that she longed to put her arms round them and mother them. No wonder Krishna wrote to Leadbeater on May 26 that Oxford "was very cold indeed and we did not enjoy ourselves at all." Mrs. Besant reported some difficulty in getting Indians into Oxford but hoped "things would be better in four years' time." In August their names were put down for Balliol and New College. They expected to take up residence in October 1914.

In June Mrs. Besant took the boys with her to Paris for a few days where on the 12th she lectured at the Sorbonne on "Giordano Bruno, Theosophy's Apostle in the Sixteenth Century." As Mrs. Besant herself had been Bruno in one of her past incarnations her lecture must at least have been convincing, so it is not surprising that the amphitheatre holding four thousand people was packed and that hundreds had to be turned away. Krishna told Leadbeater next day, "The Sorbonne lecture was a great success. I saw the Count there."[1]

Krishna recorded only one other occult experience while he was in Europe: he remembered going with George Arundale to the house of the Master Kuthumi on the night of June 27 and the Master accepting George, who was already on probation, as his pupil. Krishna wrote to Leadbeater asking for confirmation of this and received a cable to say that it was so.

Mrs. Besant gave three lectures at the Queen's Hall in London in June and July on "The Coming of the World Teacher." The hall was so full that, as at the Sorbonne, hundreds of people were turned away. In India she always wore a white sari but in Europe confined herself to a long white gown. With her short white curly hair she was a striking figure on the platform in spite of her small stature; her rhetoric was inclined to be flowery but she possessed to an extraordinary degree that vital quality for

[1] It is uncertain whether the Count (the Master, the Comte de St. Germain) was in his physical body or materialized astral body when Krishna saw him. Although the Count is said to have died in about 1784, Leadbeater in *The Masters and the Path* (1925), claimed to have met him in his physical body walking down the Corso in Rome. The Count took him up into the gardens of the Pincian Hill and sat talking to him for over an hour about the work of the Theosophical Society. Leadbeater does not record the date of this meeting.

an orator—magnetism. After her last lecture Krishna wrote to Leadbeater, "She is indeed the finest speaker in the world." Enid Bagnold, the playwright and novelist, remembers Mrs. Besant speaking at the Queen's Hall in 1912: "When she came on to the platform she was burning. Her authority reached everywhere."

Krishna too was made to take a small share in the work of propaganda. On May 28, at the first meeting at the T.S. Headquarters in London of the Round Table, an offshoot for young people of the Order of the Star, he said a few words. "George and I had prepared Krishna to speak," Mrs. Besant told Leadbeater on May 31. "He was very nervous and forgot much of it, but everyone was delighted and he looked very charming." The trite words he brought out are only interesting as being the first speech he made in his life.

By September 15 she was able to report that he had grown "very manly" and had spoken "to over 200 people at a meeting of the Star in the East, had really spoken very well. It seemed wise to take the opportunity although it was rather an ordeal for him."

In August the boys had been with Mrs. Besant to stay at Esher in Surrey with the Brights, who had a cottage there. They were able to play croquet every afternoon, though they still had to study algebra and be taken to London twice a week for riding lessons and exercise at Sandow's. Lady Emily visited them several times at Esher with Robert, who was the only young person Krishna met in England that year whom he considered at all "promising" —that is, likely to get on the Path. Lady Emily recalled that the boys had fun together on the river as far as the terrible indigestion Krishna suffered from at that time would allow.

Acute pains in the stomach would keep him awake half the night. C.W.L. [Leadbeater] had laid down a system of diet for him, supposedly under the direct orders of the Master K.H. It was a cruel diet for anybody suffering from indigestion. Innumerable glasses of milk had to be consumed during the day, and porridge and eggs for breakfast. I can see Krishna now, after a sleepless night of pain, struggling to eat his prescribed breakfast under Mrs. Benant's stern eye. How I longed to snatch the plate from him and give

his inside a rest. This digestive trouble, with acute
pain, persisted until about 1916.

On the other hand Lady Emily also recalled that they
found the unspiced food so tasteless that they deluged it
with salt and pepper. Nitya remarked one day, "I do not
think Miss Bright quite understands how much we like
rice." Miss Bright found Nitya "a charming little fellow,
such a serious face and keen, friendly, inquiring eyes; a
fine, big nature in that small Indian body."

The last event before the boys went back to India was
the laying of the foundation stone on September 3 for a
new Theosophical headquarters in Tavistock Square (now
the headquarters of the British Medical Association). Mrs.
Besant asked Edwin Lutyens to prepare plans for the
building. This he did, though more for love of his wife
than of Mrs. Besant or Theosophy, which was already beginning to eat into his home life. An appeal was launched
and £30,000 collected of the required £40,000, most of it
donated by Miss Dodge.

Although Miss Dodge, Lady De La Warr and Lady
Emily were all deeply involved in Theosophy by this time
it was not until the following year that they began to play
a prominent part in Krishna's life. Lady De La Warr,
small, wiry, smartly dressed and remote from her own
three children, was in constant attendance on Miss Dodge,
whose intimidating deep gruff voice belied her kindness of
heart. As her arthritis grew worse she was confined to a
wheel-chair and unable to do anything active for Theosophy apart from giving financial help and hospitality at
Warwick House. Lady Emily, tall and warmly impulsive,
was, on the other hand, able to lecture and write articles
as well as entertain fellow Theosophists at Bloomsbury
Square. Writing came easily to her but, being a very shy
person, speaking in public was at first a torture. Deter-
mination, however, and enthusiasm for her subject—the
imminent coming of the World Teacher to which everything in her nature responded—triumphed over her self-
consciousness and she was able to train herself to become
a fine speaker. Indeed so good did she become that eventually Mrs. Besant accorded her the status of International
Lecturer for the T.S. Her marriage suffered as a result of
being so much away from home but she felt really fulfilled
for the first time.

7

Legal Guardianship

Mrs. Besant, with Krishna and Nitya, rejoined Leadbeater
at Adyar on October 7. George Arundale had returned to
India with them but had gone back to the Central Hindu
College at Benares. After only two months at Adyar they
all went to Benares where the Theosophical Convention
was to be held that year. At the end of the Convention
something occurred which seemed to Leadbeater of "such
transcendent importance" that on December 31 he sent an
account of it to Fabrizio Ruspoli who had remained at
Adyar:

A good many members have joined the Order of
the Star in the East during the Convention, and somebody suggested (quite casually) that it would be a
great pleasure to them if the Head of the Order
[Krishna] would himself hand them their certificates
of membership. The idea was taken up with enthusiasm, and other older members also asked to be allowed to return their certificates in order to receive
them again directly from the Head. So a time was
fixed (6 p.m. on December 28th) and we went down
to the Indian Section Hall. We thought of it merely
as a formal little ceremony, and I even doubted
whether the President would come, as she was tired
after her lecture at 4.
Only Star members were admitted, but the Hall
was full; I suppose there were about four hundred
people. Mostly they sat on the floor, but there was a
line of benches round the walls, and a few chairs at
the upper end. The President and I sat there, with
Miss Arundale [George's aunt] and Nitya and a few
others, and the benches were occupied chiefly by European ladies. The arrangement was that the Head
was to stand just in front of us, with Telang [the Na-

tional Representative for India] beside him. The
members were to file past in a line, each handing his
certificate to Telang, who read out his name, and
then passed the paper to Krishna, who returned it to
its owner ... the first two or three members took
their papers with a bow and a smile, and passed back
to their places.

All at once the Hall was filled with a tremendous
power, which was so evidently flowing through
Krishna that the next member fell at his feet, over-
whelmed by this marvellous rush of force. I have
never seen or felt anything in the least like it; it reminded one irresistibly of the rushing, mighty wind,
and the outpouring of the Holy Ghost at Pentecost.
The tension was enormous, and every one in the
room was most powerfully affected. It was exactly the
kind of thing that we read about in the old scriptures,
and think exaggerated; but here it was before us in
the twentieth century.

After that each one prostrated himself as his turn
came, many of them with tears pouring down their
cheeks. The scene was indeed a memorable one, for
the stream of devotees was remarkably representative
in character. There were members from almost every
country in Europe, from America and from all parts
of India, and it was most striking and beautiful to see
white and black alike, Brahmins and Buddhists, Parsis
and Christians, haughty Rajput princes and gor-
geously apparelled merchants, grey-haired men and
young children, all prostrating themselves in rapt devotion at our Krishna's feet. The blessing poured
forth was so obvious that every one present yearned
to share in it, and those who had no certificates with
them tore off their Star badges and handed them in,
so that they also might receive something at his
hands.

He stood all the time with perfect grace and self-
possession, smiling gently upon them, and holding out
his hands in benediction over each prostrate form in
turn. I think the culmination of the strangely affecting
scene was when our dear Nitya threw himself at his
brother's feet, and the whole congregation burst into
enthusiastic applause—I hardly know why, but some-

how it seemed at the moment not at all irreverent, but entirely appropriate and natural.

When the last of that great company had made his reverence, Krishna returned to his seat between us, and there were a few minutes of silent rapture, of strange hushed awe and expectancy.

Then the President whispered to Krishna to close the meeting, and he rose and held out his right hand over the heads of the audience, and said solemnly: "May the blessing of the great Lord rest upon you forever." And so we came down to the ordinary world again, and left the Hall, feeling that we had passed through one of the greatest experiences of our lives, and that indeed it had been good for us to be there, for that this had been for us none other than the house of God and the gate of heaven. . . .

At a meeting [of the Esoteric Section] on the 29th the President said for the first time that, after what they had seen and felt, it was no longer possible to make even a pretense of concealing the fact that Krishna's body had been chosen by the Bodhisattva, and was even now being attuned by Him.

Thereafter December 28 became a sacred day for the Order of the Star in the East. On the 30th the scene was repeated, though with less force. On that occasion Mrs. van Hook and Hubert were among those who prostrated themselves before Krishna. One does not know what Hubert's feelings were on this occasion but the one person who voiced his displeasure was Krishna's father, who complained to Mrs. van Hook that this deification would make him and his sons the laughing stock of India. Mrs. Besant had many enemies amongst orthodox Hindus and anti-British extremists who saw a way of damaging her through Narianiah; they worked him up, therefore, by insinuating that her intention was for the boys to break caste altogether and forsake Hinduism for Theosophical Christianity; they also raked up the Leadbeater scandal of 1906.

At Calcutta on her way back to Adyar in January 1912, Mrs. Besant received a letter from Narianiah threatening to bring a lawsuit to deprive her of the custody of his sons. At Adyar, in the middle of the month, she sent for Sir Subramania Aiyar and one or two others, and in their presence asked Narianiah what were his true wishes with regard to the boys. He replied that there should be complete separation between them and Leadbeater, that even written communication between them should cease. According to Narianiah Mrs. Besant agreed to this condition and therefore on January 19 he signed a document to say he had no objection to her taking them to England to be educated. Poor Narianiah must have been badly torn between his loathing and mistrust of Leadbeater and the social and financial advantages of an English education for his sons, especially if they became Oxford graduates, for this would also reflect great glory on himself in spite of the inevitable breaking of caste.

Leadbeater believed that the time had come for Krishna to take his second Initiation and he had wanted to take the boys for a few months to Ootacamund in the Nilgiri Hills to prepare Krishna for this step. Narianiah's attitude now made this impossible. Neither Mrs. Besant nor Leadbeater, however, was going to allow Narianiah to interfere with Krishna's spiritual progress, so towards the end of January Leadbeater was sent off to Europe to find a suitable place for Krishna's preparation, Narianiah's supporters suggesting that he had fled the country for fear of arrest.

Mrs. Besant was now very anxious to get the boys out of India before Narianiah changed his mind. "I shall not feel safe until we are out of Indian waters," she wrote to Leadbeater on January 23. Taking advantage of Narianiah's absence—he had gone to Cudappah for a week—she hurried the boys to Bombay, giving out that she was sailing from there on February 10. In fact they sailed on the *Salsette* on the 3rd. Mrs. Besant wrote to Narianiah on the 7th from the Indian Ocean asking him to leave Adyar immediately and stating that she intended to keep the boys in Europe until they had finished their education.[1]

This time Dick Clarke and Jinarajadasa went with them as their tutors; George Arundale was to join them later. Jinarajadasa—Raja as he will be called hereafter—was, it

[1] This came out afterwards in the court case and was, according to the judge, "a declaration of war." Narianiah had been living with his two other sons in the house in the Compound, near the Theosophical Press, which had been prepared for Krishna and Nitya but where they never lived. This house is still standing, but the "hovel" in which they lived when they first came to Adyar was demolished several years ago. Narianiah moved to Madras.

may be remembered, the Singalese pupil Leadbeater had
brought with him to England in 1887. Now thirty-seven,
he had become one of the leaders of the Theosophical Society. His charm and proficiency in languages made him a
most valuable lecturer for Theosophy in all parts of the
world. Although his home was at Adyar, he had been
abroad lecturing when Krishna was "discovered."

Lady Emily went to Dover to meet them on February
16 (they had come overland again from Brindisi) and
remembered thinking how much darker both boys looked.
Krishna now had his hair cut to a conventional length.
Her recollection of that time was of Nitya, dressed in an
Eton jacket, always leaning up against a wall reading a
book or magazine. Neither of the boys ever seemed to sit
down; Krishna was always in a cloud and would jump if
spoken to suddenly.

They stayed again at Drayton Gardens with the Brights
and the same old routine of lessons and exercise at Sandow's was resumed. Then after a few weeks they were off
again—this time to Holland with Mrs. Besant, Raja, Dick
Clarke and Lady Emily. Leadbeater meanwhile had settled
on a place with the right magnetism and atmosphere for
Krishna's preparation—Taormina in Sicily. On March 25,
the boys, accompanied by only Raja and Clarke, left Holland and after a night in Paris arrived next day at Taormina where Leadbeater was waiting for them. On the 27th
they were joined by George Arundale direct from India.
They all stayed at the Hotel Naumachia, where they occupied the whole of the top floor.

Mrs. Besant obviously realized that Narianiah would be
outraged if he knew the boys were again with Leadbeater,
for back in London she wrote to the latter, "I do not think
Krishna should write to India from Sicily. If it gets about
that he is there, we may have interruptions of some sort.
Besides, the atmosphere should be kept clear from useless
thought-forms."

They stayed nearly four months at Taormina, Mrs.
Besant being with them there from May till July. Although
Leadbeater wrote an account of Krishna's second Initiation which took place on the night of the full moon of
May 1, Krishna himself only mentions it in a birthday
message for members of the Order of the Star in the East
which he sent on May 25 to Miss Arundale in Benares:

This year from our Order there have been put on Probation five people and from the Group [the Purple Order] four, and I think this ought to encourage you and make you realize that *you* can also do it. Also, as you know, Raja and I have taken the second step and that should encourage you and give you strength. I hope ... that George and Nitya will pass their first Initiation very soon, and that then there will be seven Initiates at the heart of the Society.

Mrs. Besant, Leadbeater, Krishna, Raja, George and Nitya would make six Initiates. The seventh is uncertain. Although by this time the year of Krishna's birth had been established—he was now known to be seventeen—the day was still thought to be May 25 instead of May 11.

Leadbeater received further instructions from the Master after Krishna's second Initiation:

> I must again emphasize special care of the feet ... there is even a slight commencement of distortion.... Dress them always in material of the best ... and remember that both head and feet should be uncovered when possible. Do not allow your original watchfulness in these matters to diminish.... Do not let yourself regard anything as insignificant which helps provide a perfect vehicle for the Lord.

On May 29 Krishna was telling Miss Arundale that he had written a new book called *Education as Service* which was to be published in London. In it he described the life of an ideal school where love rules and inspires, where the students grow into noble adolescents under the fostering care of teachers who feel the greatness of their vocation. Lady Emily states that this book was "obviously the work of George Arundale" just as Leadbeater had been "the real inspiration" for *At the Feet of the Master*. However, in view of Krishna's letter saying he had written it, Lady Emily seems to have overstated George's part in its composition. No doubt George helped him and did some editing, and Krishna's style would almost certainly have been influenced by George just as a child models his writing on the author he currently admires.

Mrs. Besant returned to London on July 4 and George went back to India on the 12th having taken his first Initiation. (Presumably Nitya took it at the same time, though there is no record of it.) The rest of the party left two days later to stay at the Villa Cevasco near Genoa, with old friends who had been at Adyar when Krishna was first "discovered"—Mr. and Mrs. William Kirby.[1] At the end of July, Krishna and Sitya with Raja and Dick Clarke returned to England while Leadbeater remained in Genoa with the Kirbys. Leadbeater never returned to England again. It was said by his enemies that he feared prosecution, but if that were so, how had he dared to remain in England for nearly three years after the 1906 scandal?

On July 30 Mrs. Besant told Leadbeater from London that by the last mail she had received a registered letter from Narianiah "cancelling his assignment to me and the boys, and calling on me to produce them and hand them over at the end of August. My answer will run: 'Sir, I beg to acknowledge the receipt of your letter, dated -ult. Sincerely Annie Besant.'" Narianiah's letter was later published verbatim in the Madras paper the *Hindu*, one of the most influential papers in India, which was to launch a bitter attack on Mrs. Besant, Leadbeater and the Theosophical Society. No doubt the secret of Leadbeater's close association with Krishna and Nitya for the past four months had leaked out in India. Mrs. Besant now feared that Narianiah's adherents might attempt to kidnap the boys; before returning to India, therefore, to fight an expected lawsuit, she made sure they were safely hidden in England. After some weeks with the Brights at Esher, where Nitya had congestion of the lungs rather badly, they went to Old Lodge, Ashdown Forest, a large house put at their disposal by Lady De La Warr, Miss Dodge's great friend. There they remained for five months, from November to April 1913, closely guarded by Raja, Dick Clarke and two other young Englishmen, former pupils of Leadbeater's—Basil Hodgson-Smith (an Oxford graduate) and Reginald Farrar, with Mrs. and Miss Bright in charge of the household. At Old Lodge there were compulsory runs in the Forest for the boys every day before breakfast, even when there was snow on the ground, regular hours of study and afternoon motor drives, and twice a week Krishna's body-

[1] Maria-Luisa Kirby was an Italian and an artist. She had painted portraits of the Masters from recollections on the astral plane which hung in the shrine-room at Adyar. William Kirby worked in an English bank in Genoa.

guard brought him to London to get his teeth straightened.

Lady Emily visited Krishna several times at Old Lodge and felt he was glad to see her, as well he might be. He much preferred female to male society and although he was very fond of Raja he never got on as well with him as with George. Raja was a much sterner teacher and a great disciplinarian.

Before this, in September, Lady Emily had been invited to Genoa with Barbara and Robert to meet Leadbeater for the first time. Lady Emily was fascinated by him though shocked by the disloyal way in which he discussed Mrs. Besant with the Kirbys, giving instances of her lack of judgement in her choice of the people around her. However, Lady Emily found his manner to the children "perfect." "He is very affectionate—reads to them—talks to them—takes a great deal of trouble to draw them out and make them at their ease—and is evidently devoted to children, though bored with grown ups." Very much to Lady Emily's surprise he was far more attracted to Barbara than he was to Robert.

The importance of this visit, though, was that for several months after his return to India Leadbeater wrote to Lady Emily by every mail, and his letters give a detailed record of the lawsuit brought by Narianiah against Mrs. Besant for the recovery of his sons. In October Leadbeater wrote from Adyar:

Krishna's objectionable old father has at last filed the suit against Mrs. Besant which he threatened, professedly in order to recover possession of his sons and remove them from my evil influence. It is of course a farce because it is brought when he knows that they are actually separated from me for a period of four or five years because of their university education in England. The truth is that the man is a tool of the political party here in India which is disaffected to the British Government, and he is simply being used as a weapon of attack upon Mrs. Besant and upon the Theosophical Society, because that organization has always stood for law and order. Mrs. Besant has specially roused the enmity of that section of the people because she refused to allow the preaching of seditious doctrines to the students in the Central Hindu College and has consistently thrown the whole

weight of her great influence against their propaganda
of bombs and murder. . . . We know that attempts
have been made upon her life, and this newspaper
campaign [the attack in the *Hindu*] is an attempt
upon her reputation and her influence from the same
quarter. Those people have got hold of this unlucky
man, and it is reported that he himself says he is
forced to bring this suit.

In the original plaint Narianiah alleged that he had
witnessed with his own eyes an act of sodomy between
Leadbeater and Krishna, but this charge he withdrew in
the course of the preliminary hearings. Mrs. Besant, however, pinned him down and demanded a statement of time
and place.

In reply [Leadbeater informed Lady Emily in a
letter of January 3, 1913] he has now (under oath
remember) watered it down to an entirely different
and much less important matter. We have now, therefore, before the Court two sworn statements of his on
this important point which are absolutely irrecon-
cilable. As it happens we are able to prove irrefutably
that even this modified charge is a pure invention, for
two ladies were present in my room at the time he al-
leges he saw certain objectionable things. When the
President [Mrs. Besant] saw his affidavit, she remarked with glee: "The Lord hath delivered mine enemy into mine hands!"

Narianiah had watered down the charges to certain "improper" and "unnatural" acts which he claimed to have
witnessed between Leadbeater and Krishna about the second week in April 1910, in the Octagon Bungalow when
the boys went there for a glass of milk before going for
their bicycle ride. Leadbeater stated when giving evidence
in court that Mrs. van Hook and Dr. Mary Rocke (an English doctor and social worker living in Adyar at the time
Krishna was "discovered") had been in his room every
morning from 5:30 onwards from October 1909 till the
end of April 1910.
Mrs. Besant, who was a born fighter, seems at first to
have enjoyed the case. She conducted her own defense just
as she had done thirty-six years before when fighting to re-

tain the custody of her daughter, but now with far greater vigor and far more experience. In November 1912 she had written to Lady Emily, "Ruspoli is sending you the papers in the suit against me. I am quite happy about it, and glad to have, at last, the opportunity of meeting the enemy in the open." She signed herself "Your very warlike Heracles (who, wicked thing, is enjoying herself immensely à la Irish)." Heracles was her pseudonym throughout *The Lives of Alcyone* and she was always proud of her Irish blood on her mother's side. She felt very strongly that it was not only herself and Leadbeater but the whole Theosophical Society that was under attack.

Where Krishna's sympathies lay is shown in this letter to Mrs. Besant written from Old Lodge. His own spelling and punctuation have been retained in all his letters.

Jan. 5, 1913.

My own dearest Mother,

I am so glad you think that my handwriting is improved and I am very careful about it.

Dear Mother, you must be going through a very hard time and I wish I was with you physically and be a loving son to you in the time of trouble. It is so hard for you at your dear age fighting with those awful people. I suppose it will end sometime! Anyway, you know my devotion and loyalty for you and I love you so much as my dearest Mother. I suppose these are all your trials for the 5th Initiation and it must be very hard for you to bear all these trials. Even if all the world turns against you there is one who will *never never* abandon his beloved Mother.

I am sending you my few rememberings,

Your old dearest and devoted
son
Krishna

Krishna never missed a mail in sending Mrs. Besant a loving little note. It was on the instructions of the Master, as relayed through Leadbeater, that he now always underlined his signature. It was an invariable practice of Leadbeater's also, the significance of which was never explained any more than the practice of all pupils of the Master being required to part their hair in the middle.

8

The Lawsuit

Owing to various delays and postponements the case did not come up in the High Court of Madras until March 20, 1913. It was then heard by Mr. Justice Bakewell, the presiding judge of that court. The case for Narianiah was that in the document he had signed on March 6, 1910, transferring to Mrs. Besant the guardianship of his sons, it was not open to her to delegate that guardianship to another. He had conferred that power on her alone for the sake of the boys' education and it could not be transferred to a person against whom he had the strongest aversion; he had signed the document at a time when he was completely under Mrs. Besant's influence and control, and his delay in taking legal action was due to his belief, shared by many people, that Mrs. Besant was semi-divine. It was not necsesary to prove conclusively the charge against Leadbeater of having an improper relationship with the elder boy; a well-founded suspicion, a resonable fear, were sufficient for the father to insist on his inherent right to the guardianship and custody of his children until the age of twenty-one. (His charges against Leadbeater were too indecent to be given orally; he wrote out a portion of his evidence and handed it to the court.) He also objected to the fact that the elder boy had been deified by Mrs. Besant's announcement that he was to be the Lord Christ, with the result that a number of respectable persons had prostrated before him. Moreover, knowing the boy intimately as he did he did not believe he was capable of having written *At the Feet of the Master*. Narianiah was willing to deposit Rs. 10,000 under such conditions as the judge might determine for the education and upbringing of the two boys. He was also willing that some person of undoubted respectability should be associated with him in their guardianship. (Narianiah's financial backing was believed by Mrs. Besant's supporters to come from the

Hindu, while Mrs. Besant's costs were born by the Theosophical Society.)

Mrs. Besant in her defense refuted the charge that she had broken the contract by placing the boys under a guardianship other than her own; they were in England and Leadbeater was in Adyar. She maintained that the court should be concerned only with the welfare of the minors. The elder boy would be eighteen in five weeks' time when, according to the common law of England, he would be entirely free from her authority and nothing could prevent him from returning to India and to his father if he so wished. That, in her view, constituted the fundamental absurdity of the case.

So far as the intellectual welfare of the boys was concerned, if they were left with her, the father's wishes would be carried out in full, and the object of the letter of guardianship of March 6, 1910, would be fulfilled. The removal of the boys from England to India would defeat the object for which the father had signed the letter of guardianship and they would be deprived of education in an English university. She then mentioned five witnesses who supported her plea that she had given no promise to the father to keep the boys entirely away from Leadbeater when the father gave his consent on January 19, 1912, to their removal to Europe.

A more important factor which she stressed was that of the boys' moral welfare. The character of the elder boy would be irretrievably ruined if by an order of the court he was brought back to Madras. Returning him to his father would be an endorsement of the father's accusations against him, not to speak of the misery the boy must endure if he was placed back in the power of a father who had made such terrible accusations against him. In England the boys were surrounded by people who treated them with care and love—refined and cultured people, eminent in intellectual, moral and social life.

The point had been raised that Krishnamurti was being prepared for the life of a Hindu *sanyasi.* Mrs. Besant declared that this was an altogether misleading idea. She did not believe he would marry, but there was no such outer compulsion placed upon him. He was suited for a religious life, which meant that he would not be shut out from any of the learned professions, only from party politics.

Mrs. Besant held that under the guise of a civil suit for

the custody of minors, the trial was practically a criminal trial of two, if not three persons charged with a very serious crime—the elder son, Leadbeater and herself. Having brought the suit and given publicity to a terrible accusation, the father was not fit to exercise his duty. As to the charge against Leadbeater, she had voluntarily placed all documents connected with the custody of the boys and everything else connected with the matter at the disposal of the plaintiff's lawyer because she wanted to throw full light on the subject and hold nothing back.[1] The evidence of the father was contradictory and highly improbable, she maintained. Although different stories were told about the alleged offense, the place where it was said to have occurred remained unchanged, yet a number of witnesses had testified to the fact that it was impossible for anyone to see the sofa on which Leadbeater was said to be lying at the time the plaintiff alleged to have seen it. No human father having the welfare of his sons at heart would have concealed the matter from others if it were true, as this father had done. Even after the alleged offense he had allowed the boys to associate with the alleged criminal until 1912. She asked the judge for nothing more than a decision based on the welfare of the two boys. If the judge granted the suit, Krishnamurti, as well as Leadbeater, would be branded as a criminal with a dark stain on him for the rest of his life.

"Our case is over at last [Leadbeater wrote to Lady Emily on April 11 before judgement had been delivered], and we are all delighted to be freed from the worry of it. I went up myself on Tuesday [April 4] and Wednesday of this week—the first day to give my own evidence, and the second to hear the President's closing speech, which was both masterly and magnificent. She dealt first with various legal points. . . . She then took up the evidence, and told

[1] These documents, including private letters exchanged between Mrs. Besant and Leadbeater in 1906, and the incriminating "cipher" letter, somehow fell into the hands of Dr. T. M. Nair, one of Theosophy's bitterest enemies, who published them in a Madras paper, *Justice,* of which he was editor. In 1918 he was to include them in a book, *The Evolution of Mrs. Besant.* Dr. Nair had already, in 1910, published a vicious article entitled "Psychopathia Sexualis in a Mahatma" in a local medical journal, the *Antiseptic,* attacking Leadbeater and suggesting he had been Onan in a previous incarnation.

the whole story as it appears to her, unravelling one
by one the threads of the great skein of falsehood
which the plaintiff's malignance had constructed. This
was done with wonderful cleverness, for she had the
whole matter at her fingers' ends; my only doubt was
whether the judge's mind was quick enough to follow
her through all the intricacies. He was, however, very
kindly and helpful to her, and went out of his way to
put to her some points which she ought to answer. He
specially gave her an opportunity to speak about me
and she took advantage of it to deliver a most eulo-
gistic little speech intended to undo the effect of her
E.S. pronouncement in 1906. [Her circular to the
Secretaries of the Esoteric Section.] Then she wound
up with an eloquent appeal to the justice of England
to save her ward from the stigma cast upon him by
the wickedness of an unnatural father. This was in
her best style, and produced a tremendous effect upon
the crowded audience in the Court.

In my own evidence I had an opportunity not only
of denying these recent falsehoods, but also of clearing up some part of the unpleasant matter of 1906.
The report of that London Advisory Board was cast
aside as obviously valueless, though the opposing
counsel asked me two or three questions about it,
which I answered very plainly. The forged cipher letter [the letter picked up in the flat in Toronto] was
put into the hands of our opponents by the President,
but they were afraid to produce it in Court, so I did
not get an opportunity of actually repudiating it. The
general impression seems to be that this evidence has
cleared up matters a good deal and put a much better
complexion on them.

Every day the Hindu newspaper has systematically
falsified the evidence in the most glaring manner. It
seems to me amazing that neither the Court nor the
Government interfere in such a case. They tell us
that we have our remedy in a prosecution for libel;
but the fact is that we have had enough of prosecu-
tions and do not care to undertake another."[1]

[1] Mrs. Besant had sued the *Hindu* for publishing part of Dr. Nair's
articles about Leadbeater from the *Antiseptic*, and also, belatedly,
the *Antiseptic* itself of which Nair was editor. She had lost both
actions.

They had to wait until April 15 for the judgement. In the course of his summing up the judge discussed at length the charge of improper relations between Leadbeater and the elder boy and observed that from the father's demeanor in the witness-box he appeared to be of "an emotional temperament, prone to tears and not capable of much self-control." The judge accepted the statement of some of the witnesses on Mrs. Besant's behalf that Narianiah showed himself to be a jealous and suspicious father. He was an orthodox Brahmin and therefore naturally suspicious that a European might lead his sons into some violation of caste rules. There was no doubt that at the time of signing the deed transferring the custody of the boys to Mrs. Besant, he was influenced by several considerations, including the advantage to them of an English education; there was no evidence, though, of any undue influence having been exercised on him by Mrs. Besant.

The charge of improper relationship made in the original plaint was a criminal offense alleged to have occurred in or about the latter part of March 1910 but this charge had been abandoned in the amended plaint and the date of the occurrence was given as the second week of April 1910. The judge added:

> If the plaintiff originally believed that a disgusting crime had been committed upon his son or even that his son's person had been treated indecently, as he now alleges, and that by a man whom he would have regarded as a pariah, it is difficult to believe that he would not have gone weeping to his house with his sons and complained to his household.

In evidence he said that he had merely scolded the elder boy for being naked. No complaint of the alleged occurrence was made to Sir Subramania Aiyar who was Vice-President of the Society and represented Mrs. Besant during her absence from Adyar, though the father had consulted him on several matters connected with the Society. He also allowed his sons to be associated with Leadbeater during the following months and even left them in his charge during a short absence of himself and Mrs. Besant from Adyar.

Pointing out that there were discrepancies in regard to the date of the alleged occurrence and the changes in the nature and the date of the occurrence in the amended plaint, and the inconsistent conduct of the father at the time, it was clear that his evidence was not to be relied on. Leadbeater's denial of the story was confirmed by the public nature of the room in which the act was said to have occurred and the daily routine of which Mrs. Besant's witnesses had spoken.

Mrs. Besant's servant, Lakshman, had been called as a witness at the request of both parties. The judge referred to his evidence in the course of which he had said, "Hindus usually do not bathe naked. It is sinful. I do not think Mr. Leadbeater was doing wrong." The judge accepted Leadbeater's explanation that he found it necessary to teach the boys bathing in English fashion without clothing. The father had asked Sir Subramania Aiyar about the legal effect of the guardianship letter and was advised that by that action he had waived his right as a father and would not be able to revoke it at will. The judge concluded that this opinion must have induced the father to search for something which would influence the court into revoking the agreement and that he had, therefore, revived the charges first made against Leadbeater in 1906. All the same, Leadbeater's own admission of the views he held rendered him a highly dangerous associate for the children, even though he had promised Mrs. Besant not to express or practice them. The father had certain legal and moral duties towards his children with respect to their education, maintenance and upbringing; he had no doubt attempted to strengthen his case with lies against Leadbeater, but that could not be said to render him unfit to have the custody of his children. His wishes having been disregarded, he could demand restoration of the boys to his custody.

With regard to the jurisdiction of the court the boys were subjects of the King-Emperor domiciled in British India, only temporarily resident in England, where they were taken by Mrs. Besant for their education. She had, in the opinion of he court, broken the understanding by which she was allowed to take them out of India. In these circumstances the judge claimed that his court had jurisdiction to pass orders as to the custody of the children. He added that for the reasons given it was necessary in the interests of the boys and for their future protection that they should be declared Wards of Court. The judge, therefore, directed Mrs. Besant to hand over the custody of the two boys to their father on or before May 26, 1913. With regard to the costs of the case, the trial having been unduly protracted through the allegations against Leadbeater, the judge called on Narianiah to bear the responsibility, not only for himself but also for Mrs. Besant.

The judge's decision in our case was a mixed one as we had expected [Leadbeater informed Lady. Emily on April 19]. We were warned that in order to obtain full investigation of the facts we must risk adverse judgement on legal points—which, however, could afterwards be reversed on appeal; so the President waived various points on which she might have insisted. The Judge absolutely cleared Krishnaji from any imputation of crime, saying most emphatically that the alleged abominations had been invented by the father because of his jealousy of me, and that their impossibility was clearly shown. But he said in so many words: "The fact that the man is a liar does not deprive him of his right to his children." (I should have thought that such a lie *did*.) So he said he was compelled to make an order that the boys should be restored to him, but they should be Wards of Court, in order that it might exercise supervision over them. Of course we cannot accept this, so we have promptly appealed against the decision, and we shall no doubt succeed. But the President is so overjoyed at our overwhelming victory on the facts that it quite overweighs for the moment the legal difficulties. We are getting up a big festivity and feeding a vast crowd of poor to celebrate the vindication of Krishnaji. As the matter stands, the President is ordered to produce the boys by the end of May—which is of course beyond her power; but Sir Subramania Iyer tells us that the judgement is inconsistent with itself and contrary to law, and must inevitably be reversed on appeal. The Appellate Court will not touch the questions of fact, so nothing can interfere with the definite verdict that we have on that point. The Judge, by the way, expressed an opinion that my views on sex questions were immoral and dangerous, which I thought an unnecessary remark! *The Hindu* newspaper suggests that the Government ought to deport me from the country as a dangerous person—which would be an amusing end to the controversy, for I suppose there is in the whole of India no more loyal subject of the King than I, and that law was intended for political offenders! However, the Judge decreed that all costs should be borne by the plaintiff, which indicates his private opinion of him pretty clearly.

Leadbeater added that it seemed strange that "after Bakewell had stated in Court, 'This is a plain charge of perjury against the plaintiff and of perjury of a most aggravated and infamous character' the Court should feel that the welfare of the boys would be served by returning them to the custody of such a parent." Although these words of Bakewell's are not in the official report of the case he must have uttered them, for the Madras *Standard,* in criticizing the verdict, reminded its readers that out of the judge's own mouth had come the words, "This is a plain charge of perjury . . . ," quoting exactly what Leadbeater had written.

Leadbeater was annoyed, as he told Lady Emily on May 27, that both the Madras *Mail* which he considered the best of the Madras papers, and the London *Times* had reported that the judge had "characterized" *him* as immoral instead of merely his opinions. The *Mail* published a handsome apology, but he supposed it was "too much to expect the infallible *Times* to do likewise."

In fact *The Times* published a letter from Mrs. Besant on June 2, 1913, drawing attention to this inaccuracy in reporting the case. "Everyone who knows Mr. Leadbeater personally," she wrote, "is aware that his conduct is impeccable, whatever his academical opinion may be." And that opinion, she went on, was "based on the desire to shield women from ruin by a sin which destroys the woman for life while the man goes scot free." Mrs. Besant never lost an opportunity of defending a colleague or of fighting for women's rights.

9

"The Herald of the Star"

Mrs. Besant asked for a stay of execution pending her appeal, which was to be heard when the courts reopened in July. Having heard on April 25 that this had been granted, she set off for Europe to fulfil an engagement to lecture in Stockholm. She took with her George Arundale, who had just resigned from his post as Principal of the Central Hindu College at Benares in order to tutor Krishna and Nitya until they passed into Oxford.

The boys left Ashdown Forest in April and went with Raja to stay at Septeuil near Paris, where Monsieur Charles Blech, General Secretary of the T.S. for France, had a house. On May 7 Krishna was writing from Septeuil a rather hurt letter to Leadbeater: "You hint as though I will not stand loyally to her [Mrs. Besant] and I don't think you need to be afraid about that. I love her *too* much and I am very devoted to her. Please don't think I am ungrateful for what she and you have done to me. I don't think you ought to have hinted that I should [not] loyally stand by her." Three weeks later, still at Septeuil, he was expressing his devotion to her himself:

My dearest Mother,

May 29th, 1913.

On the 25th of this month I attained my majority [according to Mrs. Besant. He was eighteen]. I want to thank you for all your loving care of me since you saw me first on the platform at Madras in 1909. I know that the only thanks you want is that I should help others as you have helped me, and I shall remember this always now that I am of age and free to follow my will without your guardianship.

Though I am now my own master I shall remain always

Your devoted Son
Krishna

Mrs. Besant had gone straight to London on her arrival
from India, but as she was now to pay a short visit to
Paris the boys and Raja went to Calais to meet her at the
beginning of June. She had not seen them since the previous October. Back in London she was able to report to
Leadbeater on June 6, "Our beloved Krishna is as delightful as ever, but has gained immensely in self-confidence
and dignity. He is no longer shy and is quite self-reliant.
He grasps the present situation fully, and takes his own
view quite steadily. . . . Nitya is much grown and in every
way developed." Nitya was now fifteen.

On June 28 the boys went to Varengeville on the coast
of Normandy, where Monsieur Guillaume Mallet had put
his house, Les Communes, at their disposal for the summer. George Arundale and his aunt, Miss Francesca Arundale, a formidable-looking spinster with screwed-back hair,
very old-fashioned in all her ways, as well as Raja and
Dick Clarke were part of the household there. Lady Emily
with her five children took lodgings in the village for the
whole of the summer holidays, and Dr. Mary Rocke, one
of Mrs. Besant's witnesses who was now living in England,
also took a room in the village. Dr. Rocke's name exactly
suited her. With her short iron-grey hair, upright angular
figure and pleasing though rugged features, she was utterly
reliable and much loved in Theosophical circles.

Although, at first, lessons continued relentlessly in the
mornings for the boys, it was a comparatively happy time
for them as there was plenty of young company. Lady
Emily took Barbara and Robert every day to Les Communes for Shakespeare readings, and in the afternoons
there would be tennis and rounders at the Mallets' other
house, Les Bois des Moutiers, with some young Mallet cou-
sins joining in. Krishna had always been very fond of
Robert Lutyens, and now Nitya and Barbara, who were
the same age, became devoted friends. As for Lady Emily,
she had by this time come to regard Krishna as both her
son and her teacher.

He drew out all my maternal tenderness [she
wrote]—he seemed so lonely and unhappy. He was
now seventeen [as she still thought] but very young
for his age in some ways and very dreamy. He was
never allowed to be alone. One day he wandered off
alone along the cliff and a search party was sent out

after him. George was desperately anxious because orders had been given that he was always to be attended by two Initiates.

Krishna could be very critical and reproving, though. He told Lady Emily that her two youngest children, Betty and Mary, aged seven and five, had very bad manners which must be corrected.

Lady Emily was radiantly happy when she was put on probation by the Master Kuthumi on the night of August 11. This step was taken entirely on Krishna's authority. It was confirmed by Leadbeater in a cable but only after Krishna had "brought through" exactly what had occurred.

> So far I have been successful with our stay here [he wrote to Leadbeater on August 21]. Lady Emily has been put on probation and I sincerely hope that Barbie and Robert will also get on. I mean to get them on probation before we leave this place and I have a sort of feeling that they will be put on. *I will do my best*. . . . I really love Lady Emily. She is very nice. She is very devoted to me and thinks that I am her Master.

Krishna's hopes were realized, for Barbie and Robert were put on probation on September 18.

But most of Krishna's letters to Leadbeater from Varengeville—and he wrote to him every week as he did to Mrs. Besant—were concerned with the reconstruction of the *Herald of the Star* which Mrs. Besant and Leadbeater had decided was to become from the beginning of 1914 an enlarged monthly magazine printed in England. The total world membership of the Order of the Star in the East was now about 15,000, with 2,000 in England, not all of them Theosophists, and it was felt that a magazine of a more international character was needed. It would be an expensive undertaking, however, for printing costs were far higher in England than in India. An appeal was launched and, as usual, small donations poured in, though it was the ever-generous Miss Dodge who made the largest contribution—£200 a year for the next five years. Neither the Theosophical Society nor the Order of the Star ever seemed to be prevented from carrying out any of their projects through lack of funds, and the magazine duly appeared in its enlarged form on January 1, 1914. From being little more than a pamphlet it now consisted of sixty-four glossy pages with twenty-four full-page illustrations, some in color. Though George Arundale did most of the work, Krishna was the nominal editor with his name prominently displayed on the cover. Krishna did in fact for some months write the editorial notes under the title "In the Starlight."

Krishna's letters from Varengeville about the new *Herald* were short and factual. Lady Emily conveyed what was probably the real atmosphere surrounding the venture:

> George worked us all up to feverish excitement. Krishna was to be the nominal editor with George the acting editor. It was to be printed in blue ink with a blue cover and a silver star. It was to review all the events of the world in the light of the Lord's coming.... George and Dr. Rocke also planned to open a star shop and George was full of plans for the construction of things to be sold there—Alcyone birthday books, calendars, blue blotting paper, stamp boxes in blue paper with silver stars.[1] All ordinary studies were abandoned. Shakespeare was relegated to the bookshelf and we spent all our time in hectic activity over blue and silver paper. Jinarajadasa was in despair and tried in vain to bring us back to a calmer and more studious atmosphere.

George, who, according to Lady Emily, was clairvoyant, "brought through" a message about the new magazine from the Lord Maitreya himself who desired George "to undertake no further activites or responsibilities beyond the education of my children [Krishna and Nitya] and the issue of my *Herald*."

They were all at this time anxiously awaiting the result of the appeal which was being heard in Madras under Mr. Justice Oldfield. Months were spent in reviewing the first case and no doubt the Varengeville party were glad to

---

[1] Edwin Lutyens was in fact very genial to Krishna, and Krishna liked him and enjoyed his jokes. Rather unfairly Lutyens put the blame for his wife's absorption in Theosophy entirely on Mrs. Besant.

have something as exciting as the new *Herald* to occupy
them during this period of uncertainty.

They returned to London at the end of September, and
from that time onwards Krishna became Lady Emily's
"entire life." Her husband, her home, her children "faded
into the background." This exclusive and intense devotion
was to cause problems for Krishna as well as for herself.

In October Krishna reported to Mrs. Besant and Leadbeater from Drayton Gardens, where he was staying, that
Miss Dodge was putting a car at his disposal and settling
on him £500 a year for life, and £300 on Nitya while he
was at Oxford. She also settled an income on Mrs. Besant,
gave Lady Emily, who was far from rich, £100 a year so
that she could be free to travel about on Star business and
helped many others in the Star movement. Krishna wrote
that Miss Dodge was "a wonderful woman" and "extraordinarily kind" to them. He also reported in this letter of
October 10 that the doctor considered George to be on the
verge of a nervous breakdown. There had been friction between George and Raja and between George and Lady
Emily owing to his growing jealousy of her, and this seems
to have affected his nervous system. Krishna was having a
very unhappy time between the three of them.

Miss Dodge had also offered him a house on top of
Hampstead Heath. It was his own wish to live there as it
had a garden, the air would be good and it would be convenient for the new *Herald* office at 19 Tavistock Square.
Besides, he wanted to live in London, he told Mrs. Besant,
because Lady Emily was there. But it was not to be, and
after a few days at a cottage near Crowborough in Sussex,
where Krishna first learned to play golf, and a conference
of Star workers in London which he successfully conducted himself because George was indisposed, the boys were
taken off by Raja and George to stay with the Kirbys at
the Villa Cevasco near Genoa. It was there, on October
31, that a distressing cable reached them from Mrs. Besant
in Adyar, forwarded from London by Miss Bright: "Appeal failed. Boys must see Pole London without fail." Pole
was Major David Graham Pole, a Scottish lawyer and
Theosophist, later an M.P., whom Mrs. Besant had taken
with her to India to help with the appeal. Not only had
the decision of the High Court been upheld in the Appeal
Court, but the order as to costs had been reversed. Mrs.

Besant immediately decided to appeal to the Privy Council in England.

Krishna wrote next day to Mrs. Besant from the Villa Cevasco:

My own beloved Mother, I am very sorry that this case has gone against us. . . . I am afraid you must be very tired of it and I wish I could be with you and love you. You know I love you very much and I am very devoted to you. Words cannot express my devotion towards your dear self. George has written to C.W.L. [Leadbeater] explaining all our difficulties here. I quite agree with what George says. C.W.L. is going to show you the letter. I am writing to him myself which he will show you.

This letter of Krishna's to Leadbeater, dated October 31, 1913, is a very important one because in it he suddenly sounds a completely new note of authority, an awareness of his own power over people. One wonders whether his income from Miss Dodge had given him an added self-confidence, a sense of independence.

My Dear Brother [as Leadbeater's pupils usually addressed him]

You will have received two letters—one from Raja and one by George which I enclose, I have read both of them and wish to express my own views. I think it is time now that I should take my affairs into my own hands. I feel I could carry out the Master's instructions better if they were not forced upon me and made unpleasant as they have been for some years. If I feel that I am responsible I shall do my best, for being now about 18 years old, I think that with advice I could manage. Of course I shall make mistakes, but I know generally the nature of my duty. I have not been given any opportunity to feel my responsibilities and I have been dragged about like a baby. I have not written about this before because I did not wish to worry Mrs. Besant but I think that you both know now the whole position.

What I propose is this: If the case [the lawsuit] permits I should like to have a house on the sea coast of Devonshire. I think it would be better to have Miss

Arundale [George's aunt] in charge of the household
arrangements, but I have been provided with sufficient money to meet all expenses. The next important
matter would be as regards studies. Sanskrit would be
the difficulty for I do not feel that I can study the
subject under Raja. Arrangements could be easily
made for all the other subjects and if George relieves
himself of all save the most important matters connected with the Herald he could probably do all that
is needful in mathematics, etc. Study has been much
neglected lately and we must now pay great attention
to it. To tell you the truth, I think all would go well
if Raja were relieved of his duties. I know I could
control and guide George and the rest of the party.
Part of George's difficulties, as explained to you in
his letter, are due to the fact that it has not been possible for me to look after him as I should wish, and
he much resents Raja's attitude towards me. The
result has been that I have been passing through a
very difficult time and the only way, it seems to me,
to make things run smoothly will be for me to take
charge. I wish this could be arranged as soon as possible. If we cannot live in England the same arrangements would hold good abroad. I know that all that
has been done for the best but it has not worked.

This letter is as much for Mrs. Besant as it is for
you. I send it to you that you may show it to her and
talk it over at a favorable moment. . . .

I feel very much for Mrs. Besant that she should
have done so much and that the outer result should
be a failure. I suppose that Pole [Major Graham
Pole] will tell us what she wishes done, but I am determined to make it quite clear that I know what I
am about and that nothing will induce me to return
to my father, nor will Nitya.

George is always my first pupil and first in my love
but he has not quite understood my relations with
Lady Emily. No doubt this is largely due to the fact
that he has had too much work to do and has not
been able to see things clearly. I do love them both
very much and nothing of these trivial things will alter it. I do feel that Lady Emily is my mother and
pupil and George is my son and pupil. Now that he is
free he is beginning to understand.

There is not much news. I hope you will both very carefully consider what I have written.

With very much love,
Yours affectionately,
Krishna

They were back in London by November 14 after a tour of Rome, Florence, Venice and Milan. On the evening of their return they saw Graham Pole as they had been instructed to do. They stayed in London at the Gwalia Hotel in Great Russell Street near Lady Emily in Bloomsbury Square, and there was hardly an evening when she did not dine with them or they with her. This freedom to see Lady Emily whenever he wanted to without their meetings being immediately reported back to Mrs. Besant by the Brights must have been a great joy to Krishna. He found complete relaxation in the Lutyen's nursery—he was always most at his ease with children—where the little ones regarded him and Nitya as brothers far kinder to them than their own brother Robert, who was a cruel tease.

Lady Emily's own lawyer, Francis Smith, had been engaged by Mrs. Besant, who was still in Madras, to collect statements from Raja and the two boys as to whether any misconduct had taken place between them and Leadbeater. Lady Emily did not believe that Krishna so much as understood the nature of the questions.

There seems to be little doubt that Narianiah had been the tool of Mrs. Besant's political enemies in bringing the case, for on November 21 Leadbeater was writing to Lady Emily, "The old villain of plaintiff approached the President with a view to a compromise, asking her to take the eldest brother and educate him also in England—rather a comical proposition, when you think that he has all this time been asserting so vigorously that the other boys have been ruined by her."

On December 1, Mrs. Besant lodged her petition in Madras to appeal to the Judicial Committee of the Privy Council in London; this was granted. It might be months before the appeal was heard, but she hoped that a stay of execution, pending the appeal, might be granted by the Privy Council in January.

10

Doubts and Difficulties

As a result of Krishna's letter to Leadbeater of October 31, 1913, Raja was recalled to India, but the letter itself had evidently not been well received, for Krishna was writing to Mrs. Besant on December 12:

> I think there has been some misunderstanding about the letter which I wrote to C.W.L. I don't think that my nature is to be ungrateful and I know how much you all have done for me. I also know how much happier and better I am since four years ago. I did *not* mean to be ungrateful to C.W.L. I only meant that Raja and I can't get along well together and please don't think that I am ungrateful either to Raja.
>
> Above all, dear Mother, for God sake don't think for a single moment that I am ungrateful to *you*. You have been so kind and so good to me and have borne so much for me. Now it seems that I am ungrateful to you. It could *never* be. I may be bad in many ways but I can never be ungrateful to you. I wish I could see you and then I could explain everything.
>
> Raja will explain to you all our difficulties. He has with him what we think we want in writing. Of course this is to your subjection. Of course I am not what I should be. In one way or another we all have difficulties here. I am doing my best. I think Raja is rather glad to be relieved of his position and to be going to India. He has had many difficulties with us and I hope he will be better off at Adyar.
>
> My dearest Mother even though I may be ungrateful, I love you very much.

It was at about this time that the lawyers, fearing again an attempt to kidnap the boys, asked George to take them off to a hiding place so secret that not even Mrs. Besant was at first informed of it. Only Basil Hodgson-Smith in London was entrusted with their address so that he could forward letters. The date of their departure is uncertain, but by January 16, 1914, they were certainly again at Taormina in Sicily, for on that day Krishna was writing to Mrs. Besant, "Now you know where we are. I would never have gone away in this fashion on my own ideas. . . . Raja will probably have explained to you about our hiding by now." He added that the lawyers wanted them to be in London by January 27, when the plea for a stay of execution would be heard.

Lady Emily was desolate at the prospect of being parted from Krishna. Then just before their departure she was let into the secret of their hiding place by George, no doubt at Krishna's insistence, and invited to follow them on condition that she told no member of her family where she was going. This caused great resentment in Barbara and Robert. As her husband was in India, having been appointed architect of New Delhi in 1912, there was no need to tell him of her secret journey.

The party at Taormina consisted of Krishna, Nitya, George, Dr. Mary Rocke, Miss Arundale and Lady Emily. They again occupied the whole of the top floor of the Hotel Naumachia. Lady Emily recorded that one evening while they were there Krishna, who had been gazing at a picture of the Buddha in *Myths of the Hindus and Buddhists*, suddenly looked up and said, "The Lord Buddha is here." His whole face changed completely and he rushed from the room. Soon he came back and told them that he had seen the Lord Buddha standing beside him.

They were all very excited at the expectation of great events taking place on the night of January 10, for the 11th was the anniversary of Krishna's first Initiation. As they were sitting down to supper on the 10th, Krishna said very decidedly, "Something will happen tonight, I am sure of it. I feel so excited." They all expected to take a further step on the Path. However, nothing much was remembered by any of them in the morning, so Krishna cabled to Leadbeater, "Last night's recollections vague. Wire event." The reply was deeply disappointing: four people had been accepted and eight put on probation—all members of the Star in India. According to Lady Emily, she, George and Krishna "went through a bad fit of de-

pression." Could Krishna's letter to Leadbeater from
Genoa, showing for the first time a spirit of independence,
have been the reason for the failure of the Taormina party
to take any occult steps? It seems quite likely since the
letter had evidently caused deep offense.

They left Taormina on January 23 to be back in London for the Privy Council hearing on the 27th. It took
place in the Privy Council Chamber in Downing Street
and was presided over by the Lord Chancellor, Lord Hal-
dane, who was a friend of Mrs. Besant's. She did not come
over for the hearing but both boys were present. Nitya
was astonished, as he wrote to Leadbeater on January 30,
"to see the highest judges of the land, one of the greatest
powers in England, taking everything casually, easily and
without the least formality." The boys, who had been
added as interveners by Order in Council, were represented by the Lord Advocate (Robert Munro); two K.C.'s appeared for Mrs. Besant, while Narianiah was represented
by Mr. Kenworthy Brown. The Lord Advocate, in answer
to a question by the Lord Chancellor, stated that he had
entirely satisfied himself personally as to the boys' wishes:
"They are passionately desirous of staying in this country
and extremely averse from going back to India." A stay of
execution was granted. The Lord Chancellor said that as
he thought their Lordships would probably advance the
hearing of the appeal, it would be absurd to send the boys
to India as they would only have to be brought back
again, but he asked them to remain in England pending
the hearing which, it was understood, would probably be
heard in May.

Lady Emily soon had to pay for the joy of being with
Krishna in Taormina by Mrs. Besant's and Leadbeater's
disapproval. She received a stern letter from Mrs. Besant
reproving her for leaving her children, who were her responsibility, to go off with Krishna, who was not. George,
although undoubtedly feeling that Lady Emily had ousted
him in Krishna's affections, seems also to have been genuinely worried by the emotional effect her love was having
on Krishna. Krishna certainly loved her and wanted constantly to be with her, but she herself realized that it was
only as a mother that he loved her.

His mother having died when he was very young,
he was always yearning to be back in her arms [she

wrote]. He had seen a picture in the *Daily Mirror*
one day of a small boy seated on a bench in the Park
and dreaming that he was sitting on his mother's lap.
He cut out this picture and told me that he felt he
was that little boy.... I longed to compensate him
for his loss.

She believed that Krishna had lost his mother when he
was about four, whereas in fact he had been ten.

George was also very depressed at this time by a letter
from Leadbeater from Adyar describing a new "find," a
thirteen-year-old boy called Rajagopalacharya (son of V.
K. Deskacharya), an Ayyangar Brahmin from South India
who was later to play a leading part in Krishna's life. This
was one of the Indians who had been put on probation on
January 11; he was said to have had a wonderful past,
having been St. Bernard of Clairvaux in his last life, and
an even more wonderful future: he was to become a Buddha, probably succeeding Krishna on Mercury. Not unnaturally George was very upset as this great position had
already been promised to him.

After a few weeks at Drayton Gardens, following the
stay of execution, the boys moved, on the Master's instructions, to Shanklin, a seaside resort on the Isle of Wight.
George was with them and also A. E. Wodehouse, who
had been sent from Benares to take Raja's place as a second tutor. Miss Arundale took charge of the household at
The Leasowes, Victoria Avenue. Krishna reported to Mrs.
Besant that he was doing English composition, literature,
history, mathematics and science. Nitya was doing the
same with the addition of Latin. They intended to stay at
Shanklin for two months and study really hard.

Lady Emily, who was deputizing for George in editing
the *Herald* found excuses to go frequently to Shanklin to
consult him on editorial matters, but judging from her diary no editorial business was discussed: she spent her time
walking with Krishna on the beach or in the woods. "He
only really cared for poetry in those days," she recalled.
"He was especially fond of Shelley and Keats and was
constantly murmuring the line, 'I am half in love with
easeful death'." In the woods at Shanklin one day he
asked her, "Do you see that little fairy?" and he described
to her a little fairy creature hopping about; he seemed surprised that she could not see it too.

Mrs. Besant arrived in England on May 1 for the hearing of her appeal three days later. (Narianiah had not come over for it.) The boys went to Dover to meet her. Although she had enjoyed the fight at the beginning, the case had now dragged on for over eighteen months and she was worn out. Lady Emily went to see her next day at Drayton Gardens and told her that she loved Krishna as a son and as a teacher. Mrs. Besant replied that it was a very curious relationship but she raised no objection to it so long as Lady Emily was discreet and did not make trouble for him. Krishna then came into the room and knelt down beside Mrs. Besant while she gave them her blessing.

The boys were not present in the Council Chamber when on May 5, after a two-day hearing, Mrs. Besant won her appeal. Complete judgement was not given until May 25. The grounds on which the appeal was allowed were chiefly that the boys' wishes had not been consulted nor had they been represented in court. In their Lordships' opinion the suit in the High Court of Madras was entirely misconceived. The boys did not wish to return to India and the order of the Madras Court could not be carried out without their consent. Had Mrs. Besant complied with the Madras Court's order and brought the boys back to India against their will she would have been at once exposed to proceedings in England on writ of *habeas corpus*. No court ought to make an order which might lead to these consequences. The suit was dismissed, therefore, with costs, but without prejudice to any application that the respondent (the father) might think fit to make to the High Court of England which would consider the interests of the boys and ascertain their wishes. Narianiah, of course, knew that he was beaten and took no further action.

So delighted was Mrs. Besant by her victory that she decided not to claim the costs awarded her nor those she had already paid for both parties by order of the Appeal Court in Madras. On hearing the good news Krishna went off to Hatton Garden to buy her a pearl brooch as a loving gesture of appreciation for all she had done and suffered for him. On May 13 he went alone with her to Paris for three nights.

While she was in London Mrs. Besant gave five lectures at the Queen's Hall which were packed out as usual. Before returning to India at the end of June she must have

talked seriously to Krishna about his need to study hard
for Oxford, his relationship with Lady Emily and the importance of making George happy, for it was in a contrite
mood that the day after she left he went down to Bude, a
seaside place in north Cornwall, with Nitya, George, Dick
Clarke and Miss Arundale. (Wodehouse remained in London to help Lady Emily in editing the *Herald*.) They had
rented the Vicarage and a new program of study was
drawn up for them. For enjoyment there were golf lessons
every afternoon with an excellent professional; but, far
more exciting, Krishna had been allowed to buy a motor
bicycle, a Williamson, in London to take with him to
Bude. Every week he wrote dutiful little letters to Mrs.
Besant telling her that lessons were going regularly and
well and that he was doing his best to make George happy.
As well as the £500 a year from Miss Dodge, Krishna
was now receiving £125 a month from Mrs. Besant for
living expenses.

On July 16 Shiva Rao, then aged twenty-three, arrived
at Bude, having been sent from India by Mrs. Besant to
teach the boys Sanskrit. Shiva Rao had first met Krishna
and Nitya in Benares in 1910 and had got to know them
well when he moved to Adyar to help Leadbeater in the
compilation of *The Lives of Alcyone*.

The outbreak of war (quite unforeseen, apparently, by
the Masters, though explained by Mrs. Besant as the great
convulsion among nations that always preceded the coming of the World Teacher) did not at first make any difference to the pattern of life at Bude. "The Germans are not
so bad as the papers make them out to be," Krishna told
Mrs. Besant in a letter of September 3, "and I have a
great sympathy for them. They are very brave. I wonder
whether I ought to join the war and I want to know what
you think of it?" Mrs. Besant thought it a very bad idea,
not so much because he might have to kill someone as
because he would have to pollute his body by eating meat.

It is perhaps significant that Krishna did not tell Mrs.
Besant that Lady Emily with her five children took a
house at Bude in September close to the vicarage where
she spent most of her time with Krishna. Her close proximity caused the usual upset, aggravated now by George's
falling in love with Barbie and making Nitya, who himself
loved Barbie, very miserable. Krishna too was miserable.

He certainly believed in the idea of the Masters [Lady Emily said of him at this time], and would frequently "bring through" interviews with the Lord [Maitreya]. He accepted his position but never derived any personal satisfaction from it. He never wanted anything for himself—money, power or position. George was always urging him to remember what had happened on other planes. *"Please* bring through," he would keep saying, but Krishna remained unmoved and only "brought through" when he really did remember something.

He was, she believed, desperately unhappy. He hated publicity; he longed for a normal life. He often said to her, "Why did they ever pick on me?" The only real pleasures he found at Bude were in golf and his motor bicycle. He enjoyed nothing more than polishing the bicycle and tinkering with the engine, and, according to Dick Clarke he was a first-class mechanic. He was a rather erratic driver, though, and when he took Lady Emily for a drive in the sidecar she had to cling to the thought that he was divinely protected.

Nitya went off in the autumn to study with a tutor at Oxford while Krishna remained at Bude deprived even of Lady Emily's visits, for when she returned to London at the end of the summer it was agreed between them that she should stay away from him for a certain length of time in order to become more self-reliant. It was not until the following January 1915 that to her great joy she was summoned to Bude by George in order to bring Krishna a dog, "a white Siberian," and managed to stretch out her visit to a week. That her stay was not a success, however, is shown by a letter she received afterwards from George telling her that she was hindering "the Master's work by emphasizing Krishna's lower nature *at the expense of his higher"* and that she knew very little of Krishna as he really was.

George must have relayed to Mrs. Besant his anxiety concerning Krishna and Lady Emily without revealing how much his evaluation of their relationship was influenced by his own jealousy, for in February Krishna had a letter from Mrs. Besant in which she said, "Your happiness lies in the work, and you will be restless and unhappy if you turn away from it. Nothing else will last, you

will find. A man called to the highest service loses 'the
lower life,' and if he is brave enough to let it go, he finds
a splendid and changeless happiness." Krishna was impressed enough with this passage to copy it out and send
it to Lady Emily, who copied it into her diary on February
6.

Mrs. Besant was at this time almost exclusively absorbed in political work, having been directed by her Master, just before the outbreak of war, to join in the fight for
Indian Home Rule. This tremendous task, which included
editing a daily paper she had taken over, *New India* (the
old Madras *Standard*), was to engage more and more of
her energy. Had she been less occupied with politics she
might have had deeper insight into the loneliness and bore-
dom of her Indian ward, stranded in a gloomy rectory by
the sea in winter wartime England, with no young companionship now that Nitya had gone, and with the prim
and proper Miss Arundale as the only feminine influence
in the household since George had succeeded in banishing
Lady Emily.

Leadbeater also had absorbing new interests at this time.
Being a staunch British Imperialist he was out of sympathy with Mrs. Besant's political activities, so she was only
too glad when in 1914 he had set off on a lecture tour of
Burma, Java, Australia and New Zealand. This tour
proved so successful that she gladly gave him permission
to remain indefinitely in Australia where he believed the
new sub-race was growing up which would be ready to
serve the World Teacher when he came. Leadbeater even
went so far as to say that it was a great blessing to be
killed in the War, for it was helping the plan of the occult
hierarchy to draw old egos from the West for speedy rebirth to Theosophical families in bodies of the new race.
By the beginning of 1915 he was living in Sydney and had
gathered round him a group of young people whom he
considered ripe for special training. For the time being
there was nothing more he could do for Krishna. Plans for
the immediate future of "the vehicle" had been carefully
laid down and the boy's only duty now was to study hard
in order to pass into Oxford as soon as possible. Leadbeater was concentrating on his new pupils and had even
given up writing to Krishna.

But although Leadbeater and Mrs. Besant seem temporarily to have lost interest in the vehicle, it did not pre-

vent them from continuing, month after month, to herald
in the most flowery language the advent of the World
Teacher in the various Theosophical publications, seldom
without warnings to their readers of the danger of failing
to recognize the Lord when he came or of rejecting him as
he had been rejected in Galilee because he was sure to say
things unacceptable to closed minds and prejudiced hearts.

The vehicle himself, however, now felt the compulsion
to reopen communication with Leadbeater after a long
silence on both sides. Mrs. Besant's admonition about "the
highest service" must have weighed with him, and also
Lady Emily's frequently reiterated distress that she had
not yet been accepted by the Master; moreover on the eve
of Leadbeater's sixty-eighth birthday on February 17,
1915, while Lady Emily with Barbie and Robert happened
to be staying at Bude for a week-end, Shiva Rao had spoken to them all about the early days at Adyar and had evidently explained to Krishna some of Leadbeater's harsh-
seeming actions at that time. This resulted in Krishna's
sending a birthday telegram, signed by the whole party,
and in his writing a letter which is fascinatingly revealing,
not only of his own current difficulties but of the existence
of friction between him and Leadbeater in the early days
of which there is no other record since Krishna himself
remembers little about those years:

Bude. February 18, 1915

It is quite a long time since I wrote to you last and
I am *very* sorry. I am afraid I am *not* at all good at
lessons and I have not got the brains for them and so
I plod along rather slowly. Miss Arundale, George,
Dick, Shiva Rao and I are here. She looks after the
household affairs. Shiva Rao teaches me mathematics
and Sanskrit, George teaches me English. So you
know what we do here.

I want to tell you *everything* and I do not know
where to begin as there is such a lot. Many things
have happened since I last saw you at Genoa, physically I mean.

First of all I want to know how *you* are and all
about your self. You have not written to me now for
a long time and I suppose you are too busy! When I
was with you, I did *not* appreciate what you did but
now it is *all* different. You are the same old C.W.L.

to me and I love you *very* much. I was foolish and an
idiot not to see it and love you when I was with you.
I am devoted to you too. Of course now I know you
did what was good for me and I did not see it. I want
to forget all that and turn over completely a new
page. You were the first person who picked me up
and I am grateful and you brought me to great things
and I owe *all* that to you my dear C.W.L. It is very
difficult for me to write what I feel but you will understand what I mean. When I was with you I hurt
you in many ways and now I see it all and I am *very*
sorry. Let us forget the past, except the happy bits,
and I hope I shall make you happy yet. I wonder
whether you understand what I mean about all this? I
want to be worthy of you and make your name shine
like a light to *everybody*. I want everybody to know
what you really are.

We have been talking about you and I feel I have
behaved towards you like a brute, but I did not understand you then as I do now. Anyway I am going
to try to make up for all that.

As to George, he is in a difficult position. You see
he has been so busy with the C.H.C. [Central Hindu
College] and working from morning till night and
surrounded by young people, who were eager to learn
and enthusiastic. Now he comes down here and has a
frightfully dull life. There are not many boys to help
and nobody to look up to him and he feels all that
very much. I am *not* enthusiastic about *anything* and
he feels a bit hopeless. He is tremendously interested
in the work and I am not but I am trying hard to do
what is expected of me. He thinks that I do not love
him just as before but that is all nonsense and as you
know I don't change my affections so easily. He does
his Star work by himself and I don't help him in that
in the least and he feels that rather. I am sorry for
him and I want to do the best. It is all very difficult
and by no means is it easy and I do not know what
to do. I know I ought to be interested in the work
and all that, but at present moment I am afraid I am
not. I am trying hard to do my duty and it is very
difficult. I *know* I will get it all back and serve the
Master and in the meantime it is not easy. I will go
on trying hard all the same. George is not very good

in health as he had a nervous breakdown and that has
rather upset him in many ways. He wants me to get
interested in the work all at once and I am afraid he
has not got the patience for it. He feels that the Master is not near him and this house is not Master's
house as it ought to be. He thinks I ought to take the
lead but I don't feel like it all and I want to be quiet.
He also thinks that he is responsible for my actions
and my life here. Do you understand what I mean.

Then comes Lady Emily. I suppose you have heard
from other sources all about her and myself. So you
know their side and now I want you to know my
side. When I first really met her at Varengeville in
1913 during the summer, we met *very* often while we
were playing tennis and during Theosophical talks. I
became very fond of her. I told her that I felt like a
son to her and that I love her very much. When I
came to London I wanted to be with her and all that
which you can understand. Then the eternal people,
who can't mind their own business began to talk and
made fairly a lot of trouble. Then Mrs. Besant came,
and she told Lady Emily and me that we must not
show our affections openly as it might create trouble.
I suppose we two have been selfish but I have been
trying hard not to and she is too. You *know* all about
her and me on the other planes and so in a way you
know it all but all the same I must tell you. Then her
husband who is not specially fond of Theosophy began to say that she ought not to be so friendly with
me, as I am an Indian. He is an anglo-Indian and
you can understand that.[1] He dislikes Theosophy and
thinks it is all bad and the usual nonsense as most
people believe when they *don't* think about it. So you
see how she stands. We have put each other before
the work and that has been the difficulty. Now we
have realized that the Masters and the work come before everything and we have made up our minds to
that and we are trying *hard* to do it. Then George
thought that I did not love him any more and that
has been *very* hard on me. I want both of them to be

[1] Edwin Lutyens was in fact always very genial to Krishna, and
Krishna liked him and enjoyed his jokes. Rather unfairly Lutyens
put the blame for his wife's absorption in Theosophy entirely on
Mrs. Besant.

very great friends as I love them both *very* much. She
has helped me a *very* great deal and made me certainly very happy. Then George said that she has
done me harm and all that and that is *not* so but on
the contrary she has helped me through hard times
and I am very grateful to her. I love in the *whole*
world four people and they are, you, Mrs. Besant,
George and Lady Emily and that will never change
whatever happens. She has not been accepted by the
Master last year and it is our fault not to please the
Master. She has been trying very hard lately and I
hope the Master is pleased with her. She wants that
too very much and I hope He is. This year she *must*
be accepted and I am going to help her to the best of
my ability and not be selfish.

You know I love her *very* purely and I don't do
anything else but that. I do really love her very much
and I want to help her and make her happy. I want
your help to this too as in everything. You are my
eldest brother and I want your help. You must help
her and me.

Lady Emily is here for a week end and I am glad
to say she has, I think, been doing what the Master
wishes. She is not so selfish as she used to be and I
think I am too better in that respect. She *does* want
to do her best and I hope she will succeed. I have
been noticing that George and she are alright now.
Lady Emily does like him very much and thinks he is
a big person and all that. They both are very fine
people in their way and I love them very much.
George was a bit jealous of her but now, thank goodness, it is all over. I love her *very very* purely and I
am glad that I am not like usual people in that respect. I am *not* that way and *never* shall be.

Then Barbie and Robert. George likes Barbie very
very much and I think she does too. She is the latest
fashion and in all the worldly things and I am sorry
for that. She does not like Theosophy for the *moment,* of course, but I know, like myself it will all
pass. I believe she is considered very nice looking and
all that sort of thing but that's nothing. Nityam and
she were once six months ago very great friends.
They loved each other and helped each other along
but then George came along and Barbie liked him

and poor Nityam became jealous and Barbie in a way dropped him and he feels awfully badly about it.

Then Robert. He is just the same and very devoted to me. He is the opposite of Barbie in everything, I think. I like and love him *very* much. He has got very fine qualities but he is very young and is very boyish. . . . He is very artistic, which is a great thing, I think. Robert and I have got more or less the same qualities and are much alike in many ways.[1]

Now I must tell you about Nityam. Poor Nityam, I am afraid is not at all happy. He has been studying a lot and got his eyes in a terrible state. He has been to see the oculist and he says he must not over work and must work an hour a day and not more. Do you see, Mrs. Besant wanted Nityam to pass his London Matriculation in July and it is frightfully stiff. So he has been overworking with his tutor in Oxford. He is very poor in health and his eyes are bad, altogether he is in a bad state. Nityam and I are now much more intimate and he tells me all his troubles and that helps him a bit. Of course he is *very* devoted to you and you could help him much more than anybody and I wish he could see you. He feels very lonely, like most of us do, and there is nobody whom he specially likes or loves and it makes double harder. He is very bitter and hard and cold. He suffers a lot I am afraid and I can't help him much. He wants somebody to love him first and foremost and to whom he can pour out all his troubles. He wants a mother to love as I have Lady Emily. I am afraid he does not like many people. Like me he is at *present* not interested in the work but I think it will pass soon. He has grown but he is not at all well for his age. He has been here twice and little separation from me has brought us closer and he likes me now and so do I like him too. Brothers and you can understand. He is awfully clever as usual and smart. He is now in London as Mr. Fleming, a doctor, is looking after him and I

[1] Robert reacted strongly against Theosophy but remained very friendly with Krishna for many years. Barbie had loved Nitya at Varengeville but never cared for George at any time. She was very jealous of her mother's love for Krishna and reacted far more strongly than Robert against Theosophy.

think it will do him good.[1] Robert and he are great
friends and they like each other. He is staying at 82
Drayton Gardens with Miss Bright. Her mother is *very*
unwell and at any moment may die. [She died on
March 12.]

Miss Arundale is just the same and very old fashioned.

I do hope this letter will reach you safely. You
must answer all my things.

My dear C.W.L. I love you *very* much and I hope
this will bring us closer together.

Leadbeater's response to this appeal is not known, but
that Lady Emily's love for Krishna was still causing anxiety a month later is shown by a letter to her from Mrs.
Besant of March 20. This letter must have hurt Lady
Emily dreadfully, especially coming on top of all her efforts to be less selfish:

I am glad things are getting better. The matter has
caused me great grief and distress, and the real
Krishna has not been able to get through for so long
that it has been very sad. An effort to affect the lower
consciousness is again being made, and there is a
little more response. His health cannot be good when
his real life cannot reach the body and he is in a
whirl of passion for which his delicately poised frame
is wholly unfit. I wrote once to you during this unhappy time, but recalled it, as I had said all I could
say before I left, and felt any more was useless. His
exquisite nature has been all jarred and thrown out of
tune, and he blames himself, poor dear lad. I do hope
all will go better.

Towards the end of March Nitya was able to escape to
France as a dispatch rider to join Dr. Haden Guest (afterwards Lord Haden-Guest), a Theosophist, who was chief
medical officer of a hospital unit in Paris. Krishna, longing
to get away from the claustrophobia of Bude, wrote to

[1] Fleming was a healer living in Half Moon Street. Later Krishna
got to know him very well, as did Lady Emily who went to him
regularly to be treated, unsuccessfully, for the migraines from which
she suffered all her life. He also treated Miss Dodge without much
success.

Mrs. Besant in April asking if he could go too and was thrilled when he received a cable giving her permission. "We will have to wear a uniform, which I like very much," he told her. "I will take my motor bicycle and I shall much more be useful then I believe." He left Bude, for good as he thought, went up to London and got his uniform, but the plan held fire; then after a month's waiting in London he heard that it was off altogether as Dr. Guest had given up his French hospitals in order to run a military hospital in London. This was to be in the Endsleigh Palace Hotel, Bloomsbury. Krishna, Nitya (back from France with Dr. Guest), George and Lady Emily all went to work there before it opened, scrubbing floors, scraping grease off the stove, a particularly odious job for vegetarians, and doing other menial tasks.

One Theosophical magazine when reporting that Krishna was to work in this hospital, commented, "Fortunate indeed, nay, happy the wounded, who are privileged to be ministered to by such hands," but in fact, as soon as the hospital opened, the committee who were running it decided that Krishna's services were no longer required. In the next four weeks he tried very hard to get other war work; it seemed, though, that as an Indian no one wanted him, which he found "most extraordinary." At last he got a chance to work in an English hospital in Dunkirk, only to hear that Mrs. Besant refused to let him go. It was not until the end of September that he was told by Lady De La Warr that Mrs. Besant would much prefer him to give up all idea of war work and continue quietly with his studies. He then heard the same thing from Mrs. Besant herself. His disappointment is very evident in the letter he wrote to her from Drayton Gardens on October 7:

> Thank you very much for your long letter. You don't know how sorry I am if I have caused you any anxiety. I will see to it that it does not occur again. I am really very sorry.
> I know I have not taken my life seriously so far and I am going to do it from now. I am beginning my studies from next Monday. I had settled to study after the letter you had written to Lady de la Warr. I am going to study Sanskrit, English, Mathematics, History and French. I am having tutors for each and I mean to get into Oxford as soon as I can. I will

study for all my worth and after Oxford there is my
work laid out for me by the Masters and yourself. I
honestly mean to do this and I *will* do this at all
costs. I *will* take my life *very* seriously, help and
make others happy. I know too that I have been
thinking about my happiness too much, which is very
silly really and now from last night when I got your
letter I have really made up my mind to do what you
say in your letter. I have been playing too much and
I shall stop. I promise to you that you won't hear any
more from others any complaints of my wasting my
time away. I know I have been a fool in playing
about, instead of getting ready for my future work. I
will do my best, my holy mother, and no man can do
more.

I thought you really wanted me to go to France
and work there. If I had known that you really
wanted me to settle down and study I should have
done it without the least hesitation. I really didn't
know what *you* wanted me to do till now. I am very
unhappy if I have caused you any worries as I really
love you very much. Everybody else has been writing
to you about me and I have been a fool not to write
myself first.

I will try to get into Oxford as soon as I really can
and I will do my best. Next week I will be able to
give you my time table. I would like to go into a college instead of being a [non] collegiate student as
that is neither the one thing nor the other. Of course,
that is, if *you* approve of it.

Dear Mother, I love George just the same and my
love for Lady Emily will be the same. She has *not*
drawn me away from George. He was jealous at first
about it and that has been a wall between us two. It
is really stupid because I love them both very much
and it is silly to say that I must *not* love anybody
else. I hope you understand what I mean? Anyway
George is happier now and I think everything will be
alright. I will do my best and I hope people write to
you again telling that it is all better.

Krishna was obliged to give up Sanskrit because he
could not find another Sanskrit teacher when Mrs. Besant
sent for Shiva Rao to help her in editing her Madras daily

paper, *New India.* At this time Edwin Lutyens was writing to Lady Emily from Delhi, where he was now spending every winter: "I wonder whether when Krishna comes of age [he would not be twenty-one until the following May] he will submit to the unnatural surroundings and his methods of education etc.: spoon and apron fed he must be becoming quite unfitted for work except esoteric and his poor India cries aloud for reliable men of action—not priests or politicians."

Yet for the time being Krishna had no alternative but to submit, and so in October the dreary life began again for him and Nitya. They stayed at Drayton Gardens with Miss Bright and had private tutors, while George, in a smart uniform of the Anglo-French Red Cross, was working at the Endsleigh Palace Hotel Hospital.

One bright new influence, though, had recently come into the boys' drab lives in the shape of Harold Baillie-Weaver, a barrister married to a widow much older than himself. Tall, with a very fine head and a commanding presence, he had been a great beau in his day, but after marriage and conversion to Theosophy he had given up high living and settled down in a cottage in Essex. He continued to dress with extreme elegance, however, and had kept his *joie de vivre.* He instilled into Krishna and Nitya a great love of good clothes, introduced them to the best tailor and shirt-maker, taught them how to polish their shoes and, for the next few years, took charge of their finances as well as helping them financially. He was the first man of the world they had ever come in contact with and they became greatly attached to him. Moreover, he was fun to be with and they could be themselves with him. Whenever they were able to escape from the holy atmosphere of Theosophy they liked to go shopping or to cinemas, particularly Westerns, or just laze around in dressing gowns. In Baillie-Weaver ("Padre" as they called him) they found a friend after their own hearts. He was a wholly good and humanizing influence on them.

At the beginning of November George Arundale was appointed General Secretary of the Theosophical Society for England and Wales. Thereafter he threw himself into his new duties as well as continuing to work at the hospital, and Krishna saw comparatively little of him. Their relationship was never again to be a close one.

By the third week in November both boys had de-

veloped such bad coughs that the doctor ordered them into
the country. They went back to Bude, therefore, accompanied only by Wodehouse. This time they stayed in lodgings, at No. 9 Sumerleaze, as money was short; Mrs.
Besant was having difficulty in wartime in keeping up her
monthly payments. They found a Belgian priest to teach
them French. By hard work Krishna hoped to pass Responsions the following October 1916, two years later than
was originally intended.

With George out of the way Krishna and Nitya drew
closer to each other; besides, Nitya was much happier after his time in France where he had been presented with
two gold medals for his work for the French Red Cross.
"He is quite different from what he was last year,"
Krishna told Leadbeater in January 1916. "He is not so
hard, in fact he is much better in all ways. He is going up
to Oxford before me, I think as he is so clever;" and a
fortnight later Nitya was writing to Mrs. Besant about
Krishna:

Jan. 26, 1916

My dear Mother
    ... Krishna has changed tremendously. He has a
great deal of insight into character and he is able to
judge for himself. He stands much more on his own
feet than he used to, and although he is not ag-
gressive and never will be, some people are irritated
by what they call his sudden firmness and attribute it
to the influence of the person who happens to be
nearest to him. I think they forget that his judgment
is not likely to be far wrong. His love for Lady Emily
is no longer an infatuation but a very steady love
which I do not think will change for he is not a
changeable temperament.
    I am writing all this for I know he would never
write himself and I know no one who would put it
impersonally, for I have not been in all the late troubles.

Your devoted son
Nitya

This accusation that Krishna was influenced by "the
person who happens to be nearest to him" is one that has
followed him all his life. It has seldom been understood

that the influence people have had on him from time to time has been entirely superficial. When he was first "discovered" at Adyar it must have struck Leadbeater that the boy's empty mind was ideally fertile soil for the implanting of Theosophical ideas. So it was, but what was not realized was that these ideas never took root. The scattered seeds came up dutifully as little platitudinous annuals of Theosophical occultism. All these years of study and Theosophical conditioning have left hardly a mark on Krishna's mind. What is in him today was there at the beginning. His true being was all the time slowly, secretly unfolding, hidden even from himself.

11

Cramming

Krishna's scrappy letters to Mrs. Besant for the first few months of 1916 were all to do with his hopes of getting into Oxford. "My difficulty at present," he told her from Bude in January, "is that my brain, whatever there is, is not very developed and it shows when I work." He was to reiterate this about the insufficiency of his brain throughout the year. Passing Responsions was not the only difficulty, however. New College had struck off the boys' names at the time of the lawsuit, and now Harold Baillie-Weaver, who knew the Dean of Christ Church, was trying to get them into that college or into Balliol through the influence of a friend of his, Sir Robert Younger.

The boys left Bude for good at last at the end of April when Wodehouse joined the Scots Guards, and after two months in London went to a tutor, found for them by Baillie-Weaver—John Sanger, whose wife was a Theosophist, at The Little Hermitage, near Rochester, Kent. It was a large house with a beautiful garden and a tennis court, and with a golf course close by, and only three other students. Krishna found Mr. Sanger an excellent tutor and he quite enjoyed the place, though he was disappointed when Sanger told him that there was no hope of his passing the examination until March 1917. It was decided, therefore, that both boys should stay on at The Little Hermitage until then.

On November 11 they went up to London for the wedding of Raja, who had been on a lecture tour in Europe, to an English lady, Miss Dorothy Graham, whom he had met in Adyar. Krishna thought the marriage "most extraordinary; he is the last person I would have thought of as getting married." Indeed, the idea of an Initiate marrying was deeply shocking to most Theosophists, many of whom had ruined existing marriages by abstaining from sex. A week later the boys went up again to see the newly

married couple off to India. Two days after returning to
Rochester Krishna was writing to Lady Emily. Although it
is known from her diaries that after leaving Varengeville
in September 1913 they wrote to each other almost every
day when separated, this is the first of his letters to her to
have survived, therefore it is given in full:

Nov: 19: 16.
11:30 A.M.

My dearest Mummy,

It was awful to leave you mother and I knew you
would be sad & I was sad too. I thought of you all
the time in that carriage where there were 8 soldiers
and all the windows shut. They were rude when I
asked them, very politely, if I might open the window
a little. Anyway I got my way in the end. Mummy
dear there will be so very many partings in this life
that we must get used to it, if we want to be happy.
Life is really one huge separation if one loves anybody *very* much and *purely*. In this life we have got to
live for others and not for ourselves & not be selfish.
My mother you don't know how much you helped me
lately, it is you who have created a desire in me to
work and to do what the Master wants me to do. It is
also you who have made me live purely and think of
pure things & cast away those thoughts which bother
so many. You see, my *holy* mother, that you have
helped me even though you very often think that you
have been a hinderence to me. Now it is my turn to
help you and make you, as the Master wants you to
be, I want Him to see that my beloved mother is not
like the rest of the world and that you will come up
to his expectations. Don't think I am preaching
mother, only I want to help you as you are helping
me, I don't want to receive everything and in my turn
not give anything. My love for you is very great and
that love will go through everything to help you in
the least little bit. You know there are very few
things that I would not do for you. I am not boasting
myself mother but I want you to know that I would
& will do everything for you. There! No more
preaching or we will both get bored with it.

I got your dear letter this morning and before answering it I will tell you what I have been doing.

When we came back on Friday we made some coffee
& did a little work and went up to bed. It was awfully
cold & fortunately they had given us both hot water
bottles. All yesterday it snowed & rained, on & off
and in the afternoon we all sawed wood and tried to
get warm. Prentice, that long faced dirty fellow has
gone away for good & we shan't see his unearthly face
any more. Everybody is very pleased about it. This
morning I have written to Mrs. Besant & to the rest
of them and I read a little bit from the two papers
which you sent us [the *New Statesman* and the *Nation*]. We are going to keep them all & if you or we
want to bind them we can do so. Nityam is immersed
in them. After lunch I shall go through them thoroughly and mother if you want me or Nityam to read
any special article please mark it & also the ones
which you think or [are] interesting. It will be a
great fun.

Now I shall answer your letter of to-day. Mummy
don't worry about us as we are really very warm and
we really don't want eider downs as there are plenty
of things here & it would be a wicked waste. I
promise you mother we shall take care of ourselves.
You need never worry about that my dear mother.
There is nothing much to answer in your letter.
Please let me know how much we owe or else *please*
tell Mr. B.W. & he will pay it back. You *must* let me
know and we can't sponge on you my dear mother.

You know that I think of you all the time & send
you all my love & devotion. I hear the other boys
coming back from the church & so I will stop. I shall
write again on Monday or Tuesday. Oh! my mother
you are very holy and very loved by me

Your most devoted son
Krishna

After a long holiday spent partly with Miss Dodge at
West Side House on Wimbledon Common, which she had
now bought in addition to Warwick House, and partly
with the Baillie-Weavers in Essex, the boys returned to
Mr. Sanger's in Kent in January 1917. Nitya's eyes were
so bad by this time that he could no longer work in artificial light, so he had to work all the harder in the day-time.
They intended to sit for Responsions at Oxford on March

20 and Krishna was hopeful of passing. By the beginning
of February, however, all hope of getting them into Christ
Church was over ("The Dean is scared," as Krishna put it
to Mrs. Besant). Baillie-Weaver tried other colleges as well
as Balliol, but by the beginning of March it was certain
that no Oxford college would take them. Mr. Sanger now
hoped to use influence to get them into his old college at
Cambridge, St. John's, although for this they would need
new subjects which would entail another eight months'
study. But by June it was realized that there was no hope
of Cambridge either; there was nothing for it now but to
try for London University, for which the entrance examination would be even stiffer than for Cambridge.

It was not surprising that Oxford and Cambridge refused
to have an Indian boy who had not only been proclaimed
as the coming Messiah but had been accused of homosexuality by his own father; but it was very disappointing for
Krishna who had worked really hard, though more to
please Mrs. Besant, it would seem, than for any value he
himself attached to book-learning. He never apparently
went for an interview with the heads of any of the colleges. Had he done so the results might have been different.

Meanwhile Mrs. Besant, with the help of George Arundale who had now returned to India, had been campaigning so vigorously for Indian Home Rule that towards the
end of June 1917 she and George were both interned for
three months at Ootacamund in the Nilgiri Hills. Mrs.
Besant never advocated separation between India and the
British Raj; what she was fighting for was Dominion
Status for India—that is, self-government—and if she had
won her campaign much bloodshed might have been
avoided. As it was, both the British Government and the
Indian extremists, who wanted to get rid of the Raj altogether, regarded her as a dangerous enemy.

Krishna's letters to Mrs. Besant were now failing to get
through so he began writing to Raja who was allowed to
go up to Ootacamund to see her. He told Raja on July 8
that they hoped to sit for Matriculation the following January and that he was taking English, Latin, French and
history. Afterwards he would go on with literature while
Nitya read for the Bar. "So you see, dear Raja," he added,
"I shall be *educated* properly, not dragged along the path
of Education." He owned to being "rather a nib at

French," but seems to have forgotten mathematics which
he also had to take and which was his worst subject. A
week later he wrote, "I hope, my dear Raja, you have for-
given all my misconduct & my foolishness of bygone
days," and in a later letter: "As you know I am a bit of a
Puritan but I do like to have some fun & a 'bust up' occasionally which you also know to your cost."

Mrs. Besant had a tremendous reception when she returned to Madras on September 21 after being unconditionally released. Although her health had suffered,
primarily from the enforced inactivity, her three months
of martyrdom had only succeeded in greatly increasing her
already considerable influence and prestige with the advo-
cates of Home Rule. Krishna, naturally, was all for Home
Rule. He also evinced at this time an interest in English
politics, his sympathies being entirely with Labour. George
Lansbury, the Labour Member of Parliament, whom he
had met through Mrs. Besant, became a great friend and a
member of the Order of the Star in the East. "I am a
great pacifist and I want to be a complete cosmopolitan,"
Krishna had told Mrs. Besant in April. He refused to believe in the stories of German atrocities.

Although Krishna had always abhorred violence in any
form and continued to do so, he had no real interest in
political movements any more than in books. How bored
he must have been by this time with the interminable
dreary cramming in subjects for which he had no aptitude;
but one of his own inherent powers was now beginning to
develop.

> You may be glad to know I am doing Nitya's eyes
> [he told Raja on November 11]. They have im-
> proved tremendously and he can see with his left eye.
> Mr. Fleming has given me a few lessons on the sub-
> ject of healing and personally I am very keen on
> it. . . . Here [at Mr. Sanger's], when anybody has a
> headache or toothache comes to me so you can imag-
> ine I am fairly popular.

And some weeks later he was writing to Mrs. Besant:

> I have been thinking of you such a lot lately and I
> would give anything to see your dear face again.
> What a funny world it is! I am so very sorry you are

feeling rather weak and I expect you are over-work-
ing as usual. Only I do wish I was there to look after
you and I believe I would make you all right again. I
am developing that power of curing people and I do
Nitya's eyes every day and they are much better.

In December they went up to London where they had
taken a flat at No. 2 Robert Street, Adelphi, and on January 14, 1918, they sat for the four-day Matriculation. On
the 17th they were in great spirits feeling they had done
well, and celebrated by going with Lady Emily to the re-
vue *Yes Uncle*. Krishna told Mrs. Besant on the 20th that
the papers had been stiff but that in Latin, his weak subject, he was certain he had got fifty per cent. But by the
beginning of March they heard that although Nitya had
passed with honors, Krishna had "come a cropper." So
back he had to go to Sanger's to work for another attempt
in June. Nitya's name was entered at Lincoln's Inn and in
June he began to eat his dinners, dining a number of times
in Hall being a necessary preliminary to becoming a member of an Inn of Court and so a barrister.

Mr. Sanger was very disappointed for Krishna. He had
observed that while Nitya had the sharper mind, Krishna's
mind was the bigger of the two; he had a wider grasp of a
subject though was handicapped by not being able to
express his thoughts readily.

12

After the War

Since George's return to India Lady Emily had been responsible for editing the *Herald,* and in accordance with Krishna's sentiments had been sounding a pacific note. Krishna's name as editor had been taken off the cover in September 1917 and there was no word in the magazine either from him or about him from the beginning of the war until 1919. In a letter from Australia Leadbeater had voiced to Mrs. Besant the Lord Maitreya's grave disappointment in the magazine (certainly one article sent in by Leadbeater had not been published in it); the Lord's displeasure was relayed to Lady Emily in a long cable from Adyar which she received on May 5, 1918, suggesting among other things that Wodehouse, who had been wounded in the leg and invalided out of the army, should replace her as editor. "Another bitter blow for me, another failure," she noted in her diary. She immediately wrote off to Krishna and was comforted three days later by "a dear letter" from him, "so wise." It was the kind of letter that it would fall to him to write many times in the future:

> I am in a way *very* glad you have had this shock, because personality will be knocked out, and it is by that way alone, I am positively certain, that one can really serve the Lord.... Personality is the curse of Theosophists and do not let that be one of yours. Life is hard and through hardships we grow to a better and happier state. In the meantime suffering must be endured and not allowed to interfere with anything. There!!

He told her at the same time that he would not be ready to sit for the examination in June after all; he would have to wait until September.

All the same he thankfully left Mr. Sanger's for good on May 24, and on the 30th, at a meeting in London which he attended, it was decided that Wodehouse and Lady Emily should work together as joint editors of the *Herald*. Krishna reported this to Raja on the same day, adding that he felt the magazine ought to be "international." "By using the word 'international' I mean include one's enemy as well as one's ally. It is most important to bear this in mind, as I feel there won't be any distinction between the ally and the enemy when the Lord comes & he will have a message for the so-called enemy as well as the ally." In saying this Krishna was pitting his will against Leadbeater's. The latter was whole-heartedly anti-German and had conveyed in the message he had "brought through" from the Lord Maitreya complaining of the deterioration in the *Herald*, that the sympathy of the Occult Hierarchy was also entirely with the allies.

Krishna and Nitya spent the summer partly at Old Lodge, Ashdown Forest, where they had stayed in 1912, and partly at West Side House, Wimbledon, which Miss Dodge shared with Lady De La Warr. In this large house with its beautiful garden, including two tennis courts, the boys were surrounded with every imaginable luxury, for Miss Dodge lived in great style.[1] Their enjoyment of this after the cheap lodgings at Bude and the Little Hermitage was rather flawed, though, by a sense of restriction. They had to behave very formally and were conscious that their misdeeds, such as undue frivolity or the frittering away of time, might be reported back to Mrs. Besant by Lady De La Warr. Miss Bright had now also moved to Wimbledon Common, to a lovely Georgian house given to her by Miss Dodge, and she too was in constant communication with Mrs. Besant.

On September 9 Krishna sat again for Matriculation, and although he felt he had done quite well in all but Latin, he found on going to inquire at London University on October 1 that he had failed in maths. The Baillie-Weavers now took a house on Wimbledon Common, The Brockencote, Burghley Road, where the boys lived with greater freedom than at West Side House, and Krishna

---

[1] West Side House on West Side, Wimbledon Common, built in the reign of George III, has now been turned into flats. The façade has not been altered, nor have the hall and staircase, though most of the garden has now been incorporated into Cannizaro Park which is open to the public. It is still possible, however, to trace the old boundary of the West Side House garden.

travelled up every day by bus and Underground to London University to attend lectures. This daily journey by crowded public transport after the quiet routine with private tutors was a severe strain on his sensitive nervous system (as he later wrote to Raja, "I am a democrat but I don't like people too near me"), and in November he went down with the influenza that was then rampant. As by the time he had fully recovered there were only a few days of the term left he gave up work and went into the country with Nitya who had also been ill. Krishna knew it was no good sitting again for the examination in January as he had intended.

Before leaving London he told Mrs. Besant in a letter of December 15 that Nitya's eyes were better but not quite right yet. "He is a thundering good fellow even though I should not say so," he added. He also told her that the previous day, election day, he had been to Bow "to help Mr. Lansbury with his polling." (Lansbury was narrowly defeated by the Coalition candidate Major Blair. The Coalition won the election with a 262 majority.) Krishna hoped that Mrs. Besant was coming to London in February 1919.

> I cannot tell you what I am feeling at the thought of your coming over here and also at seeing you [he wrote in this same letter]. It has been more than four and a half years since I last saw you and a great many things have happened since then. You will find a great change in me except in one thing, namely that my devotion and love for your dear self has never changed. Words are so futile and cannot by any means convey what is one's real feeling although he be a master of words. So mother dearest, I, who am not a conjurer with words as yet, cannot unfold to you on paper, or in words, those thoughts which are constantly in my brain and in my heart. To me it will be a new life, give me a different point of view on life and my aspect on human nature will be so completely changed.
>
> You can give me anything that's enobling and yet be a mother which, in my opinion, cannot be found in modern civilization, especially over here. I can do but mighty little in comparison to what you have done for me, I can and will give you, mother dear, all

my pure love and devotion and be a true son on whom you can lean. So much for my innermost thoughts.

It was to be another five months before Mrs. Besant arrived. When the boys returned to London they shared the flat in Robert Street again, as the journey from Wimbledon had proved too much for Krishna; he went every day to London University while Nitya continued to read for the Bar. Although Krishna was now nearly twenty-four and Nitya nearly twenty-one they were still referred to as "the boys."

Mrs. Besant arrived on June 6. She was now so deeply involved in her work for Indian Home Rule that she had deliberately set aside the last vestiges of her psychic powers and thenceforth relied entirely on the people she trusted for occult communications; nevertheless she continued to proclaim the coming of the World Teacher at every opportunity both in her lectures and through the *Theosophist*. Leadbeater too was heralding the Teacher in *Theosophy in Australia,* though seldom communicating with the "vehicle."

On June 14 Krishna presided over a Star meeting that Mrs. Besant addressed in London, the first work of the kind he had done since she was last in England. As restlessly energetic as ever, she travelled all over England and Scotland that summer of 1919, speaking on a variety of subjects, though her chief concern at this time was to press the Government of India Bill on Parliament and start an Indian Home Rule League in England.

In July the boys went to stay with Lady De La Warr at a house she had taken by the sea in Scotland, at Gullane in East Lothian, on the outskirts of the famous championship golf course at Muirfield; playing golf every day, Krishna became a scratch player. According to Mrs. Jean Bindley, National Representative of the Order of the Star in the East for Scotland, Krishna won a championship at Gullane which, he told her, was the proudest moment of his life. Krishna himself maintains that he was never able to play well in competition.

On their return to London Krishna and Nitya made a new friend in Jamnadas Dwarkadas, a rich Bombay cotton merchant who had been converted to Theosophy in 1912 and had now come to England especially to see Krishna.

They met at lunch on August 1 at the house of Dr. Haden Guest, and as far as Jamnadas was concerned it was "love at first sight." They became such immediate friends that early next morning Jamnadas went to West Side House, Wimbledon, where Krishna was staying with Miss Dodge, and was shown straight up to Krishna's room. Jamnadas was much taken aback to find the future World Teacher sitting cross-legged on the floor cleaning his shoes and asked why one of the servants could not do this task. Krishna replied that he did it much better himself and that if Jamnadas would give him his shoes he would make them shine as they had never shone before. Jamnadas became very good friends with Nitya too and introduced him to his own favorite sport of horse racing.

In September the Lutyenses moved to a large Adam house in Mansfield Street near Cavendish Square where Krishna and Nitya were such frequent visitors that Mary, the youngest daughter, now eleven, would look hopefully every afternoon when she returned from school for their pale grey Homburg hats and gold-knobbed malacca walking-sticks lying on the hall table. They wore pale grey spats, had their shoes made at Lobb's (their feet were far too narrow for ready-made shoes), their suits at Meyers and Mortimer, their shirts at Beale and Inman, bought their ties at Liberty's, and had their hair cut at Trumper's. As Nitya was shorter than Krishna they could not wear each other's suits, but their shirts, socks, handkerchiefs and underclothes were interchangeable and all neatly embroidered with their joint initials JKN.

Mary recalled that they were lapped in a charm they created around themselves wherever they went.

> For one thing [she wrote], they were so much cleaner than anyone else I had ever come across. . . . their neat brown shoes were always so beautifully polished, and their straight black hair, which was parted in the middle and smelt of some delicious unguent they both used, so sleek. . . . These two brothers seemed more alike than two English brothers because their foreignness set them equally apart. Their English accent had an identical lilt and their laugh the same rather high-pitched tinkle. . . . They were both able to bend the first joints of their fingers without bending the second. Nitya was not as classically good

looking as Krishna but his face had great charm and his smile was irresistible.

Their extreme physical cleanliness and the care they took with their clothes were apt to make Mary feel dirty and ill-groomed. She took particular trouble with her appearance and washed particularly carefully when she knew she was going to see them.

At this time Krishna had just discovered P. G. Wodehouse and Stephen Leacock, and Mary remembers him in the drawing-room at Mansfield Street reading *Nonsense Novels* and *Piccadilly Jim* aloud, "laughing so much that he spluttered over the words." He would stand, leaning against the bookcase, while he read aloud. He never seemed to sit down except at meals.

In October Mrs. Besant took Krishna and Nitya to Paris on a short visit; on their return the boys moved into a flat at 33 Duke Street, St. James's, from where, on November 3, Krishna wrote to Sacha de Manziarly, a new friend he had made in Paris:

I asked Mrs. Besant if she had any objection to my living in Paris or anywhere in France to learn French and generally enlarge whatever brains I have. She, luckily, had no objection whatever, so I hope I shall turn up in the spring. I *must* learn French and lengthen our friendship. I am very bad at expressing my feelings but I hope you understand. Do come over before Spring. I was describing to Lady Emily all about you and how nice you were even though you were a great friend of mine.

Sacha was the twenty-year-old only son of a family with whom Krishna was soon to become very intimate; he was a delightfully gay young man in spite of having lost a leg in the war. It appears from this letter to Sacha that Krishna had now given up hope of getting into London University. Nevertheless he continued to attend lectures there that winter but does not seem to have studied very seriously, as he was frequently at Mansfield Street in the afternoons, and every week-end he and Nitya would go to cinemas with Lady Emily and the younger Lutyens children, usually to the New Gallery in Regent Street.

Nitya had had a great bit of luck in November. Jamna-

das, who was still in London, had dreamt that a horse with
the initials K.J. (the reverse of J.K.) was going to win a
race. He found that a horse called King John was running
in the November Handicap at Manchester. He was further
encouraged to believe his dream when he saw that the
jockey had the initials E.A.W. (Ernest Armine Wodehouse). Jamnadas told Nitya about the dream and they
both backed the horse in London at 8 to 1. They also went
secretly together to Manchester and put on more money
on the course. It won, netting Jamnadas about £1,300 and
Nitya, too, a considerable, though lesser, sum. (The race
was run on Saturday, November 22. King John won at
13-2. The jockey was E. Wheatley.) They did not get back
to Duke Street until after eleven that night. Krishna, quite
worried, demanded to know where they had been all day.
Feeling very pleased with themselves they told him that
they had been to the races at Manchester, to which he retorted, "You both look very dirty; you need a good bath."
They then told him gleefully about the money they had
won. "That's why you are looking and feeling filthy," he
replied. "Many people must have lost for you to make all
that money."

But for Nitya the race had an even more deflating
dénouement than this: with his winnings and the contribution of some of Jamnadas's, he bought an Isotta Fraschini
car, only to be ordered by Mrs. Besant to get rid of it as
soon as she heard about it. One does not know what happened to the money; probably he was made to give it to
Theosophical funds. Anyway, the chief outcome of this
windfall was to fire Nitya with the ambition to make some
money he could call his own.

13

Life in Paris

Nitya passed his examination in Constitutional Law and Legal History on January 13, 1920. Krishna sat for Matriculation again on January 20 but realized that he had no chance of passing. His own recollection is that he left the papers blank. Mrs. Besant had already agreed that it would now be best for him to study languages with a view to being able to speak in all parts of the world when the time came for him to start his life's work, so without waiting to hear the result of the examination he left London for Paris on January 24. On the same day Nitya moved into a flat on his own at 69 Piccadilly and began to study Criminal Law and eat more dinners at Lincoln's Inn.

Krishna went first to stay with Madame Zelma Blech and her sister Mademoiselle Aimée Blech at 21 Avenue Montaigne where he was given his own sitting-room. Madame Blech, the widowed sister of Charles Blech, was the National Representative of the Order of the Star for France. She had reverted to her maiden name, and now she and his sister lived with their brother who was in hospital at this time undergoing an operation.

Krishna wrote long letters to Lady Emily every two or three days, giving detailed records of all his doings and most intimate feelings. At first he was terribly homesick for her. On January 25 he wrote about his departure from Victoria Station:

> As soon as the train started my heart was in my throat & I had to swallow a great lump but I could not prevent tears & was obliged to put a paper in front of my face. Like all things it passed but the wound is still there which will *only* be cured when I shall see you again.... What did you do after I left? You must tell me *everything, everything* you do, you think, you buy....

On February 1 he was writing, "I can *never* realize my dream, the more wonderful it is the more sadder and unobtainable. You know my dream mother which is being with you—ad infinitum. But I am a lusus naturae (freak of nature) and nature enjoys its freak while the freak suffers."

One of the first people Krishna saw in Paris was Fabrizio Ruspoli, who had been at Adyar when he was 'discovered.' Ruspoli had rejoined the navy on the outbreak of war and was now in Paris as head of the Italian Naval Delegation to the Peace Conference.

> Ruspoli and I lunched at a little restaurant [Krishna told Lady Emily in this same letter of February 1]. We two talked a long time. He is very upset, like me. Poor old Ruspoli.... He, at the age of 42, feels homeless, believes in none of the things which C.W.L. [Leadbeater] or Mrs. Besant have said.... He does not know what to do, has no ambition. In fact we are both in the same unfortunate boat.... He thinks and feels all that I feel, but as he says What's to be done? We both felt miserable.

And ten days later: "Oh! mother I am young, must I grow old with sorrow as my eternal companion? You have had your youth & your happiness and you have that which can be given by man and God, a home. We all have our moments of depression so excuse." And on February 20: "You ask me whether I am happy? Are the flowers happy without their own dear sun? So we will pass over that question as nothing can come of it. I am interested in my new life but am not carried away by it."

He was soon to find interest in his new friends. There was Isabelle Mallet, whom he had met in November, a cousin of Guillaume Mallet, a beautiful and talented young woman who was confined to a chair as a result of paralysis; then there was the de Manziarly family who had a flat close to the Blechs at 2 rue Marbeuf. Madame de Manziarly (née Irma Luther), a Russian married to a Frenchman much older than herself, was a woman of great beauty, culture, erudition and vitality, four years younger than Lady Emily. She had been one of the first members of the Order of the Star in Europe and had made her four children members when they were quite small. The eldest girl,

Mima, was at a university in America when Krishna first went to Paris; Sacha now had a job at Viviez in the South of France and rarely came to Paris; so it was the two younger girls, Marcelle and Yolande (Mar and Yo), aged nineteen and fifteen, who became Krishna's constant companions. Mar was a fine musician, a pianist and composer. The de Manziarlys had much more vitality and natural gaiety than the Lutyens's and were far more extroverted. Sacha in particular was tremendous fun to be with and Krishna loved going about Paris with him, while Mar and Yo treated him with a mixture of playfulness and reverence which he found very endearing.

The girls met him for the first time on February 29 at Isabelle Mallet's flat at 33 rue de Miromesnil. "Our contact was immediate," Mar remembers; thereafter they saw him every day and helped him greatly with his French. Madame de Manziarly, whom he had met first, was more serious; she gave him French lessons, took him to picture galleries, the Comédie Français and the Russian ballet, and introduced him to the many interesting and important people she knew. "I like Mme de Manziarly *very* much," he had told Lady Emily on February 8, "& she is very nice to me & she takes such a lot of trouble." She had taken him to the Louvre and "instructed" him as she knew such a lot about painting. He considered this good for him, but, he added characteristically, "I much prefer beautiful scenery." Lady Emily had certainly never tried to instruct him; they had always been to comedies or cinemas together and she shared his passion for Westerns.

Isabelle Mallet was very unhappy because the man she loved had recently died. Krishna was troubled as there was nothing he could do to comfort her.

When a most critical moment comes [he wrote to Lady Emily], Theosophy and all its inumerable books don't help. She [Isabelle] wants to see the Masters physically or mentally & does not believe what A.B. and C.W.L. have said, in fact she feels what we [he and Nitya] have felt for the last two or three years.... I tried to persuade her from not waking occult powers & all that kind of things but she is longing for it.... When I left I kissed her poor hand & I felt awful.... Poor Isabelle longing to see the Mas-

ter, Madame de M. also the same, I, you know, don't
care a damn.

Krishna was embarrassed to find that Madame de Manziarly, Sacha and Isabelle all felt "inspired" by him. He assured them that there were thousands of people like him
only they had not met them. Madame de Manziarly had
told him, he informed Lady Emily, that when first she had
met Mrs. Besant ten years before her life had changed
completely and now that she had met Krishna another
turning point had come; he was "a living flame" to her.

Suddenly while she was talking [he continued in
this letter], I became unconscious of her & the room
& toutes les choses, toutes. It was as though I fainted
for a second & I forgot what I had been saying and
asked her to repeat what I had been saying. It is absolutely indiscribable mother. I felt as though my
mind & soul was taken away for a second and I felt
most strange I assure you. Mme de M. was looking at
me all the time & I said that I felt very strange & I
said 'Oh! the room is *very* hot isn't it?' For I did not
want her to think that I was 'inspired' or anything of
that kind but all the same I *felt* really inspired & very
strange. . . . I had to get up and stand a bit & collect
my ideas. I assure you mother it was most strange,
most strange. Between ourselves *absolutely*, in the
Theosophical language, there was someone there but I
did *not* tell her.

Before meeting the de Manziarly girls he had gone to
the South of France on February 12 with Captain Max
Wardall, an American Theosophist to whom Sacha had introduced him and who knew Leadbeater. He had to leave
the Blechs anyway as Monsieur Blech was coming out of
hospital and Madame de Manziarly promised to look for a
flat for him while he was away. He and Max Wardall
stayed first at the Hotel Astoria at Nice for three days. On
the first day they drove into Monte Carlo and had tea at
the Casino but were not allowed into the gaming rooms
because they had not got their passports. One woman in
the Casino smiled at Krishna, followed him and did everything to attract his attention. He assured Lady Emily that
he "never twiched once," he was "like a stone," and after

about fifteen minutes she left him alone. Back at Nice they
spent the evening with two Russian girls, friends of Wardall's, with whom they "went to a club and danced! They
could not dance, nor could I, so I was relieved, but we
danced all the same. Nothing happened mother dear &
don't laugh mother."

On the last afternoon, while having tea at the Nice Casino, Krishna suggested to Wardall that

> it would be splendid if we controlled the ball by will-
> power and then we could bet as much as we liked &
> ruin the Bank. We both rushed to the table & began.
> I imagined putting a small elemental in the middle of
> the table who caught hold of the ball & put it in ei-
> ther 3, 4 or 5. It did work and at one time we had
> 100 francks & we only started with 10 francks but
> lost it. We were frightfully keen on it.

In the end they lost 20 francs. Could there have been a
trace of envy in Krishna's reaction to Nitya's happy and
successful day at Manchester with Jamnadas?

On February 17 they moved to the Hotel Savaurain at
Cagnes where they was a golf course and where they were
able to stay for 25 francs a day with full pension, the exchange being then 45 francs to the pound. Krishna wrote
to Lady Emily from there:

> I left the beastly & ugly town behind me and
> walked up the hill. Every step I took reminded me of
> Taormina. The smell of rain and the rather fresh
> wind from the Alps brought before me such
> memories of joy that I almost believed you were
> there. . . . I have had no letter from you for a week,
> unheard of during the last 6 years. . . . Oh! mother
> mine how I do want you but I can never have you. It
> is a very depressing thought & I had better drop it.

Although he continued to love Lady Emily, he was
never again to miss her so much after this time at Cagnes.
From then on she had no more influence in his life, yet
for the next fifteen years or so she remained his chief con-
fidante; he was able to let himself go in his letters to her
as to no one else.

Before leaving for Paris on February 27, Krishna and

Wardall moved to Monte Carlo for a few days. It was
probably there that a certain incident occurred. Wardall
went off and left Krishna on his own in the hotel. While
he was alone a married woman spoke to him and asked
him to go up to her room to have a talk. In good faith
and innocence he went with her as she seemed very nice
and not at all like "that kind of woman." When they got
to her room she locked the door and started to embrace
him. He was so terrified that she unlocked the door at
once, saying, "You are not like that, are you?" It was only
afterwards that it was pointed out to him, by whom he
does not remember, how dangerous his position would
have been if the woman's husband had found him there.
No doubt she thought he was a homosexual. All his ten-
dencies were in fact heterosexual but at that time he believed, with the majority of Theosophists, that sex was
something unclean that must be sublimated. Part of his at-
traction for Lady Emily was his horror of sex, for by the
time she met him she had come to shrink from that aspect
of married life.[1]

Krishna had an intensely loving nature, but he was still
innocent about women and very frightened of them. "I
have had no adventures," he had told Lady Emily soon after his arrival in Paris, "and don't particularly want any
and I carefully avoid when I see a woman either to walk
away from her or keep my eyes on the ground.... These
women are appalling, painted, rouged and smelling like
chemists shops—whew," and when, later on, he went to
Quo Vadis, he left early "before the naked lady
appeared." But that he was physically a very normal man
is shown in his letters: so close was he to Lady Emily that
he was even able to tell her, touchingly, of his "bad"
dreams which he found "beastly" and could not understand because his thoughts were always perfectly pure during the daytime.

Krishna found Nitya in Paris when he returned there on
February 28; indeed Nitya had been there since the 21st.
In London he had been hatching some money-making
scheme for forming a company to import cars and tractors

[1] Krishna's letters to Lady Emily between February 20 and April
7 are missing, therefore one can assume that this incident with the
woman took place at Monte Carlo, for had it occurred at Cagnes
he would surely have told her about it. At that time he seemed to
keep no detail of his life from her, however intimate.

into India. In connection with this he had sent several cables to Jamnadas who was now back in India, although it was a friend of Jamnadas's, Ratansi D. Moraji, another rich Bombay cotton merchant and Theosophist, who was chiefly involved in it. At the London end Nitya had been given a reference by Lady Churchill and introduced by her to the Master of Sempill, Lord Sempill's heir, who was giving the scheme encouragement.[1]

Nitya was very happy in Paris where he had met Isabelle Mallet and the de Manziarlys. (In the "memoranda" of his diary for the week ending February 19, he wrote that Marcelle's playing was "wonderful" and that he and Isabelle "discovered how nice we both were and became friends. If she were well!!! What would she not be able to do with men.") But it was Madame de Manziarly and Nitya who were to become particularly attached to each other; he began to feel that at last, in her, he had found a friend of his very own who loved him not just because he was Krishna's brother. Yo de Manziarly also loved him very specially and so did Mary Lutyens, but they were only children. It was a mature love he needed.

He returned to London on March 8 and wrote to Madame de Manziarly on that day to say that "business was too wonderful for words," so his scheme must already have matured. On the 18th Ratansi himself arrived in England. The next day there was a meeting to talk business with Ratansi and the Master of Sempill. By this time Nitya had made up his mind to go back to India with Ratansi; he had cabled to Mrs. Besant to tell her of his intention and had booked his berth on March 12. Ten days later he left London for Paris with Ratansi, having given up his flat and noted in his diary, "Exam for criminal law will have to be laid aside till later."

As soon as Nitya arrived in Paris he received a cable from Mrs. Besant ordering him to remain in England: his first duty was to look after Krishna; if Krishna got into any difficulties in Paris, Nitya could easily reach him from London. This destruction of all his hopes and plans must

---

[1] The Master of Sempill (1873–1965) was a pioneer in aviation and was also keenly interested in motoring. Lady Churchill, a daughter of the Earl of Lonsdale, was a follower of Mrs. Besant. She had married the 1st Viscount Churchill in 1887. Her husband was not as long-suffering as Edwin Lutyens and in 1927 obtained a divorce from her on the grounds of desertion.

have been a terrible blow; he had been so excited over the whole adventure, yet he merely noted in his diary, "A.B. the all powerful."

He stayed on in Paris, comforted by the de Manziarlys, while Ratansi, who had decided not to return to India without him, went back to London. In the middle of April Nitya went off to Turin for a week, probably to settle some business about a car; his state of mind can be judged from the entries in his diary while he was there: "Hell, Hell, Hell" for three days, and then in the "memoranda:" "Turin the most miserable in my life." To Madame de Manziarly he wrote from Turin on April 17, "It is a very extraordinary thing, but I've never yet enjoyed anything for which I've not paid dearly, I think it must be because my enjoyments are among the forbidden ones, and those that are permissable are not enjoyable."

He went back to Paris and stayed there until April 28 and then returned to yet another lonely furnished flat in London, 22 Hans Court, Hans Road, near Harrods, to resume work and eat more legal dinners. With his keen intelligence, less spiritual nature and stronger physical impulses than Krishna, and his longing for financial independence, it must have been desperately hard for him to fulfill the role assigned to him by Mrs. Besant. He had lost all faith and felt even more lost and unhappy than Krishna did at this time.

14

Critical and Rebellious

Krishna meanwhile was enjoying his independence in a little one-room flat, a *garçonnière,* at 4 rue du Colonel Renard, which Madame de Manziarly had found for him while he was in the South of France. He ate mostly by himself at a small Italian restaurant near his flat (Lady Emily maintained that he half starved himself from economy) but he had many meals with the de Manziarlys. One day he went to Fontainebleau with them, another to Versailles. He enjoyed these expeditions but complained that the de Manziarlys were so energetic that they tired him. Normally he found the greatest difficulty in getting dressed in the mornings; he and Nitya when left to themselves would lounge about in dressing-gowns till lunch time.

He told Lady Emily on April 7 that two days before (Easter Monday), "Madame de M, Marcelle, my love!!! & Yo (another love) came here bringing tea with them. I changed into Indian dress and they went into raptures. (If I allow myself I could be most conceited fool on earth but thank God & you I shall never be that." The next day, at tea with the de Manziarlys, "A Slave [Slav?] man played the flute. It was really wonderful. He had been a real sheapard and he played all the sheapard songs. I had goose skin the whole time. It was really perfect.) I was so moved I asked him to teach me & he is going to. 'Krishna playing the flute'." He added in this same letter:

I am *more* in 'lofe' & they are all in 'lofe' with me. As I said if I allow myself I could be seriously in love but tell me honestly mother, I want your opinion if it is the right thing. Of course I shall *never* marry, that is not for me in this life, I have something better to do. Don't laugh, I mean seriously I like Marcelle, my love, *very* much but I don't know whether I am in

love with her. So don't worry. Do you seriously think
I shall forget you, after 8 years?

One does not know what Lady Emily's advice was
about falling in love but later Krishna expressed surprise
when she told him she was jealous. He was becoming
reconciled to being without her. ". . . it is the question of
the sun & the moon—never can they be together so the
less said about it the better," he wrote on April 18. In the
same letter he told her that he was going to get a professor
and work really hard as well as taking flute lessons every
Thursday. These flute lessons did not last long, nor did the
resolve to work hard.

On May 6 he was writing after being with Sacha de
Manziarly who had come to Paris unexpectedly, "Curiously all day I have been *very* dreamy, more dreamy than
usual and in my heart there has been a continual thought
of Lord Buddha. I was in such a state that I had to sit
down & meditate. Think of me meditating. Extraordinary."

On June 6 he went to London and stayed with Nitya at
Hans Court for five weeks. Mrs. Besant did not come to
Europe that year so there seems no reason for his going to
England except to see Lady Emily. Ratansi was still in
London; Nitya had been riding with him every day in
Richmond Park, going to theatres with him and drives in
his Rolls-Royce, though evidently not enjoying himself,
for, as he wrote to Madame de Manziarly, "Pleasures
taken seriously become miserable duties."

On July 11 Krishna and Nitya went with Ratansi to
Paris where they stayed in comfort for once at the Hotel
Claridge. The de Manziarlys had already gone to Amphion on the Lake of Geneva, near Evian; they had taken a
villa there for the summer holidays where Krishna was to
join them. He begged Lady Emily to go too, but as she
felt she could not leave her children nor afford to take
them abroad that year because Barbie had been married in
May, she had to sacrifice this pleasure. After an amusing
week at Viviez with Sacha and a Spanish friend of his,
Krishna joined the de Manziarlys on July 20 for two
months. He stayed at the Hôtel des Princes opposite their
villa and had his meals in the hotel, but spent all day with
them, walking, rowing, swimming, playing tennis and
golf—speaking French all the time. In the evenings they
played bridge or poker, with beans for counters, and paper

games. Isabelle Mallet joined them at the end of July;
Sacha came for a few days and Nitya paid them two visits
in August and September.

This holiday at Amphion was probably the happiest normal time Krishna had ever spent. He wished Lady Emily
were there: "How you would enjoy all the childish and
joyish side." His first letter to her from Amphion was pep-
pered with pencil crosses—kisses from the two de Manziarly girls whom she had met during a visit to Paris. He
told her about an expedition to Chamonix and the Mer de
Glace: "So calm & so dignified those mountains
looked. . . . I longed for you to see that which to me is the
manifestation of God himself." This was the first time he
had been in the mountains and he has never lost his love
for them. When Sacha came, he and Krishna went together to the Casino at Evian. Krishna "longed to dance"
but had no partner, and even if he had would have been
"too timid."

He was reading aloud to the de Manziarlys *The Buddha's Way of Virtue* and was so struck by one passage
that he copied it out for Lady Emily: "All conquering and
all knowing am I, detached, untainted, untrammeled,
wholly freed by destruction of desire. Whom shall I call
Teacher? Myself found the way." And the de Manziarlys
were reading to him Turgenev and Bergson, which he
found rather difficult to understand. The two books he had
read in Paris that year which had most impressed him
were *The Idiot* and *Thus Spake Zarathustra*.

Part of his happiness at Amphion was that no one in
the hotel knew his history, though he was so embarrassed
by all the women ogling him in the dining-room that he
kept his eyes on his plate. But this kind of embarrassment
was nothing to the torture his reputation as the coming
Messiah caused him from time to time. He reported that
Yo de Manziarly thought him, "God on earth—better than
Mrs. Besant or C.W.L." "I told her not to turn my head &
mother dearest don't worry about it as they are not likely
to turn my head. I am not worth it." All the same, it may
have been the de Manziarlys' treatment of him, or his
reading about the Buddha, that suddenly reawakened in
him an interest in the role he was intended to play.

Raja had come to London in July and Krishna supposed
that now Raja was there it would "all begin again"—

meaning the past lives and the occult steps on the Path.
He wished he could

> stir up the b—Theosophists! I do hate this mamby-
> pamby affair we are at present. . . . What rot it all is
> & to think that it might be. We will have to do it.
> Change it from top to bottom and knock the personal
> element into thick air. I should like to know what
> Raja thinks of it all but I suppose he is of the old
> school. *Damn*! I am really fed up with that crowd but
> at present it is not my affair. One day, as I am really
> at the bottom very keen on it all, I shall take it up
> and do what *I* think is right and hang everybody who
> has got any personal element in it. Oh, mother what
> rot it is. Don't laugh. *Damn*!! Sacré nom d'une pipe,
> it means the same thing! We will change the world
> together with the help of Mme de M, Mar & Yo.!!!

Raja had brought with him to England Rajagopalacharya, Leadbeater's "discovery" of 1914 with the
wonderful past and marvellous future. Krishna told Lady
Emily that the de Manziarlys wanted to know what her
personal feelings were about

> this blinker Rajagopalacharya (what a name. They
> ask me if I have any fear of my rival!!? They think I
> am jealous! Poor chap, he can accept my notorious
> place for two sous. Personellement je m'en fiche de
> Raja, Rajago!!!) I wonder what he is going to do. I
> hope they won't rater [spoil] his future. If so I can
> condole him. Please if you see him give him my
> blessing and ask him for his. (Lord what fools we
> mortals are. We believe in anybody that shouts
> loudest & the so called T.S. birds cry in a jungle of
> fools and fools swallow what it pleases them most
> and it does them no good.)

A few days later he heard that Raja wanted to introduce some form of ceremonial into the Theosophical Society.

> I am going to write to Raja & tell him that as long
> as he does not use his blinking ceremony in the Star
> it is all the same to me. . . . Why not clear up the

mess we are in *first* & then start new things?[1] All this
only adds to the existing chaos making it more cum-
bersome. We have got something magnificient & when
we have the biggest we add to that human creations.
It makes me mad. Why are we like this? Because we
can't face the Bigness of life & so we create Little
Bigness which we can see.

And on August 7:

I wrote a long letter to Raja saying rather straight
that all these sideshows kill the main show. . . . I hope
he won't get annoyed with me! He sent me an advance copy of the *Disciple*.[2] My hair stands on
end. . . . As you know I really do believe in the Masters etc and I don't want it to be made ridiculous. A
beautiful idea or an object can never be ugly but we
human beings can make it monstrously unwholesome.
That's what the Disciple does. It is so damned petty
and unclean. What I want to do is this, that A.B.,
C.W.L., Raja, one or two others and myself should sit
round a table and discuss and lay out a plan, big &
clean, and follow that plan putting aside all personalities and all our petty things. But I don't see how it
can be done. We are all so far apart. . . . I can talk to
Raja but what can we two do mother dear among so
much chaos. . . . I am going to write to Raja about
the Disciple and then I shall thoroughly be in good
odeur!! I am in a most rebellious mood as you can
imagine and personally I don't want to belong to anything of which I am ashamed. . . . Thank you for telling me about Rajago & I I am sure he is 'au fond'
like everybody. Thank you for telling me that he is
not my 'Rival'!! There is nobody to tell to these
people not to be damn fools. They ought to have a
brother, especially like Nitya. There ought to be one
for Raja. Of course *if* [underlined four times] I am
to occupy a leading position in the T.S. it will be be-

[1] Dissident elements within the Theosophical Society were making trouble again at this time.
[2] One of several journals issued by the Esoteric Section of the T.S.
Started in May 1913 it came out only irregularly. There was no issue
between May 1920 and January 1922. Perhaps the advance copy
Krishna was shown was suppressed after he gave his opinion of it.

cause of [what] *I am* and not what other people think of me or have created a position for me. . . . I personally must work hard at my studies and get my mental condition into smooth running order. As you say when I get to Paris I shall go to elocution classes.

And on August 25:

Extraordinary chap Raja and I suppose he believes what Lady D [De La Warr] says about us and our debts. Raja is like the rest of us and if he had told me that they had spent so much on me in 'educating' (?) me & that I must return it in 'service' to the T.S., I should then tell him that I never asked him to take me out of India etc. Anyhow it is all d—d rot & I am fed up with it.

In writing to Mrs. Besant he did not allow any of this rebelliousness to appear:

Sept. 10. 20

I just want to write for your birthday [her seventy-third on October 1]. There will be thousands of people who will be writing to you from all parts of the world and sending you their love or devotion and I assure you mother, even though I may not be able to express my sentiments in a flowery language I have got profound love and devotion for your personal self. . . .

I am going to stay here till the end of this month and then shall go to London for a few days to see Raja etc. Then I shall come back to Paris. . . . I intend to go to the Sorbonne as now I can understand and read French with facility and take up philosophy. I have got the reading craze on me and I want to study *very* hard for the next two or three years. If I may say so, my education has been somewhat neglected and I want to rectify this neglect. . . . I want to gain everything that the West can give and then turn my face to India where I am sure I shall work. I hoped I am not boring you with all my plans . . . my love and my devotion are always at your disposal.

That he was fully reconciled to the fact that his work would lie in India is shown by his writing to Lady Emily on the same day as he was writing to Mrs. Besant: "Mother dear it has got to be sometime in this life. Mrs. Besant has not yet sent for me. If she does we *all* have to put our feelings in our respective pockets and I shall certainly go to India."

15

In Love

Krishna and Nitya arrived in London from Amphion on
the last day of September. They went to stay at a very
pleasant flat, No. 1 Robert Street, Adelphi (next door to
the previous flat they had had in the same street), which
had been taken for them by Lady De La Warr. Nevertheless they hated the dirt and noise of London and the black
smoke.

Nitya sat for his examination in Criminal Law on October 5 and heard on the 19th that he had passed, "though
badly." By this time Krishna had seen a great deal of
Raja. He had also met Rajagopal whom he described in a
letter to Mar de Manziarly as "a nice boy," though he had
not yet had much chance to talk to him, but by the 14th
he was able to tell her that he had had a long conversation
with him and found him "very nice" and that Rajagopal
had told him that he would like to work for him. Nitya
was not too pleased, however, when he heard that Rajagopal, while studying to get into Cambridge, was to share the
Robert Street flat with him after Krishna returned to
Paris. There was only one sitting-room and Nitya had
hoped to have it to himself.

There may well have been something in the idea that
Rajagopal was being considered as a possible "rival" to
Krishna, for Leadbeater must have been aware, not only
astrally, of Krishna's disenchantment with his role at this
time. Leadbeater had indeed already given an indication
that he was prepared to limit the importance of the chosen
"vehicle," even if not to supplant him altogether, when he
had written the previous year: "I have been given to understand [by the Lord Maitreya himself no doubt] ...
that in addition to the body He will use most of the time,
and in which He will travel about, He will probably
choose some one person in each country, whom He will
sometimes inspire when He wishes, whom He will guide
and direct as to what He wants done." These words were

evidently addressed to his young Australian pupils, for after saying that the Lord was not expected to come for fifteen or twenty years, and that therefore he, Leadbeater,
would not see him in his present body, he went on, "Do
you realize that if He is going to choose a young person
through whom to speak, say here in Australia, it will have
to be a person who at the present moment is about the age
of some of you?" He neglected to say what might happen
if all these different people in the various countries, who
believed themselves to be personally inspired by the World
Teacher, were directed to say and do contradictory things.

Krishna did not return to Paris until December 8. During those weeks in London his interest in the Star work
was stimulated, probably under the influence of Raja, and
he again undertook to write the editorial notes for the Star
magazine, the *Herald*. Wodehouse was now married and
was returning to India as Professor of English at Deccan
College, Poona, so the editorship of the *Herald* was once
again left entirely to Lady Emily. Wodehouse had resigned
from his position as Organizing Secretary of the Order of
the Star in the East and Nitya was appointed in his place.
Wodehouse never lost touch with Krishna and in 1926 returned to work for him at Adyar.

Even with the favorable currency exchange Krishna
had to be very economical in Paris. He stayed first with
the Blechs and then moved to a small hotel where Ruspoli
was living, the Victor Emmanuel III in the rue de Pon-
thieu, but he took most of his meals with the de Manziarlys
as Monsieur de Manziarly was ill in the South of France.
Krishna wrote to Lady Emily for her forty-sixth birthday
which was on December 26: "Do you remember mother
darling that a long time ago I wrote to you that as each
birthday passed my love would increase rather than de-
crease? Well I can honestly say that my love for you is immense without any exaggeration. There is a tie between us
which will *never* be broken.... I love you with all my
heart & soul & that love is my best & purest."

Nevertheless his letters to Lady Emily in 1921 were far
shorter and less frequent than before, and usually began
with an apology for not writing sooner. Following her advice he was having elocution lessons, and on December 28
he took the important step of speaking voluntarily at a
Theosophical meeting in Paris. It was not on the program
that he should speak but he suddenly discovered that he

wanted to. He spoke for ten minutes in English which was translated.

> Just before I got on the platform, naturally I was quaking & my nerves were awful & as I got on to the platform I was as calm as an experienced speaker. People clapped and grinned all over their faces.... I told them not to be sentimental etc. Politics & Religion must go hand in hand etc.... I am going to speak now as I like it and I am very glad as I have to do it some day.

Krishna's letter to Mrs. Besant from Amphion had evidently hurt her, for on January 12, 1921, he was writing to her:

> My letter about my education must have made you unhappy. Please mother that was *not* my intention when I wrote it and it was far from it. If my education was neglected it was *not* your fault, it was the war and other things and please don't say that you are sorry as it hurts me profoundly. Nobody in the world could have been more thoughtful and motherly to Nitya and me. What has happened is finished and after all why should I or you worry about it. You have enough as it is, God knows. So please don't say you are sorry.... I am going to write the editorial every month and for me it will be very difficult. My French is getting on splendidly and in a few months I ought to be quite good. I go to the Sorbonne [which was free] and I have taken up Sanskrit which will be useful in India. My one desire in life is to work for you and for Theosophy. I shall succeed. I want to come out to India as Raja will have told you and take my part in the work. Anyhow mother remember that I love you with all my heart and soul and no man can be more devoted to you.

Mrs. Besant was delighted to hear that he was going to write the editorial notes in the *Herald*. It was a terrible strain on him and he came to dread them more and more each month, but they made a great difference to the sale of the magazine which was again in financial straits, for Miss Dodge had given up her guarantee. Krishna himself

wrote to several people asking for donations. Mrs. Percy
Douglas-Hamilton, another rich Star member, daughter of
the tobacco millionaire, Frederick Wills, and a devotee of
Mrs. Besant, guaranteed £1,000 for a year, and Joseph
Bibby of *Bibby's Annual,* a Theosophist of long standing
though not a Star member, guaranteed £100. In April
Robert Lutyens, who was now a professional journalist
working on the *Daily Mail,* undertook to edit the *Herald*
and made a great success of it.

At the beginning of February Krishna fell ill with a
sinus infection that turned to bronchitis. He had a very
high temperature and became delirious. Madame de Manziarly insisted on his moving to the rue Marbeuf where she
and the girls lovingly looked after him until she was called
away to the South of France where her husband was now
desperately ill with pneumonia. Krishna then moved to the
Blechs as it was not *convenable* to remain alone with the
girls. Nitya was also ill in London at this time. He had
chicken-pox so badly that it was thought at first he had
smallpox. Krishna was very worried and hoped that Lady
Emily was looking after him as well as the de Manziarlys
had looked after *him.*

Monsieur de Manziarly died on February 10. After his
death Madame de Manziarly was able to devote herself
entirely to Krishna and Nitya. As Krishna was still conva-
lescent and Nitya did not think he himself would ever be
well until he got away from London which he hated, the
brothers went off alone together on March 4 to Antibes
for three weeks. They stayed in a pretty cottage by the sea
with a Madame Rondeau where they seem to have been
very happy. Nitya then went back to London to study for
his finals while Krishna returned to Paris to live with the
de Manziarlys.

Krishna had had time to think and look into himself at
Antibes. "I am very glad you have faith in me," he wrote
to Lady Emily soon after returning to Paris. ". . . We will
all be someday, great teachers & we must get to that stage
as soon as we can. I don't know why you should have
faith in me for I have done *nothing* and yet you and everybody says that they have faith in me. God knows why.
I am *not* fishing & you know me." And soon afterwards:

> I *must* take my self in hand & work hard. I am do-
> ing it. I have taken myself in hand & I mean to do

things. I do a vague kind of meditation but I must do
it more rigorously and regularly. That's only the way.
I don't know the phylosophy of my life but I *will*
have one. . . . I have been thinking a great deal about
the Order & the T.S. mais surtout de moi-même. I
must find myself and then *only* can I help others. In
fact, I must make the Old Gentleman come down &
take some responsibility. Probably he wants to but
finds that the body & mind is not spiritual enough &
now I must waken them for 'his' habitation. If I am
to help I must have sympathy & a complete understanding & surtout infinite love. I am using well worn
phrases but to me they are *new*.

By "the Old Gentleman" Krishna meant his ego—he
must make his body and mind spiritual enough for his
ego's habitation. This differentiation between body and the
ego, the soul, was very much emphasized in Theosophy.
The body was something at a lower stage of evolution
which had to be looked after like a child or a domestic animal. Krishna was seeing a great deal of Ruspoli again,
who was much happier, and bringing down "the Old
Gentleman" was originally Ruspoli's remark about his own
ego.

As Krishna was still feeling far from well—he had pains
in his stomach and some kind of unspecified trouble with
his nose from which he had suffered on and off all his
life—Madame de Manziarly took him to see a friend of
hers, Dr. Paul Carton, a naturist, who put him on a
régime which he followed very strictly. He has always
been interested in new diets, though has never ceased to be
a vegetarian.

It was Nitya, however, who was really ill. One afternoon in the middle of May when he had been with Lady
Emily to the New Gallery Cinema, he gave a sudden
cough and brought up blood. It was diagnosed that he had
a patch on the left lung. Krishna immediately sent for him
to come to Paris to be treated by Dr. Carton, and on May
29, with the permission of his London doctor, he arrived.
Krishna and Madame de Manziarly took him off next day
to see Dr. Carton who lived at Boissy-St. Leger, an hour's
journey from Paris. The doctor found the infected spot
with difficulty, put him on a strict diet and said he must be

taken care of as if he were at the last stage of the disease, for that was the only way to cure him.

As Dr. Carton wished to see him frequently it was arranged that he should go to Boissy-St. Leger for the summer. A Dr. Schlemmer, a pupil of Dr. Carton's, had a house there which he put at Madame de Manziarly's disposal, and on June 14 she took Nitya to Boissy for a period of complete rest and freedom from all excitement.

Krishna meanwhile had gone on June 3 to London where Mrs. Besant would soon be arriving. He had a busy time travelling about with her, eventually returning to Paris with her at the end of July for the Theosophical World Convention. This Convention was followed by the first Congress of the Order of the Star in the East which Nitya was considered well enough to attend. There were now more than 30,000 members of the Order in all parts of the world. Some 2,000 attended the Congress, many of whom had made great financial sacrifices to get to Paris.

Nitya sent a report of the Congress to Leadbeater:

The main feature of the whole Congress was Krishna's presence and influence. He has been a revelation to everybody, and even Mrs. Besant was very interested to watch his unfolding. She and Krishna opened the Congress together [both speaking French] and afterwards he took everything into his own hands; he took the chair at the debates and conducted them with great skill concentrating the attention of the people on the relevant arguments, and not allowing the debates to wander from the point in question.... Krishna spoke several times informally to the delegates and the members, and gave a lecture at the Theatre des Champs Elysées, everyone as you may imagine, wondering what he was like and what he could have to say to them as the head of the Order. Mrs. Besant, all in white, was in the chair and watched him the whole time that he was speaking; he was a very slender figure in evening dress, and the two made a beautiful contrast on the enormous stage of the theatre.

Mrs. Besant also wrote enthusiastically in the September *Theosophist* about the way Krishna conducted the Congress:

... he astonished all present by his grasp of the questions considered, his firmness in controlling the discussions, his clear laying down of the principles and practices of the Order.... But the biggest thing about him was his intense conviction of the reality and omnipotence of the Hidden God in every man, and the, to him, inevitable results of the presence of that Divinity.

It was resolved during the Congress that there should be no ceremonials in the Order. "A ritual, however beautiful and magnificent," Krishna declared, "would inevitably tend to crystallize the movement and narrow down its scope of action." In his editorial for the August *Herald* he was writing: "An open mind is essential if we are to understand Truth;" the Star members should not be like the Pharisees of old, unable to grasp the Truth when it was spoken. Raja also was emphasizing in the *Herald* at this time the need for intellectual detachment from all traditions, ideas and customs. "When He speaks to us," he wrote, "shall we be free of all our previous notions and realize that if He says something novel which is contrary to all traditions, it is for us to drop all the traditions, and start afresh to understand Him?" How often this warning, echoing Krishna's words, was to be reiterated by the older leaders of Theosophy and how little they themselves heeded it when the time came.

After the Congress Krishna and Nitya went to Boissy on August 1. Four days later Lady Emily, who had rented a house there, arrived with her two youngest daughters, Betty and Mary, now aged fifteen and thirteen. Mar de Manziarly, Rajagopal and an Austrian friend of Krishna's, John Cordes,[1] stayed with Lady Emily, while Yo was with her mother, Krishna and Nitya at Dr. Schlemmer's house close by. Nitya led an invalid life and was seldom seen. The other members of the party, except for Madame de Manziarly who never left Nitya, played rounders in the afternoons and childish games like Russian Whispering, Blind Man's Buff and Statues in the Lutyens's garden in

[1] National Representative of the Star for Austria. Cordes was a sturdy old man with white hair and a very healthy complexion. He was something of a naturist himself, his panacea being ice-cold hip baths. He had been at Adyar in 1910-11 where he had been in charge of Krishna's physical exercises.

the evenings. It was a very hot summer and the mosquitoes were a torment.

The long rest at Boissy had not brought down Nitya's temperature so at the beginning of September he went to Montesano in the Swiss Alps above Montreux with Krishna, Rajagopal and John Cordes. From Montesano on September 9 Krishna wrote to Lady Emily expressing all his former love after those weeks together at Boissy: "I must be sentimental to you as I *shall* not be to any other. My love for you is as pure & as lasting as the snow on Mont Blanc."

They knew they were soon to part because, before Mrs. Besant returned to Adyar in the middle of August, it had been arranged that Krishna and Nitya should go to India that winter for Krishna to begin his life's work; but Lady Emily could not have guessed how soon she would have to share his love. Leaving Nitya at Montesano with Cordes, he went to Holland on September 15 at the invitation of Baron Philip van Pallandt van Eerde who had offered to make over to the Order of the Star his beautiful eighteenth-century ancestral home surrounded by 5,000 acres of woodland—Castle Eerde (pronounced Airder) at Ommen, not far from Arnhem. Krishna was away for only a fortnight, but during that time he met an American girl of seventeen, Helen Knothe, a niece of Miss Cornelia Dijkgraaf, National Representative of the Star in Holland, and daughter of Frank Knothe who had a successful clothing business in New Jersey. Helen was staying with her aunt in Amsterdam studying the violin. Krishna was greatly attracted by her; indeed, according to Lady Emily, he fell really in love for the first time.

On his way back to Montesano Krishna stopped in Geneva and attended a two-and-a-half-hour session of the Assembly of the League of Nations of which Ruspoli was now a representative.

All sorts of old fogies spoke [he told Lady Emily on October 3], including Lord Robert Cecil. He spoke about stopping the poison gas. They never go to the bottom of things, stopping *all* wars; they are a lot of insincere and money grubbing lot of people. . . . I know how much better we Theosophists could manage the League of Nations for I think we are more disinterested. We must some day have in the T.S. a

true League of Nations which included *all* nations.
We shall too & as a matter of fact we are but we
don't function properly. You wait, when we get going
we shall make a hum & beat them all at their own
game.

Soon after returning to Montesano it was decided, with
the help of Harold Baillie-Weaver who made their travelling arrangements, that if Nitya's health permitted
Krishna and Nitya should sail from Marseilles to Bombay
on November 19. Nitya was certainly much better. He
was able to walk for three hours every morning and play
croquet in the afternoons. When Lady Emily heard that
the date was fixed she must have sent Krishna a very
miserable letter, for he replied from Montesano on October 19:

What a letter you have written me!! I don't *want* to
weep and it is going to be hard for us both, so we
must make the best of a very bad job; by grinning
and bearing it. Easy thing to do!! Really you write to
me as though I was going away to some far off desert
island from which I shall never return. You compare
yourself to a man who is about to be hanged. Darling
Mother, you know even if I go away, say for many
years, that my love for you will *never* cease. . . . It is
all going to be very difficult anyway . . . you know
mother it *won't* do for us to be weak for we won't
help each other. . . . There is a bigger side, as you say,
to all this & that is essential & from which we must
not budge an inch.

Then to Lady Emily's joy her husband told her that he
wanted her to go to Delhi with him that winter: she hoped
to get to Adyar to be with Krishna during her stay in India.
On October 20 Krishna left Montesano while Nitya
went to Leysin with Madame de Manziarly to consult a
famous lung specialist, Dr. Rollier. Krishna, after a fortnight in London saying good-bye to various people, including Mr. Sanger and Rajagopal who was now reading Law
at Trinity College, Cambridge, went to Holland for a
week, this time for a Theosophical and Star Convention in
Amsterdam. There he met Helen Knothe again. On

November 17, the day he left for Marseilles, he wrote to
Lady Emily from the Blechs' flat in Paris a short letter
which could have done nothing to make the parting easier
for her:

> I am very miserable as I am leaving you and Helen
> for a long time. I *am* awfully in love & it is a great
> sacrifice on my part but *nothing* else can be done. I
> feel as if I had an awful wound inside me; don't
> think I am exagerating. I shall not see Helen for God
> knows how long & you know mother dear what I am.
> I think, I know, she has felt it too but what else is
> there to be done. It is not going to be easy; on the
> contrary, a thousand times worse. Oh! well, no good
> grumbling about it. I shall see *you* soon any way
> thank goodness but—!!! I hope you are not jealous,
> dear old Mum?? I shan't receive a letter from you or
> from her for at least a month. Cheerful. Stop it,
> damn you, Krishna. You don't know how I am
> feeling. I have never realized it all before & what it
> all means. . . . 'Enough of idle wishing. How it steals
> the time.' How one is miserable!! God bless you.

Unfortunately for Nitya, Dr. Rollier pronounced him
well enough to go to India. Madame de Manziarly went
on ahead to be there in time to meet him, leaving Cordes
to escort him to Marseilles where he met Krishna on
November 18. The next day the brothers sailed for Bombay on the *Morea*.

16

Return to India

Mrs. Besant with Madame de Manziarly, Ratansi, Jamnadas and a great crowd of Theosophists and Star members were there to meet Krishna and Nitya when they docked at Bombay on December 3. Mrs. Besant with two garlands was the first up the gangway. As she wrote in the *Theosophist* "the two brothers who left as boys have returned as men after an absence from their native country of almost ten years." They arrived in European clothes but by the afternoon, at a garden party at Ratansi's house on Malabar Hill, where they were staying in Bombay, they had changed into Indian dress. Part of Krishna's natural wish to efface himself has always been to appear as inconspicuous as possible, therefore he wears Indian clothes in India and Western clothes in Europe and America, except occasionally in the evenings when he may change into Indian dress.....

After going with Mrs. Besant to Delhi, Agra, Benares and Calcutta they reached Adyar in the second week of December, where they had "a royal welcome." Mrs. Besant tried to say a few words of welcome at the Adyar Hall but speech was difficult "so overpowering was the feeling of the closing of one chapter and the opening of another." Mrs. Besant had built a large room with a veranda for the brothers on the top of what had been Mrs. Russak's house which was connected at first-floor level with the Headquarters building. Their veranda had the most beautiful view in the whole of Adyar.

Krishna wrote to Lady Emily from Adyar on December 12 welcoming her to his country, where she was to arrive on the 17th, and telling her that life was not "over pleasant," that he had not been "particularly happy" and that "things" were "going to be damned difficult in the future." As well as this letter of greeting, he and Nitya went to Bombay to meet her. "They looked very strange," she

141

recalled, "in their India dress—Krishna in a mauve tur-
ban, a long tussore coat and a dhoti (a long muslin gar-
ment draped around the legs), and Nitya in a little round
velvet cap." Lady Emily managed to escape from Government House, Bombay, where she and her husband were
staying with Sir George and Lady Lloyd, to go with
Krishna and Nitya to Benares to join Mrs. Besant for the
Theosophical Convention that was being held there that
year.

In 1914 Mrs. Besant had handed over the Central
Hindu College, and the boys' and girls' schools attached to
it, to some leading Hindus who developed it into the
Hindu University. During the Prince of Wales's visit to India in 1921, he went on December 13 to Benares where an
honorary doctorate was conferred on him by the Hindu
University. The next day Mrs. Besant was accorded the
same honor. She was very proud of this and liked thenceforth to be referred to as Dr. Besant. She must have returned to Benares to receive her doctorate the day after
Krishna's welcome at Adyar. Her energy at seventy-four
was amazing.

Krishna gave one of the four Convention lectures in
Benares, his subject being "Theosophy and International-
ism." In speaking, he was "very halting in those days,"
Lady Emily recalled,

and obviously had great difficulty in putting his
thoughts into words although he thoroughly prepared
his lectures. His technique is now most impressive
and he has complete command of his audience, but
that is due, I think, more to the force of his personality than to his power of oratory. He always speaks in
English, which a large proportion of his audience, at
any rate in India, cannot understand, and yet they listen spellbound. I believe he speaks to some inner consciousness that is not dependent on words.

That was written nearly twenty years ago, yet many
would say the same of him today.

Shiva Rao was in Benares and also George Arundale
with Rukmini Devi, the beautiful Brahmin wife he had
married the previous April when she was just sixteen, the
daughter of a well-known Sanskrit scholar and engineer.
(This marriage had met with a good deal of opposition

which Rukmini had bravely faced.) Another person there
was Barbara Villiers, a cousin of Lady Emily's through the
Clarendons and almost an adopted daughter of Lady De
La Warr, whom Krishna had known well in England and
who had travelled out with them on the *Morea*. She became very ill with typhoid during the Convention, causing
grave anxiety. As soon as they thought she was out of
danger, Krishna and Nitya, with Mrs. Besant, Madame de
Manziarly and an Indian friend, Jadunandan Prasad
(called Jadu for short),[1] went to Adyar at the beginning
of January 1922, while Lady Emily was obliged to join
her husband in Delhi.

On January 11, Mrs. Besant, Krishna and Nitya all
spoke at a meeting at Adyar, Krishna for thirty-five
minutes. "A.B. said to me after the lecture that I spoke
well," Krishna was able to tell Lady Emily, "more control
over myself & my ideas clear etc!! By jove I prepared it
for two days and sweated over the damn thing." In this
talk he foreshadowed what was to come when he said, "I
want to point out to you this morning that He is not going
to preach what we want, nor what we wish, nor give us
the sop to our feelings which we all like, but on the contrary He is going to wake us all up whether we like it or
not, for we must be able to receive knocks as men." In
this same letter to Lady Emily he added:

Adyar is a *very* gossipy place, and if I began to
narrate them to you there will be no end to them. . . .
Helen sent me a big photograph of herself, not *very*
good; I showed it to Mrs. Besant & she said, 'Do you
want it framed?' She was going to have it done. I
said, 'I think I had better not, as I don't want to start
gossip about myself & lots of people come to my
room'. She smiled and understood. . . . It is not all
beer & skittles here. Curse. What a life.

It is interesting that not only was Krishna able to tell
Mrs. Besant about his feelings for Helen but that she
seemed to have no objection to this human love and no

[1] Jadu had been born in Bihar and educated at the Central Hindu
College where Krishna had first met him in 1910. He had then gone
to Cambridge where he had taken a degree in Natural Science. He
had been at Varengeville in 1913, and was to become very close to
Krishna.

fear of its "emphasizing his lower nature" or in any way interfering with the mission to which his life was dedicated.

Krishna was distressed to find so many jealousies and warring factions at Adyar. Determined to bring everyone together in harmony and "smash their cliques" he began to give daily tea parties in his room, each time for different people. He then started giving Sunday lunch parties on the ground-floor of the Russak house for about twenty people at a time. This floor was now occupied by Dwarkanath Telang, an Oxford graduate and manager of *New India*, the daily paper in Madras which Mrs. Besant edited. Rich and very generous, Dwarkanath was the real host at these Sunday luncheons. The first floor was occupied by Raja and his wife. Mrs. Russak herself was now remarried and lived in America.

Krishna had a heavy correspondence to deal with as well as having to write his editorial notes for the *Herald*, which he was finding more and more difficult although "as usual Nitya helped" him. He rested and read for an hour every afternoon; Madame de Manziarly was giving him French lessons and he took up Sanskrit again, so it was a busy life. Nitya rested for three hours every afternoon and was putting on weight. Every evening after playing tennis Krishna walked down to the sea just as the sun was setting and found it "really wonderful." He has always had a passion for sunsets. He and Nitya both thought Adyar the most beautiful place they had ever seen.

It had been Nitya's idea before going to India that they should see their father again and try to make friends with him. This meeting took place some time in January at Triplicane, a district of Madras, where Narianiah was living. Nitya wrote to Mar de Manziarly, "Nous avons vue nôtre père qui est gaga, nôtre frère ainé qui est vraiment pas mal, nôtre frère cadet qui est fou." All that Krishna remembers of this meeting is that he and Nitya prostrated themselves before their father and touched his feet with their foreheads, whereupon Narianiah immediately went and washed his feet because they had been touched by pariahs.[1]

[1] Narianiah died in February 1924. His eldest son, Sivaram, became a doctor. He died in 1952, leaving four sons and four daughters. His eldest son, Giddu Narayan, now teaches mathematics at a Rudolph Steiner School in Sussex. Krishna's youngest brother, Sadanand, lived

Towards the end of January news came that Barbara
Villiers had had a relapse and was now desperately ill.
Krishna immediately set off for Benares. "When she knows
that I am there, an old friend, a healer etc, it might cheer
her up & help her," he wrote to Lady Emily from the
train. "I *am* going to cure her; my pride is touched." But
in Calcutta, where he had to break his journey, he received a telegram to say she was dead.

> Isn't it awful? [he was writing from Benares].
> Poor old Barbara has gone & for ever too. I felt
> stunned. . . . This is the first time in my life someone
> has died whom I have really loved [he seems to have
> forgotten his mother] & it feels very strange & rather
> depressing. But one must be a philosopher, specially
> when one is in sorrow. . . . Barbara was like a sister,
> & like the tender rose of morning, she has gone!

Nitya was not so philosophical when writing to Mar de
Manziarly from Adyar:

> Poor Barbara, it was an awful shock to us. . . . It is
> awful to see how life goes on, how no one is really
> necessary for the world's existence or for our exis-
> tence; it does not matter who dies, we should go on
> and on and on. It is so tiring all this, and then Theo-
> sophy, it is the most tiring thing of all. Krishna est un
> grand success ici et moi aussi, mais tout ça au fond
> change très peu. You are very lucky, you have your
> music, and you can forget everything occasionally. La
> vie prochaine, I shall go in for music of some sort,
> even if only beating the drum.

Krishna did not see much of Mrs. Besant while they
were at Adyar. She went off every morning at ten o'clock
to Madras to the offices of *New India,* and did not return
until 6.30, and in the early mornings she did not like to be
disturbed. Naturally Krishna kept Indian hours, as did everyone at Adyar, and adopted Indian habits, such as sitting on the floor cross-legged for meals and eating with his

---

with Sivaram until his death in 1948. Remaining mentally a child, he
was very playful, enjoyed games and was much loved by his nephews
and nieces.

fingers off plates of large banana leaves. He got up at 5.45, had breakfast with Mrs. Besant at 6.30, lunch at 10.30, tea at 3.30, dinner at 6.30 and bed by 8.45. In the mornings many people sought private interviews with him. "Every body is very anxious to see me & talk to me & take my advice," he told Lady Emily on February 14. "Lord only knows why; I certainly don't. Mrs. Besant listens to my gibber very attentively when I do speak to her & says I will be a great help to her etc. No, mother, don't be afraid I won't have a swollen head."

Lady Emily herself was able to escape to Adyar from Delhi for about a month from the end of February before returning to England. Mrs. Besant put a room at her disposal at Headquarters and for once she had a time of un-diluted happiness with Krishna. She fell in love with the beauty of Adyar as so many people have done before and since.

It had been decided almost as soon as they arrived in India that Krishna and Nitya should go on to Sydney, where Leadbeater was still living, to attend a Theosophical Convention there in April. On March 22 they duly sailed from Colombo on the *Omar* with Raja and his wife, to be followed by Mrs. Besant three weeks later. Mrs. Besant felt she could not go with them, although it would mean missing the Sydney Convention, for Gandhi had just been arrested, and she hoped, by remaining in India, to use his influence to avoid bloodshed. Madame de Manziarly stayed on in India until September when she returned to Paris.

The journey to Colombo and the damp heat of Ceylon had been very bad for Nitya and he had started to cough again during the voyage. The offensive curiosity of the passengers disgusted Krishna; "the two belles" on board tried to flirt with him and he found himself "down in the dumps."

> What a life & is it worth it? [he asked Lady Emily a week after they sailed]. This striving striving. For what I don't know. . . . I dream and dream of a dif-ferent life. . . . I wish you & Helen were with me I would be perfectly happy. . . . Vain & empty desires. It makes me a bit crazy at times but like all things, either good or bad, it will soon pass. . . . You don't know what I am going through; there is a rebellion

within me, surging quietly but surely. To what purpose I don't know. A continuous fight, fight & then some more fighting. I would like to weep, a good long weep & relieve a bit of this tention but what's the good; it will but return soon. Dearest mother mine, I want to go away away from everybody to some beautiful cool secluded spot but alas!

This was part of a very long letter, with a few pages written almost every day. It was a dreary voyage enlivened only by games of poker, though he does not say with whom he played.

On April 1, the day before they reached Fremantle, Krishna received a radiogram from Perth saying, "The Brothers of the Star welcome you."

I had a cold shiver down my back [he wrote], here are people waiting to welcome me, have you ever heard of such a thing—welcome me—& I am wishing I was anywhere but here. It is awful & I can't give any precise explanation. In a way it is a shame; I am not one of those that longs for these kinds of things and yet it will be like this all my life. Oh! Lord, what have I done. Also I am so shy & ashamed of what these people will think, these fellow passengers, not that I care a damn but oh! how I dislike it all. Mother do tell me, what am I to do? I feel like a child, wanting to escape to its mother. Oh! heavens what am I talking about.

He then described how the evening before Raja had gone "to sit beside an Englishman on the sofa & the man said, 'It is engaged.' Raja said, 'Oh, sorry,' & went away. The man turns round to his friend & explains in an injured tone 'What b. . . .y cheek!' I felt like thumping his ugly head but I had too much of sense unfortunately to do it. What's one going to do with these ignorant barbarians?"

From Fremantle they drove to Perth where Krishna had to undergo "the torture" of speaking twice. "I never wanted to speak & all the people were so pleased & thanked me for what I said. You don't know how I abhor the whole thing, all the people coming to meet us, the meetings & the devotional stuff. It all goes against my nature & I am not fit for this job." Before the final evening meeting (the ship sailed at 11 p.m.), in a room given to them in which to rest, he and Nitya tried for an hour to put their point of view to Raja. Krishna told him that T.S. people did not appeal to him, he did not feel he belonged to their circle and yet in the outside world he was a "crank of the superlative degree." Raja was unable to understand. "He follows the current. . . . So when two people are fighting against the beastly current, Raja is stupified & amazed & cannot understand the strugglers." All Raja said at the end was, 'The best thing for you is not to give so many lectures'!!! So we begin again at Adelaide, Melbourne & Sydney etc. Oh! cus."

It was the same at Adelaide and Melbourne—meetings, hand shakings, devotion and smiles, while Krishna became "more and more morose and depressed," and reiterated his longing to get away somewhere where no human being had ever been before. Yet in his editorial notes for the July *Herald*, posted from Adelaide, he gave a lyrical description of the beauty of the twelve-mile drive from Fremantle to Perth and a sense of excitement at being in a new country. Reading these notes no one would guess he was not the happiest young man in the world.

17

Trouble in Sydney

They arrived in Sydney on Wednesday, April 12, and were met by Leadbeater surrounded by a small group of boys, and the usual crowd of Theosophists and Star members. "C.W.L. is just the same," Krishna told Lady Emily; "he is much whiter in hair, just as jovial & beaming with happiness. He was very glad to see us. He took my arm & held on to it & introduced me to all with a 'voilà' in his tone. I was very glad to see him too."

Krishna, Nitya and the Rajas went to stay with Mr. John Mackay and his wife, prominent Theosophists, at "Malahide," Elamang Avenue, Kirribilli, about two miles from where Leadbeater was living at "Crendon," Neutral Bay, with a Dutch family called Köllerström. Leadbeater had been living in Sydney for nearly six years. He now had about a dozen young people round him, mostly boys, ranging in age from fourteen to twenty-one.

> You know he is really a marvellous old man [Nitya wrote to Ruspoli]; he is absolutely unchanged, except that he has grown milder, and less cruel to old ladies; he goes out of his way now to talk to all the old ugly women. . . . Yet occasionally he lets fly and he is the old C.W.L. of Adyar. But just as in Adyar he takes everything for granted, never a question of doubt, never a question that anyone else can doubt; he is always sure that everything is as real to everybody as it is to him.

There was, however, one important change in him since Krishna and Nitya had seen him last in 1912—he had become a bishop in the Liberal Catholic Church. At this point another flamboyant character enters this story— James Ingall Wedgwood, a descendant of the master-potter, Josiah Wedgwood. Born in 1883, he had trained as an

analytical chemist and studied organ construction; he was
a pupil of the organist of York Minster and was intending
to take Holy Orders in the Anglican Church, when, in
1911, he had heard Mrs. Besant speak at York and was
immediately converted to Theosophy. He became General
Secretary of the T.S. for England and Wales, before
George Arundale held that position, and he introduced
into the Order of the Star, soon after it was founded, a
short-lived ceremonial called the Rosy Cross. When that
failed he looked round for some other outlet for his ceremonial proclivities and found it in the Old Catholic or
Jansenist Church, called after Bishop Cornelius Jansen, a
seventeenth-century reformer who had broken away from
the Church of Rome because he would not subscribe to
the doctrine of papal infallibility. The Old Catholics
claimed apostolic succession, and Wedgwood was ordained
a priest in 1913 by the Old Catholic bishop, Bishop Ma-
thew. Three years later, after consultation with Mrs.
Besant and Leadbeater (for he had not ceased to be an active member of the T.S. and Star), Wedgwood was made
a bishop by another Old Catholic bishop, Bishop Wil-
loughby. Wedgwood then at once set off for Australia, and
on July 15, 1916, with the Lord Maitreya's blessing, consecrated Leadbeater as Regionary Bishop for Australasia
in the Liberal Catholic Church, as the Old Catholic
Church was now called. The Mass followed the Roman
Catholic ritual, but the liturgy, which Mrs. Besant had
helped Leadbeater to compose, was in English; there was
no confessional; and celibacy was not required of the
clergy. The priests as well as the bishops were decked out
in gorgeous vestments.

It is strange that Leadbeater should have wanted this
particular form of elevation, but maybe he had all along
been hankering after his old calling, for on July 25, 1916,
he had written to Mrs. Besant:

> An interesting little glimpse of occult ways came to
> me the night after my consecration. My own Master
> [Kuthumi] referred very kindly to it, and spoke of
> the additional power to help that it had given me;
> and then He remarked: 'You thought you had given
> up all prospect of a bishopric when you left your
> Church thirty-two years ago to follow Upâsika
> [Madame Blavatsky]; but I may tell you that it

would have been in this very year that you would
have reached it in your original work, so you have
lost nothing except the emoluments and the social
position, and have gained enormously in other ways.
No one ever loses by serving Us!'

Wedgwood had returned to England after Leadbeater's
consecration to work as a Theosophical lecturer and
writer as well as to fulfil the duties of a bishop in the new
Church, but when Mrs. Besant went to London after the
war she heard that charges of sexual perversion were being
made against him by the police. Her decision that he must
resign immediately from the T.S. had to be reversed when
she received a cable from Leadbeater saying that this
would be impossible as Wedgwood had recently been
made an Initiate. The police charges against him were not
pressed, it seems, and he remained in England for a time.

Krishna and Nitya were astonished to find what a large
part the activities of the Liberal Catholic Church played in
the lives of Leadbeater's followers. The old man had more
power than ever now, for he was able to create priests as
well as give out occult advancements. Krishna's attitude to
the Church was expressed in his first letter to Lady Emily
from Sydney:

> Sunday morning [April 18] I went to the L.C.C.
> church [in Regent Street, Redfern] & C.W.L. was the
> acting priest. He did it all *very* well but you know I
> am *not* a ceremonialist & I do not appreciate all the
> paraphanalia with all those prayers & bobbing up &
> down, the robes etc; but I am *not* going to attack it,
> some people like to so what right have I to attack or
> disapprove of it? The church lasted 2½ hours & I was
> so bored that I was nearly fainting. I am afraid I
> rather showed it. I must be careful or else they will
> misunderstand me & there will be trouble. They are
> like cats & dogs over this church affair. They are
> fools anyway. Their over-zealousness & the lack of
> tact is the cause of all the trouble here.

This trouble within the T.S. had been fermenting for a
long time between Leadbeater's Church party and the
anti-Church faction led by T. H. Martyn, General Secretary of the T.S. and head of the Esoteric Section in Aus-

tralia, a rich man who, for years before Leadbeater went
to live in Sydney, had financially supported the Australian
Theosophical Lodge. Martyn was now campaigning
against Leadbeater in a "Back to Blavatsky" movement—
Blavatsky Theosophy being regarded by many as pure
Theosophy untainted by the Leadbeater cult of personalities, occult advancements given out like university degrees,
the World Teacher, and now this upstart Church. Martyn
formed a Loyalty League—loyal, that is, to Madame
Blavatsky. Wedgewood, in London, as well as Leadbeater
was at the centre of the storm; the former was accused of
heterosexual as well as homosexual misbehavior and had
outraged Mr. Martyn by making love to his wife while a
guest in his house, and Mrs. Martyn even more so for
dropping her at Leadbeater's insistence. The whole unhappy business came to a head at the T.S. Convention
which opened on Friday, April 16, two days after
Krishna's arrival. If Mrs. Besant had been present she
might have prevented it from erupting, at any rate in such
a very unpleasant form.

According to Krishna the trouble only started on the
19th when a prominent Australian Theosophist brought in
a resolution to the effect that the Convention should pass a
vote of confidence in their two teachers, Dr. Besant and
Bishop Leadbeater.

> There was a huge uproar on the part of the Loy-
> alty League. A man got up, frightfully coarse & vul-
> gar & said that he had no confidence in C.W.L. as he
> was an immoral man & began to rake up all the lies
> about C.W.L. Raja who was the chairman said that
> all this had nothing to do with it etc. Then there were
> those who spoke for C.W.L. and those against him.
> He was there all the time. The storm of accusation &
> defending went on for about 2½ hours. Martyn spoke
> & said C.W.L. could not be trusted because he was
> associated with Wedgewood [sic]. Then Fritz Kunz,[1]
> Nitya & I finally spoke. We thundered at them. I said
> I knew C.W.L. better than most of them & so I could
> speak with some authority. I declared he was one of

[1] An American from Illinois who had come from Adyar with
Krishna and his party. As a boy of seventeen he had travelled with
Leadbeater and had been one of his secretaries in 1906 at the time
of the inquiry in London into Leadbeater's conduct.

the purest & one of the greatest men I had ever met.
His clairvoyance may be doubted but not his purity.
As to his style Bishop, a man can call himself what
he liked etc. Finally I said that being Theosophist we
behaved worse than the ordinary man & that we lost
all gentlemanliness when we were attacking etc. Martyn went out immediately after the vote was taken.
For 85 & against 15. Only delegates voted.

Two days later Krishna and Nitya dined with Mr. and
Mrs. Martyn and did their best to reconcile them with
Leadbeater. Martyn said that he believed in Leadbeater's
purity but had irrefutable proof of Wedgwood's immorality. Krishna had met Wedgwood, of course, but had no
knowledge of his character. He asked Lady Emily to find
out what the charges had been against him in England.
The chief accusations against him in Sydney were that he
had been seen by a private detective to enter "public con-
veniences" sixteen times within two hours; the charges in
England, it transpired, were of acts of immorality with one
of his priests. Meanwile Wedgwood had resigned in
March from the T.S., "weary of the campaign of slander
and malicious intrigue against" him; he refused to reply to
the personal attacks on him and said that he intended to
retire into private life.

After the Convention, Nitya, who had been very pulled
down by the sea voyage, went to see a doctor in Sydney
who discovered by X-ray that not only was his left lung
diseased but that his right lung was now also affected. This
was a terrible shock to both brothers, for Dr. Rollier had
not only assured them that the left lung was cured but that
his right lung was perfectly healthy. The doctor ordered
Nitya to leave Sydney immediately, so on April 29 he and
Krishna went to the Carrington Hotel at Katoomba in the
Blue Mountains, some sixty miles from Sydney.

Before going to Katoomba, Krishna tried to talk to
Leadbeater alone but complained that this was impossible
as there were always too many boys round him. Krishna
did not feel drawn to any of the boys but he had a chance
to make friends with an English girl who was also staying
with the Mackays at "Malahide"—Ruth Roberts, a niece
of Dr. Mary Rocks who was now living in Sydney as
Leadbeater's medical attendant and had brought Ruth with
her to be helped along the Path by Leadbeater. "She

[Ruth] is very nice, *very* tall & nice looking," Krishna
told Lady Emily. "No, I am not in love & I don't think I
will be either." Ten days later he wrote again about Ruth:

> Well, I admit she is very nice & I like her; she
> wants to get on Probation & she doesn't know why
> she can't. She is just 17 & I have had a long talk with
> her. Somebody told me that a rumor was afloat that
> I was in love with her & that it would turn her head
> etc. What an idea! Me in love! How, besides, can I
> be. All the same it showed how darn careful I must
> be in all this kind of thing or else I will have 'some'
> reputation & Theosophists are so gullible.

Had he forgotten his declaration of being in love with
Helen on the eve of his departure for India? If so, he had
not forgotten Helen herself, for in his next letter he wrote,
"Now I must stop & write to Helen. I have written to you
for half an hour & half an hour for Helen," and a few
weeks later he was to write after hearing that Lady Emily
had met Helen, "I am *very very* glad that you like Helen.
I am glad you approve of my taste."

As Krishna and Nitya went back to Sydney to meet
Mrs. Besant who arrived on May 9, Nitya had been allowed barely ten days in the mountains where he had im-
meidately begun to feel better. Krishna was delighted to
see Mrs. Besant. "She is really great," he told Lady Emily,
"& far nicer than the whole lot of us."

Nitya described in a letter to Ruspoli what happened in
Sydney after Mrs. Besant arrived:

> Martyn asked for an investigation of Wedgwood,
> the Church & C.W.L. Martyn gave all his documents
> to one of the big daily papers [the *Daily Telegraph*].
> A.B. received a very friendly welcome when she ar-
> rived, all the papers boosted her, so of course Mar-
> tyn's accusations were a tremendous bombshell and
> all the papers took it up. They dragged in everything,
> H.P.B. [Madame Blavatksy], C.W.L., Alcyone, the
> Star, the Church, the Masters, everything was
> dragged up, and for about a fortnight we had huge
> columns in the papers. Everybody wrote, A.B. an-
> swered some letters, C.W.L. in his usual way paid
> very little attention to it. A.B.'s lectures were packed,

and her sermons in the church attracted about 1500
every time. We got a huge advertisement without
spending a penny.

Nitya's commercial sense was strong. He and Krishna
and some of Leadbeater's current boys wrote to the *Tele-
graph* in Leadbeater's defense but the paper refused to
print their letters. Krishna minded the publicity far more
than Nitya did.

> Awfully vulgar articles have appeared [he reported
> to Lady Emily on June 2], such as 'Where Lead-
> beater bishes', 'The Mahatmas', 'Dandy colored
> Coons', meaning us. [Another headline was 'Lead-
> beater a Swish Bish with Boys'.] One of them asked
> where I got my clothes, as they are so well cut. . . .
> Heavens how I hate it all; it is not pleasant to have
> such notareity. As I go about the street the people
> nudge each other & point me out; the other day one
> chap said to the other, 'There goes that chap printed
> in the papers, the Messiah!' Then they burst out
> laughing. I should have laughed too if I hadn't been
> there or involved in anyway. Sydney is having a great
> time at our expense & at the expense of Theosophy,
> thanks to Mr. Martin and his crew. . . . The other day
> as I was walking along, someone said, 'Hallo, there
> goes that fellow with 30 lives.' I nearly collapsed on
> the floor. Lord! how I hate it all and I dislike all the
> publicity and I shall have it all my life. Heavens,
> what have I done to deserve all this.

So great was the uproar in the papers that the Minister
of Justice was obliged to order an inquiry into the allegations against Leadbeater, and on May 25 (the day that
was still thought to be Krishna's birthday—his twenty-sev-
enth) he and Nitya, Raja, Fritz Kunz and some of Leadbeater's other "boys" went voluntarily to the Executive
Office of the Police Department to be cross-examined by a
detective. They went in one by one except for Krishna and
Nitya who, being brothers, were allowed to go in together.
Krishna described this ordeal in his letter of June 2; he
was "shaking life a leaf" and so nervous that he was
nearly "dotty." "I have become more sensitive & you can
imagine what I went through." There were two detectives

and four reporters present. He gained the impression that the detectives were not biased in any way but really wanted to find out the truth. He and Nitya gave a very definite "no" to all the questions, such as whether they had ever seen any immorality or ever been taught immoral practices by Leadbeater. "They asked the most appalling questions," Nitya told Ruspoli, "which the youngest boy did not even understand."

As the charges against Leadbeater were denied by all his "boys," past and present, the inquiry was closed. Nothing has ever been proved against Leadbeater. He never for a moment denied advocating masturbation as a prophylactic but in doing so he was no more than ahead of his time, and he certainly did not teach this practice to either Krishna or Nitya. Moreover, there is no evidence that any of his "boys" grew up to be homosexual; indeed most of them made happy marriages.

It was now felt to be imperative that Nitya should leave Sydney as soon as possible to return to Switzerland where he must remain until he was cured beyond all doubt. To go via India or South Africa would be too hot for him; there was only one alternative—to go by way of San Francisco. Mr. A. P. Warrington, the General Secretary of the T.S. in America, who was in Sydney for the Convention, suggested that they should break their journey by staying in the Ojai Valley (pronounced O-high), some eighty miles north of Los Angeles, which was said to have an excellent climate for consumptives. A friend of his was willing to lend them a house there where they could stay for three or four months and then go on to Switzerland in the late autumn. "I had a talk to Amma [Mother: Mrs. Besant] about myself," Krishna had written to Lady Emily on May 19; "I told her that my mental body was not developed enough and that I wanted to study quietly & uninterruptedly. . . . Of course I shan't do any Star or Theosophical work as I really want to study." He intended to take eighteen months off in California and Switzerland to study philosophy, economics, religion and education. Mrs. Besant and Leadbeater both approved of this plan and therefore it was settled that, accompanied by Mr. Warrington and Fritz Kunz, they should sail on June 14 for San Francisco.

Mrs. Besant returned to India a fortnight before their departure. "Amma left last night," Krishna told Lady

Emily on June 2, "amidst great cheers and personally I
was *very* sad to see her go off and Lord knows when we
shall see her again, especially we two. I don't think I have
ever loved her more that I do at present. She is really marvellous." Before she left she and Leadbeater had had long
private talks with Krishna, Nitya and Raja about "the
whole thing, Wedgwood, Initiates etc" which Krishna
thought best not to commit to paper. Krishna also told
Lady Emily in this same letter of June 2 that he had received a message from the Master Kuthumi, "brought
through" by Leadbeater. Krishna copied it out for her:

> "Of you, too, we have the highest hopes. Steady &
> widen yourself, and strive more & more to bring the
> mind & brain into subservience to the true Self
> within. Be tolerant of divergences of view & of
> method, for each has usually a fragment of truth
> concealed somewhere within it, even though often-
> times it is distorted almost beyond recognition. Seek
> for that tiniest gleam of light amid the Stygian
> darkness of each ignorant mind, for by recognizing &
> fostering it you may help a baby brother."

Krishna added, "It is just what I wanted as I am inclined to be intolerant & not look for the brother!" This
message was to have a profound effect on Krishna.

Krishna and Nitya reached San Francisco on July 3 after a very dull voyage during which female passengers of
all ages sought Krishna's acquaintance while some of the
men were extremely offensive. Krishna overheard one Australian asking why "a dark man" was allowed to travel
first class. In San Francisco they stayed with a T.S. member, Miss Miklau, who was a professor at Berkeley University. Nitya, who had been very sick during the voyage
but was on the whole better and coughing less, wanted to
see a doctor in San Francisco so they were obliged to stay
two nights as the 4th was Independence Day, a public holiday. The doctor took an optimistic view, said that he did
not think Nitya's right lung was affected and assured him
that Ojai was an excellent place for him.

Miss Miklau showed them all over Berkeley University
where there were 14,000 students of all nationalities.
Krishna was entranced with it:

There was not that dreadful distinction between men & women which creates that peculiar atmosphere so particular in England & elsewhere [he told Lady Emily]. People look one another full in the face, not that sidelong glance so painful in the older countries. I wanted to live there & relive some of my life. The laisser aller of everybody was my particular delight. . . . I wanted to help them all; I felt so friendly, so amiable not caring even if they knew my history. There was not that aloofness that exists between the godly Englishman & the humble Indian. That arrogant spirit of class & of color was not to be found there ... one breathed the air of freedom of equality which is the equality of opportunity & of ability irrespective of class, creed or color. I was so thrilled that I wanted to carry the physical beauty of the place with me to India for the Indians who alone know ... how to create the proper scholastic atmosphere. Here this atmosphere was lacking they were not dignified as we Indians are ... oh, for such a university to be transplanted to India, with our professor[s] for whom religion is as important, if not greater, as education.

On the night of July 5 they left by Pullman train for Ventura, where they arrived at ten next morning and were met by their hostess, Mrs. Mary Gray, and driven the twenty miles or so inland to the far end of the Ojai Valley, 1,500 feet above sea level. Mrs. Gray had two empty cottages set in the midst of orange groves; one of these she lent to the brothers, and the other, two minutes away, to Mr. Warrington. The temperature was 95° when they arrived but the air was very dry and the nights cool. A woman came in to cook their breakfast and lunch but they cooked their own supper. Krishna was amazed that the woman received $5.30 a day, about 25/—. "Awful, isn't it? we don't pay, we are guests of Mrs. Gray!!!!" There were wonderful vegetables, fruit and cream. They took to riding in the mountains twice a week which did not tire Nitya, performed regular physical exercises and found a stream in which to take a daily hip bath. On July 20 Krishna was able to tell Lady Emily that they could now cook pancakes, scrambled eggs and chipped potatoes,

though Heinz "came in very useful." Nitya was getting on
well and hardly expectorating at all.

But a week later the whole picture had changed. Nitya
had started running a temperature and coughing badly;
Krishna had had several scares because they were alone in
the house.

> Nitya is such a temperemental person [he wrote to
> Lady Emily on July 28], & being his brother he gets
> very irritable with me & won't do anything I tell him.
> Miss Williams, a sister of one of Mrs. Gray's friends
> came the other day on a visit to Mrs. G's house.
> Well, anyway, we both like her & she likes us; she is
> not a Theosophist but *very* nice. To make the story
> short, Nitya does what she tells him & the conse-
> quence is he does what I have been telling him for
> the last ten days. She is only a girl of nineteen but
> these Americans are capable from the moment they
> are born & what's more she is *very* cheerful, gay and
> keeps N in a good humor which is essential. Her sis-
> ter is a T.S. person & so she knows all about it & in
> spite of all that she is very nice. She went away yes-
> terday & is going to find out from her mother if she
> may come back & so in a way look after Nitya. I
> read to him about three hours a day; he doesn't read
> at all which is very good. . . . *Don't* worry; everything
> will be allright. I am more than certain of it. We are
> reading O. Henry & the Bible, a good combination!

The Song of Solomon was Krishna's favorite book in
the Bible, then parts of Ecclesiastes, and Ecclesiasticus
from the Apocrypha. He maintains he has never read the
Gospels.

What Krishna did not mention was that Rosalind Williams was a very pretty girl with fair wavy hair and eyes of
the most unusual blue, like those of a Siamese cat. She did
get permission to return to Mrs. Gray, rather surprisingly
it would seem in view of the nature of Nitya's disease.
Perhaps her Theosophical sister persuaded their mother
that tuberculosis was a small price to pay for the privilege
of looking after the brother of the coming World Teacher.
It was understood from the beginning that Rosalind was
Nitya's special friend rather than Krishna's.

Many people had been writing to Mr. Warrington urging that Nitya should try the treatment of Dr. Albert Abrams who claimed to be able to diagnose and cure tuberculosis, cancer, syphilis and many other diseases by means of an electrical machine which he had invented. It was Dr. Abram's contention that the smallpox vaccination was the cause of most diseases, especially syphilis; he maintained that only two per cent of the world population was free of syphilis, either contracted or hereditary. All that was necessary for diagnosis were a few drops of the patient's blood on a clean piece of blotting-paper. The brothers decided to try this treatment. Nitya's blood was sent to a pupil of Dr. Abrams in Los Angeles, Dr. Strong, without any details at all except his name; two days later the report was received: Nitya had T.B. in his left lung and both kidneys (this last was a great shock) and syphilis in his spleen. Mr. Warrington, through a friend, managed to get hold of one of the rare Abrams machines called an "Oscilloclast." Plates were strapped on to the affected parts (left lung, kidneys and spleen) and wires then attached from the machine to the plates, and Nitya had to sit for so many hours each day undergoing this boring though completely painless treatment. The contents of the box were a close secret; when switched on it made the noise of a loud clock but produced no sensation whatever in the patient. The method of cure was to send electrical waves through the affected parts which vibrated at the same rate as the disease.

Albert Abrams (1863–1925) had been born in San Francisco of very rich parents. Far from being a quack, he had the highest medical qualifications. Sir James Barr, a distinguished Scottish physician, believed Abrams to be a genius born before his time. Upton Sinclair, a great believer in Abrams, wrote, "Take my advice, wherever you may be those that are suffering, and find out about the new work and help to make it known to the world." Abrams's method of diagnosis was by percussion on the torso of a perfectly healthy young man connected electrically in some complicated way with the patient's blood.

After two and a half weeks a sample of Nitya's blood was again sent to Dr. Strong to be tested; the report now was that there were no more T.B. germs in his body and no more syphilis; all the same he was to continue with the treatment for forty-five minutes a day and must take great care of himself. Krishna told Lady Emily that for the first

time since contracting the disease Nitya had lost the taste
of his sputum.

Krishna, who now believed absolutely in the machine,
sent in a sample of his own blood and was told that he
had slight cancer in his intestines and left lung, and syphilis in his spleen and nose. "Curious about my nose, wasn't
it?" he wrote to Lady Emily. "Do you remember how it
used to bother me & the doctors couldn't make it out what
it was. . . . Of course I haven't written to anybody about
my diagnosis & Nitya's; it would undoubtedly make an
awful row." He meant, of course, the diagnosis of syphilis.
In telling Mrs. Besant and Leadbeater about Dr. Strong's
diagnosis and the treatment Nitya was having from the
Abrams machine, Krishna mentioned everything except
the syphilis. He too was now having treatment from the
"Oscilloclast" and was soon able to report to Lady Emily
that his nose was much better.

18

The Turning Point

There is no doubt that Krishna had been greatly influenced by the message from the Master Kuthumi "brought through" before he left Sydney. On August 12, about five weeks after their arrival at Ojai, he wrote to Lady Emily:

> I have been meditating every morning for half an hour or 35 mins. I meditate from 6:45 to 7:20. I am beginning to concentrate better even though it be for sometime & I meditate again before I go to sleep for about 10 minutes. All this is rather surprising you, isn't it? *I am going to get back* my old touch with the Masters & after all that's the only thing that matters in life & nothing else does. At first it was difficult to meditate or to concentrate & even though I have been doing it for only a week, I am agreeably surprised.

It was only five days after writing this that he underwent an experience that changed his life, though it was to be some weeks before anyone outside Ojai heard about it. Both Nitya and Krishna wrote accounts of this experience which began on August 17. Nitya's account was written for Mrs. Besant and Leadbeater a fortnight after the event:

> In a long and narrow valley of apricot orchards and orange groves is our house, and the hot sun shines down day after day to remind us of Adyar, but of an evening the cool air comes from the range of hills on either side. Far beyond the lower end of the valley runs the long, perfect road from Seattle in Washington down to San Diego in Southern California, some two thousand miles, with a ceaseless flow of turbulent traffic, yet our valley lies happily, unknown and forgotten, for a road wanders in but knows no way out. The American Indians called our valley the

Ojai or the nest, and for centuries they must have
sought it as a refuge.

Our cottage is on the upper end and no one else
lives near except Mr. Warrington, who has a cottage
all to himself a few hundred yards away; and
Krishna, Mr. Warrington, and I have been here for
nearly eight weeks, taking a rest and getting well. We
have an occasional visitor in Mr. Walton, the Vicar-
General of the Liberal Catholic Church for America,
who has a house in the valley, and Rosalind, a young
American girl, stays a week or two near by, spending
her time with us. About two weeks ago happened this
incident which I want to describe to you, when all
five of us chanced to be here together.

Of the true meaning of what happened, of the exact importance of it you of course will be able to tell
us if you will, but here we seem to have been
transported into a world where Gods again walked
among men for a short space of time, leaving us all
so changed that now our compass has found its lode-
star. I think I do not exaggerate when I say that all
our lives are profoundly affected by what happened.

Krishna himself, properly speaking, should relate
the sequence of events, for all of us were mere spec-
tators, willing to help when necessary; but he does
not remember all the details, as he was out of his
body a great part of the time, and everything remains
clear in our memory, for we watched him with great
care the whole time with a feeling that his body was
entrusted partly to us. Mr. Warrington is not in perfect health, and I am not yet allowed to move about
much, so it was Rosalind's good fortune to look after
Krishna, and I think she has already received her reward [by being put on probation].

On the evening of Thursday the seventeenth
Krishna felt a little tired and restless and we noticed
in the middle of the nape of his neck a painful lump
of what seemed to be a contracted muscle, about the
size of a large marble. The next morning he seemed
all right, until after breakfast, when he lay down to
rest. Rosalind and I were sitting outside, and Mr.
Warrington and Krishna were inside. Rosalind went
in at Mr. Warrington's call and found Krishna apparently very ill, for he was lying on the bed tossing

about and moaning as if he were in great pain. She went and sat with him and tried to find out what was the matter with him, but Krishna could give no clear answer. He started again moaning and a fit of trembling and shivering came upon him, and he would clench his teeth and grip his hands tight to ward off the shivering; it was exactly the behavior of a malarial patient, except that Krishna complained of frightful heat. Rosalind would hold him quiet for a bit, and again would come the trembling and shivering, as of ague. Then he would push her away, complaining of terrible heat and his eyes full of a strange unconsciousness. And Rosalind would sit by him until he was quiet again, when she would hold his hands and soothe him like a mother does her young. Mr. Warrington sat at the other end of the room, and realized, so he told me later, that some process was going on in Krishna's body, as a result of influences directed from planes other than physical. Poor Rosalind, who at first was very anxious, raised questioning eyes and Mr. Warrington assured her that all would be well. But during the morning things got worse, and when I came and sat beside him he complained again of the awful heat, and said that all of us were full of nerves and made him tired; and every few minutes he would start up in bed and push us away; and again he would commence trembling. All this while he was only half conscious, for he would talk of Adyar and the people there as if they were present; then again he would lie quiet for a little while until the ruffle of a curtain or the rattling of a window, or the sound of a far-off plough in the field would rouse him again and he would moan for silence and quiet. Persistently every few minutes he would push Rosalind away from him when he began to get hot, and again he would want her close to him.

I sat near, but not too near. We tried our best to keep the house quiet and dark, but slight sounds which one scarcely notices are inevitable, yet Krishna had become so sensitive that the faintest tinkling would set his nerves on edge.

Later as lunch came he quieted down and became apparently all right and fully conscious. Rosalind took him his lunch which he ate, and while we all finished our meal he lay quiet. Then a few minutes afterwards he was groaning again, and presently, poor fellow, he could not keep down the food he had eaten. And so it went on all the afternoon; shivering, groaning, restless, only half conscious, and all the time as if he were in pain. Curiously enough, when the time came for our meals, even though he ate nothing himself, he became tranquil and Rosalind could leave him long enough to have her food, and at bedtime he was quiet enough to sleep through the night.

The next day, Saturday, it recommenced after his bath, only in a more acute form, and he seemed less conscious than the day before. All through the day it lasted, with regular intervals to give him a rest and allow Rosalind to have her food.

But Sunday was the worst day and Sunday we saw the glorious climax. All through the three days all of us had tried to keep our minds and emotions unperturbed and peaceful, and Rosalind spent the three days by Krishna's side, ready when he wanted her and leaving him alone when he wished it. It was really beautiful to see her with him, to watch the way she could pour out her love unselfishly and absolutely impersonally. Even before all this happened we had noticed this great characteristic in her, and though we wondered then if a woman should be near by at that moment, yet the eventual happenings showed that probably she was specially brought here at that moment to help Krishna and indeed all of us. Though she is only nineteen and knows little of Theosophy she played the part of a great mother through these three days.

On Sunday, as I've said, Krishna seemed much worse, he seemed to be suffering a great deal, the trembling and the heat seemed intensified and his consciousness became more and more intermittent. When he seemed to be in control of his body he talked all the time of Adyar, A.B., and the members of the Purple Order in Adyar, and he imagined himself constantly in Adyar. Then he would say, 'I want to go to India! Why have they brought me here? I don't know where I am,' and again and again and again he would say, 'I don't know where I am.' If anyone moved in the house he nearly jumped off the bed and every time we entered his room we had to give him warning. Yet towards six o'clock when we had our evening meal he quieted down until we had finished. Then suddenly the whole house seemed full of a terrific force and Krishna was as if possessed. He would have none of us near him and began to complain bitterly of the dirt, the dirt of the bed, the intolerable dirt of the house, the dirt of everyone around, and in a voice full of pain said that he longed to go to the woods. Now he was sobbing aloud, we dared not touch him and knew not what to do; he had left his bed and sat in a dark corner of the room on the floor, sobbing aloud that he wanted to go into the woods in India. Suddenly he announced his intention of going for a walk alone, but from this we managed to dissuade him, for we did not think that he was in any fit condition for nocturnal ambulations. Then as he expressed a desire for solitude, we left him and gathered outside on the verandah, where in a few minutes he joined us, carrying a cushion in his hand and sitting as far away as possible from us. Enough strength and consciousness were vouchsafed him to come outside but once there again he vanished from us, and his body, murmuring incoherencies, was left sitting there on the porch.

We were a strange group on that verandah; Rosalind and I on chairs, Mr. Warrington and Mr. Walton opposite, facing us sitting on a bench, and Krishna to our right a few yards away. The sun had set an hour ago and we sat facing the far-off hills, purple against the pale sky in the darkening twilight, speaking little, and the feeling came upon us of an impending climax; all our thoughts and emotions were tense with a strangely peaceful expectation of some great event.

Then Mr. Warrington had a heaven-sent inspiration. In front of the house a few yards away stands a young pepper tree, with delicate leaves of a tender green, now heavy with scented blossoms, and all day it is the 'murmurous haunt of bees,' little canaries, and bright humming birds. He gently urged Krishna to go out under that tree, and at first Krishna would not, then went of his own accord.

Arrival at Charing Cross Station, London, May, 1911, Nitya, Mrs. Besant, K, George Arundale.

Mrs. Besant, Leadbeater, K, Raja, wearing the insignia of the Purple Order. Benares, December, 1911.

Taormina, January, 1914. *Standing:* George Arundale, Dr. Mary Rocke, Nitya; *seated:* Lady Emily, K, Miss Arundale.

K at Amphion, summer 1920.

The Octagon Bungalow, Adyar, looking down the river to the sea.
Photograph by courtesy of Mark Edwards.

The Headquarters Building, Adyar, from across the river,
showing Mrs. Russak's house on left, then Octagon Bungalow.
Photograph taken by K in 1911.

The Banyan Tree, Adyar. *Photograph by courtesy of
Mark Edwards.*

K's father, Narianiah.

K, Sivaram and Nitya. The first photograph, Adyar, 1909.

Nitya and K. After the first Initiation, Adyar, 1910.

Arundale's consecration as bishop, Huizen, August, 1925.
From left: Bishop Mazel, Oscar Köllerström (as priest),
Bishop Arundale, Rajagopal (holding crozier), Mrs. Besant,
Bishop Wedgwood, Bishop Pigott.

K speaking at the Ommen Camp.

K on the roof of the
Sheraton Hotel, Chicago,
September, 1926.

K under the Gobelin tapestry,
Castle Eerde, July, 1926.

Madura   Nov. 21:27

Ah! the symphony of that song

The innermost shrine
Was breathless with the love of many.
The flames flickered with the thoughts of many

The scent of burnt camphor fills the air.
The careless priest drones a chant,
The idol is pastless meaning to most
Weary of such boundless adoration.

The still silence holds the air
And on the instant
A melodious song of infinite beauty
Brings ~~forgotten~~ tears to my eyes

In a fuchite robe,
A woman sings to the heart of love
Of the travail that she knew not
Of the laughter of children around her
Of the love that died young
Of the sorrow in a barren love
Of the solitude in a still night
Of life fruitless amidst the ...

I cried with her.
Her sorrow became mine

Part of a poem by K. A pencil page from his notebook, 1927.

K dissolving the Order of the Star, Ommen Camp, August, 1929.

Castle Eerde, Ommen, Holland.

Arya Vihara, Ojai, California, in 1924.

Pergine, August, 1924. *Back row*: Helen, Rama Rao, Rajagopal, Cordes; *front row*: K, Lady Emily, Betty, Mary, Sivakamu, Malati, Ruth.

K under the apple tree, Pergine, 1924.

Arrival in Bombay, November, 1924. Nitya, Mrs. Besant, K.

Now we were in a starlit darkness and Krishna sat under a roof of delicate leaves black against the sky. He was still murmuring unconsciously but presently there came a sigh of relief and he called out to us, 'Oh, why didn't you send me out here before?' Then came a brief silence.

And now he began to chant. Nothing had passed his lips for nearly three days and his body was utterly exhausted with the intense strain, and it was a quiet weary voice we heard chanting the mantram sung every night at Adyar in the Shrine Room. Then silence.

Long ago in Taormina, as Krishna had looked with meditative eyes upon a beautiful painting of our Lord Gautama in mendicant garb, we had felt for a blissful moment the divine presence of the Great One, who had deigned to send a thought. And again this night, as Krishna, under the young pepper tree, finished his song of adoration, I thought of the Tathagata [the Buddha] under the Bo tree, and again I felt pervading the peaceful valley a wave of that splendor, as if again He had sent a blessing upon Krishna.

We sat with eyes fixed upon the tree, wondering if all was well, for now there was perfect silence, and as we looked I saw suddenly for a moment a great Star shining above the tree, and I knew that Krishna's body was being prepared for the Great One. I leaned across and told Mr. Warrington of the Star.

The place seemed to be filled With a Great Presence and a great longing came upon me to go on my knees and adore, for I knew that the Great Lord of all our hearts had come Himself; and though we saw Him not, yet all felt the splendor of His presence. Then the eyes of Rosalind were opened and she saw. Her face changed as I have seen no face change, for she was blessed enough to see with physical eyes the glories of that night. Her face was transfigured, as she said to us, 'Do you see Him, do you see Him?' for she saw the divine Bodhisattva [the Lord Maitreya], and millions wait for incarnations to catch such a glimpse of our Lord, but she had eyes of innocence and had served our Lord faithfully. And we who could not see saw the Splendors of the night mirrored in her face pale with rapture in the starlight. Never shall I forget the look on her face, for presently I who could not see but who gloried in the presence of our Lord felt that He turned towards us and spoke some words to Rosalind; her face shone with divine ecstasy as she answered, 'I will, I will,' and she spoke the words as if they were a promise given with splendid joy. Never shall I forget her face when I looked at her; even I was almost blessed with vision. Her face showed the rapture of her heart, for the innermost part of her being was ablaze with His presence but her eyes saw. And silently I prayed that He might accept me as His servant and all our hearts were full of that prayer. In the distance we heard divine music softly played, all of us heard though hidden from us were the Gandharvas. [Cosmic angels who make the music of the spheres.]

The radiance and the glory of the many Beings present lasted nearly an half hour and Rosalind, trembling and almost sobbing with joy, saw it all; 'Look, do you see?' she would often repeat, or 'Do you hear the music?' Then presently we heard Krishna's footsteps and saw his white figure coming up in the darkness, and all was over. And Rosalind cried out, 'Oh, he is coming; go get him, go get him' and fell back in her chair almost in a swoon. When she recovered, alas, she remembered nothing, nothing, all was gone from her memory except the sound of music still in her ears.

The next day again there was a recurrence of the shuddering and half-waking consciousness in Krishna, though now it lasted but a few minutes and at long intervals. All day he lay under the tree in samadhi[1] and in the evening, as he sat in meditation as on the night before, Rosalind again saw three figures round him who quickly went away, taking Krishna with them, leaving his body under the tree. Since then and every evening he sits in meditation under the tree.

I have described what I saw and heard, but of the effect of the incident upon all of us I have not spoken, for I think it will take time, at least for me, to

---

[1] A Sanskrit word, here used probably as a state of trance. A simple definition is: "The excellent process of Samadhi destroys death, leads to eternal happiness and confers the supreme Bliss of Brahman [Reality]."

realize fully the glory that we were privileged to witness, though I feel now that life can only be spent in one way, in the service of the Lord.

Krishna's own account follows. It was sent at the same time as Nitya's but the latter part was written only two days after the events described:

Ever since I left Australia I have been thinking and deliberating about the message which the Master K.H. gave me while I was there. I naturally wanted to achieve those orders as soon as I could, and I was to a certain extent uncertain as to the best method of attaining the ideals which were put before me. I do not think a day passed without spending some thought over it, but I am ashamed to say all this was done most casually and rather carelessly.

But at the back of my mind the message of the Master ever dwelt.

Well, since August 3rd, I meditated regularly for about thirty minutes every morning. I could, to my astonishment, concentrate with considerable ease, and within a few days I began to see clearly where I had failed and where I was failing. Immediately I set about, consciously, to annihilate the wrong accumulations of the past years. With the same deliberation I set about to find out ways and means to achieve my aim. First I realized that I had to harmonize all my other bodies with the Buddhic plane [the highest plane of consciousness] and to bring about this happy combination I had to find out what my ego wanted on the Buddhic plane. To harmonize the various bodies I had to keep them vibrating at the same rate as the Buddhic, and to do this I had to find out what was the vital interest of the Buddhic. With ease which rather astonished me I found the main interest on that high plane was to serve the Lord Maitreya and the Masters. With that idea clear in my physical mind I had to direct and control the other bodies to act and to think the same as on the noble and spiritual plane. During that period of less than three weeks, I concentrated to keep in mind the image of the Lord Maitreya throughout the entire day, and I found no difficulty in doing this. I found that I was getting calmer and more serene. My whole outlook on life was changed.

Then, on the 17th August, I felt acute pain at the nape of my neck and I had to cut down my meditation to fifteen minutes. The pain instead of getting better as I had hoped grew worse. The climax was reached on the 19th. I could not think, nor was I able to do anything, and I was forced by friends here to retire to bed. Then I became almost unconscious, though I was well aware of what was happening around me. I came to myself at about noon each day. On the first day while I was in that state and more conscious of the things around me, I had the first most extraordinary experience. There was a man mending the road; that man was myself; the pickaxe he held was myself; the very stone which he was breaking up was a part of me; the tender blade of grass was my very being, and the tree beside the man was myself. I almost could feel and think like the roadmender, and I could feel the wind passing through the tree, and the little ant on the blade of grass I could feel. The birds, the dust, and the very noise were a part of me. Just then there was a car passing by at some distance; I was the driver, the engine, and the tires; as the car went further away from me, I was going away from myself. I was in everything, or rather everything was in me, inanimate and animate, the mountain, the worm, and all breathing things. All day long I remained in this happy condition. I could not eat anything, and again at about six I began to lose my physical body, and naturally the physical elemental[1] did what it liked; I was semi-conscious.

The morning of the next day (the 20th) was almost the same as the previous day, and I could not tolerate too many people in the room. I could feel them in rather a curious way and their vibrations got on my nerves. That evening at about the same hour of six I felt worse than ever. I wanted nobody near me nor anybody to touch me. I was feeling extremely tired and weak. I think I was weeping from mere ex-

---

[1] The part of the body that controls its instinctive and purely physical actions when the higher consciousness is withdrawn. It is at a low stage of evolution and needs guidance.

haustion and lack of physical control. My head was
pretty bad and the top part felt as though many
needles were being driven in. While I was in this state
I felt that the bed in which I was lying, the same one
as on the previous day, was dirty and filthy beyond
imagination and I could not lie in it. Suddenly I
found myself sitting on the floor and Nitya and Rosalind asking me to get into bed. I asked them not to
touch me and cried out that the bed was not clean. I
went on like this for some time till eventually I wandered out on the verandah and sat a few moments exhausted and slightly calmer. I began to come to myself and finally Mr. Warrington asked me to go under
the pepper tree which is near the house. There I sat
crosslegged in the meditation posture. When I had sat
thus for some time, I felt myself going out of my
body, I saw myself sitting down with the delicate tender leaves of the tree over me. I was facing the east.
In front of me was my body and over my head I saw
the Star, bright and clear. Then I could feel the vibrations of the Lord Buddha; I beheld Lord Maitreya
and Master K.H. I was so happy, calm and at peace.
I could still see my body and I was hovering near it.
There was such profound calmness both in the air
and within myself, the calmness of the bottom of a
deep unfathomable lake. Like the lake, I felt my
physical body, with its mind and emotions, could be
ruffled on the surface but nothing, nay nothing, could
disturb the calmness of my soul. The Presence of the
mighty Beings was with me for some time and then
They were gone. I was supremely happy, for I had
seen. Nothing could ever be the same. I have drunk
at the clear and pure waters at the source of the
fountain of life and my thirst was appeased. Never
more could I be thirsty, never more could I be in utter darkness; I have seen the Light. I have touched
compassion which heals all sorrow and suffering; it is
not for myself, but for the world. I have stood on the
mountain top and gazed at the mighty Beings. Never
can I be in utter darkness; I have seen the glorious and
healing Light. The fountain of Truth has been revealed
to me and the darkness has been dispersed. Love in all
its glory has intoxicated my heart; my heart can

never be closed. I have drunk at the fountain of Joy and eternal Beauty. I am God-intoxicated.

Mr. Warrington also wrote an account of the experience. He stated that he had read Krishna's and Nitya's accounts and could vouch for their truth. He added only one detail of interest—that he knew the bed was clean because he had helped to make it himself with "clothing freshly taken from the linen closet that evening."

On September 2 Krishna was writing letters to Mrs. Besant, Leadbeater and Lady Emily. To Leadbeater he wrote:

I sent you sometime ago a cable asking you to confirm my impressions that Lady Emily was accepted on the night of Aug. 12th. Since I have no reply, I presume she has not been. I am sorry. I am sending you photographs of Helen Knothe and Rosalind Williams. We talked about Helen when I was in Australia and I am sure she is going to work for the Masters and besides you have once said she was Piet Meuleman.[1] Do please write to me about her as I am very much interested in her. (I was almost in love with her when I saw her in Holand!!!!).

Miss Williams is 19, an American girl, very nice and on the night of 21st August, I had the impression that she was put on probation. Please tell me if she is.

Nitya is writing in some detail the extraordinary experience I had on the night of 20th of Aug. and the way the two previous days had been leading up to it. I am sending you, Mrs. Besant and Raja a copy each. As you well know, I have not been what is called 'happy' for many years; everything I touched brought me discontentment; my mental condition as you know, my dearest Brother, has been deplorable. I did not know what I wanted to do nor did I care to do much; everything bored me in a very short time and in fact I did not find myself. By what Nitya has written and by what I have added to it you will see I have changed considerably from what I was in Australia. Naturally I have been thinking clearly and deliberately about the message Master K.H. gave me

---

[1] Mrs. Petronella Catharina Meuleman-van Ginkel (1841–1902). She started the T.S. in Holland in 1891. Helen was born in 1904.

while in Australia. I had begun to meditate regularly
every morning for about half an hour. After a few
days of meditation, I began to see clearly where I had
failed and where I was failing and as you know me
of old, I began consciously and deliberately to destroy
the wrong accumulations of the past years since I had
the *misfortune* of leaving you. Here let me acknowledge with shame that my feelings towards you
were not what they should have been. Now, they are
wholly different, I think I love and respect you as
mighty few people do. My love for you when we first
met in Adyar has returned bringing with it the love
from the past. Please *don't* think that I am writing
mere platitudes and worn out phrases. They are not
and you, my dearest brother, know me, in fact better
than myself. I wish, with all my heart, that I could
see you now.

After Aug. 20th I know what I want to do and
what lies before me—nothing but to serve the Masters and the Lord. I have become since that date
much more sensitive and slightly clairvoyant as I saw
you with the President, the other night while I was
sitting in the moonlight. Such a thing has not happened to me for over seven years. In fact for the last
seven years, I have been spiritually blind, I have been
in a dungeon without a light, without any fresh air.
Now I feel I am in sunlight, with the energy of many,
not physical but mental and emotional. I feel once
again in touch with Lord Maitreya and the Master
and there is nothing else for me to do but to serve
Them. My whole life, now, is, consciously, on the
physical plane, devoted to the work and I am not
likely to change.

Please tell me, without any reservation, what you
think of all that I have written and felt.

His letter to Mrs. Besant was more or less a repetition.
To Lady Emily he expressed his feelings more intimately:

I have not written to you a long letter for over a
fortnight; I am sorry but I could not help it as you
will see when I go on explaining. I have been ill and
you will see by what I have sent to Miss Dodge that I
have not been exactly ill. I have had the happy for-

tune of getting back, I think, into the consciousness
of the Master & my old touch with Lord Maitreya. I
have sent my written statement to Miss Dodge, first
because we can't get many copies here & also I
wanted to send it to her because she is not well &
perhaps it might cheer her up & help her. I knew you
wouldn't mind my sending it to her & I hope you
won't! I am going to write to her to finally give it to
you. I think it would be better that one of you should
read it out when you are all together & I will write to
Miss Dodge to that effect. By that you will see that I
am 'changed' & that I am happy beyond human happiness. I feel & live in exaltation; not the exaltation of
pride. Nitya & Mr. Warrington have written too & I
have written mine unaided. Specially the latter part
was written two days after the event & when I was
still in the spirit of exaltation & adoration. I feel like
that still when I think about it. All that I have written
is absolutely genuine & profound. I can never be the
same. I am not going to stop loving you mother dear
ever but my attitude towards life is changed; there is
nothing for me but the work. I certainly have more
energy mental & emotional but not yet physical &
that will come. I feel as though I am sitting on a
mountain top in adoration & that Lord Maitreya is
close to me. I feel as though I am walking on delicate
& perfumed air. The horizon of my life is clear & the
sky-line is beautiful & precise.

So mother you see I have changed & with that
change in me, I am going to change the lives of my
friends. I want them to climb the same mountain &
look at the glories of the Great Ones from there. . . . I
want you to be up there with me. . . . I am going to
help the whole world to climb a few feet higher than
they are & mother you must help me & to help you
must have climbed so as to direct the peoples along
the path. You must change, change with deliberation
& with a set purpose. . . . I hope you do not think that
I am preaching to you, but since I have changed &
now that I consider that I have found myself, I want
to help you to realize your own self & become great.
You must be for there is nothing else in the world
but to tread the glorious and sacred Path & mother
dear I am going to help you. There is nothing else to

do but become like Them in all things & to follow &
serve Them by serving the world. You don't know
how I have changed, my whole inner nature is alive
with energy & thought & I am sure my ego has come
down decidedly. I am slightly clairvoyant.

Will you, when you get finally the manuscript of
my experience, what Nitya, Mr. Warrington and I
have written, manage to get 4 copies of it? . . . I don't
want it to be gossiped about & besides *very* few
people ought to know about it. Do be careful by
whom it is typewritten. Can you think of somebody
absolutely trustworthy? I want you to send, all
marked 'Absolutely Private. Please show no one,' to:
—Cordes, Ruspilo, Madame Blech, Miss Dijkgraaf?
I hope you don't mind but choose somebody really
trustworthy, please be *careful*. I leave it to your
judgment.

In a later letter he told Lady Emily that he was not
sending a copy to Helen as he did not think she would understand it all, but that as she was going to be in Holland,
Miss Dijkgraaf could read it to her.

Lady Emily asked Rajagopal to type the manuscript. In
sending a copy to Ruspoli she wrote to him:

I hope the reading will make you as happy as it has
done me. Knowing K. and his absolute honesty it is the
more striking. . . . For you and I who have known how
unhappy K. has been—isn't it wonderful to think of him
happy and at peace—having found himself? It has certainly changed the whole current of life for me and I
hope it may for you also.

Nitya too felt his life had changed. As be told Leadbeater on September 1: "I am afraid I have not been as
much help to Krishna as I ought to have been, probably
I've been a hindrance, but I will help him all I can from
now on. . . . If you can tell me of any way I can help
Krishna, please remember that I should be grateful." And
to Mrs. Besant Nitya wrote: "The whole world has so
changed for me since these things have happened, I feel
like a bubble which has suddenly become solid, and life
has become simple, thank goodness. I feel as if I have

never really lived before, and now I could not live unless I
served the Lord."

Leadbeater had no doubt that Krishna's experience was
the passing of the third Initiation, yet he was puzzled, as is
shown by this letter to Mrs. Besant of October 21:

You will by this time have received copies of the
accounts written by Krishna and Nitya of the wonderful experience which came to the former. It was
indeed marvellous and beautiful, though I wish that it
had not been accompanied by so much physical
sickness and suffering. I should like very much to
hear your comment upon all this. We have ourselves
passed through very similar experiences, except that,
in my own case at least, there has never been any of
these terrible physical symptoms, the body being usually left peacefully resting in a trance condition, or
else fully awake and taking part in what was passing,
but without any pain or sickness.

Oddly enough it was not for another month that Leadbeater wrote to Krishna himself. Had he waited to hear
from Mrs. Besant before writing? On November 14 he
wrote from a house called The Manor, at Mosman, a
suburb of Sydney, where he was now living:

My dear Krishna,
    I congratulate you with all my heart. The step you
have taken is of extreme importance, and makes it
certain (so far as mere human beings can ever be
certain!) that you will take the next also before many
years are over. I understand all the happiness that
you feel, the certainty, the wonderful increase of love
and energy. For she and I have been through all
this—though I did not suffer physically nearly as
much as you seem to have done. I think that *she did*
so suffer, but she has said very little about it. Compared with the way in which progress goes with most
pupils, things have moved wonderfully quickly since
that day, now nearly fourteen years ago, when we
met for the first time in this incarnation at Adyar.
And I am very, very thankful that we have come thus
far on the way without serious mishap, for at one
time I had a little anxiety, even though I *knew* all

must be well in the end. You *should* be absolutely
firm and unshakable now; yet all occult tradition
warns us that there are still dangers and temptations
up to the very threshold of Divinity. May the LORD
[Maitreya] grant us to remain ever faithful to
Him—to forget outselves utterly in our love for Him!

It was a most wonderful and unparalleled opportunity for Rosalind Williams to be with you and to be
able to serve you on that most important occasion,
and we need not be surprised that as a result she was
at once put on probation. May her progress be
worthy of this marvellous and sublime beginning!
You were quite right in supposing that Lady Emily
was accepted. Helen Knothe was a tiny baby when I
saw her; I do not know much about her now, though
I admired her greatly as Piet Meuleman. . . .

What will be your next move? Were you thinking
of coming here again? We should all be more than
delighted to see you, and unquestionably you could
do much good—but of course that is equally true of
every other country in the world! Very much love to
Nitya and yourself, and kindest regards to Mr. Warrington.

I am,

Yours ever most affectionately,

C. W. Leadbeater.

About a month before he received this letter Krishna
had heard from Mrs. Besant that he had passed the third
Initiation, but by that time he was undergoing a strange
and agonizing process which was to continue on and off
for years.

19

The Process Begins

Krishnamurti's friends and followers call him Krishnaji, the suffix -ji being a term of affectionate respect in India. He always refers to himself now in the third person as K. The change in him after his experience at Ojai was too great not to be marked by some new form of respect, so after consultation with him it has been decided to call him K henceforward in this book.

The strange process referred to in the last chapter had been going on since that Sunday of August 20. K described it to Mrs. Besant in a letter of September 16 but gave many more details in writing to Lady Emily the following day:

I have not written to you for over ten days. . . . I have, I think, a very substantial excuse; ever since I had that memorable experience I have not been 'well.' Every evening at about 6:30 I become semi-conscious; I have no food but go to bed; from 6:30 to 7:30 or 8, or even 8:30 it lasts. I toss about, groan & moan and mutter strange things, in fact almost behave like one possessed. I get up, thinking somebody is calling me and collapse on the floor; I rave considerably, see strange faces & light. All 'he time, I have a violent pain in my head & the nape of my neck & can't bear the touch of anyone. Also during that time, I become very sensitive, can't bear a sound, however small it may be. I feel so tired & exhausted, while the thing is going on. Sometimes the whole thing becomes *very* acute & force has to be used to keep me down & other times it is quite mild. After it is over, I remember some parts of the scene I had been creating; then I have my food & retire to bed. I don't know what's the cause, nor what it's for; now it has lasted for nearly a month, practically everyday

except when I went to Los Angeles. It may be that I
may become clairvoyant when it is all over or merely
that I am gradually going mad!!! For the last five or
six days I have been seeing my dead mother. Whenever I shut my eyes & especially during the evening
when Rosalind, who looks after me during that
period, is with me, I see her very clearly, in fact, I
call to her aloud & mistake Rosalind for my long lost
mother. It may be that she uses R. or that R. is the
reincarnation of my mother. I don't know which it is,
nor is it of any importance. While I am in that state,
I remember long-forgotten boyhood scenes, such as
when I was ill with my mother, how I used to rest on
her stomach!!, the beggars we used to feed & how I
used to be waked up by her, & the going to the school
etc. I can't account for all this but I am going to find
out from C.W.L.—that's if he will tell me. So that's
how I spend my evenings. Nitya streatched out on the
deck outside on the verandah, Rosalind inside the
room to prevent me from falling down.

In the mornings, I am writing an article of rather a
curious nature. I have written so far 23 pages, absolutely unaided & I won't tell you what it's all about as
you will see it.[1]

On September 25 the process came temporarily to an
end, as K had felt sure it would because the moon was too
bright; he believed, though, that it would begin again as
soon as the moon waned, and indeed it did, more pain-
fully than ever and leaving him completely exhausted.
Their cook had now left and Rosalind was doing the cooking with a little help from K.

Nitya also told Leadbeater about the process in a letter
of October 2:

Every evening about 6.30 to 8, Krishna has gone
into a state of semi-consciousness when the ego seems
to leave and the physical elemental is allowed enough
consciousness to suffer, to talk and even transmit in-

[1] This "article," a sort of prose poem, runs to 12,000 words. Under the title *The Path* it was published in the *Herald* in three parts,
October, November and December 1923. In 1924 it appeared as a
booklet (Theosophical Publishing House, Adyar).

telligently any piece of information that may be necessary. He complains of agonizing pain while he is in this state, centering mostly in the spine; so we have surmised that his kundalini is being awakened.

According to Yoga philosophy certain force centers in the human body are awakened at various stages of evolution. The *kundalini*, sometimes called the Serpent Fire, is the force center at the base of the spine. Right living, high thinking and unselfish activity are said to be essential conditions for the awakening of *kundalini*, which is part of the practice of true Yoga. The awakening brings with it a tremendous release of energy and the power to see clairvoyantly.

Nitya went on to tell Leadbeater in this same letter that Krishna, when in this strange state, was convinced that Rosalind was his mother. It was true that Rosalind was nineteen and their mother had died only seventeen years ago, so it was difficult to see how she could be a reincarnation of their mother, "but the discrepancy can I suppose be accounted for, if the Great Ones considered unusual steps necessary. She has been a perfect Godsend to him during these days, for she has enormous vitality and a great love for Krishna, she also likes me." This last remark was an understatement, for there was a very special mutual love between Rosalind and Nitya.

The excitement of the last two months had not been good for Nitya's health. It was now thought advisable, therefore, that he should have more Abrams treatment. As they had left the "Oscilloclast" go and could not get another, the brothers went to Hollywood on October 26 for Nitya to be treated by Dr. Strong's machine. They stayed with Dr. John Ingleman, a Swedish Theosophist and dietician, who put them both on a very strict régime. Dr. Strong discovered that Nitya still had a patch of tuberculosis in the old spot in the left lung, which he guaranteed to cure in a fortnight or so (actually it took two months) and, as K still had a trace of syphilis in his nose, they both had daily treatments from the machine. K experienced the greatest difficulty in not "going off" every evening and felt sure that if Rosalind had been there the process would have been resumed: he was, however, free from pain all the time they were in Hollywood.

They were still there when Leadbeater's letter of

November 14, congratulating K on passing the third Initiation, at last arrived. K answered it on December 14:

I can hardly realize that I have taken such a step; while I was having this remarkable experience, I did not consider the importance of it, as much as I do now. It was like a magnificent dream and now I am realizing the grand reality of it. I am glad that I have been honored with this Initiation for now I can be of more use to the Master and to you two, to her and to you.

My difficulty is, I feel so small and incapable to do the mighty work; I still lack confidence in myself and I don't think I shall ever be conceited. I do not feel that way. I must improve both in writing and in speaking as I am rather backward. I am going to lay special stress on these two things. Henceforth, there is but one thing for me and that is work and I hope to do it utterly unselfishly. . . .

I am so glad about Lady Emily and Rosalind Williams and I will do everything I can to help them. With regards to Helen Knothe, she wants to come to Australia and be under you. She has written to her parents, if she can go out to you; she is still in Amsterdam, studying music. A.B. [Mrs. Besant] wrote to her suggesting that she should go out to Australia and she is doing her best to take this opportunity.

As soon as he received Leadbeater's letter K sent off to Lady Emily the good news of her acceptance. He had not hinted at it before Leadbeater confirmed it. It was nine years since Lady Emily had been put on probation at Varengeville (August 11, 1913) and even now she had had to wait another four months before receiving the news of her acceptance because of Leadbeater's dilatoriness in writing. He had certainly punished her for whatever harm she had done to Barbie and Robert by following K to Taormina in 1914, though he, of course, would have said that it was the Master's displeasure she had incurred.

K and Nitya returned to Ojai in December with a clean bill of health for Nitya from Dr. Strong, but with the injunction that he should be re-examined every month or so. They had also consulted an orthodox specialist who said the lung was healing but that Nitya must do no work for at least six months. "Poor fellow," K wrote to Mrs. Besant, "he is so keen to get into active life and he knows that he must not overdo anything for a while as that would be disastrous." And to Lady Emily he had written, "Nitya has made progress all round, both mentally & morally. One wouldn't think he was a sick man, to a certain extent he radiates health & also he is happy which is a great thing." Nitya had also been to an oculist who had helped him so much that he was beginning to see with his blind eye. He now weighed 118 pounds, the most he had ever weighed in his life.

Ojai had been parched when they left in October; now, after heavy rain, everything was "a sparkling and tender green." K was enraptured by the beauty of it: "... the green of England is nothing compared to this ... this is a truly wonderful country," he told Lady Emily.

He was soon to receive an unpleasant shock when he heard that Mar de Manziarly was engaged to be married. "What awful news about Mar," he wrote to Lady Emily on December 26. "She might just as well commit suicide." And two days later:

> It is the biggest shock I have had. I can hardly believe it; it is like some fearful nightmare. Whenever I am not doing anything my mind reverts to Mar & the calamity for it is a calamity. What a fool she is. . . . Just think what Mar could do for the Master etc & now. Oh! God, it is really a pitiable thing. . . . I suppose it is impossible to stop it & if I interfered, Mar would never again speak to me.

The engagement was later broken off painlessly by mutual consent and without any interference from K. Indeed Nitya had written to Mar that although her news had been a shock, if she felt there would now be two to help the Masters, he was very glad she was going to be married.

In the New Year of 1923 K really began to work for the Star and for Theosophy. As well as his editorial notes for the *Herald*, which had become even more of a burden since his August experience, he began to write a monthly message for the Self-Preparation groups which had been started in every country throughout the Star movement. He was answering dozens of official letters and putting the Star on a new basis in California with Ernest Wood, from

the old Adyar days, as the new National Representative.
He went to Hollywood to speak on Leadbeater's seventy-
sixth birthday, February 17, and collected nearly £100. He
spoke to the women's college at Pasadena and at
Thatcher's, an exclusive boys' school in the Ojai Valley.
He had also agreed to tour America in May, lecturing,
and to attend the Theosophical Convention in Chicago at
the end of that month as well as Theosophical and Star
Congresses in Vienna in June.

K's "process" meanwhile continued on and off at Ojai,
though in a much milder form. Rosalind was still there but
seldom mentioned. He was constantly pressed for time; his
letters to Lady Emily that year were short and infrequent,
and he told her he did not have time even to write to Hel-
en. His experience had, however, brought him closer to
Mrs. Besant and almost every week he assured her how he
longed to be with her in India.

In the middle of February they had the opportunity of
buying their cottage at Ojai and six acres of land with another, larger, house on it. "I cabled to Baillie-Weaver that
it will be a pity to lose this place after all that has happened here," K wrote to Mrs. Besant on February 28. "He
says that we can buy it & that the money will come. . . . In
a few days it will be ours. . . . I thought it would be better
to form a trust to hold this & I think it will be a magnificent center." He did not say where the money was
coming from or how much they would have to pay for it,
but probably it came from Miss Dodge. Later, another
seven acres were added to it which were certainly a gift
from Miss Dodge. The Trust holding the property was
called the Brothers Association.

After a week's drive to see the redwood trees in
northern California as the guests of Mrs. Gray, and three
weeks in Hollywood for a final course of Abrams treatment, K and Nitya set off on a tour of Theosophical and
Star centers in various towns including Kansas City, De-
troit, Rochester and Washington, before finally going to
Chicago for the T.S. Convention there from May 27 to 30.
They were staying in hotels, something to which they were
quite unaccustomed and which K found "the God's limit."
At each place he spoke three times, at a T.S. meeting, an
Esoteric Section meeting and a Star meeting; he also had
to attend receptions. At every meeting he tried to raise
funds for Indian education, one of his deepest and most

abiding loves. He particularly hoped to raise Rs. 21,000 to buy land for the extension of a Theosophical school at Guindy, about a mile from the T.S. Headquarters at Adyar, which had been started soon after the war.

Nitya did not attend any of the meetings during the tour as it was essential for him to preserve his strength, not only for the train journeys across the continent but for the voyage to England. Their passages had been booked from New York on the *Paris,* sailing on June 6. Rosalind was to join them in New York but not to go with them to England although Lady Emily had offered to put her up in London.

As K told Mrs. Besant in a letter from Washington on May 23, he was worried about his physical condition. His "process" was continuing all the time he was travelling. He was in constant pain, with a throbbing and burning at the nape of his neck and at the base of his spine. He frequently went out of his body when, Nitya told him, he would groan and weep and call out for his mother. He did not know what best to do for the future. When he had gone to Ojai the year before he had seriously intended to study but then the process had started which had made that impossible. He was very conscious that he was not sufficiently prepared intellectually for his future work. He wished to have a holiday somewhere in Europe after the Vienna Congress; after that he was quite in the dark as to whether the Master wanted him to go to India, as he longed to do, or return to Ojai to study.

Nitya evidently attended the meetings in Chicago for he reported to Mrs. Besant:

> The Convention was a record success, thanks to K's presence and I think the greatest thing that can be said is that he more than came up to everyone's expectations ... everyone whom Krishna has come into touch with feels a new revival of their enthusiasm. Krishna now talks like someone who has found his goal, and his purpose in his talks has been to make the existence of the Masters an intense reality and in this he is really inspired.

Neither Leadbeater nor Mrs. Besant was able to account for K's strange condition. The former was particularly mystified as is shown in this letter to Mrs. Besant of May 12, 1923:

It is evident that in all higher matters the methods of progress differ for each individual. I do not understand why such terrible physical suffering should come to our Krishna. Surely the Brahmin body is exceptionally pure, and should need less in the way of preparation than the average European vehicle. In my own case I have no recollection of anything in the least commensurate with this when I was passing through the same stage, though there was certainly a great deal of excessive discomfort in the development of the Kundalini. It may be, as you suggest, that this is part of the preparation of that body for its Great Occupant, yet nothing has been said as to any hastening of the Coming. But it might well be that years must elapse after the completion of this preparation, in order that the body might fully recover from it before having to undergo the strain of the actual occupancy. The case is so unique that I suppose the truth is that we can only wait and watch.

20

The Process Intensified

Lady Emily was at Plymouth to meet K and Nitya on June 11. They went to stay at West Side House, Wimbledon, with Miss Dodge and Lady De La Warr, and Lady Emily was invited to stay there too for the first night. She vividly remembered having breakfast with the brothers alone the next morning and beginning to talk to K about his experience, whereupon he immediately went off into a dead faint. Nitya told her that K could not talk about it; if anyone mentioned it he just put his head down and became unconscious.

Now that I have seen more of Krishna & Nitya [Lady Emily wrote to Mrs. Besant ten days later], I can say more of the impression they make upon us all. Krishna seems outwardly little changed though perhaps more beautiful, but one is conscious at every moment of a controlled but immense concentrated power flowing from him. His E.S. talk last Sunday was an immense advance on anything he has given before. He had no notes & spoke for 45 mins, fluently, easily & yet with such tremendous earnestness & force it was like listening to the throbbing of a great machine. Already he is working great changes and settling up many tangled problems. Nitya has grown from a boy to a man, with all his sweetness intensified but with an immensely added strength. For both of them now only the work counts & is of interest. You would be happy to see them.

After a strenuous month in London giving interviews and speaking at various meetings, K and Nitya went off to Vienna via Paris and Monsieur Blech's country house at Septeuil, where they were able to have a few days' rest. Mrs. Besant, to K's intense disappointment, was not able

to come to Europe that year because she had been seriously ill as the result of a scorpion bite, so although Raja
was there to preside over the T.S. Congress, which started
on July 19, the whole weight of the second international
Star Congress which followed fell on K. Many of his
closest friends, however, including Lady Emily and Helen,
were there to give him support, and immediately afterwards a chosen number of them went off with him and
Nitya for a seven-weeks' holiday to Ehrwald, a village in
the Austrian Tyrol near Innsbruck, where a friend of John
Cordes had put a chalet, the Villa Sonnblick, at K's disposal.

The party consisted of Helen, Lady Emily with Betty
and Mary, Rajagopal, Mar de Manziarly (no longer engaged), Cordes, Ruth Roberts (the girl K had met in Sydney) and a young Indian woman, Malati Patwardhan, and
her husband. Isabelle Mallet joined them on August 10.
(Miss Dodge was too crippled ever to go abroad.)
Krishna, Nitya, Lady Emily, Helen, Rajagopal and Cordes
stayed at Sonnblick, where the whole party had meals,
while the rest of them were lodged in a nearby chalet. It
was an ideal place for walks; there was a flat field for
rounders and a stream for daily hip baths—with the sexes
carefully segregated. The first fortnight was a real holiday;
Krishna and Helen were certainly happy, but there was
some heart-burning among the other girls who could not
fail to realize how much of a favorite Helen was. Although she was not pretty, whereas Ruth was really beautiful, she had exceptional charm and vitality.

Then, in the middle of August K's "process" started
again even more severely. On August 15 Lady Emily began to write a diary letter to Mrs. Besant describing these
strange evening occurrences:

On Monday [August 13] we went for rather a
long walk up the mountains into a pine forest. We all
scattered & took sun baths & presently we heard
Krishna's voice chanting & Nitya & Rajagopal answering him back. I cannot tell you how beautiful it
was, so full of power echoing through the forest. . . .
At dinner time he was obviously hardly conscious &
almost directly afterwards he went right 'off' and the
body began to sob & groan. We all sat very quietly
outside except the faithful Nitya—who presumably

sent for Helen as he thought she might help him. It lasted till 9 o'c. when he came round & went off to bed. But at 12 o'c. he began again, & again Helen & Nitya sat by him till 1 o'c. & once again in the early morning. He said that Helen was very nervous & naturally so as at first it is awful to witness such suffering & to realize his consciousness is not there. It is very curious that he seems to need a woman's presence & also that the vitality of Americans seems to supply something that he needs. I asked him if I could not help him as I felt that I could keep very calm, but he explained to me that being married would make it undesirable—that when in this state he is very particular that everything round him should be of the purest. I was very grateful to him for telling me this as I could quite understand & now I can try & give him all the help I can by my loving & pure thoughts & Helen will help him in the other ways. . . .

Yesterday he was naturally very tired & we spent the morning quietly in the woods reading & he seemed very happy . . . again at dinner only Krishna's body was there—& very much tired by any loud talk or voice. Dinner was over by 7. My two children & Ruth went off at once to the house where they sleep—and the rest of us sat quietly watching the sunset & meditating. Krishna went to his own room with Nitya & Helen & was 'off' again until 9 o'c. This time he seemed in much less pain & did not groan much, but when he woke up at 9 o'c. he was very dazed & confused. . . .

When he is himself he likes the young ones about . . . I try to be Mother to them all & fit in when I am wanted. . . . With so many girls an older woman is rather necessary, & I think I can help Helen as the strain on her is rather severe. *Thursday* [August 16] Yesterday was rather a curious day as at lunch time Krishna was very boisterous & full of jokes. Then a thunder storm came on & it poured with rain & we could not go out so we played a game ['Up Jenkins']. It is very curious to watch the phases through which Krishna passes. Sometimes he is just a frolicsome boy with apparently not a serious thought in the world. Then swiftly he changes & becomes the Teacher—stern & uncompromising, urging his pupils

onward towards swift progress. Again he is just tortured with the pain in his spine—not speaking & just
wanting quiet—or most strange of all the figure that
comes to dinner—beautiful, with unseeing eyes
mechanically eating his food & shrinking at every
sound. Most beautiful of all when he sits in meditation chanting mantrams—his soul going out in worship. These phases succeed each other in such swift
succession that it is something of a strain to be always prepared for them.

Last night ... by 7 the house was quiet & Krishna
had gone up to his room. We sat quietly meditating
but presently Nitya came to say he felt our thoughts
& they were upsetting him—& would we just go on
with ordinary occupations. This is not easy to do—
but of course we shall. It seems so much more
natural to keep quiet & think of the Master but I suppose that any intensity of feeling upsets him & we are
not wise enough to know just how to guide our
thoughts aright. Krishna was away for just two
hours—not in much pain apparently but just talking
vaguely. He said that his body must not eat so much
at night & must take more exercise.

Sat [August 18]. Last night just as he went off
Krishna said that they must wake him up at 8.30.
Then almost immediately some of the Great Ones
came. Nitya apparently saw & heard Them on the
balcony in front of Krishna's room. Krishna himself
goes now to Nitya's room as it is quieter & darker.
Nitya says he has never before been so conscious of
the presence of Master K.H. & when They left he felt
something of himself go after Them and then he
fainted. Krishna was conscious of this & called to him
& he came round at once. Apparently Krishna's body
faints off & Helen & Nitya have to revive it. Sometimes he will come back if they just call him, sometimes they have to pour water on him but he asked
them not to do this if they could help it as it hurt
him so much. Before he came back his elemental [see
p. 170] said: 'Krishna is standing there & laughing. I
wonder what he is laughing at.' Nitya suggested that
he should ask him, but he said 'Oh, no I couldn't'....

Sunday.... When Krishna went up last night he
again said they must wake him at 8.30 & then he said

that Someone was coming & asked Helen & Nitya to
wait outside. This they did for about five minutes
when they heard him fall with a bang & went in. He
seems to have been in great pain last night & swooned
a good many times. He told them at the end that he
was too tired for more to be done, but it would be
continued tonight. . . .

Monday. We had a very quiet day yesterday. Nothing
special happened in the evening. Krishna went a long
way off & the little child came talking of his childhood, his hatred of school etc. I think Nitya had a
message two nights ago which he is trying to remember. . . . I hope that as the experience happens nightly
it means that the conditions here are all right for him.
It is a wonderful privilege to be here & to share a
little bit in these great events. I only pray to be
worthy of it all.

The next day, Tuesday, August 21, Lady Emily started
a second letter:

Krishnaji . . . went away as usual at 7, & was off
till 8.40. He suffered a very great deal & his body
groaned & wept.

Wed. Yesterday . . . Krishnaji went off at the usual
hour & suffered terribly. Helen was very tired & not
very well & the physical elemental seemed conscious
of this & tried to control his groans—but at one time
they were so bad that Krishna came back & asked
what was happening. They said nothing & when he
had gone again the physical elemental or whatever is
in charge of the body was dreadfully distressed at
having brought Krishna back & said Krishna had told
him to control himself & he had done his best &
could not help it.

The Church bells begin to ring always at 8 o'c. &
their noise causes him agony. Last night he fainted
twice while they were ringing. . . .

Nitya told me of the message Master K.H. gave
him. He said Krishna was wasting energy & that he
ought to read books which would increase his vocabu-
lary but not give him set opinions. [After this they all
tried to learn a Shakespeare sonnet by heart every
day.] Nitya & I have thought out some books but at

present he is not fit to do any kind of mental work.
Nitya understood that these experiences will not be
very long continued. Nitya also told me that he thinks
Helen was put on probation on the night of the 17th.
This will be a splendid achievement as Krishna was
so eager about it & it means that our stay here has already been amply justified. They have cabled C.W.L.
for confirmation.

Thursday. Yesterday ... the evening performance
was very bad, the worst that has yet been. An hour of
concentrated agony. Krishna sent Nitya & Helen out
of the room once as it was so bad. Downstairs we
could hear him banging himself on to the floor & his
awful groans & it was hard to keep one's thoughts
resolutely turned away. When I went up afterwards
he looked so tired & his poor eyes all bloodshot. The
pain has been chiefly in his head during these days
here. ...

Friday. The evening performance was again excrucia-
ting. He had to send Nitya & Helen out of the room
several times & we could hear his poor body falling
repeatedly. He lies upon the floor upon a rug but sits
up in his agony & then faints away & falls with a
bang. Happily he seems to sleep soundly & in the
morning he is not too tired. This morning we had a
good walk & to see him leaping down the hills so full
of grace & beauty & vitality it is almost impossible to
believe what his poor body has endured each night.

I think Nitya is feeling the strain a good deal. Hel-
en is not such a support I fancy as Rosalind was. She
is very nervous & highly strung, but she is taking herself in hand firmly. It is a curious experience for a
young girl.

Sat. Last night was bad as usual but he seemed more
controlled & did not have to send them out of the
room. Helen thinks this was because she was more
controlled. He told her one night that if she was so
nervous the whole business would have to stop & that
her attitude should be kind but indifferent. Ruth was
not well yesterday & we kept her in this house to
sleep. She sat below with me while the process was
going on, & the elemental seemed at once conscious
of a fresh person & asked who was there. ...

Sunday. Yesterday the evening performance was

more than usually agonizing ... just when he was at
his worst the Church bells rang & caused him such a
shock of agony that Krishna had to come back & apparently consulted with them if anything more could
be done to the body that night. The physical elemental begged them to continue. Afterwards he said 'That
was a very narrow shave. Those bells nearly tolled for
my funeral.' When they rang again later Helen called
Krishna to come back & take charge till they stopped
again. He seemed very nervous all the rest of the
time & even when I went up afterwards Krishna kept
saying 'What is the matter? I feel so uncomfortable
tonight.' He [the physical elemental] also told them
that Krishna must go out & take exercise even when
it rained.

Monday. Last night was very bad. We could hear his
dreadful cries & apparently he said 'It has never been
as bad as this'. After the worst is over he generally
has about half an hour when he is a little child again.
He then thinks that Helen is his Mother. This seems
very curious. Does he confuse her with Rosalind—or
does his Mother influence him through both? ...

I think I have told you everything about Krishna.
Nitya is I am afraid a good deal strained, he is
coughing a good bit, but we make him rest as much
as possible.

On September 7 Lady Emily began a third letter:

With this week a new phase of intensity seems to
have begun in Krishna's nightly experiences. On
Monday [September 3] he suffered terribly or rather
the body & was twice sick. On Tuesday he was in
great pain all day & was sick again after every meal
keeping nothing down except his evening milk.
Wednesday he was told he must eat nothing but fruit
& this he kept down. Thursday he was told to fast all
day only drinking water. This reduced him to such a
state of weakness that the evening's work was wasted
as nothing could be done to the poor exhausted body.
He had to be given food & hot bottles to revive him,
& when I went to say goodnight his poor face looked
so thin & haggard. ...

Krishna was very much annoyed at the waste of

time & reproached Nitya & Helen for letting him fast,
but of course they were following his own instructions. Now he is to use moderation—he no longer
eats the evening meal, but has his bath while we eat,
& then has his food after all is over. This seems to
answer better. They seem to work on him the last two
nights with greater concentration & intensity—it has
been very awful to hear his cries & sobs. It sounds
like some animal in awful pain. But he has his food
now soon after 8 o'c. & seems very cheerful & happy
when I go up to say goodnight to him. . . . It is wonderful how quickly Krishna's body recuperates. Even
after that day of fasting when he seemed too weak to
move, next morning he walked and played rounders
as vigorously as ever.

There are no more letters from Lady Emily about the
evening process but it is known from her diary that it continued, though in a less severe form, until September 20.
On that evening K brought through a message from the
Master Kuthumi which he relayed to Nitya who immediately wrote it down:

Nitya Listen.
    This is finished here, this is the last night. It will be
continued in Ojai. But this depends upon you. You
both should have more energy. On what you do in
the next month will depend the success. You have to
be exceedingly careful. Let nothing stand in the way.
You have both of you to put on more fat, in order to
have more energy. Let everything be consecrated to
the success of this. It has been a success here. But
Ojai depends entirely on you, there it will be continued with much greater vigor if you are ready.
Helen—She has learnt well, come on well. She will be
used later. We are all very grateful to her.
Nitya—They want you especially. They do not say to
you they are grateful for you are too near. When you
leave this place you have to be exceedingly careful. It
is like a fresh vase, just out of the mold, and any
bad vibration may crack it, and this will mean repair-
ing and remodelling and this would take a long time.
    You have to be careful; if you fail it will mean be-

ginning everything from the beginning. Consecrate
everything. 'Do it as unto Me.'

Please thank the happy household for their courtesy and thought; they've been happy. God has been
with them when they knew it not. May they be happy
hereafter.

This house is sacred, it should be used for Austria.
[The Villa Sonnblick is now a guest house.]

The whole party left Ehrwald on September 22 when
some of them, including the Lutyens's, Rajagopal, Helen
and Ruth, went with K and Nitya to stay at Castle Eerde,
Ommen, as guests of Baron Philip van Pallandt, who in
1921 had so generously offered K as a gift the Castle and
5,000 acres of land. As K did not want to own any
property personally a Trust was formed, with K as
President, to which the estate was made over, and Eerde
became the international headquarters of the Order of the
Star in the East. It was planned to hold a Star Congress
there the following year, so this was the last occasion on
which the Baron acted as host. The Castle, surrounded by
an inner and an outer moat, fed by a small river, was a
perfect example of early eighteenth-century Dutch ar-
chitecture, as unspoilt inside as out, with all its original
furniture, including four Gobelin tapestries made for the
drawing-room in 1714; closets leading off each bedroom
contained oubliettes going straight down into the moat
where gigantic ancient carp acted as scavengers. The setting of the Castle was ideal for a religious center for it
was isolated in acres of woodland, interspersed with lakes,
where no creature had been killed by man ever since the
Baron, a Practical Idealist, came into his inheritance.

21

Climax of the Process

K had reluctantly decided that he could not go to India that autumn, as he longed to do, but must return to Ojai to complete the work of preparation on his body. During that time, however long it took, he did not feel he would be able to do any more public work. Nitya, while at Ojai, could study for his finals. So after a week or two in London following their stay at Eerde, the brothers sailed for New York on Ocotober 22 and eventually reached Ojai on November 8. Helen had travelled with them on the ship but they parted from her in New York. "Helen was very miserable when she left us & joined her family," K told Lady Emily. "I think she is having a bad time. Good for her though." This last remark, apparently so heartless, was characteristic of K: to go through a bad time was an essential preliminary to change and growth; contentment was stagnation which led to mediocrity.

Nitya felt it was necessary to have another Initiate at Ojai besides himself to help look after K; Rajagopal, therefore, who had been made an Initiate before he came to England in 1920, was asked to take a year off from Cambridge to go with them. Koos van de Leeuw, a Theosophist and Star member belonging to a rich family of coffee merchants in Rotterdam, and a member of the Eerde Trust, also accompanied them. They now went to live in the larger house at Ojai included in the property they had bought in February, while Rosalind, who was so delighted to see them that she "almost cried," was in their former cottage with her mother. They called their new house Arya Vihara, meaning Noble Monastery.[1] It was not at all comfortable, as it had hardly any furniture apart from a hideous dining-room suite and four wicker chairs.

---

[1] The house still bears that name. The cottage, now called Pine Cottage, is at the end of Pine Lane. It has been enlarged (spoiled, according to K) and the "young pepper tree" is so grown that it completely dominates the cottage.

The outside, which was white, needed painting, and since they were extremely short of money, they started doing this themselves; moreover they did all their own cooking and cleaning which K found "past a joke"; nor were they allowed to neglect the housework, for Rajagopal, who was irritatingly tidy himself, insisted on everything being in perfect order. Eventually they engaged a cleaning woman to come from the village twice a week, and a gardener.

On November 20, less than a fortnight after their arrival, K's "process" started again. It was so bad that for the first time Nitya became worried, wondering whether everything was as it should be. He naturally turned to Leadbeater for advice and on the 27th wrote him an anxious letter. After telling him about everything that had happened at Ehrwald and saying that he was enclosing a copy of the message the Master had given them on the last night there, he continued:

> During the last days in Ehrwald They tried the experiment of leaving Krishna conscious while the pain was still fairly strong, but this consciousness was only for 10 or 20 seconds at a time, and as soon as the pain became too intense, Krishna would leave the body.
>
> Seven days ago the process began again only now Krishna is fully conscious and the pain is growing more and more intense, tonight has been the worst night for pain. I started this letter while he was suffering and he has just come out of the room after an hour of fierce pain. Nowadays, there is no Helen with him nor Rosalind, though R is here in Ojai next door to us. He does not seem to want her; after the pain is over Krishna leaves the body and the body weeps heartbrokenly with exhaustion. He calls for his mother, and I've discovered that he wants Helen, not Rosalind.
>
> As far as I can make out from what Krishna's body occasionally says, there is still a great deal of work to be done on the body, perhaps it means many months.... We came back here to Ojai for we thought that this place was most suitable, since these things began here last year. While we were at Ehrwald, Krishna and I wired to you inviting you to Ojai for as long as you wished. But apparently the

wires (for we wired twice, the first was a reply paid)
never reached you, for we had no answer. I felt that
it would be wonderful if you, who could see what
was happening, could have been with him during this
time. Of course you know what a great joy it would
have been for us, to have been with you, we might
have even had the Adyar days over again. Now the
point is this. Do you think that Krishna should be
with you during this period? If you could only tell us
this, you know we would take the next boat to Australia. Would you not cable us your opinion? Please,
please tell us what you think is best for Krishna. Of
course the Great Ones will look after everything for
the best. We hardly like to leave Ojai and set sail for
Sydney till we have definite instructions or expression
of opinion from you. Now I want to ask you some
questions. . . . Is Rosalind our mother? Shall we come
out to Sydney, and shall we bring Rajagopal?

The next day he added as a postscript:

Krishna's body repeated this message on the night
of 26th, immediately after the process was over for
the evening.
'The work that is being done now is of gravest importance and exceedingly delicate. It is the first time
that this experiment is being carried out in the world.
Everything in the household must give way to this
work, and no one's convenience must be considered,
not even Krishna's. Strangers must not come there
too often; the strain is too great. You and Krishna
can work this out.
Maintain peace and [an] even life.'
I have a feeling that the reference to the 'experiment' is not only to the fact that this kind of thing is
generally done in a monastery, but also perhaps that
They are trying something new in the preparation of
the body.
Do you know at all if something similar to what is
going on now, was part of the preparation of the
body of Master Jesus when the Lord came last time?
Could you not tell us something of this. I wish so
heartily that we were with you; Krishna's sufferings
tonight were worse than last night—of course, I know

that the body is in the care of the Masters yet I wish
you were here on the physical plane. It would be a
great blessing upon us all.

It was just as well they did not go to Sydney before
hearing from Leadbeater because they would not have
been at all welcome. Leadbeater could not give any explanation for what was happening, nor any reassurance.
As he wrote to Mrs. Besant on January 1, 1924:

I have just received a letter from Nitya in which he
tells me that all this terrible business of preparation
has been resumed. . . . I am very much troubled about
the whole affair, for I have never met with anything
in the least like it, and I cannot feel sure that it is
right or necessary. Certainly he obtained a step last
year along very similar lines; yet all this is so utterly
opposed to what I myself have been taught. I hope
that you can assure me that you know all is well.
    Krishna and Nitya seem to have no shadow of
doubt, and I think they they must know; and yet two
messages which they have received (copies of which I
enclose, though they have no doubt already sent them
to you) are not in the least in the style of either of
our Masters. I suppose that all is well, and that they
are being led along the way which is right and best
for them; yet it certainly seems very strange. I feel
quite clearly that, although this is a very powerful
center, it would not be at all a good place for exercises of this description; it is far too near to a big
city, and there is so much work always going on that
it would be impossible to obtain the perfect quiet
which seems to be so necessary.

Part of Leadbeater's letter to Nitya, also written on January 1, is given below:

I do not understand the terrible drama that is taking place with our beloved Krishna, but I want to
have frequent news of it, for indeed I am very anxious about it. It is very hard to believe that all this
frightful pain can be right or necessary for him.
There was nothing of all this in the future that
stretched itself before us in those happy days at

Adyar so long ago. The body then needed preparation, but not *this* kind of preparation; what has been
done to it since that has made all this necessary.
However it seems from what you write that you have
been specially sent to that secluded spot in Ojai Valley in order that this work should be done; if that be
so, surely you will have to stay there until it is ac-
complished. I certainly dare not take the responsibility of advising you to come here while it is going on;
nor would I take the other and more mundane responsibility of bringing *you,* with your delicate chest
and lungs, into the sea air which suited you so ill at
Malahide. When all these strange agonies are safely
over, we shall be more than delighted to see you in
Sydney if your health will stand it; but even then you
ought to have a reliable doctor's opinion as to the
question of air.

I do not see how Rosalind can be your mother, for
I understand that she was born before your mother's
death. As Krishna seems to have used the same language to Miss Knothe, we can only consider it as
symbolical, unless we suppose that your mother was
allowed to use the bodies of both these young women
as mediums through whom she could help her son in
his appalling sufferings. I think that that is by no
means improbable, and it would account for his action in turning to comparative strangers in that curiously intimate manner.

Mrs. Besant, rather strangely as she had laid aside her
clairvoyance for the sake of her work for India, apparently had no doubts, for on January 8 Leadbeater was
able to write to her,

I am very glad to receive your letter of December
7th enclosing a copy of one of the messages which
Nitya received through Krishna. It is a very great relief to me to see that you are fully satisfied that the
whole proceeding is under authority, and that everything is being rightly done. It seemed to me that that
must be so, and yet the whole thing is so utterly at
variance with all that happened in my own case and
with anything whatever with which I am personally
familiar, that I could not be sure about it, and where

anything concerns Krishna of course I want to be very sure. I suppose that we may take it that the physical body will be carefully protected, but certainly the accounts are of the most alarming character.

From this time onwards Leadbeater seems to have left all responsibility for K to Mrs. Besant. This was totally unlike him; one would have thought he could have asked the Master Kuthumi, or the Lord Maitreya, or particularly the Master Jesus, what was happening to K's body. Unfortunately there is no way of knowing what was going on in his mind. It is one of the many mysteries of this strange story. Yet it may be felt that his uncertainty in this matter gives authenticity to his clairvoyance rather than the reverse.

K's torture meanwhile went on unabated.

I am getting more & more irritable & I am getting more & more tired [he told Lady Emily], I wish you & the others were here. I feel like crying so often nowadays & that used not to be my way. It's awful for the others & myself. . . . I wish Helen were here but that is an impossibility & also probably They don't want anybody to help me along. So I have to do it all by myself. . . . However hard one may try, there is a loneliness, that of a solitary pine in the wilderness.

It seemed that only when he became a child again was he able to relax and thereby obtain some relief from the pain, which was with him all day now as a dull ache as well as intensely in the evenings. But he could not become a child without a "mother" to look after the body. Rosalind was no longer able to fulfill this role for some unexplained reason and Helen's father, not unnaturally, would not allow her to go to Ojai. ("I suppose it's difficult with a blinking family," he conceded to Lady Emily. "God, I'm glad I haven't got one"—yet, when he first went to Paris in 1920, a family was the one thing he longed for.) All the unanswered letters piling up, his monthly message to the Self Preparation groups and his editorial notes weighed heavily on his mind; his official writings never had to be in a very finished state because Lady Emily invariably

corrected them for him, but the slightest mental exertion
now started up the pain in his spine.

He gave Lady Emily only a few glimpses of their daily
life: playing golf which failed to relax him, Rajagopal trying to teach Rosalind algebra and their squabbling over it.
"We are all fed up with ourselves so thoroughly that nothing at present amuses us or at least everything does. We
laugh at the least thing to almost tears."

By February 7 Nitya told Mrs. Besant that they had had
seventy-six nights of the process without cessation and had
been for three months at Arya Vihara.

> The evening business is more of a strain than it
> has ever been, now all the excitement and the fun, if it
> ever was fun, have gone. . . . Krishna I think has al-
> most forgotten to smile. . . . The pain is getting more
> and more intense, though his capacity to bear pain is
> growing with it. . . . I had a letter from C.W.L. the
> other day, all about this business. He said he did not
> understand what it was all about. His letter made us
> feel a little anxious if everything was alright so we
> cabled him. His reply was very characteristic—'Presi-
> dent says all right.'

All this time K continued to write touchingly loving
little letters to Mrs. Besant by almost every mail. He was
very anxious, he told her, for Helen to go to Sydney to be
"brought on" by Leadbeater, by which he meant helped
along the Path of Discipleship, but her father would not
let her go and Leadbeater would not have her without his
consent. K was worried about her, fearing she was wasting
her life by remaining with her family.

At the beginning of March K confided to Mrs. Besant
that John Ingleman, the Swedish doctor he had stayed
with in Hollywood the year before, had given him a car,
but as he did not want anyone to know about such an expensive present he had asked Dwarkanath Telang to be its
"official owner." Dwarkanath was at Adyar and K intended to ship the car out there when next he went to India.
(He did not in fact do this.) The car arrived at Ojai on
March 2 and caused intense excitement as it was the first
car he had ever owned. It was a pale blue convertible
seven-seater Lincoln with "silver lamps"—"as good as a
Rolls," he told Lady Emily. "It does easily 70 miles an

hour and climbs like a bird." It was the only joy he had during those agonizing months, apart from the fact that in spite of the strain Nitya seemed to be completely free from his disease.

Towards the end of February K's "process" reached a climax which he described to Lady Emily:

> Don't worry about me, because I think, this all has been arranged, so that I could go through it by myself. Probably the feminine influence was not wanted & They took care that I should not have it. Last 10 days, it has been really strenuous, my spine & neck have been going very strong and day before yesterday, the 27th, [February] I had an extraordinary evening. Whatever it is, the force or whatever one calls the bally thing, came up my spine, up to the nape of my neck, then it separated into two, one going to the right & the other to the left of my head till they met between the two eyes, just above my nose. There was a kind of flame & I saw the Lord & the Master. It was a tremendous night. Of course the whole thing was painful, in the extreme. Last night, I was too tired to have anything done but I suppose it will continue but I am sure we are going to have a holiday soon.

He described this experience to Mrs. Besant also, though without mentioning the feminine influence, and Nitya too gave her an account of it. Nitya presumed it meant the "opening of the third eye." In treatises on Yoga the "third eye" is often referred to as the Eye of Shiva. It is in the middle of the forehead and, like *kundalini*, is associated with clairvoyance. "Krishna's clairvoyance has not begun yet," Nitya added, "but I imagine it is only a question now of time. So far we've had 110 nights of the process since we've been here." He went on to say that they had just received a cable from Sydney from Dr. Rocke announcing that she was arriving at the end of March for a short visit. Although they would be very glad to see her they could not understand why she was coming. "C.W.L. in one of his letters said that he wished a doctor could be here to see the physical body was not overstrained, adding that he supposed an ordinary doctor would condemn the whole business. So it may be that he had asked her to come here."

Dr. Rocke did go to Ojai and was there for over a week observing K's process every evening. She was still there for the last evening on April 11—"a marvellous night for us all," as Nitya told Mrs. Besant a fortnight later. K was given a message on that evening which he repeated to Nitya who wrote it down at once and enclosed it in this same letter to Mrs. Besant on April 25. Nitya believed that the first part of the message was from the Lord Maitreya himself. K had told them that a few days before the process stopped, the Lord Buddha had come one evening. "In the message they refer to His coming in the most beautiful way," Nitya wrote.

This was the message:

April 11th, 1924, (6.30 to 7.15 p.m.)
My Sons, I am pleased with your endurance and bravery. It has been a long struggle and as far as We have gone, it has been a good success. Though there were many difficulties We have surmounted them with comparative ease. There have been many chapters in the progress of the evolution, and each stage has its trial. This is but the beginning of many struggles. Be equally brave, and endure it with the same grace in the future, with the same power and with the same cheerfulness. Then only can you help Us.

You have come out of it well, though the entire preparation is not over. The part that has been done is done well and successfully. We are sorry for the pain, long drawn out, which must have seemed to you apparently endless, but there is a great glory awaiting each one of you. It has been like living continuously in a dark cell, but the sun outside is awaiting you.

My Blessing be with you.

Though We *shall* begin at a later date I do not want you to leave this place for Europe until after Wesak [the great occult festival of the full moon of May which fell that year on May 18], when you shall all see Me. Though We have guarded the three places in your body there is sure to be pain. It is like an operation; though it may be over you are bound to feel the effects afterwards.

You may go for your long expected holidays but
be wise in your freedom. Do not go for a while yet.
During your stay here, before you sail, both of you
must prepare your bodies. Though it has been somewhat neglected you must now turn your thoughts
completely in that direction. Plenty of food, plenty of
open air and exercise should be sufficient. Do not go
into crowded places unnecessarily, and keep in the
open air as often as you can. Do not do all this immediately but go slowly and gently, or you might
break the body which has been under a tremendous
strain. It must be treated with great care.

The body cannot be relaxed properly until it gets a
little time with its supposed mother. If it has an opportunity let it see her.

Though We may not be so consciously with you
remember that you have had the tremendous privilege
of many visitations from Us. Though Krishna had occasional doubts and misgivings We were always
watching. Do not worry about that side for We are
always with you.

For the next months be happy in the knowledge
that you have seen Him, Who gives happiness to all
things, to Us and to you. [This was the reference to
the Buddha's presence.]

These messages may not have been in the style of either
of the Masters, as Leadbeater said, but they were not in
K's style either.

It turned out that Dr. Rocke had been sent specially by
Leadbeater who wanted a report on K's general physical
condition from "a sane person." "We were awfully glad to
see her," K told Lady Emily, "as we also wanted a confirmation that we are not entirely mad. . . . She was tremendously struck by the whole thing & we are not entirely
mad."

Unfortunately there is no other record than this of Dr.
Rocke's opinion of what was going on. She was the only
medical practitioner ever to witness K's "process." K himself never really seemed to doubt that the pain was a
necessary part of the preparation of his body. He never
considered consulting a doctor or so much as taking an as-
pirin. The opinion of a psychiatrist or of an orthodox doctor would, of course, be interesting if not illuminating. The

chances are, though, that nothing would have happened if a strange doctor had been in the house, whereas Dr. Rocke was not only an old friend but an Initiate. Such was the sensitivity of K's body that the physical elemental had been aware, it may be remembered, of another presence in the house of Ehrwald when Ruth had stayed the night there. It is hardly conceivable, therefore, that the process would have gone on with the vibrations of a stranger anywhere close enough to K to be able to observe him, let alone examine him.

22

Teaching at Pergine

Lady Emily and Mary had spent the winter in India where they had had the joy of occupying K's own room at Adyar for several weeks, and were returning to England with Edwin Lutyens and Mrs. Besant in the second week in May. K wanted to be there to meet them—he had not seen Mrs. Besant since June 1922 when she left Sydney—but as he would not have dreamed of disobeying the Master's orders not to leave Ojai until after Wesak, and as Nitya then had to have a few more Abrams treatments in Hollywood, they did not arrive at Plymouth until June 15. Rajagopal, and Helen whom they met in New York, travelled with them, while Rosalind and Koos van de Leeuw went to Sydney to be "brought on" by Leadbeater.

K very much hoped, as he had told Lady Emily more than once, that they might all spend the summer holidays together again, and the possibility of going to Italy had been mentioned. He begged her to talk it over with Mrs. Besant before he arrived and see what could be arranged.

Once in England K and Nitya were immediately caught up in the whirlpool of Mrs. Besant's activities; they accompanied her on her lecture tour of provincial towns, and then, in July, on a flying visit to Paris (it was the first time that any of them had been in an airplane); then back to London for a T.S. and Star Convention, culminating on July 23 in a massive meeting at the Queen's Hall to celebrate Mrs. Besant's fifty years of public work, attended by all her old friends and co-workers as well as her large following in Theosophy.

On August 4 the brothers went with Mrs. Besant, by air again, to Hamburg and then flew on to Holland for a T.S. Congress at Arnhem. This was immediately followed by the third international Star Congress, also at Arnhem, and then the first Star Camp at Ommen, a mile from Castle Eerde on part of the land made over to the Star by

Philip van Pallandt. This first Ommen Camp, which lasted two days, was very small; only about five hundred members attended it, all sleeping under canvas, seven to a tent, in very primitive conditions, with nowhere to wash except in a small river. Mrs. Besant returned to India directly after the Arnhem Congress so she was not present at the first Ommen Camp, but George Arundale and his wife were there. The Camp was held in a large clearing surrounded by pine-woods. On both evenings a bonfire was lit just as it grew dark. Everyone gathered round the fire while K talked; then afterwards he, Nitya and Rajagopal chanted in Sanskrit some of the songs of Sri Krishna.

K's emphasis this year in his talks was on the need to *feel*: an intellectual conception merely of a divine Teacher was not enough for those striving to attain the Path of Discipleship; passionate feeling was essential, a burning energy which he could only compare with falling in love. It was this power to fall in love, to give oneself completely, that he found so lacking, particularly in older people.

Lady Emily, in accordance with his wishes, had arranged that after the Camp certain friends should go away with him again for a holiday. The Kirbys had found accommodation for them in an eleventh-century Castle-hotel on top of a steep hill above the village of Pergine, about ten miles from Trento. Mar de Manziarly and Isabelle Mallet could not be of the party this year although K had invited them, but all the others from the Ehrwald holiday were there—Lady Emily, Betty, Mary, Helen, Ruth, Rajagopal, Cordes and the Patwardhans. In addition there were two other Indians—N. S. Rama Rao[1] and a gentle doctor, Sivakamu, the eldest sister of George Arundale's wife Rukmini. They arrived at Pergine on August 18, the Kirbys joining them at the end of the month.

The Hotel Castello was most beautifully situated with views of snow-capped mountains and terraces of vines immediately below. K, Nitya, Lady Emily, Helen and Rajagopal occupied a square tower, quite separate from the

---

[1] Rama Rao (no relation to Shiva Rao) had, like Jadu, been at Cambridge where he had taken a degree in science. As a boy he had run away from his home in Mysore to Benares, longing to be educated at the Central Hindu College. George Arundale had given him a scholarship and he had become one of George's brightest pupils. He too had been at Varengeville in 1913.

main body of the hotel, at one corner of the old battle-
ments; the other members of the party were scattered in
other parts of the Castle where they all had meals together
in the vast dining-hall, screened off from the other guests
and with their own vegetarian Austrian cook engaged by
Cordes.[1]

They all went into K's tower at eight every morning for
half an hour's meditation before breakfast; K would then
read aloud to them a passage from *The Gospel According
to Buddha,* after which he, Nitya and Rama Rao would
join in singing a mantram. Later in the morning they
would walk down through the vineyards to a flat field for
the inevitable games of rounders or volley-ball.

They were all there for a definite purpose that summer—to be helped along the Path of Discipleship. The
Manor at Sydney, presided over by Leadbeater, was recognized as the greatest of occult forcing-houses, and Lady
Emily, Betty, Mary, Helen and Ruth were all hoping to go
to Sydney as soon as possible in accordance with K's ear-
nest wish. Lady Emily had written to Dr. Rocke, the only
person close to Leadbeater whom she knew in Sydney, to
ask whether he would approve of her going there with the
four girls. On August 30 Dr. Rocke replied, giving Leadbeater's consent to the plan. It was agreed, therefore, that
Lady Emily and the four girls should travel out to India
with K and Nitya in November and then go on to Sydney
after some weeks at Adyar.

Now that they were definitely going to Sydney, Lady
Emily begged K to try to prepare them for this great opportunity, so instead of playing games all the morning K
began to talk to them of the purpose for which they were
gathered there. "He was very shy at first," Mary recalls,
"and so were we, but this soon wore off and he talked
more and more openly." He would sit under an apple tree
at the edge of the field a little apart from the others, his
knees hunched up to his chin, his fingers playing in the
long grass at his feet. Nitya also talked to them occasionally; he felt he might be able to help because at one time
he had been "drawn away from all these things" but had
found his "way back again."

---

[1] The Castle is still a hotel but a very much more luxurious one.
The square tower is now an annex with separate numbered rooms,
one on each floor, whereas in 1924 it had been like a small house.

Lady Emily and Mary both noted in their diaries some of the things K said in these talks: the qualities they all needed to acquire for discipleship were unselfishness, love and sympathy; they must all take a leap into the dark; they must live dangerously; they should feel so acutely that they would be able to jump out of the window; they must change radically: it was "so easy" and "such fun" to change. He told the girls that it was only human nature for them to want marriage, companionship and a home of their own, but they could not have those things *and* serve the Master too; they had to make their choice; they could not try and play at both lives; that way they would only become bourgeois; anything was better than being mediocre; but they must not destroy emotion and become hard; to grow by love and radiant happiness was the only way to grow. He defined true devotion as the power to respond instantly.

As well as the morning talks K now began to have private conversations with some of the girls in Lady Emily's room in the afternoons. Mary has published an account of some of the talks she had with him which she recorded at the time in her diary. Her last entry was:

> I have had more wonderful talks with Krishna—in one of which he made me weep—urging on me the need for immediate effort in case the vision of the mountain top should fade away ... he finished by saying that no one would ever love me so much as he does—that none of us know what real love, real devotion, is, that he wanted to see me great, happy and beautiful. He was moved so greatly at times by his own exertions and desire to help that he cried.

No doubt K talked to the other *gopis* (as the girls called themselves) in much the same strain, making each of them feel that her advancement was the only thing that mattered to him, just as Sri Krishna, eternally young and eternally wise, had multiplied himself to dance with all the *gopis* (the milkmaids) at the same time in the Forest of Brindaban. Betty Lutyens in her autobiography maintains that these private talks with K destroyed her self-confidence for years, but then she makes no secret of the fact that she had always been jealous of her mother's love for him. Certainly he often reduced them all to tears, including Lady Emily, by the unpalatable home truths he told them about their appearance, behavior and character. It seemed to Mary, though, that these criticisms were necessary, however unpleasant, if they genuinely wished to change themselves radically as they assured him they did, but no doubt he sugared the pills more for Mary who had been a pet of his ever since she was three years old.

K found them all dreadfully unresponsive. On September 13 he told Lady Emily it was like talking to a lot of sponges who just sucked it all in; he wished he could "bruise them" more. The next day he said he felt desperate because there was so little change in any of them and he wondered whether he was the right person to help them. "You are like people in a dark room waiting for someone to turn on the light for you instead of groping in the dark and turning it on for yourselves." Lady Emily reminded him of what St. Paul had said: "My little children for whom I travail in pain till Christ is born in you," to which he retorted, "You bet I have the pains right enough!"

He might well say this because his "process" had started again on August 21 and was more agonizing than ever although this had not seemed possible at Ojai. Nitya wrote to Mar de Manziarly on September 14 that the process had been a greater strain for the past three weeks than he could ever remember.

Instructions were given through K on September 4 that his room must be closed by 3 p.m. and that no one must touch him after that hour and that everything and everyone must be exceptionally clean; nor must he eat before his ordeal. At 6 p.m. he would have his bath and put on Indian dress and go into his "torture chamber" as Lady Emily called it. Only Nitya was allowed to go in with him. Lady Emily, Helen and Rajagopal, having had an early supper, usually spent the hour while the process was going on sitting on the stairs outside his door. After his ordeal they would sit with him in his room while he had his supper.

On the evening of the 24th, Lady Emily recorded that K had a presentiment that it was going to be an "exciting night," and sure enough the Lord Maitreya came and remained with K for a long time and left a message for the whole party. This message was read aloud to them by Nitya the next morning:

Learn to serve Me, for along that path alone will you
    find me

Forget yourself, for then only am I to be found

Do not look for the Great Ones when they may be very
    near you

You are like the blind man who seeks sunshine

You are like the hungry man who is offered food and
    will not eat

The happiness you seek is not far off; it lies in every
    common stone

I am there if you will only see. I am the Helper if you
    will let Me help.

These could well have been K's own words; they were
very much in the vein of the poems he would soon be
writing. Or it could, of course, be argued that it was the
Lord Maitreya who was to inspire K's poems. At any rate
this message was very different in style from the other
messages that had been brought through.

The process stopped after September 24 and for the last
three evenings of their stay at Pergine K had dinner with
the rest of the party in the hotel. He relaxed completely,
sang comic songs and told rather vulgar jokes at which he
laughed explosively. Lady Emily was deeply shocked at
such sacrilege after the wonderful evenings in the square
tower; K's sudden changes from the sublime to the ridiculous always disconcerted her. For the humbler members of
the party, however, who had not been privileged to be in
the square tower, it was a joy to have K and Nitya with
them on those evenings, playing the fool and enjoying
themselves.

23

"The Travelling Circus"

"The travelling circus," as Lady Emily called their party, left Pergine on Sunday, September 28, and travelled together as far as Milan. K and Nitya then went to Geneva where they had some trouble to sort out in connection with the Star, and from there to Holland to settle the final arrangements for the transfer of Eerde to the Trust. They arrived back in London on October 7 and stayed with Lady De La Warr at a house she had taken in London, 10 Buckingham Street, Westminister, as Miss Dodge had now given up Warwick House; then towards the end of October they went to Paris while Rajagopal returned to Cambridge for his final year before taking his degree in Law.

On the evening of October 28 Lady Emily joined them in Paris with Helen, Ruth, Betty and Mary, and they all went on together to Venice from where they were to sail for Bombay in a ship of the Lloyd Triestino Line which was cheaper than the P & O. Miss Dodge, with her usual generosity, was paying the return fares to Sydney for Lady Emily and the four girls. Had it not been for this, Edwin Lutyens might have been able to veto the plan, which he deplored, for Lady Emily could not have afforded it herself. On October 13 her second daughter, Ursula, who never came under the influence of Theosophy, had been married with the full panoply of St. Margaret's, Westminster, so her father must have been feeling particularly disinclined to send the rest of his family on an expensive jaunt to Australia, quite apart from his fears of Betty and Mary coming under the influence of Leadbeater. It is a mystery how Lady Emily managed to make all the arrangements for Ursula's wedding when she did not return from Pergine until the end of September, having been abroad since the begining of August.

Lady Emily wrote in her diary on October 28, "Off on the great adventure. Where will it lead?" It might well have led to disaster, for in spite of the warnings of Barbara Villiers's death from typhoid in Benares, Lady Emily seemed quite unmindful of the risk she was running in not having herself or the girls inoculated or vaccinated before departure. K did not hold with injecting poisons into the body (particularly now he knew of Dr. Abrams's opinion of vaccination) so she did not hold with it either. Perhaps her faith was as effective as any other protection against infections.

After four bitterly cold days sightseeing in Venice, where they stayed at the Luna Hotel, they embarked on November 2 on the *Pilsna*. Rama Rao and the Patwardhans joined them in Venice and travelled with them. The latter part of the voyage brought bliss to Mary. Now sixteen, she had been in love with Nitya ever since she could remember and had come quite close to him at Pergine. One evening in the Red Sea, leaning over the ship's rail together watching the sunset, he told her that he loved her. He said that he had first loved her eldest sister, Barbie, then Madame de Manziarly, then Rosalind ("When I first saw Rosalind something seemed to break inside me"). "And now there is you," he added. But Mary's happiness was to be as brief as the Eastern twilight: two days before they reached Bombay, when they met on deck to watch the sunset as had become their habit, Nitya told her that he had coughed up blood again that morning. This sudden hemorrhage came as a terrible shock to him as he had believed himself cured, and the worry was all the greater knowing that he was on his way to the damp heat of Adyar. He dreaded having to tell K.

They reached Bombay on November 18 where they were met by Mrs. Besant and a throng of Theosophists, including Raja, Shiva Rao and Ratansi with whom they all went to stay for a few days. K and Nitya immediately changed into Indian dress. Nitya had warned Mary that "things would be different" when once they arrived in India but she had not been prepared for quite such a sense of separation. There were so many people perpetually around him and K that there was no chance of a word alone with him the whole time they were in Bombay. She did not believe that he had as yet found the courage to tell K about his hemorrhage on board ship.

They arrived at Adyar on November 24. There the whole de Manziarly family, including Sacha, who had been in India since the end of October, were waiting to greet them. Lady Emily had rented what was called the Arundale House close to Headquarters and facing the river. (Miss Arundale, who had died in March of this year, had built the house in 1910). Helen, Ruth, Betty, Mary and Shiva Rao stayed there with Lady Emily, and K and Nitya had lunch and supper with them every day in the bare, tiled dining-room, sitting on the floor with banana leaves for plates. Naturally there was a Brahmin cook. After supper Lady Emily would read aloud to them, reading aloud being one of her greatest gifts.

Mrs. Besant was very kind to all the girls. She did not have much to say to them but when she saw them she would take their hands in both of her own and look at them with such smiling love that they would have died for her. She had a really extraordinary gift for inspiring devotion. Always wearing white saris in India she looked somehow right in them, unlike the other European women residents at Adyar who followed her example and looked ridiculous. Fortunately neither Lady Emily nor any of the *gopis* attempted to wear anything but Western clothes even though they adopted Indian hours and habits, such as sitting on the floor for meals, eating with their fingers and taking their shoes off before entering a room.

At seven each morning K held a meeting in his room, attended, among others, by all the *gopis*. He spoke in much the same way as at Pergine, but as there were about forty people at these meetings they were much more formal. Then in the cool of the evening a large party of young and not so young would play exciting games of volley-ball on the old tennis court.

It was generally known by this time that Nitya was ill again. He was running a temperature and did not attend the morning meetings or join in the games; sometimes he felt too ill even to go to Lady Emily's house for supper. (Black evenings, these, for Mary.) Nevertheless, he went for a fortnight in the middle of December with Mrs. Besant and K to a Theosophical Convention in Bombay which certainly did his health no good. K gave a public talk there on "The Citizen as a Divine Agent."

Meanwhile Ruth and Helen had gone on ahead to Sydney on December 11. K had written to Leadbeater on the day of their departure, before going to Bombay:

We are all, once again, back in dear old Adyar,
and there is no place like it in the world. Even California doesn't come up to the magnificent level of
Adyar. All that I wish is that you were here as of old
but I greatly hope that you will come for the great
Convention of 1925 at Adyar [the fiftieth anniversary
of the founding of the T.S.]. . . .

I am glad that Ruth is going back to you; I think
you will find her greatly changed and I hope for the
better. Of course you will be able to help her better
than any one of us and I am more than happy that
she is going.

With regard to Helen. I have been urging and con-
triving to facilitate her going to you. That has been
my dream, ever since I met her and I have been trying to prepare her to take full advantage of her being
with you. I think she is somebody and will be of use
later and for that I have done everything to make it
possible for her to go. I pray that she will fit in and it
is in her own hands and in the laps of God and in
yours.

Lady Emily and her daughters are coming in
March.

My process is slowly beginning and it is rather
painful. The back of my head and the base of my
spine are active once again and when I think or write,
it is almost unbearable. The moment I lie down, it's
very painful and when I wake up in the morning, I
feel as though it had been going on all the night. It is
altogether very curious and I don't understand it in
the least. . . . I have an intense desire to see you and I
wonder when it will be fulfilled.

His desire was to be fulfilled much sooner than he expected. He and Nitya had been invited to attend the T.S.
Convention in Sydney in April, and when John Mackay,
their host of 1922, offered to pay their fares they decided
to go at the same time as Lady Emily if Nitya were well
enough.

On January 9, 1925, Lady Emily with Betty and Mary
went to Delhi to join her husband. Soon afterwards Nitya
became so ill that it was proposed he should go up to the
hill station of Ootacamund for a few weeks and then return to Ojai via Sydney for another course of Abrams

treatment. Mrs. Besant, who was in Delhi staying with the
Lutyens's, approved this plan, so on January 23 Nitya
went up to "Ooty" with Madame de Manziarly, Yo and
Rama Rao. They stayed at a house there called Gulistan
("Place of Flowers") where Mrs. Besant had lived during
her internment in 1917. Built by Colonel Olcott in 1890, it
was the summer home of the President of the T.S., but
Mrs. Besant hardly ever used it.

After informing Mrs. Besant of Nitya's departure, K
went on to tell her about his own pain which was "getting
worse and worse."

> I suppose it will stop some day but at present it is
> rather awful. I can't do any work etc. It goes on all
> day & all night now. Also when Helen was here, I
> was able to relax & now I can't. I feel as though I
> want to cry my heart out but what is the good. I wish
> Helen were here. I had a letter from her from Sydney
> & C.W.L. seems to have welcomed her, talked to her
> and been very nice. So I am very glad.

A few days before writing this he had been to Madanapalle, his birthplace, looking for a suitable site for a
university which it was one of his most cherished dreams
to found in India. He had discovered a lovely place in the
Tettu Valley, about ten miles from the town and 2,500 feet
above sea level, and hoped to be able to acquire 1,000
acres there.[1]

How worried he had been about Nitya is shown by a
letter he wrote to Mrs. Besant on February 10, recounting
a dream he had had:

> I remember going to the Master's house and asking
> & begging to let Nitya get well & let him live. The
> Master said that I was to see the Lord Maitreya and I
> went there and I implored there but I got the im-
> pression that it was not His business & that I should

[1] The plan did not materialize until the following year and then
he was able to buy only about 300 acres. A school was founded
there, not a university, and the valley was renamed Rishi Valley
because it was dominated by the Rishikonda mountain. The Rishi
Valley Trust was formed on the same lines as the Eerde Trust with
K as one of the trustees. The school, based on his ideas of education, still flourishes and he stays there for some weeks whenever
he is in India, talking to the students and teachers.

go to the Mahachohan [see p. 39]. I went there. I
remember all this so clearly. He was seated in His
chair, with great dignity & magnificent understanding,
with grave & kindly eyes. My futile description is so
absurd but it's impossible to convey, the great impression of it all. I told Him that I would sacrifice my
happiness or anything that was required to let Nitya
live, for I felt this thing was being decided. He listened to me & answered 'He will be well.' It was such
a relief and all my anxiety has completely disappeared.

Nitya did recover somewhat at "Ooty," though on February 19 he was writing to Mary who, with Lady Emily
and Betty, had just returned to Adyar from Delhi:

I've been in bed for four weeks and my bones are
wearing through my skin. The number of times I
walk to the precipice of death, look over and walk
back again! It is becoming a habit with me. When I
really do die at the mature age of 90 or so, I shall by
force of habit continue to live ... it's been the worst
four weeks I have ever spent. To feel ill, feeble and a
failure is a horrible combination. [He gave Mary
some comfort by adding] whatever you do or don't
do I shall always love you.

He returned to Adyar on March 11, and two days
later he and K with Raja, Rama Rao, Lady Emily, Betty
and Mary left for Sydney, while the de Manziarlys remained in India, with the exception of Sacha who had
gone to take up a job in Pekin. It was a sudden decision
on Raja's part to go with them to Sydney to share in the
responsibility of looking after Nitya, and one that greatly
relieved K who was dreading the journey. Nitya was looking terribly thin and ill; the bad crossing to Ceylon exhausted him and he had to lean heavily on Raja's arm as
they queued for passport inspection when embarking at
Colombo on the *Ormuz*. He left his cabin on the voyage
only to lie on deck. Mary was not allowed to go near him.
It had been decided that he must go on to Ojai as soon as
possible, and that Rosalind, who was still in Sydney where
she had gone when the brothers left for England the year
before, should be asked to go with them to look after him.

Mary, who was so jealous when she heard this a few days after sailing that she wanted to kill herself, was told by K, characteristically, not to be "a damned fool." He could not tolerate pettiness, and what could be more petty than jealousy, especially where Nitya's wellbeing was concerned? K claims never to have suffered from jealousy in his life. It could be said that he has never had cause for it, yet it is hard to imagine his allowing any feeling so inconsistent with nobility and greatness, so utterly mediocre and contemptible, to dwell in him for more than an instant.

In Fremantle, Perth, Adelaide and Melbourne, Star meetings were held at which K, Raja and Lady Emily spoke. At all these places plots of land, on which buildings could be erected for the work of the World Teacher, were presented to K. These Star Lands, as they were called, were being dedicated to him not only in Victoria but in New South Wales, Queensland and Tasmania. As usual he requested that the land should be held by Trusts. In Sydney itself a great white amphitheatre to seat 2,500 people in twenty-six tiers had been built—an inspiration of Dr. Rocke's. It was on a truly magnificent site, on the edge of the rocky coast overlooking the harbor at Balmoral. Dr. Rocke herself had made a generous contribution to the cost, though the bulk of the estimated £13,500 for its construction and the land had been raised by selling Founders' seats—£10 for seats at the top and £100 for those near the arena. The first sod had been turned by Leadbeater in June 1923 and it was finished in good time for K to speak there during the Convention which opened soon after his arrival in Sydney.

Fears for Nitya

The party reached Sydney on April 3, and were met by
Leadbeater and his whole entourage, including Dick
Clarke who was now in constant attendance on him. Leadbeater "came prancing down the wharf like a great lion,"
as Mary described it, "hatless and in a long purple cloak,
holding on to the arm of a very good-looking blond boy of
about fifteen." This was Theodore St. John, an Australian
boy of great charm and sweetness, who was Leadbeater's
current favorite and who slept in his room. It would have
been difficult not to notice Leadbeater in a crowd, for
apart from his dress and snow-white hair he was very tall
and had a long white beard. He "had the merriest of twin-
kling blue eyes, a joking manner and a very loud though
pleasant voice and an air of sparkling health, as if every
faculty, mental and physical, was kept in perfect working
order for immediate use." Under his cloak he wore a red
cassock with a large amethyst cross round his neck and on
the third finger of his right hand a huge amethyst ring. He
was now seventy-eight but seemed very much younger,
giving the impression by his enormous vitality that there
was "nothing he would not do or dare." His only unpleasant feature was a pair of very long yellow eye-teeth
that inevitably brought vampires to mind.

K and Nitya were immediately whisked off by Mr.
Mackay and Rosalind to the former's house, Myola, David
Street, in Mosman, a suburb of Sydney, close to The
Manor where Leadbeater had lived with his community
since 1922. The Manor was a hideous great house in a
beautiful position overlooking the harbor, where some
fifty people of all ages and nationalities endeavored to
live in harmony, eating in a communal dining-room over-
looked from a dais by Leadbeater who, although allowing
muted conversation, would wince at the dropping of a
knife or the scraping of a chair.

Lady Emily and her daughters were privileged to be given a room on the ground-floor next to Leadbeater's own. The only people they knew there, apart from Dick Clarke, were Dr. Rocke, Helen, Ruth, Ruth's mother, Mrs. Roberts, and Koos van de Leeuw who was now a priest in the Liberal Catholic Church and in charge of the community's finances. Leadbeater formed a special little group of Theodore St. John, Lady Emily, Betty, Mary, Ruth and Helen whom he invited into his room every evening, where he would talk to them about the Masters with a most infectious conviction of their reality. The atmosphere was not at all holy; he would relate anecdotes of the Masters in a matter-of-fact way as if they were close neighbors. He had a large cat to which he always courteously offered the best chair; it was said to be in its last animal incarnation, and indeed so human was it that when one evening it wandered into Lady Emily's room just as she was going to bed she was too shy to undress in front of it.

On a walk, Leadbeater's conversation was at its most fascinating. He would comment on everything he saw clairvoyantly around him, such as the *devas,* or nature spirits, who could not bear vulgar human lovers or the smell of alcohol or tobacco but who crowded round The Manor people because they did not smoke or drink or eat meat and were "united by a real affection." One day Leadbeater pointed out a large rock in Taronga Park which had once fallen in love with one of The Manor boys; when the boy sat on it all the life in the rock gathered into that part on which the boy was sitting. To be loved by rocks and nature spirits was not perhaps a substitute for human love but it seemed very enviable to Mary.

Two days before the Theosophical Convention opened on April 9 Nitya had been to see a specialist who diagnosed cavities at the apex and base of his left lung, said that his right lung was also affected and that he would need all his strength to pull through; he must leave Sydney immediately. Dr. Rocke at once went up to Leura in the Blue Mountains, 3,000 feet above sea level, and found a five-roomed furnished house for him, a kind of superior log cabin. Directly after the Convention he moved up there with K, Rosalind, Rama Rao and Mrs. Roberts as chaperone and housekeeper. As it was only about an hour by train from Sydney, K was able to go backwards and forwards. Almost immediately Nitya's temperature went down in the comparatively cold dry air, but he was told that he must stay in the mountains until he was well enough to travel to California. As Raja was committed to returning to India, K cabled to Dr. John Ingleman in Hollywood to come and help look after Nitya on the voyage. (Ingleman arrived in Sydney on May 5.) K was certain that Nitya would get well; he wrote to Mrs. Besant on May 3, "There is no longer that sick man feeling about him; he's much more cheerful and what's excellent he feels he's getting better."

This was a restless and boring time for K who was now virtually commuting between the Mackays at Myola and "Nilgiri," as they called the house at Leura which Mr. Mackay had now bought. Although it had been K's own wish, his "dream," that the *gopis* should go to Sydney, he could not resist making fun of them now that he saw them there. Life at The Manor was geared to the Liberal Catholic Church and Co-Masonry.[1] Mass was celebrated by Koos van de Leeuw every morning before breakfast in a private chapel, and there was Benediction every evening, while on Sundays there were two services at the L.C.C. church, St. Alban's in Regent Street, at which Leadbeater officiated and which all The Manor people were expected to attend. Non-attendance would certainly have impeded their occult progress. The church was so alien to K's nature that although he tried to be respectful and uncritical, all his instincts rebelled against it. He longed for Nitya to get well so that they could be off to Ojai.

Mary felt that K was as much out of place in that mediocre community as a gazelle in a flock of sheep, whereas Leadbeater was as much at home there as a happy shepherd. All the same, she thought it was unfair of K to mock their efforts to conform, for, after all, it was he who had urged them to go to Sydney, impressing on them

---

[1] Another offshoot of Theosophy. In 1879 several Masonic Chapters under the Supreme Council of France had revolted. One separated Lodge, *Les Libres Penseurs*, admitted a woman in 1881, Mlle Marie Desraimes. Twelve years later, in collaboration with Georges Martin, she formed a Lodge, *Le Droit Humain*, to which sixteen women were admitted. Miss Francesca Arundale was the first Englishwoman to be initiated in 1902. She aroused Mrs. Besant's interest in the movement and the latter was initiated in Paris that same year. Mrs. Besant founded Lodges in Benares and London, and in 1910 built a Masonic temple at Adyar.

over and over again what a marvellous opportunity it was,
and if they did not fall in with the ways of The Manor
what was the point of their being there? She remembered
one occasion particularly well: all the young people at The
Manor were sitting in a circle during a regular weekly
meeting, with closed eyes, holding hands and meditating
on their unity, when she suddenly opened her eyes to find
K grinning and winking at her through the window. It was
almost more than she could bear. What a contrast to Pergine, with Nitya apparently cured and K sitting under the
apple tree talking to them, and yet everything he had said
in those happy days had been directed towards this unique
opportunity of going to Leadbeater to be "brought on."

Mary would not have been so unhappy in Sydney if she
had had anything definite to do—Betty at least was able to
play the organ in church and go swimming, which terrified
Mary because of the danger of sharks—but apart from the
evening meetings in Leadbeater's room and an occasional
walk with him there was nothing to do but try to teach
herself shorthand and typing. Mrs. Besant, a great believer
in higher education for women, had been shocked, when
she had seen Mary in India in 1923, that she had been
taken away from school at fifteen and had made out a list
of books for her to study. Leadbeater had no such feelings
about education; any kind of individual work was looked
upon by him as a deplorable self-indulgence. Shorthand
and typing only were permissible for they might be used in
the service of the Masters.

Leadbeater had a way of appearing unexpectedly on the
veranda which ran round the house, ready to go for a
walk, and anyone who happened to be there might be invited to go with him. To miss such an opportunity was
considered detrimental to spiritual progress; therefore most
of the young people hung about on the veranda all day in
the hope he would emerge from his room. Betty had made
great friends with Theodore St. John, who was also Ruth's
best friend, and so close was he to Leadbeater that to go
swimming with him was as good as going for a walk with
Leadbeater himself. Theodore played the violin, so he and
Betty and Helen could also have musical sessions together.

Leadbeater must have found K a very disturbing influence and it was quite apparent to everyone that his visits
to The Manor were not welcome. Nevertheless, Leadbeater
wrote about him to Mrs. Besant on April 21, "He cer-

tainly is a wonderful and beautiful person and seems much changed in many ways since he was here three years ago—as is after all only natural, considering what he has passed through."

K had been longing to talk to Leadbeater about his process and they did have several private talks, but it is doubtful whether Leadbeater was able to help much; indeed he seemed reluctant to discuss it at all. He told Lady Emily that it was quite outside the range of his experience and certainly not a necessary part of the preparation for Initiations: "It seemed to be the forcing of the spirillae in each atom." When pressed for an explanation of this he would say no more than that men of the fifth root-race had only a certain number of spirillae functioning in each atom of the brain; in order to prepare K's body for the Lord Maitreya, additional spirillae had to be opened—spirillae that would be present in men of the sixth root-race. Awakening sixth root-race spirallae in a fifth root-race body must inevitably be a very painful process.[1]

Leadbeater did not like being out of his depth. At The Manor, where he was thoroughly in his element, all the activities were directed towards the taking of occult steps along the Path. These steps were more likely to occur at the great occult festivals, especially that of Wesak—the full moon of May—which in Sydney in 1925 was at 1:43 a.m. on May 8. For weeks beforehand The Manor was throbbing with excitement and expectancy as the members of the community frantically worked on themselves to develop those qualities considered necessary for discipleship with all the intensity of cramming for a vital examination. The results were not put up on a notice board but they soon filtered through and gave rise to a great deal of mortification, snobbery and spiritual pride. The only important question asked of anyone at The Manor was, "How far on are you?" Leadbeater made out lists beforehand of pos-

[1] According to Mrs. Besant's and Leadbeater's clairvoyant investigations into the structure of matter, the Anu was the "ultimate atom" out of which all physical things were composed. The life force flowed through the Anu. Seven spirillae were present in each Anu, only four of which were normally active. There were 1,600 coils or spirals in each spirilla. The spirillae in an individual could be forced by Yoga practice. (*Occult Chemistry* by Annie Besant and C. W. Leadbeater, Theosophical Publishing House, Adyar, 1908.)

sible advancements, while Theodore St. John gave hints to
his special friends as to what they might expect. Two days
before Wesak K was able to write to Mrs. Besant to tell
her of some of the steps that were to be taken.

Altogether there were seventy advancements in all parts
of the world at Wesak, even more than Leadbeater had
anticipated. Lady Emily, Ruth, Ruspoli, Mrs. Kirby and
Shiva Rao all took the first Initiation; Helen was accepted
and Betty and Mary put on probation. Rosalind had
already been accepted and Rama Rao was already an
Initiate. The de Manziarlys, Isabelle Mallet, Harold Baillie-
Weaver, Cordes and the Blechs must also have taken some
step or other because K wrote to Mrs. Besant to say how
happy he was for them. Yet in spite of this letter he was
in truth extremely irritated by the absorption of everyone
at The Manor in his or her spiritual progress. On May 25
(still thought to be his birthday, his thirtieth) he dined at
The Manor and spoke afterwards to the community "most
beautifully," according to Lady Emily's diary, and looked
"wonderfully beautiful" too. He spoke of the importance
of "what you *are* and not of any labels"—a most necessary thing to impress on The Manor people who were
chiefly concerned with their spiritual tags. (He had written
in his editorial notes for the January *Herald*, "Merely putting on a badge or calling oneself a member of the Star is
like having in your possession a checkbook without a
banking account.")

It struck Mary as strange that K, who was to play the
leading role in the great drama for which they were all re-
hearsing, should be so aloof from it all. She felt he was
like a beautiful rose growing in some lovely garden while
everyone else at The Manor was a paper imitation manu-
factured inside stuffy rooms by hands practiced to turn out
such shoddy counterfeits by the dozen. No doubt, when
urging Helen and the other *gopis* to go to Sydney, K had
been remembering the Leadbeater of the old Adyar days,
training a handful of exceptional pupils, or even the Leadbeater of three years before with only ten pupils round
him; he had not realized until this visit what a factory it
had all become.

K had little chance while he was in Sydney of seeing
any of his friends alone, although Helen went up once to
Leura when he was there. It is possible, though, that he
did not feel quite so much in tune with her now, for she

and Ruth had become deeply entrenched in The Manor
way of life before he arrived. Perhaps he felt closer to
Mary, knowing her to be miserable and as anxious as he
was about Nitya. One evening, when Mary returned to the
room she shared with her mother and Betty after a meeting in Leadbeater's room, she found K fast asleep on her
bed. She had never seen anything so beautiful as his sleeping face; she felt her bed had been blessed. "Why is he
always so delicious?" she wrote in her diary. "He makes
me feel more unselfish than anyone. I wish I could love
everyone as purely as I love him."

He was beginning to look tired and worn. For the first
time he was doubtful of Nitya's chances of survival.

Lady Emily planned to return to India with Raja on
June 7, leaving Betty and Mary at The Manor, and then
to travel back to England with Mrs. Besant in time for the
birth of Ursula's first baby. She had a great struggle with
her conscience when K asked her to go with him to Ojai
as soon as Nitya was well enought to travel. She consulted
Leadbeater, hoping that he would see it as her first duty to
go with K, but to her intense disappointment he ruled
unhesitatingly that she should return to England as
planned because Mrs. Besant and Ursula needed her more
than K did. So reluctantly she went off. She hoped to see
K again in England in the autumn but would not be
seeing Betty and Mary until December when they would
all join up at Adyar for the Golden Jubilee Convention of
the T.S., which Leadbeater and most of his community
would be attending.

The specialist, having been up to Leura to see Nitya,
pronounced that he would be fit to travel by the middle of
June. Krishna had been worried that if Rosalind went with
them she might miss some chance of occult advancement.
Leadbeater reassured him, according to Lady Emily's diary: "The next step [Initiation] is anyhow a very big
one—but remember if she goes with you and helps Nitya
she will also be serving Them." This seemed to Mary a
most unfairly easy way of serving "Them." Mary had met
Rosalind once when she had come down to The Manor
for the night, and Rosalind had been so sweet to her, perhaps at Nitya's instigation, that her jealousy had melted;
nevertheless, in nursing Nitya, Rosalind was doing the
only thing in the world that Mary really wanted to do herself.

On June 24 Nitya and K, Rosalind, Rama Rao and Dr. Ingleman embarked on the *Sierra* for San Francisco. Mary was allowed to see Nitya for five minutes alone in his cabin, the first time she had spoken to him since she had left Adyar for Delhi in January. He had grown a full black beard while he was at Leura which hid his look of ill health. This was just as well since they were afraid of his being turned back by the authorities at San Francisco.

K wrote to Mrs. Besant from Hawaii on July 11:

This fearful voyage is coming to its end. We reach San Francisco on the 14th and Ojai on the 15th. We have had a greater anxiety on this voyage than ever before. When we came down from the mountains two days before we sailed, Nitya's temperature, owing to all the excitement, went up very high and it kept up, with slight variance, till about a week ago. This high fever had reduced him nearly to complete exhaustion and he used to cry after his bath as it tired him. A week ago we had a kind of crisis. His heart began to beat very feebly and began to grow weaker and weaker and his feet got colder. He felt as though he was slipping away; he feebly asked Rosalind, who was with him, and we all take turns to be with him, to hold on to his feet. She clung to them and thought of the Master. In about five minutes he recovered and since that day he's a different person. He has hardly any fever and as soon as we are at Ojai, we shall be thankful. He is fearfully thin and incredibly weak.

We will pull through and Nitya *will* be well once again. It has been and is a most anxious time, my own beloved mother, but you and the Masters are there.

As soon as K and Nitya arrived at Ojai they hired an Abrams machine and after only a fortnight of daily treatments K was able to assure Mrs. Besant and Leadbeater that Nitya was already much better.

25

The Self-appointed Apostles

In the meantime extraordinary things were taking place in Holland. George Arundale, after travelling round the world on a lecture tour with his young wife, Rukmini, had proceeded to Huizen, a few miles from Ommen and the center of the Liberal Catholic Church in Europe, presided over by Bishop Wedgwood. A modern house, De Duinen, in an estate with a beautiful garden, had just been made over to the work of the Church by Mrs. van Eegen-Boissenvain who had built a little chapel there, St. Michael's, for Wedgwood. Oscar Köllerström, a young Dutchman and a former pupil of Leadbeater's, who was now a priest in the Liberal Catholic Church, was also at Huizen at this time. When Mrs. Besant, accompanied by Lady Emily and Shiva Rao, arrived at Marseilles on July 17, she received a telegram from George announcing that Oscar had just taken his third initiation, Wedgwood his second and Rukmini, he believed, her first. Further important occult developments were expected at Huizen and he begged Mrs. Besant to come there immediately. She telegraphed back that she could not possibly go to Holland before the beginning of August as she had a commitment to give some lectures at the Queen's Hall in London.

Mrs. Besant and Shiva Rao stayed in London at Buckingham Street with Lady De La Warr; three days after their arrival they went round to Lady Emily and read aloud to her "a wonderful letter" Mrs. Besant had received from George all about the occult happenings at Huizen; *kundalini* had been awakened in Wedgwood and Rukmini (George and Oscar Köllerström were already clairvoyant) and there was a suggestion of a possible visit on the physical plane to the castle of the Master the Count, somewhere in Hungary. In this same letter George asked Mrs. Besant's permission to become a priest. Mrs. Besant was very disturbed by this last request and affirmed very strongly that such a step would destroy all his usefulness in India. Nevertheless, two days later, after another "even more wonderful" letter from George, Mrs. Besant postponed her Queen's Hall lectures and went to Huizen. Lady Emily, Shiva Rao, Rajagopal and Miss Bright went with her among others.

Next day, July 25, Mrs. Besant decided to reawaken her *kundalini*, but this, apparently, she was unable to do. On the 26th George was ordained; that night Miss Bright and Rajagopal took their second Initiations and next day Rajagopal was made a deacon. On the night of August 1 George and Wedgwood took their third Initiations and Rukmini her second. It was stated in a message from the Mahachohan that every advancement and Initiation must be confirmed by Leadbeater on the physical plane, but this order, it seemed, was not obeyed.

Lady Emily had to return to London for Ursula's confinement on July 19 but was back again at Huizen in time for George's consecration as a bishop on August 4. For the unusual procedure of becoming a bishop a little over a week after ordination Leadbeater's permission had been requested by cable. No reply had been received by the appointed day, but as George assured them all that Leadbeater had given his "cordial consent" on the astral plane, Wedgwood went ahead with the consecration ceremony. On returning from the chapel they found a cable from Leadbeater strongly disapproving of such a step. It struck Lady Emily that Mrs. Besant looked grave when she read the cable.

K meanwhile had asked Mrs. Besant if Rajagopal might be sent to Ojai to help look after Nitya, who was very ill again. She gave her consent and Rajagopal set off for America on August 5.

During those hectic days at Huizen many messages and instructions from the Masters were "brought through" by George: no Initiate was to share a room with a non-Initiate; silk underwear only was to be born by the priests; copes and gowns were to be carefully chosen but no hats worn. (This instruction about silk underwear was particularly hard on the poorer priests, and for once Miss Dodge struck when she was asked to buy vestments for the bishops.) Mrs. Besant, Wedgwood, George and Rukmini were told to give up eating eggs in any form. According to Lady Emily only Mrs. Besant adhered to this diet and in

consequence half starved herself from that time onwards
since she could not even eat a piece of cake.

The proposed visit to the Master the Count in his Hun-
garian castle was discussed at length. The importance of
such a meeting was vital, for if the Count could be visited
on the physical plane it would prove to the world beyond
all doubt the existence of the Masters. The actual locality
of the castle was a secret; George was astrally instructed
to open a Continental Bradshaw at random and conduct
the party to the place on which he happened to put his finger.

On the night of August 7, K (in Ojai), Raja (in India),
George and Wedgwood all took the fourth, or Arhat, Initiation. Leadbeater and Mrs. Besant were already Arhats.
George told Lady Emily that those who had taken this Ini-
ation were allowed to ask for a boon and that K had
asked for Nitya's life. On this same night Lady Emily and
Dr. Rocke (in Sydney) were consecrated by the Lord on
the astral plane to lead an Order of Women which he was
to found when he came. This particularly delighted Lady
Emily who had never been interested in clothes and who
now hoped she would soon be able to don an abbess's
habit.

It was also discovered that George and Wedgwood
are direct pupils of the Mahachohan [Lady Emily
noted in her diary on August 10]. Wedgwood is to be
Mahachohan of the 7th Root-Race with Amma [Mrs.
Besant as the Manu [see p. 39] and C.W.L. as the
Bodhisattva. For this reason the Mahachohan is gradually withdrawing his influence from Raja, who has
hitherto held this position in the triangle. George told
me that much help was needed for Raja, as he was
feeling much depressed in consequence of this new
appointment. George himself is to be Chief of Staff
of the 7th Race, and he told me this was his last incarnation, as henceforth he would be sent all over the
Universe and not attached to any one planet.

It may be remembered how depressed George had been in
1914 when he heard that Rajagopal was to usurp his place
on Mercury.

In the June *Herald* George had written an article an-

nouncing that K would not be attending the Ommen
Camp that year on account of Nitya's health, but he
hoped that far from Star members cancelling their reser-
vations, they would regard it as their special duty to be
present. Mrs. Besant would be there and so would he,
Arundale. Owing to this appeal there were not many
cancellations, and on August 10 the Huizen party moved
to Ommen where the Camp and Congress were opened
that afternoon. That night there was a tremendous thunderstorm and cyclone which destroyed towns and villages
on each side of Ommen, leaving the Camp miraculously
untouched. An omen at Ommen!

On the night of the 9th George had "brought through"
the names of ten of the twelve apostles whom the Lord
had chosen to work with him when he came; they were—
Mrs. Besant, Leadbeater, Raja, George, Wedgwood,
Rukmini, Nitya, Lady Emily, Rajagopal and Oscar
Köllerström. The other two were as yet undecided.

On the morning of the 11th, the day after the Camp
opened, Mrs. Besant, in the course of a very long speech,
publicly gave out the names of some of these apostles.
Talking about "Sir Krishnamurtin Christ" she told her
audience that the birth, the transfiguration, the crucifixion,
the resurrection and the ascension were the symbols of the
journey of the human spirit through the five great Initiations. She went on:

> His taking possession of His chosen vehicles is
> typified by the birth you read of in the Gospels, and
> that . . . will be soon. Then He will choose, as before,
> His twelve Apostles. . . . He has already chosen them,
> but I have only the command to mention seven who
> have reached the stage of Arhatship, which seems to
> be the occult status for the small circle of His imme-
> diate disciples. . . . The first two, my brother Charles
> Leadbeater and myself, passed that great Initiation
> . . . at the time I became President of the T.S. Our
> younger brothers here . . . have passed the four great
> Initiations. . . . They are . . . that disciple of beautiful
> character and beautiful language, C. Jinarajadasa. . . .
> My brother Leadbeater and myself were of course
> present on the astral plane at this Initiation, and also
> that of Krishnaji, and welcome the new additions to
> our band. Then my brother George Arundale, whose

consecration as Bishop was necessary, as the last step
of his preparation for the great fourth step of Initiation; and my brother Oscar Köllerström ... and
then one whom I have called my daughter, Rukmini
Arundale, this Indian girl of glorious past, will be one
in a few days. ... Young in body yet old in wisdom
and will-power; "child of the indomitable will" is her
welcome in the higher worlds.

Rukmini took her third and fourth Initiations on the
night of the 12th when Lady Emily and Shiva Rao took
their second, according to Lady Emily's diary. Mrs. Besant
only realized afterwards, when it was pointed out to her,
that she had left out Wedgwood, and in doing so had
given the impression that K was to be one of his own
apostles, for without Wedgwood she had mentioned only
six. She publicly rectified this mistake in another speech on
the 14th.

Continuing her talk of the 11th, she announced that a
World Religion was to be founded which would not be
destructive of other faiths, and a World University with its
three centers at Adyar, Sydney and Huizen. (The Huizen
estate comprised only forty acres whereas Eerde with its
5,000 acres was not mentioned at all.) She herself was to
be Rector of the World University, Arundale Principal
and Wedgwood Director of Studies.

The next morning Arundale, in a long speech, enlarged
on this new university: he had been commanded to establish it with as little delay as possible by his own great
Master, the Mahachohan. "We shall not seek for recog-
nition from without," he declared. "We shall not ask
someone to grant us a charter, so as to make our degrees
respectable and approved by the world ... the degrees that
are conferred in the name of the Master—those shall be
recognized by the world, as no degrees conferred by
human agency can ever be."

What a glorious new source of power these two institu-
tions would hold for George and Wedgwood; they would
be able to hand out degrees as well as Initiations, create
archbishops as well as bishops and devise for themselves
positions as mighty as Pope.

When Leadbeater heard from Mrs. Besant about all
these pronouncements he was "visibly distressed," according to Ernest Wood who happened to be with him in

Sydney at the time. He did not believe in any of it and
said to Wood, "Oh, I hope she does not wreck the Society."

The Camp broke up on the 14th and the party who had
been at Huizen before it opened returned there. George
kept saying excitedly all day, "I know something else has
happened but it seems impossible!" But the impossible had
happened, for the next morning Mrs. Besant called Lady
Emily, Esther Bright, Rukmini and Shiva Rao into her
room and told them very shyly that she, Leadbeater, K,
Raja, George, Wedgwood and Oscar had all taken their
fifth and final Initiation on the night of the 13th, but it
was to make no difference to the way they were to be
treated. (Rukmini later told Lady Emily that she had become an Adept—that is, taken the fifth Initiation—at the
same time as the others. She had taken three Initiations in
three days!) Lady Emily, with Miss Bright and Shiva Rao,
left for England that evening entrusted with a telegram to
send to Krishna: "Greetings from four brothers." It was
assumed that he would have known on the astral plane
about the passing of this fifth Initiation.

Lady Emily had written to K from Huizen to tell him
about everything that had occurred there and had received
a cable from him while she was in Camp asking whether
Leadbeater had confirmed all these happenings. She had
cabled back that Mrs. Besant herself was making the announcements, and added, "Put your trust in her." When
she arrived in London she found a letter from him awaiting her full of a most unhappy skepticism. Lady Emily
destroyed all his letters to her of this period at his request.
He was afraid that if they fell into anyone else's hands his
criticism of Mrs. Besant would be misunderstood.

On August 16 Mrs. Besant, George, Rukmini, Wedgwood and Oscar set off on the secret journey to the castle
in Hungary of the Master the Count. The next day Lady
Emily received a telegram from Amsterdam: "You are invited to accompany us. See Esther at once. Besant." Lady
Emily hurried to Wimbledon where Miss Bright told her
that they were to go to Innsbruck "as soon as the word
came" and there await further orders. Lady Emily obtained a visa for Hungary, cashed a large check and announced to her family that she was "going into retreat for
a while." She and Miss Bright waited and waited but no
further orders came. About a week later Mrs. Besant and

the others returned to Huizen. Shiva Rao went over there
to see Mrs. Besant who said to him, "You are the only
sensible person in this group." She made no reference to
their journey, though he gathered they had got no further
than Innsbruck.

It was not until September 12 that they all arrived in
London where Mrs. Besant was at last to give her Queen's
Hall lectures. Lady Emily met them at Liverpool Street
Station but not a word was said about the abortive journey. Mrs. Besant looked very stern and the whole party
"extremely woebegone." The next morning Mrs. Besant
merely told Lady Emily that the "black forces" had been
too strong for them. The story of what really happened on
that journey has never been told. The attempt to reach the
Count's castle cannot be blamed entirely on George Arundale, for, after all, Rukmini, Wedgwood and Oscar
Köllerström had all claimed to have developed psychic
powers by the awakening of their *kundalini*.

At the very time George was bringing through the
names of the apostles (August 10) Krishna was writing to
tell Mrs. Besant that Nitya had had a sudden hemorrhage and that for a few days they had been desperately
anxious. Nitya was so weak now that he could not move
out of bed at all and there had to be someone with him
night and day. Rosalind was there during the day while K
and Rama Rao shared the night watch. The happenings at
Huizen must have seemed very remote as well as disturbing; yet in a letter to Mrs. Besant of August 22 K managed to hide his true feelings in order not to hurt her:

> Lady Emily cables that great events have been tak-
> ing place at Holland and that many have been put on
> probation and that others have entered the Path and
> further steps by the others. I am so delighted and
> only wish I had been there—physically—to have
> witnessed it all. The most surprising thing is about
> George becoming a Bishop! I suppose it's alright
> his work in India will be interfered. Mother it cer-
> tainly is a curious world and our changes are rapid.
> How I wish I were with you and in your presence
> and for that I would forgo many things, even initi-
> ations.
> Nitya has had another hemorrhage, not the serious
> variety but we have had, so far, two within less than

a month. It has left him utterly exhausted and weak, so that I attend to his washing etc. in his bed. Poor Nitya he has suffered a lot and I sit often, for an hour or more, holding his heart or his hand. Suffering is good, as it certainly had made us strong and when we come out of it, we must be unscathed and greater. It's a most extraordinary thing all this—so long, but I suppose we must get through it. We still can laugh, thank God.

It will be a tremendous relief having Rajagopal here. He will be here in two days. How I wish I could see you for I love you with all my heart and soul. You are my most beloved mother.

It will be noted that, apart from writing that he would forgo Initiations in order to be with her, K made no mention of the Initiations he was said to have taken himself or of the Apostles, although by this time he had heard all about them from Lady Emily. He was in a terrible position, not believing in the things that were said to have taken place at Huizen yet unable to repudiate them without repudiating Mrs. Besant herself who was publicly proclaiming them. In the circumstances it must have been an extremely difficult letter to write. Did he take long to compose it, one wonders, or did his sensitivity and love for Mrs. Besant find immediate expression in words that neither committed himself nor could hurt her?

Evidently he was pressed by Mrs. Besant to confirm the advancements "brought through" at Huizen, for he was writing three weeks later, "I am afraid I do not remember any of those happenings that are taking place over there as I am much too tired and as I have to sleep with Nitya and be constantly wakeful. My head and spine have been intermitently bad." He told her in this same letter of September 16 that the last three months had

all been terrible, what with the anxiety and caring for Nitya. Poor old Nitya, he has gone through a beastly time and I suppose it's good for him but heavens, what price one has to pay to evolve and I suppose it's worth it. Sometimes he has been unconscious when his body cries and wants his Amma and at other times he's too feeble to say anything or even move. He doesn't get out of bed at all and I attend to all his

bodily needs. It's good training but I hate to see other
people suffer.

Nevertheless Nitya was slowly improving, and therefore
when Mrs. Besant cabled to K asking him if he could get
to England in time to travel back with her to India at the
end of October for the Jubilee Convention, he reluctantly
agreed. Rosalind and Rajagopal were to travel with him
while Madame de Manziarly was sent for from India to
look after Nitya with the help of Rama Rao.

26

The First Manifestation

K, with Rosalind and Rajagopal, arrived at Plymouth on
October 23. Lady Emily as usual went to meet them and
had a very unhappy journey back with them in the train
to London. Although she already knew from K's letters
that he was skeptical about the things that had happened
at Huizen and Ommen she was not prepared for "the ava-
lanche of sarcasm" that fell on her from all three of them.
Rajagopal's *volte face* must have been particularly dis-
concerting to her because he had shared in most of the
Huizen excitement and had even gone off to Ojai with a
magnetized swastika, a Theosophical emblem, to help cure
Nitya. Lady Emily herself was skeptical by this time,
though she still trusted Mrs. Besant and did not see
how she could have been so deceived.

K went to stay at West Side House with Miss Dodge
where Lady Emily had a long talk with him next day. She
found him "terribly unhappy about the whole affair, dis-
believing everything." He felt that something infinitely precious, sacred and private had been made publicly ugly and
ridiculous, cheap and vulgar. Lady Emily asked him why
he did not say openly what he felt, to which he replied.
"What would be the use?" They would only say that the
Black Powers had got hold of him. However he did try
several times to talk to Mrs. Besant, but, according to
Lady Emily she did not seem to take it in; it was almost
as if she had been hypnotized by George.

On the eve of their departure for India a meeting was
held for Star members at which both K and Mrs. Besant
spoke. The latter said, ". . . you must not any of you feel
surprised or troubled because many of the things which
have been talked of only in a comparatively small circle,
are now given out to the world at large." (Her speech, announcing the names of those who had passed the fourth
Initiation and been chosen as Apostles, had been published

in the September number of the *Herald*.) She added that
the object of such publicity was a very definite one, but
she did not say what the object was. K, speaking after her,
made no mention at all on the public utterances at Ommen, which must have disappointed his audience greatly.
He spoke about the importance of putting oneself in the
place of others who had ideas just as thrilling as one's
own. He ended his talk with the words, "Smile and be
happy."

Mrs. Besant, K, Lady Emily, Rajagopal, Rosalind,
Wedgwood and Shiva Rao set off for India on November
3. Their ship was leaving from Naples and they went by
way of Paris and Rome. In Rome, where they spent three
nights at the Hotel Bristol, they were joined by the Arundales. George and Wedgwood went about in purple cas-
socks with large pectoral crosses dangling on their breasts.
Lady Emily maintained that they treated K with a good
deal of condescension and that George brought through
messages from the Mahachohan reproving him for his
skepticism. "The suggestion was subtly made that his spirit
of criticism and unbelief was spoiling his chances." They
even went so far as to tell him that if he would acknowledge them as his diciples and confirm that they
were Adepts, Nitya's life would be spared.

On the evening of the 8th they sailed in pouring rain on
the *Ormuz*. As soon as they were on board K received a
telegram to say that Nitya had influenza. They reached
Port Said on the 13th where they went ashore; when they
returned to the ship K found another telegram awaiting
him: "Flu rather more serious. Pray for me." K was not
unduly worried by this, for, as he told Shiva Rao, "If
Nitya was going to die I would not have been allowed to
leave Ojai." His faith in the Masters' power to prolong
Nitya's life appeared to Shiva Rao to be unqualified and
unquestioning: Nitya was essential for K's life-mission and
therefore he would not be allowed to die.

As the ship was entering the Suez Canal on the night of
the 13th in a violent thunderstorm the telegram arrived
announcing Nitya's death. It was held back by the ship's
authorities as parts of the message were obscure, so it was
not until the next morning at breakfast that it was delivered to Mrs. Besant. As K always had breakfast in his
cabin, Mrs. Besant asked Shiva Rao to show her the way
to it. She went in alone to break the news to him.

According to Shiva Rao, who, with Rajagopal, shared a cabin with K during this voyage, the news "broke him completely; it did more—his entire philosophy of life—the implicit faith in the future as outlined by Mrs. Besant and Mr. Leadbeater, Nitya's vital part in it, all appeared shattered at that moment." The next ten days were agonizing for him and for those who had to watch him, particularly for those sharing his cabin.

At night he would sob and moan and cry out for Nitya, sometimes in his native Telugu which in his waking consciousness he could not speak. Day after day we watched him, heart-broken, disillusioned. Day after day he seemed to change, gripping himself together in an effort to face life—but without Nitya. He was going through an inner revolution, finding new strength.

By the time they reached Colombo he had been able to express his feelings in words:

The pleasant dreams my brother and I had of the physical are over. . . . Silence was a special delight to both of us, as then it was so easy to understand each other's thoughts and feelings. Occasional irritation with each other was by no means forgotten but we never went very far as it passed off in a few minutes, we used to sing comic songs or chant together as the occasion demanded. We both of us liked the same cloud, the same tree and the same music. We had great fun in life, though we were of different temperaments. We somehow understood each other without effort. . . . It was a happy life and I shall miss him physically all through this life.

An old dream is dead and a new one is being born, as a flower that pushes through the solid earth. A new vision is coming into being and new consciousness is being unfolded. . . . A new thrill and a new throb of the same life is being felt. A new strength born of suffering is pulsating in the veins and a new sympathy and understanding is being born out of the past suffering. A greater desire to see others suffer less and if they must suffer to see that they bear it nobly and come out of it without too many scars. I have wept

but I do not want others to weep but if they do I now
know what it means.... I have seen my brother....
On the physical plane we could be separated and now
we are inseparable.... For my brother and I are one.
As Krishnamurti I now have greater zeal, greater
faith, greater sympathy and greater love for there is
also in me the body, the Being, of Nityananda.... I
know how to weep still, but that is human. I know
now, with greater certainty than ever before, that
there is real beauty in life, real happiness that can not
be shattered by any physical happening, a great
strength which cannot be weakened by passing events,
and a great love which is permanent, imperishable
and unconquerable.

Mar and Yo de Manziarly, who had remained at Adyar
the whole year, were at the Madras station to meet them
when they arrived on November 25. Mar recalled that K's
face was radiant; there was not a shadow on it to show
what he had been through.

Leadbeater and his party of seventy, including Helen,
Ruth, Betty, Mary, Theodore St. John and Dr. Rocke,
reached Colombo on December 2, having heard of Nitya's
death when the ship stopped at Melbourne. K, Mrs.
Besant, Lady Emily, Wedgwood and Raja returned to Colombo to meet them although they had been only five days
at Adyar. Leadbeater greeted K with the words, "Well, at
least *you* are an Arhat," meaning that K at any rate had
passed the fourth Initiation.

There was a special train for the whole party back to
Madras and at every station there were crowds, garlands
and prostrations. K, who, of course, knew of Mary's
feelings for Nitya, was very sweet to her and made a point
of sitting beside her and talking to her both in the train
and on the boat crossing to India. "Krishna was perfectly
delicious," Mary wrote in her diary, "and talked to me
about Nitya. They are together all the time now. And K
himself is so much more wonderful, and much softer."

Lady Emily had the Arundale House again at Adyar
where not only Helen and Ruth but thirteen girls altogether stayed with her, sleeping on *charpoys* on the veran-
das, for Adyar was very short of accommodation during
the Jubilee Convention in spite of the erection of a village
of temporary straw huts. Rosalind was in the Headquar-

ters building where Rajagopal was also staying. Nitya's death and all they had been through together at Ojai during the last months of his life had drawn Rosalind and Rajagopal very close to each other.

Mrs. Besant herself had been deeply shocked by Nitya's death as had everyone else in close contact with K; they had all shared his faith that Nitya would not be allowed to die. There could have been few people around K at that time who were not in some way disturbed or unhappy by the extraordinary situation that had developed. Lady Emily heard through Ruth, who was told by Theodore St. John, that Leadbeater did not believe that he himself or any of the others had taken their fifth Initiation (he hoped that he and Mrs. Besant might do so in their next life), and he was very doubtful whether Rukmini had taken even three in such a short time. "It is even more than our Krishna did," he said. Occult promotions continued in his own special group, however, and within a week of his arrival at Adyar there had been twenty advancements among them. It was only out of respect for Mrs. Besant that there was not an open rift between him and the Arundale-Wedgwood faction.

Lady Emily had now been forced to the conclusion that Mrs. Besant had been deceived at Huizen as she had herself. Mrs. Besant was so honest, Lady Emily concluded, "that she was incapable of suspecting insincerity where once she had given her trust, especially with regard to George, whom she loved so dearly." There is no evidence, though, of insincerity in George. He may well have been taken in by Wedgwood or they may all have been victims of hysteria or delusion. If they believed in the Masters and the World Teacher why not the Mahachohan, if in one Initiation why not in five? Was it not only a question of degree? This could well be argued. But it was the degree that made it so absurd. By claiming five Initiations they had given themselves divinity, whereas it had never been claimed by Leadbeater that K was to be more than the vehicle for divinity.

K himself stood apart from both the Leadbeater and the Arundale-Wedgwood factions, though for Mrs. Besant's sake he joined in all the activities that meant so much to her, such as attending Mass. He even allowed himself to be made a Co-Mason on November 27 in order to please her. There was one form of ceremonial, though, to which

he seemed genuinely to respond—a reformed Hindu ritual
at which he, as a Brahmin, was entitled to officiate. The
first public celebration of this ceremony took place on December 21, three days before the Convention opened. K,
dressed only in a white *dhoti*, with the sacred thread round
his neck, looked wonderfully beautiful as with Rajagopal
as his assistant he officiated at the consecration ceremony
of a small Hindu temple recently built in the Compound.
(Zoroastrian and Buddhist shrines, a synagogue, a mosque
and a Liberal Catholic chapel were also built at Adyar
in 1925-6, though the idea of the World Religion was
quietly shelved as was also the World University.)

Mrs. Besant was in almost as unhappy a position as K
himself at this time. Her personal love and reverence for
K were no more shaken than his for her, nor was her belief that he was the vehicle whom the Lord Maitreya had
chosen, but there was a conflict of loyalties in her that she
could no longer ignore. She made one last attempt to
reconcile them soon after Leadbeater's arrival. She went
up to K's room one morning, took him by the hand and
led him down to her own drawing-room where Leadbeater,
Raja, Arundale and Wedgwood were assembled; placing
him on the sofa between herself and Leadbeater, she asked
him whether he would accept them as his disciples. He replied that he would accept none of them except perhaps
Mrs. Besant herself.

Although this discord between the leaders of the T.S.
was naturally kept very private, no secret was made of the
fact that great things were expected to take place at the
Convention; hundreds of members expected to see the
Masters in person if not even higher beings. The *New
York Herald*, the *New York Times*, the *Times of India*
and lesser Indian papers all published articles about the
arrival of the delegates from all over the world, and the
startling pronouncements at Ommen, published in the
September *Herald*, were commented on in the *Indian Daily
Mail*. More than three thousand people attended the four-
day Convention in the greatest possible discomfort, for it
rained nearly the whole time, the monsoon being late that
year, and was unusually cold. Nevertheless most of the
meetings were held under the Banyan tree where Mrs.
Besant had had amplifiers installed for the first time and
where the speakers stood on a high dais surmounted by a
canopy wreathed in flowers. Nothing at all exciting hap-

pened, however, and the Convention broke up in great disappointment.

The Star Congress followed next day, December 28 (a sacred day since 1911), and at the first meeting under the Banyan tree at eight o'clock in the morning, with the amplifiers turned off, a dramatic change took place while K was speaking. It came at the end of his talk. He had been speaking about the World Teacher: "He comes only to those who want, who desire, who long . . ." and then his voice changed completely and rang out, "and I come for those who want sympathy, who want happiness, who are longing to be released, who are longing to find happiness in all things. I come to reform and not to tear down, I come not to destroy but to build."

For those who noticed the change to the first person and the difference in the voice, it was a spine-tingling experience. Among the few who noticed nothing were, not surprisingly, Wedgwood and the Arundales. They thought he was merely "quoting scripture." As he had never quoted scripture before they must have been aware of some difference. Mrs. Besant, Leadbeater and Raja were certainly very conscious of the change, and Mrs. Besant frequently referred to it thereafter. In the final meeting of the Star Congress she said:

> . . . that event [of December 28] marked the definite consecration of the chosen vehicle . . . the final acceptance of the body chosen long before. . . . The coming has begun. . . . That there should be opposition is natural; did the Hebrews acknowledge Him or the Romans welcome Him, when first He came in the body of a subject race? History repeats itself before our eyes.

And in the *Theosophist* she wrote, "For the first time the Voice that spoke as never man spake, has sounded again in our lower ways in the ears of the great crowd that sat beneath the Banyan Tree, it was on December 28 . . . and we knew that the waiting period was over, and that the morning star had arisen above the horizon."

K himself had no doubts. Talking to the National Representatives at the end of the Star Congress he said:

You have drunk at the fountain of wisdom and

knowledge. The memory of the 28th should be to you as if you were guarding some precious jewel and every time you look at it you must feel a thrill. Then when He comes again, and I am sure that He will come again very soon, it will be for us a nobler and far more beautiful occasion than even last time.

And on January 5, 1926, he said at a pupils' meeting:

A new life, a new storm has swept the world. It is like a tremendous gale that blows and cleans everything, all the particles of dust from the trees, the cobwebs from our minds and from our emotions and has left us perfectly clean. . . . I personally feel quite different from that day. . . . I feel like a crystal vase, a jar that has been cleaned and now anybody in the world can put a beautiful flower in it and that flower shall live in the vase and never die.

A fortnight later he told Lady Emily that he felt now just like a shell—so absolutely impersonal. He used the phrase, "I feel somehow so precious now." He said he was sure "the Lord would come more and more whenever there was the occasion or the special need of Him."

Leadbeater was no less certain. In answer to a question after he got back to Sydney, "When we are asked if the World Teacher has come, what do we answer?" he replied that there was not "a shadow of doubt" that "He" had used "the Vehicle more than once" at the Jubilee Convention, just as "He" had used it at Benares on December 28, 1911. "He" would continue to use it only intermittently, though more frequently. Being "the busiest person in the world 'He' naturally would not want to use it while it was on a train journey or having a meal. Besides, 'He' would have to get the Vehicle used to Him."

Lady Emily sent an account of what had happened to her sister, Lady Betty Balfour, in England. Lady Betty, in her reply, repeated some very natural comments from her husband, from her sister-in-law and from the friend who lived with them: sister-in-law "silent and profoundly shocked, as a Roman matron of old would have been at the Christian doctrines enunciated by St. Paul;" the friend "scoffing, said no other Messiah had had the stage so carefully set for him, trained from babyhood to believe that Christ *would* inhabit him, and then his manifestation made at a carefully organized public meeting. I said that I thought the shepherds, the Magi, Simeon, the Doctors in the Temple, the public baptism, and the meeting at Pentecost were comparable;" her husband, Gerald (brother of Arthur Balfour), "very reverent, deeply interested but skeptical as to whether it is the real thing. Wants to know on what evidence it rests, apart from the world of Krishna himself, and Mrs. Besant. ... What did Betty and Mary feel?"

All those who were aware of the change felt it instantly and independently. Lady Emily, Mary and Mar de Manziarly wrote about it in their diaries as a fact and without any consultation with each other, and there are others alive today who believed it then and still believe it. But proof? Is there ever any proof of religious faith—proof of the doctrines of transubstantiation or reincarnation? Where can one draw the line between faith and credulity? Is not faith the name by which we dignify our own conviction of the truth of some unscientifically proved doctrine, and credulity our derisory word for such belief in others? But now, however great the faith (or the credulity) it had become impossible for anyone to believe in K *and* in Arundale and Wedgwood. Unless one of them accept the other, an open split was inevitable sooner or later.

27

The Kingdom of Happiness

The party at Adyar had dispersed by the end of January
1926. Lady Emily, Betty, Mary and Mar de Manziarly returned to Europe; Helen and Ruth went back to Sydney
with Leadbeater who also took with him the Arundales,
while Rosalind, Rajagopal and Madame de Manziarly,
who had arrived at Adyar with Nitya's ashes the day before the Convention, remained in India with K.

K went to Benares for a month in February where he
talked every day to the boys and girls of the Theosophical
School in the Compound, impressing on them particularly
the need for scrupulous physical cleanliness and care in
the way they dressed. He had always had a love for young
people and felt most at his ease with children. He also felt
that if he could make contact with them before they were
conditioned in racial and family traditions and prejudices
they would grow up in freedom and fearlessness.

On March 12 he was back at Adyar with a high temperature and boils all over his face as a result of food poi-
soning in Calcutta. Fortunately Madame de Manziarly was
still at Adyar; she immediately took charge of him and on
the 25th went up with him to Ootacamund to convalesce
with Malati Patwardhan and Jadu. Rajagopal was too
busy with various Star matters to accompany them, and
Rosalind also remained at Adyar. Rajagopal had been appointed Organizing Secretary of the Star in Nitya's place.
He had also become International Treasurer of the Order,
a new appointment. He used the Octagon Bungalow at
Adyar as his office, but on the afternoon of December 28
the foundation stone had been laid of a Headquarters for
the Star at Adyar, dedicated to Nitya, on land presented
by Mrs. Besant.

On the day Krishna left for "Ooty" he wrote revealingly
to Leadbeater:

I am very glad the Master wants George to stay in Australia for a year. [George stayed for two years as General Secretary of the T.S.] This will ensure us from complications and unnecessary and absurd romantic excitement. I have woken up so often with feelings of revolt and distrust that my impressions and intuitions are growing stronger and stronger and I feel that the events of the last ten months aren't clean and wholesome. Of course there's nothing to be done but wait for events to develop. Of course none of them are very important but this apostles business is the limit. I don't believe in it all and this is *not* based on prejudice. With that we shall have difficulty and I am *not* going to give in over that. I think it's wrong and purely George's imagination. Anyhow it's a trivial thing but other people are making a mountain of it. . . . Wedgwood is distributing initiations around . . . Initiations and sacred things will be a joke presently. . . . I believe in all this so completely that it makes me weep to see these sacred things dragged in the dirt.

It was little more than a year since Nitya had been at "Ooty" and K wrote to Lady Emily from there on March 31, "I am staying in the same room as Nitya. I feel him, see him & talk to him but I miss him grievously." He also told her that he was growing a beard. "I would like to grow it long as people then, I hope, won't recognize me. Oh! God the papers & crowds!!" He had just received the sad news that Harold Baillie-Weaver had died on March 18 after a long illness.

K found the reporters more persistent than ever when he went to Bombay with Mrs. Besant at the beginning of May en route for Europe. There was also a continuing amount of publicity of a mixed nature in America and England as well as in India. K told Leadbeater from the *Rajputana* on which they sailed, one of the newest ships of the P & O Line, that the passengers were "not nearly as nice as the boat." They were so curious that most of them would have "stiff necks and bulging eyes by the time they get off." Mrs. Besant, Rajagopal, Rosalind, Madame de Manziarly, Jadu and the Patwardhans were travelling with him.

K had already planned to have a gathering at Castle

Eerde before the Star Camp at Ommen that year, and a
typewritten letter, headed "West Side House, Wimbledon"
and dated June 3, 1926, was sent off to special friends, in-
viting them to this gathering for nearly three weeks from
July 3:

> The order of the day will be very much like it used
> to be at Pergine. . . . There will be only one meeting
> a day and the rest of the time will be spent in other
> ways. Please come prepared for a fairly rough time in
> the way of household arrangements; and if you have
> a typewriter kindly bring it along, for we shall have
> much work to do.

Living expenses, it was stated, would be between three
and four guilders a day (about £2 a week). A postscript
added, "If you *cannot* afford the extra expense [apart
from the Camp] this visit will entail, please write by return to D. Rajagopal Esq. at the *above address* (marked
"confidential") and we will endeavor to arrange help from
a small fund we are trying to collect for this purpose."

The wording of this letter was typical of Rajagopal who
was extremely efficient, a born organizer, fanatically tidy
and inclined to be bossy—in fact the exact opposite of K
and Nitya; yet he could be very sweet, for he had a most
affectionate nature as well as a great deal of charm. His
efficiency was certainly wanted at that time, for, as K told
Leadbeater, Ommen was "in desperate need of workers.
Huizen is now in vogue so Ommen suffers, as everyone
rushes to the latest supposed spiritual place." The year before, Huizen, not Ommen, had been named as one of the
three centers for the World University and the World Religion, and Mrs. Besant, in spite of her declarations about
the Lord speaking through K on December 28, went
straight to Huizen when she arrived in Europe.

Lady Emily would, of course, be going to the gathering
with Betty and Mary, and in the autumn Mary wanted to
go to Ojai with K, and Betty wanted to go back to Sydney. For once, however, it seems that their father put his
foot down, for K was writing to Lady Emily on June 25
from Grimalp near Basle, where he had gone with Rajagopal for a month's rest:

I was quite upset that Betty's going to Sydney

should involve breaking up the house. Please, it's not worth it. C.W.L. would certainly *not* approve of it. If I may say so please *don't* do *anything* till we meet & talk over the affair. It's too serious. . . . It's not so important that Betty should go to Australia or Mary to America. . . . Mum, dear, please don't do anything rash. Your letter made me quite worried.

K has probably kept more homes together than he has broken up. Mary had already booked her passage to New York; now on the strength of K's letter she reluctantly cancelled it.

Thirty-five people of many different nationalities joined K at Castle Eerde on July 3. Modern plumbing and electric light had now been installed in the Castle by the Trust and the large bedrooms had been turned into dormitories. Only K had one of these bedrooms to himself. It was on the first floor, at the south-east corner, with a dressing-room leading off it. Apart from the Lutyens's there were some others there from the old Ehrwald group—Mar de Manziarly, Rajagopal, the Patwardhans and John Cordes. In addition there were Rosalind, Jadu, John Ingleman, Philip van Pallandt and several other friends K had made in the course of his travels.

Life at the Castle was not at all what it had been at Pergine. For one thing, everyone was on rosters to help with the various household chores, and there was not the same sense of intimacy. On the other hand it was much less lonely for the small fry and there were enough people to make up sides for exciting games of volley-ball; moreover, K's "process" had stopped—at any rate in its former intense form, though he still "went off" sometimes, "mothered" by Rosalind who, since Nitya's death, had been able to help him again in that way.

He had caught a bad cold in Switzerland and for the first three days of the gathering he was confined to bed with bronchitis. A Swedish *gopi*, Noomi Hagge, who was a trained nurse and subsequently became a doctor, was given the privilege of carrying up his trays, but some of the old Pergine group took turns in sitting with him in his room after supper, so they did not feel he was shut away from them. On the morning of the 8th he came down for the first time in his dressing-gown and talked to the gathering in the large drawing-room at the rear of the Castle

overlooking the meadows beyond the moat. Thereafter, for
the next fortnight, he spoke every morning for about an
hour, sitting cross-legged on the sofa under one of the
Gobelin tapestries.

The weather was perfect the whole time and this contributed enormously to the success of the gathering. Most
afternoons K went for a walk by himself in the beautiful
woods surrounding the Castle to find inspiration for the
next morning's talk. Lady Emily, Mary and Mar all made
notes about these talks in their diaries which bear witness
to their independent belief that the Lord Maitreya frequently spoke through K. On the 11th, Lady Emily noted,
"Marvellous talk & I am sure the Lord was there. K told
me afterwards that he had to resist saying I instead of
Him." Mar was more emphatic with simply: "The Lord
spoke."

"There is nothing so nice in the world," Mary wrote in
her diary, "as to feel as one feels here, really alive physically, mentally and emotionally. To have, as K said, that
sense of well-being throughout." She drew very close to K
during this time at Eerde. It seemed so natural to transfer
her love to him, believing as she did that he and Nitya
were now one.

"I have seen a lot of him," she wrote (she used to see
him alone in his room after supper), "and what he has
been to me in sweetness no words can express. He said he
didn't enjoy life now except with either Nitya or me. This
evening he told me of a walk we three had been for this
morning. They are both there upstairs together—Nitya
and Krishna. He said he wished I was his sister." Mary
wished so too; as his sister she could have spent the rest of
her life with him.

The talk on the 19th, the last day of the gathering, was,
according to Lady Emily, the most wonderful of all:

Krishna spoke as never before & one feels now that
his consciousness & that of the Lord are so completely blended that there is no distinction any more.
He said, "Follow me & I will show you the way into
the Kingdom of Happiness. I will give each of you
the key with which you can unlock the gate into the
garden"—and it was no effort to him to use the personal pronoun . . . the face of the Lord shone through
the face of Krishna & His glorious aura encompassed

us in an almost blinding light. When he finished Jadu threw himself at Krishna's feet—I had a longing to follow suit but caught Krishna's eye in time.

The next day Lady Emily wrote a long and ecstatic letter to Raja, in India, telling him all about these talks, and saying that July 19 had been even more wonderful than December 28—firstly because He was there with us not for a few moments but for an hour. Secondly, whereas on the 28th one could feel the disassociation of personality between the Lord and Krishna, now it seems all to have gone and They are One. Krishna has become the Lord."

Rosalind and Mary, no doubt at K's wish, remained at the Castle with K and Rajagopal when all the others moved into Camp at Ommen on the afternoon of July 19. Mrs. Besant and Wedgwood arrived a couple of days later and also stayed at the Castle. The Convention, which opened on July 24, was attended by about 2,000 people of practically every nationality.[1] There was one huge tent for meetings, smaller tents for meals, rows of sleeping tents for one, two, three or four people, shower-baths, toilets, and well-designed permanent huts for post office, bookshop, first-aid station and information bureau. Everything was extremely well organized. In the middle of the Camp an amphitheatre had been built with circular rows of rough-hewn logs for benches. Meetings were held there in good weather, and it was there that a great bonfire was lit every evening when it was fine. K, who was still a hesitant speaker, often repeating himself and not always finishing his sentences, was at his very best when talking at the Camp fires. The smell of burning pine was a delicious accompaniment to these evening meetings which began just as the sun was setting. K wore Indian dress and as the fifteen-foot high pyramid of wood was lit he would chant a hymn to Agni, God of Fire.

According to Mar de Manziarly's diary the Lord spoke through K at the Camp fire on the first evening, and again on the 25th and on the 27th. Lady Emily and Mary, however, make no note of this until the 27th when they both wrote lyrically about it in their diaries. Wedgwood had

[1] The annual report of the Order of the Star in the East for 1926 gave the total number of members as 43,600 in forty countries. Only about two-thirds of these were also members of the T.S.

spoken in the morning of the 27th and made Lady Emily
"feel sick it was so artificial—so personal—& so tragic to
see the whole crowd purring & feeling comfortable." At
2:30 there was a Star Council meeting at the Castle at
which K spoke "too marvellously but oh! so sadly of the
lack of comprehension." A pupils' meeting followed at
which Wedgwood again spoke. K came to this for a short
while: "His eyes were the eyes of the Lord shining, &
afterwards he rushed from the room as if he could bear
no more." That evening, at the Camp fire, Lady Emily

knew that directly he appeared *He* was there. He
looked so stern & full of power—Then he spoke &
looked so magnificent & his voice thrilling with
power. He said, "I am going to speak to you as the
Head of this Order—& I will ask you graciously to
pay attention to all that I shall say to you from the
first word to the last. For I feel that all I have been
saying these last few evenings has been in vain for
you have not understood"—Then he spoke with in-
conceivable majesty & power with a flow of beautiful
words. Such sternness and such compassion.

It was a particularly beautiful talk. In part of it he said:

I would ask you to look at my point of view; I
would ask you to come and look through my window,
which will show you my heaven, which will show you
my garden and my abode. Then you will see that
what matters is not what you do, what you read,
what any person says you are or are not, but that you
should have the intense desire to enter into that abode
where dwells Truth. . . . I would have you come and
see it; I would have you come and feel it . . . and not
say to me: "Oh, you are different, you are on the
mountain top, you are a mystic." You give me phrases
and cover my Truth with your words. I do not want
you to break with all you believe. I do not want you
to deny your temperament. I do not want you to do
things that you do not feel to be right. But, are any
of you happy? Have you, any of you, tasted eternity?
. . . I belong to all people, to all who really love, to
all who are suffering. And if you would walk, you
must walk with me. If you would understand you

must look through my mind. If you would feel, you must look through my heart. And because I really love, I want you to love. Because I really feel, I want you to feel. Because I hold everything dear, I want you to hold all things dear. Because I want to protect, you should protect. And this is the only life worth living, and the only Happiness worth possessing.

Mrs. Kirby, who was there and who had known K longer than anyone else present, even longer than Mrs. Besant, said to Lady Emily afterwards as they walked in the woods, "I have always known Him, it was His voice I have always heard & it is the voice of one's own higher self."

Mrs. Kirby, after she returned to Genoa, wrote to a friend about this talk:

At first K began in the usual way, though I noticed (I was very near him) an unusual dignity in his appearance. His face had grown strangely powerful and stern, his eyes at times half veiled as if looking inwards, had an unusual fire, and even his voice sounded deeper and fuller. The power went on increasing with every word he uttered. . . . There was a strange stillness—nobody moved or made a sound even after it was over. . . . The speech you will read, and so will I, but I know I shall not find in it a tenth part of what I heard. . . . It is not to be described. What can one say? The Lord was there and He was speaking. I think I have as a rule, a fair amount of control over my feelings, but when it was over I discovered I was trembling from head to foot. . . . I don't know what the others thought and felt, as I came away the morning after without seeing anybody. [She must have been too carried away to remember speaking to Lady Emily.] I only saw Krishnaji, because he sent for me at the last moment. He was as dear and affectionate as ever, and as I was telling him how his whole appearance had changed the evening before he said: "I wish I could see it too." . . . Krishnaji looked as if he badly needed a rest. . . . What a life, poor Krishnaji! There is no doubt about his being *the Sacrifice*.

From the atmosphere of excitement in the Camp it was

evident that the great majority of those present believed
they had heard the voice of the Lord Maitreya which, of
course, they had been expecting to hear ever since the
Convention opened. One individual, though, had his own
unique explanation of the phenomenon. Wedgwood, who
was sitting next to Mrs. Besant at the Camp fire, was seen
to lean over and whisper something to her as K ceased
speaking. As soon as the meeting broke up Mrs. Besant
asked Rajagopal to take K back to the Castle immediately.
Mrs. Besant went into K's room as soon as she returned to
the Castle and told him that it was a powerful black magician whom she knew well who had been speaking through
him at the Camp fire. (It was undoubtedly Wedgwood
who had "seen" the black magician and whispered his
name to Mrs. Besant.) K was utterly astounded. He told
Mrs. Besant that if she really believed that, he would
never speak in public again. This apparently distressed her
even more than Wedgwood's revelation and she never
again made any suggestion that the black powers had influenced him. From that time onwards, however, it was a
convenient theory for Wedgwood and others to adopt:
whenever K said something they disapproved of they could
claim that the "blacks" were speaking through him.

On July 28, the evening after the black magician incident, Lady Emily recorded that she knew the Lord was
there again at the Camp fire, "but this time with tenderness instead of power. It was infinitely touching and sad.
K told us of his own inner experience, took us into his
very heart. He said 'You may take my heart and eat it,
you may take my blood and drink it & I shall not mind—
because I have so much, & you have so little.' "

Next day the Camp broke up.

28

"The World Teacher is Here"

So distressed was Mrs. Besant at this time by conflicting
loyalties that she seriously considered giving up the
Presidency of the Theosophical Society in order to obey
the dictates of her heart and follow K. She put her
dilemma to Leadbeater who, in a letter of September 21,
1926, dissuaded her from this step by pointing out that it
was not in accordance with her Master's orders. Before receiving this letter and still uncertain whether to resign or
not, she made the sudden decision to go with K to America at the end of the summer instead of returning to India
as planned. It would be the first time she had been to
America since 1909, the year K was "discovered." A lecture tour was quickly arranged for her throughout the
States at $1,000 a lecture. But before leaving she spoke in
Wales, Scotland and Ireland on the World Teacher. K
meanwhile remained at West Side House during August
and not a day passed without his seeing Lady Emily and
Mary.

On August 26 K, Mrs. Besant, Rosalind and Rajagopal
arrived in New York from Southampton. Twenty reporters
came on board with photographers and all seemed disappointed to find K dressed in a neat grey suit. One reporter
described him as "a shy, badly frightened, nice-looking
young Hindu boy, slight in figure, with straight blue-black
hair, soft brown eyes and drooping eye lashes." The head-
lines can be imagined: "Cult of Star Awaits Glory of
Coming Lord," "New Gospel Told by Annie Besant," "A
New Messiah in Tennis Flannels," "New Deity Comes in
Plus Fours," and so on.

They stayed at the Waldorf-Astoria where the next day
K was interviewed alone by more than forty reporters; he
was far less shy without Mrs. Besant there. The *New York
Times* reported that many of the interviewers "tried to trip
him up with shrewdly worded questions; he skilfully

avoided all these pitfalls and earned their admiration by coming out triumphant. "There was one dissentient voice: Maurice Guest wrote, "Here's what I think of that Oriental. I wouldn't give him a job in a third rate Chu Chin Chow company;" yet it was not long after this that K was offered $5,000 a week by a film company to play the title role in scenes from the life of Buddha. This offer gave K the satisfactory feeling that he could always earn his own living if the need arose.

A few days later the *New York Times* commented that K "was seen very little abroad, but was then usually in the company of Rosalind Williams, a blond woman who was a member of the party." The reporter quickly added that this did not mean that Krishnamurti had any real interest in the opposite sex. When asked what he thought of love and marriage K replied, "People marry because they are lonely. . . . I am never lonely. . . . I have something which you cannot take away." Later it got into the papers that he had been engaged to Helen Knothe, a rumor which Helen's parents would neither confirm nor deny. K himself, however, denied it hotly: "Any report concerning the engagement is absurd. It is really too terrible."

From New York they moved to Chicago for a T.S. Convention where the *Tribune* assigned its leading feature reporter, Genevieve Forbes Herrick, to cover their visit. She was impressed in spite of herself. The delegates, though, must have been greatly disappointed when there were no manifestations of the World Teacher at any of the many meetings. After the Convention Mrs. Besant went to Minneapolis to give the first of thirty lectures while K and Rajagopal went to Warm Springs, Virginia, for a rest. (Rosalind presumably returned home, though she was to join them later at Ojai.) From Warm Springs, K wrote a little letter to Mrs. Besant which shows that neither the "black magician" episode nor anything else had changed his love for her: "I hope I shall see you very soon my own Mother. By heaven, I want to be with you and I realize how much I really love you. One sees the greatness of a mountain, when one's further away from it."

It was not until the end of September that he met her in San Francisco at the end of her tour, and not until October 3 that he had the joy of taking her to Ojai for the first time. He had been away just about a year. Two days after his arrival he wrote to Lady Emily from Arya Vihara:

Here I am—without Nitya. We drove up here from Los Angeles with Amma. When we entered the house, I saw Nitya & felt him almost physically & when I went into the room in which he was ill & from which he went away, I am afraid my body cried. It's a strange thing the body. I wasn't really upset but my body was in an extraordinary state. After India & perhaps, even before that, he liked this place & still does. So I can feel him & see him. Life is strange. I miss him terribly—the body. I am getting used to his physical absence—which is rather a difficult thing to do, as we lived here more than anywhere, where we both suffered & where we were both happy. Well, I won't depress you. I don't feel it inside me. . . . Amma is very tired after her tour but it is remarkable how she picks up. The two days rest here has again put her on her feet; she's really marvellous & wonderful.

He went on to tell Lady Emily that for the past four weeks he had had a rather hard and painful swelling in his right breast. He had been to Hollywood to see Dr. Strong who had told him that it was glandular and that there was nothing to worry about, though it must be watched. K also told Lady Emily his plans—he intended to leave New York with Mrs. Besant on November 20 and go to India with her at the beginning of December. The T.S. Convention that year was to be at Benares and Leadbeater would be attending it.

But soon all his plans were changed. The swelling in his breast grew more painful and Dr. Strong as well as an orthodox doctor in Hollywood forbade him to go to India. To mitigate his intense disappointment Mrs. Besant decided to remain with him at Ojai. In a letter of October 22 telling this to Lady Emily, he asked her if she, Betty and Mary would also come to Ojai to be with him: "I haven't asked Amma yet if it would be alright but I am sure it will be alright. You know what I mean, papers & gossip. But Mum dearest I seriously invite (!!) you to Ojai. Won't Mary be glad. The last letter from her said how she longed to be at Ojai. . . . Do come if you can. I will pray for it."

Mrs. Besant evidently had no objection to the plan and Lady Emily, having arranged some lectures in America to

help pay her expenses, set off joyfully with Mary at the
end of November. Betty did not want to go because her
reaction against K and Theosophy had already set in;
besides, she had just joined the Royal College of Music.
Lady Emily and Mary remained at Ojai for nearly five
months, the longest consecutive time Lady Emily had ever
been with K during the whole of their long association. It
was the quietest time too, because although the swelling in
his breast had subsided somewhat, he still had to avoid exertion. Lady Emily and Mary stayed with Rosalind in an
ugly modern guest house which had recently been built in
the grounds, while Mrs. Besant, Rajagopal and K occupied
Arya Vihara where they all had meals together.

Lady Emily wrote to her husband on December 18:

Imagine Italy, the Riviera and the best parts of
India rolled into one and you have this place. . . .
Amma is so sweet here and so happy. She has not
had a quiet time like this for years. She helped me
make her bed yesterday and this morning helped to
lay the table. In the evenings we play bridge and she
writes or reads. Krishnaji is much better and is so
happy here. He loves working in the garden. Rajagopal is busy with the Star and I can help him in this.
Altogether it is just Paradise here.

The first weeks were indeed paradise. K was writing poetry at this time and every evening they would walk to see
the sunset which inspired him so much that he would return to write a poem,[1] but by January 1927, as he wrote
to tell Leadbeater, the "old business" of intense pain at the
base of his spine and the nape of his neck began again and
went on practically all day.

Mary was now able to help him to relax when he "went
off" in the afternoons. When she first went to him on February 20 the body asked her who she was and then said,
"Well, if you are a friend of Krishna and Nitya I suppose
you are all right." He became like a child of about four,
though without the restlessness of a child. Although he

[1] His first poem, *Hymn of the Initiate Triumphant*, had been published in the *Herald* in January 1923. About sixty other poems were
published, both in the *Herald* and in book form, up till 1931 when
he ceased to write poetry.

spoke English he would always call her Amma; he seemed
very frightened of K, as of a stern elder brother, and
would say things like, "Take care, Krishna's coming
back." With K away the body did not seem to be in any
great pain, though it was sometimes fractious. K, on his
return, had absolutely no recollection of anything the child
had said. These afternoon occurrences took place in the
Shrine, as Pine Cottage was then called. At the beginning
of March, K had his bed moved into the Shrine where he
much preferred to sleep, away from everyone as it was so
much quieter.

In the mornings he was teaching Mary to drive. His
Lincoln had been traded in for a Packard, and recently
The Packard had been exchanged for another pale blue
Lincoln. K became so irritable with Mary out of ner-
vousness that one day she took the car out on her own in
retaliation. Wanting to return after having gone a certain
distance, she was obliged to walk back to the house since
she could not reverse. She was then miserable to realize
the anxiety she had caused K.

Lady Emily also found him "less the teacher and more
his human self" in these peaceful surroundings and consequently it was harder for her to sublimate her love for
him. He told her that she "must not have the possessive attitude. . . . If I become necessary to you you will not be
free and it will spoil it all. We love each other and that is
sufficient." She asked him what he meant exactly by "possessive," to which he replied, "Everybody is the same—
they all think they have some special claim—some special
road to me."

There was also a certain amount of friction between the
Lutyens's and Rosalind. The Lutyens's were accustomed to
servants waiting on them, so there was no doubt much jus-
tification in Rosalind's complaint to K that they did not
clean the bath properly; however, Lady Emily was upset
that Rosalind should complain to K instead of going direct
to her. Mrs. Besant was probably quite unaware of these
undercurrents as she quietly pursued her own occupations,
writing letters and articles and making out lists of future
pupils. She was also engaged in an exciting new scheme
involving property. Like everyone else she had fallen in
love with Ojai, and soon after she arrived she had managed to buy over 450 acres in the upper valley near Arya
Vihara where K wanted to start a school. She was now try-

ing to raise money for a further 240 acres at the lower end to form a center for the World Teacher and for an annual Camp as at Ommen. A Trust was formed called the Happy Valley Foundation and an appeal launched for $200,000. A large portion of the money was subscribed and the land purchased but it took twenty years to start the Happy Valley School.

During this quiet time with K at Ojai Mrs. Besant revised her conception of the World Teacher speaking only intermittently through him and came to believe that his consciousness was now almost entirely blended with that of the Lord Maitreya. She was no doubt influenced by K's own conviction of this which he had expressed to Leadbeater in a letter of February 9:

I know my destiny and my work. I know with certainty and knowledge of my own, that I am blending into the consciousness of the one Teacher and that He will completely fill me. I feel and I know also that my cup is nearly full to the brim and that it will overflow soon. Till then I must abide quietly, and with eager patience. . . . I long to make, and will make, everybody happy.

Before leaving Ojai in April Mrs. Besant made her position unequivocal by issuing a statement to the Associated Press of America beginning, "The Divine Spirit has descended once more on a man, Krishnamurti, one who in his life is literally perfect, as those who know him can testify," and ending with the words, "The World Teacher is here."

29

Liberation

Lady Emily reluctantly left Ojai with Mary ten days before K and Mrs. Besant in order to travel back to England with her husband who was in America in connection with his recent commission to design the new British Embassy in Washington. Two days after their departure K wrote to Lady Emily:

> I am writing this in the Shrine, just after my affair of every day. . . . By jove, how I miss you but I shall see you soon. An extraordinary thing life is, always changing fortunately. My head has been extra bad & my physical body misses Mary enormously & so do I. But it's extraordinary how the body can get used to anything. First day, the day you left, it was on the verge of tears but now it's quite normal. . . . I feel so changed since I have been here & as I love you, I want you to see the glory too. Great times are ahead of us & you too must be great.

K, with Mrs. Besant, Rosalind and Rajagopal, arrived in England on May 10. He stayed a week in London and then went with Rajagopal to Eerde where a small community was now living permanently, including Miss Dijkgraaf, Philip van Pallandt and Dr. Rocke, who had left Sydney for good. From Eerde K went to Paris on May 25 and flew back to London on the 30th. He told Lady Emily that he had spoken in Paris at a meeting of the Esoteric Section and said "some strong things—that the Masters were only incidents." This was a very important pronouncement which must have greatly shocked and disturbed his listeners, for a belief in the existence of the Masters was the whole *raison d'être* of the Esoteric Section of the T.S. No one could have guessed how soon even the Lord Maitreya was to become an "incident" for K.

On June 6 Mrs. Besant gave the first of four public lectures at the Queen's Hall on "The World Teacher and the New Civilization." There was to be another pre-Camp gathering at Castle Eerde that year starting on June 19, followed by the Camp at Ommen. Mrs. Besant planned to be there for the Camp but intended to stay at Huizen beforehand.

K went to Eerde ten days before the gathering opened with Rajagopal, Mary and Koos van de Leeuw. It had been arranged some time beforehand that Mary should go with them, but at the last moment Mrs. Besant decreed that she must not travel without a chaperone. In order not to disappoint Mary, Lady Emily unselfishly went with them overnight by sea although she had to return to London the following night. Rajagopal was very miserable that Rosalind did not go too. He was very much in love with Rosalind by this time and wanted to marry her. Surprisingly, Rosalind did not go to Eerde at all that summer or even to the Ommen Camp. She remained in England, at Wimbledon for the most part, where some houses had been bought on West Side Common to form a community centre for Theosophy and the Star. Probably Rosalind needed time and distance to help her make up her mind whether or not to marry Rajagopal.

One of the great barns flanking the entrance to Castle Eerde had now been converted into small rooms on two floors so that about sixty people were able to attend the gathering this year, which was, in consequence, less harmonious. Among old friends staying there were Madame de Manziarly and her three daughters,[1] Lady Emily, Mary, Rajagopal, Ruth (just returned from Sydney), Mrs. Roberts, Dr. Rocke, Isabelle Mallet, Jadu, the Patwardhans, Philip van Pallandt, Koos van de Leeuw, Noomi Hagge and A.P. Warrington who had been with K and Nitya at Ojai in 1922.

In spite of a bad cough caught in Paris, K began his talks on June 19 "full of quiet power and certainty,"according to Lady Emily's diary, and without any shyness, but two days later he woke with a fever that turned to bronchitis and he was obliged to stay in bed for more than

---

[1] Mima, the eldest, had married an American, George Porter, in 1925, but he had tragically died in February 1927. She built a house in the Ojai Valley a few years later where she has lived ever since.

a week. This led to a quarrel between Madame de Manziarly and Noomi Haage as to which of them was more
qualified to look after him. Madame de Manziarly, who
had a very forceful character, got her way, though Noomi
was still given the privilege of carrying up his trays. Then
Madame de Manziarly and Dr. Rocke disagreed about the
best way to treat his illness. K himself, Lady Emily recorded, was "full of amusement at this fatuous quarelling
over him like dogs with a bone;" he asked Lady Emily to
hold a meeting and tell them not to be "damned fools."
While he was ill Lady Emily read his poems aloud in the
mornings to the assembled party while he lay in bed reading Edgar Wallace.

The Eerde party heard on June 25 that George Arundale (who, having left Australia, had been in England
trying to collect £10,000 to present to Mrs. Besant and
Leadbeater on their approaching eightieth birthdays) had
held a Star meeting in London at which he had stated that
he disagreed with Mrs. Besant about the blending of K's
consciousness with that of the Lord; nevertheless, he said,
a united front must be shown to the public. He and
Rukmini returned to India before the Ommen Camp.

K was well enough by the 28th to get up and sit with
the others in the drawing-room while Lady Emily read
some of his poems aloud; the next day he read aloud three
of his own poems to test his voice. On the 30th he was
able to start speaking again. His theme this year was
Liberation whereas the year before it had been The Kingdom of Happiness. Lady Emily made notes of what he
said each day:

> You must become liberated not because of me but
> in spite of me ... all this life, and especially during
> the last few months I have struggled to be free—free
> of my friends, my books, my associations. You must
> struggle for the same freedom. There must be con-
> stant turmoil within. Hold a mirror constantly before
> you and if there is anything you see there which is
> unworthy of the ideal you have created for yourself,
> change it. ... You must not make me an authority. If
> I become a necessity to you what will you do when I
> go away? ... Some of you think I can give you a
> drink that will set you free, that I can give you a for-
> mula that will liberate you—that is not so. I can be

the door but you must pass through the door and find
the liberation that is beyond it. . . . Truth comes like a
burglar—when you least expect it. I wish I could in-
vent a new language but as I cannot I would like to
destroy your old phraseology and conceptions. No
one can give you liberation, you have to find it
within, but because I have found I would show you
the way. . . . He who has attained liberation has become the Teacher—like myself. It lies in the power
of each one to enter into the flame, to become the
flame. . . . Because I am here, if you will hold me in
your heart I will give you strength to attain. . . .
Liberation is not for the few, the chosen, the select. It
is for all when they cease to create *karma*. It is you
yourselves who set in motion this wheel of birth and
death whose spokes are agonies and pains and it is
you alone who can stop that wheel so that it turns no
more. Then you are free. Most people cling to this in-
dividuality, to this sense of I. It is that which creates
karma. Liberation is life and the cessation of life. It is
as a great fire and when you enter it you become the
flame, and then you go forth as sparks, part of that
flame.

He was saying in effect that the Masters, and all the
other gurus, were unnecessary; that there was a direct way
to truth and that everyone had to find it for himself. This
caused much consternation among those at Eerde who,
even though they were not Theosophists, wanted to be told
by him just what to do, but it was far more devastating
for the members of the Esoteric Section of the T.S., of
which there were several at the gathering, who were accustomed to being informed exactly how far they had
progressed along the spiritual Path.

At this time K was longing for complete renunciation,
to become a *sanyasi* in India. He talked a great deal about
it to Lady Emily at the gathering. It was probably the last
great temptation he had to face. He had written to Raja
from Ojai on February 9, "My cup is full. . . . I have mentally and emotionally put on the yellow robe! I want to
shout from the mountain top and shake the people in the
valley. I want to give up everything and become a true
sanyasi. I may do it. Anyhow my time hasn't come yet and
I am waiting with eager patience."

There were frequent discussions during the gathering
about the reorganization of the Order, for now that so
many people believed that the Teacher had come, the objects of the Order seemed no longer valid. On June 28
Lady Emily and Rajagopal drew up new objects: "1. To
draw together all those who believe in the presence in the
world of the World Teacher. 2. To work for Him in all
ways for His realization of His ideal for humanity. The
Order has no dogmas, creeds or systems of belief. Its inspiration is the Teacher, its purpose to embody His universal
life"

The name of the Order was to be changed from the Order of the Star in the East to the Order of the Star, and
the official magazine from the *Herald of the Star* to the
Star Review. Henceforth each country was to publish its
own version of the magazine but there was to be, in addition, an *International Star Bulletin*, published by the Star
Publishing Trust which had been legally set up in Holland
in 1926 and which was for many years to publish all K's
writings. Rajagopal was to be known in future as the
Chief Organizer instead of the General Secretary-
Treasurer, and the National Representatives were to be
National Organizers.

On the morning of July 11 Raja and his wife arrived at
Eerde and spent the night at the Castle on their way to
Huizen where Mrs. Besant was staying. Instead of his
morning talk K read three of his poems aloud, after which
there was a discussion on the new objects of the Order.
Raja objected to the first object as being too definite in as-
sociating too closely Krishnamurti, the disciple, with the
Lord. Several people spoke afterwards, all attacking Raja's
objection; Koos van de Leeuw even went so far as to say
that the first object was not definite enough.

In the afternoon K took Raja for a walk and convinced
him (as K thought) that he was indeed now one with the
Teacher. The next day K wrote a little note to Mrs. Besant
for Raja to take to her at Huizen:

More and more am I certain that I am the Teacher
and my mind and consciousness is changed. I think
Raja will be able to explain. My work and my life is
settled. I have reached my goal. You need never
doubt or think that I would love you any the less. I

love you with all my heart. . . . Oh! mother, the fulfilment of many lives has now come.

On the 15th he went over to Huizen for the day with
Koos to see Mrs. Besant, who was evidently much happier
there than she would have been at Eerde where she felt
that the people round K, even if not actually hostile to
her, were not sufficiently reverential towards the past.

On this same day Lady Emily received a letter from her
husband saying that he had heard through Lord Riddell
that the Central News Agency was about to publish an announcement of Mary's engagement to K. Lutyens and had
managed to get it stopped on the grounds that it would be
libel to say that a "holy man" was engaged; nevertheless
he wanted Mary sent home immediately. Lady Emily was
far more concerned with the effect this news might have
on K if he got to hear about it than with her husband's
anger, even though Betty had also written to say that her
father had sworn that if it were true he would give up all
his work, turn the family out of the house and never see
any of them again. Mary wished it were true, but knew
that K would be just as horrified as her father if he heard
about it and would almost certainly insist on sending her
back to London; so K was never told, and Lady Emily
managed to pacify her husband by assuring him that K
would never marry: "His whole life is devoted to one
object, which is to teach; and though he has many friends
of different ages he loves no one specially." Mary, who felt
even closer to K this year than the year before, stayed on.
She managed to see him alone every day if only for a few
minutes. Lady Emily also had her private sessions with
him as did, no doubt, many other members of the party.

On July 22, Raja and his wife came again from Huizen
for a couple of nights; in the evening, after K had gone to
bed for supper, he spoke to the assembled gathering about
K as an ego. In order to understand him, Raja said, one
must know of his past lives and also of his future when he
would be a Buddha; but many, many lives lay ahead of
him before he would achieve that goal. To Lady Emily his
talk was like "a douche of cold water," and most of the
others at Eerde felt the same.

No doubt this talk was relayed to K, for the next morning he spoke in Raja's presence:

There is a person called J. Krishnamurti who has ever had in view the end he would reach and in search of that end he has passed through many struggles, sorrows, pains. He has explored many avenues thinking they would lead to the goal. And then came the vision of the mountain top which is union with the Beloved, which is liberation, and from that moment he set aside all affections, all desires, all things except the attainment of the goal. And now that goal is reached and he has entered into the flame. And what happens after that does not matter—whether the spark remains within the flame or issues forth. And you may have the Beloved with you constantly even before you have become one with the Beloved.

Lady Emily noted that this "was an answer to Raja, almost a rebuke, made with such dignity, simplicity and courtesy."

The following evening Lady Emily went for a walk with Raja who "staggered" her by saying that the gathering that year at Eerde "had been a tragedy and a failure and had almost wrecked the plan of the Brotherhood [the occult hierarchy]."

Raja, unlike Wedgwood, was very devoted to K personally but he belonged to the old school of Theosophists; he had worked all his life for esoteric Theosophy, at the heart of which was the Path of Discipleship. If K was going to deny the existence of the Masters, or even by-pass them (he had already pronounced that they were "incidents"), Raja's life's work would be nullified. The older leaders of Theosophy were to feel this more and more; their influence was being undermined. What could they travel the world lecturing about? What would happen to their authority if they could no longer train pupils for discipleship and dole out Initiations as the ultimate accolade? The direct path to truth would by-pass them as well as the Masters whom they served.

30

Revolutionary Pronouncements

The Eerde party went into Camp on August 1, and the meetings began although the Convention was not to be officially opened for another week. That year almost three thousand members attended the Camp, some of them staying in hotels in the neighborhood. George Lansbury, who was staying in Camp, wrote that it was representative of more races, creeds and sects than had ever before been gathered into one place. Rom Landau, who was also there that year, described it vividly in his book *God is my Adventure*. A young Bulgarian, who could not afford the railway journey, had taken six weeks to walk to Ommen from his native country. A subscription was raised among the other campers to pay his fare home but he preferred to stay for good and was made custodian of the Camp in winter.

On August 2, in a talk entitled "Who brings the Truth," K gave his first public answer to the question which was troubling so many—did he or did he not believe in the Masters and the rest of the occult hierarchy?

When I was a small boy [he said] I used to see Sri Krishna, with the flute, as he is pictured by the Hindus, because my mother was a devotee of Sri Krishna. . . . When I grew older and met with Bishop Leadbeater and the Theosophical Society, I began to see the Master K.H.—again in the form which was put before me, the reality from their point of view—and hence the Master K.H. was to me the end. Later on, as I grew, I began to see the Lord Maitreya. That was two years ago and I saw him constantly in the form put before me. . . . Now lately, it has been the Buddha whom I have been seeing, and it has been my delight and my glory to be with Him. I have been asked what I mean by "the Beloved". I will give a

meaning, an explanation, which you will interpret as
you please. To me it is all—it is Sri Krishna, it is the
Master K.H., it is the Lord Maitreya, it is the Buddha, and yet it is beyond all these forms. What does
it matter what name you give? ... What you are
troubling about is whether there is such a person as
the World Teacher who has manifested Himself in
the body of a certain person, Krishnamurti; but in the
world nobody will trouble about this question. So you
will see my point of view when I talk about my Beloved. It is an unfortunate thing that I have to explain, but I must. I want it to be as vague as possible,
and I hope I have made it so. My Beloved is the open
skies, the flower, every human being. ... Till I was
able to say with certainty, without any undue excitement, or exaggeration in order to convince others,
that I was one with my Beloved, I never spoke. I
talked of vague generalities which everybody wanted.
I never said: I am the World Teacher; but now that I
feel I am one with my Beloved, I say it, not in order
to impress my authority on you, not to convince you
of my greatness, nor of the greatness of the World
Teacher, nor even of the beauty of life, but merely to
awaken the desire in your hearts and in your own
minds to seek out the Truth. If I say, and I will say,
that I am one with the Beloved, it is because I feel
and know it. I have found what I longed for, I have
become united, so that henceforth there will be no
separation, because my thoughts, my desires, my
longings—those of the individual self—have been
destroyed. ... I am as the flower that gives scent to
the morning air. It does not concern itself with who is
passing by. ... Until now you have been depending
on the two Protectors of the Order [Mrs. Besant and
Leadbeater] for authority, on someone else to tell
you the Truth, whereas the Truth lies within you. In
your own hearts, in your own experience, you will
find the Truth, and that is the only thing of value. ...
My purpose is not to create discussions on authority,
on the manifestations in the personality of Krishnamurti, but to give the waters that shall wash away
your sorrows, your petty tyrannies, your limitations,
so that you will be free, so that you will eventually
join that ocean where there is no limitation, where

there is the Beloved. . . . Does it really matter out of what glass you drink the water, so long as that water is able to quench your thirst. . . . I have been united with my Beloved, and my Beloved and I will wander together the face of the earth. . . . It is no good asking me who is the Beloved. Of what use is explanation? For you will not understand the Beloved until you are able to see Him in every animal, every blade of grass, in every person that is suffering, in every individual.

Mrs. Besant, with Raja and Wedgwood, arrived the day after this, August 3, and stayed at the Castle. Lady De La Warr also came at this time and stayed in camp. Mrs. Besant had wanted to come sooner but K had persuaded her not to, saying that he was shy of speaking in front of her. In truth he was afraid that what he intended to say at the meeting on August 2 would hurt her.

The Camp was officially opened on the 7th and closed on the 12th. Although Mrs. Besant's main speech during the Camp was entitled "The World Teacher is Here" she was still finding it difficult to reconcile what K was actually saying with her preconceived idea of what the Lord Maityrea would say when he came. In all these years of preparing for the Coming she had begged her readers and listeners to keep an open mind, had warned them that what he said when he came might not be acceptable because it would be so new; now she herself was in danger of falling into the very trap she had foreshadowed for others. K's pronouncements were becoming so utterly revolutionary that the foundations of her world were rocked.

She returned to Huizen on the 14th. After her departure a two-day Camp was held for those voluntary workers who had helped in the kitchens and administration offices and had not therefore been able to attend the meetings of the Convention. K's talk to this Service Camp, as it was called, on August 15 upset a great many people. There is no printed record of it; it was probably suppressed out of consideration for Mrs. Besant. Lady Emily's diary merely records: "Krishnaji spoke at the Service Camp. Quite excellent but upset many. One fine sentence was—you cannot really help till you are yourself beyond the need of help." Some idea of the disturbing things he said can, however, be gathered from a report by Peter Freedman, M.P., General Secretary of the T.S. for Wales: "He [K] told us that he had never been able to read through a Theosophical book in his life—could not understand our Theosophical 'jargon', and although he had heard many Theosophical lectures, none of them had convinced him of their knowledge of Truth."

Lady De La Warr was evidently one of those upset by this talk, for K wrote to Mrs. Besant on August 22 from Montesano in Switzerland where he had gone with Rajagopal and Jadu for a rest and where Lady De La Warr was also staying because she had been ill:

> I am so happy to get your letter, Amma mine. I didn't know that I had caused a storm by my speech at the Service Camp Fire. I don't remember what I said but when the copy comes I will see. I am *very* sorry that Lady D. and others are upset. She has not said a word to me. I am afraid they all object to think for themselves, it's so much easier to sit, in comfort, in the thought of others.
>
> Life is curious and it's going to be difficult. It's all in the day's work. I am, more and more, certain in my vision of the Truth. These mountains and the clean air here are wonderful and I have the Beloved with me. So—!!
>
> Mother, we two must stick together and nothing else matters.
>
> I will talk to Lady De La Warr, and try to explain whatever she may have misunderstood.

And four days later he wrote again:

> I had a long talk with Lady De La Warr and she told me she was not in the least upset or worried but she said that she did not agree with all the things I said. That's quite a different thing. Anyhow, Amma mine, she said she never would quarrel with me!![1] Also please don't think or worry about it. I do not know whether that unfortunate speech was taken down; it doesn't matter. . . .
>
> In these hills and Forests, I feel more close to my Beloved than ever.

---

[1] Lady De La Warr never did quarrel with him but she never fully recovered her health and died in 1930.

I am so happy that we are going back to India together.

But Mrs. Besant was not appeased. She later talked to Lady Emily in London about her deep concern at the increasing division between the Esoteric Section of the T.S. and the Star, maintaining that K gathered round him at Eerde young people who knew nothing of the past, or renegade Theosophists, and that "his Service Camp speech had upset people dreadfully." At Adyar, she said, the words had been "I come not to destroy," but she feared the present spirit was very destructive. Lady Emily asked her whether she wanted to restrict his followers to Theosophists. She replied certainly not but that others would be of no use to him.

From Montesano K went to Paris on September 21 where he had promised to sit for the sculptor Antoine Bourdelle whom he had met through Madame De Manziarly. The sittings were begun next day. Bourdelle would have liked him to stay a month so that he could make a full-length statue, but as that was impossible K sat for two hours in the morning and two in the afternoon for eight days. "What M. Bourdelle does is going to be first class," he told Mrs. Besant on September 23, "as he is really a master in his profession. He's like Rodin but better, I think." Bourdelle, then sixty-six, was immediately conquered by K. "When one hears Krishnamurti speak one is astonished—so much wisdom and so young a man. . . . Krishnamurti is a great sage and were I fifteen years of age I would follow him," he is quoted as saying. He considered his bust of K, now in the Bourdelle Museum in Paris, among his finest works.

K flew back to London on September 30. He stayed with Lady Emily and she went with him to dinner at Buckingham Street on October 1 to celebrate Mrs. Besant's eightieth birthday. Her largest birthday present was £25,000 left to her by Mrs. Percy Douglas-Hamilton who had recently died. The Order of the Star also benefited by £10,000 in the will.

K was to go with Mrs. Besant to India in the middle of October. In the meantime, while she remained in London, he returned to Eerde. He was not present when, on October 3, Rosalind and Rajagopal were married at a Registrar's Office in London with Jadu as one of the witnesses, nor at the religious ceremony performed on the 11th at St. Mary's Catholic Church in the Caledonian Road. Mrs. Besant gave Rosalind away while David Graham Pole, the lawyer who had helped Mrs. Besant with her appeal to the High Court in Madras in 1913, was best man. Presumably Bishop Pigott, the Liberal Catholic bishop in England, officiated. K has no recollection of what he thought about this marriage. His feelings about marriage in general had, however, undergone a considerable change since 1922; he no longer considered it a complete disaster.

Rosalind and Rajagopal, after touring Europe with Philip van Pallandt, went off to Arya Vihara at Ojai which was to become their home. K meanwhile had joined Mrs. Besant at Marseilles. Raja, Jadu and Dr. Rocke were also of the party returning to India on the *China*. While the ship was in the Red Sea, Dr. Rocke fell down a companion-way and died instantly of cerebral hemorrhage. She was one of K's oldest friends and he was deeply shocked and saddened by her death.

31

The River into the Sea

Landing in Bombay on October 27, they were met by a
crowd of reporters to whom Mrs. Besant made a statement
about K:

> I bear witness that he has been accounted worthy
> of that for which he had been chosen, worthy to
> blend his consciousness with that of a fragment, an
> *amsa*, of the omnipresent consciousness of the World
> Teacher. . . . When He came two thousand years ago
> in Palestine, He chose as the body He would use that
> of a member of a subject race. . . . And when He has
> come to us . . . He has chosen from among the
> despised and the rejected of the world. . . . And to us
> now, Indians, brethren, this great joy has come. . . .
> Only a few months have passed since the long and
> steady growth attained its completion in union with
> "the Beloved". . . . And now that he has come back to
> you, to his own people, to his own race, yet trans-
> cending both, for he belongs to the whole world, you
> have the joy that your race has given a body to bring
> the great Message of help.

One can imagine the effect of this pronouncement on
Indians whose natural tendency is to prostrate themselves
in worship without the slightest embarrassment. Such a
public affirmation, however, called forth from George
Arundale an article which illustrates the difficulties with
which K was faced at Adyar that winter: "Our President
has been declaring that the Lord [Maitreya] is here. . . .
Now it is impossible for me to reconcile this statement . . .
with my own knowledge of the Lord as He is in His glorious body." Mrs. Besant, he went on, had agreed that only
a fragment of the Lord's consciousness was in Krishnamurti; he, Arundale, had doubts about even that fragment

being with Krishnamurti always. But she had said, "The Lord is here," and she must be right, for she was always right.

What were Theosophists to make of such ambiguity? Leadbeater was more subtle. In a tribute to Mrs. Besant on her eightieth birthday he had written, "Another and very wonderful department of her work has been to train and to take care of the vehicle of the World Teacher. . . . Now, she is reaping the reward of that care and is watching with joy the unfoldment of the bud which she has nurtured, the blossoming of the flower whose fragrance shall fill the world." Leadbeater had found a position from which he could retreat whenever he wanted to: the fragrance might not fill the world nor the bud fully open for many years to come.

Nevertheless, for the time being, Leadbeater was in accord with K. He arrived at Adyar on December 4 for the T.S. Convention and four days later K was writing to Lady Emily about him:

I had a long talk with him for an hour & a half. He agrees with me to an astonishing extent. He asked me what I felt like & I told him there was no Krishna—the river & the sea. He said yes, like the books of old, it's all true. He was very nice & extraordinarily reverential. . . . I haven't had much time to think about renunciation & sangha [living in a religious community]. It's at the back of my mind simmering & growing larger & larger. I want to go very slow about these things. They are important & inadvisable to rush.

During the Convention Mrs. Besant lost no opportunity of proclaiming her complete faith in K. At one meeting she said, "In August of the present year 1927 such part of the consciousness of the world Teacher as could manifest within the habitation of a human physical body descended and abode in him. . . . I, who have known him from a little child . . . now have become his devoted disciple."

After a visit to Calicut on the west coast following the Convention, K returned to Adyar for the sacred Star Day of January 11—the anniversary of his first Initiation seventeen years before. "There was a meeting & Amma & C.W.L. & I spoke," he reported to Lady Emily next day.

"They have certainly made things perfectly plain that I am
the Teacher, everyone trying to find out if I am the Christ,
the bringer of Truth. Everywhere I go that is the question
I am asked... By heavens how difficult it is going to be."
He told her in this same letter of January 12, 1928, that
his head had been terribly bad and that he must have
fainted quite often. He was evidently disappointed that
Leadbeater could give no explanation for the continuance
of this pain except that "it must be part of the work.
George is in a state about me," he added; "thinks I am
not right etc. I hardly see either his wife or him. I am not
in the least worried. I'm greatly afraid it's personal & no
great thought behind it—him, I mean. Well, Amma &
C.W.L. are 'boosting' me up, so he feels left out of it all.
I'm sorry."

A Star Camp followed—the first Camp in India, held
at Guindy School just outside Adyar—at which K spoke
twice a day as well as holding a two-and-a-half-hour question and answer meeting.

> It was *my* own fault entirely [he wrote to Lady
> Emily on January, 17], as I wanted those particular
> questions answered when once they were started ...
> on Individual Uniqueness, the Beloved and creative-
> ness. I don't know how those people stuck it out!!
> I couldn't let it go half way through. The Camp was
> on the "whole" a fair success. There were about a
> thousand. Full of devotion but I had to fight against
> a wall of everything. It was so exhausting but there it
> is. It is all so difficult but I am going to fight 'em all.
> Nothing else matters. Save them against themselves.
> It's a strange life. . . . I'm feeling absolutely done up
> & weak but it will be alright soon.

He toured India after this, speaking at every place to
packed audiences of about three thousand. Now that
Rajagopal was married, Jadu had become his close companion, traveling everywhere with him. Jadu had much of
Nitya's charm and was like him in many ways. Because of
this there was a natural affinity between him and K, and
K became very devoted to him.

By the time K and Jadu sailed from Bombay for Europe on February 29, 1928, K was completely exhausted,
having had another attack of bronchitis and given two

public lectures in Bombay. They were travelling on a slow ship to Genoa and for the first time K spoke to his fellow passengers and held discussions with them after repeated requests.

From Genoa they went to Paris, then Ommen and then on to London, where K gave his first public talk on March 31 at the Friends Meeting House, which created so much interest that hundreds had to be turned away. Four days later he and Jadu sailed for New York. K intended to have a complete rest at Ojai before the first Star Camp to be held there in May on the Happy Valley Foundation land that Mrs. Besant had acquired the year before. K was very glad to see Rajagopal and Rosalind again at Ojai, and, as he told Mrs. Besant, delighted with the growth of all the new trees she had helped him to plant at Arya Vihara. In place of the Lincoln he now had a Ford Chief which he pronounced to be as good as the Lincoln.

But before the Camp he gave his first public address in America on the evening of May 15 at the Hollywood Bowl before an audience of 16,000 who, according to the *Los Angeles Times*, listened in "apparently rapt attention" to his talk on "Happiness through Liberation."

Meanwhile, Mrs. Besant at Adyar had sponsored a new divine personality—the World Mother, as she preferred to call the Virgin Mary, just as she preferred to call the Christ the World Teacher as having a less denominational ring. Rukmini Arundale was the human vehicle chosen by the World Mother. This movement was a more specific revival of one of the many wonders "brought through" at Huizen in 1925—the special Order for Women which the Lord Maitreya was to found when he came and in which Lady Emily and Dr. Rocke had been consecrated abbesses. The story was reported in the *Times of India* under the heading "Mrs. Besant's New Fad;" it was taken up by the American papers and inevitably K was brought into it. He wrote to Leadbeater on May 4:

I hear Amma has proclaimed Mrs. Arundale as the representative of the World Mother etc. I hear also that I am dragged into it all. It is the work of George, with his messages, the outcome of his fertile brain. His machinations are innumerable. I do not want to be mixed up with any of these things. I am going to be clear of such complications. Only I wish

Amma hadn't mixed me up with it, as she did in the affair of the so-called Apostles. I suppose you have been informed about it all—the World Mother etc.— and I suppose you do not mind my being frank with you. Life is strange. It is full of complications and as I am free of it all, I do not want to be caught up once again in it.

I know definitely what I want to do here, this time, and in this world and I am going to do it. So few understand and hence it is going to be difficult and even now some of the so called 'Apostles' are creating trouble and derision. I am *not* complaining: on the contrary, it's rather amusing. Only, I want to tell you of these things, as you know how I stand, with regard to it all. I hope you don't mind.

More and more, I am certain of my union with my Beloved, with the Teacher, with the life eternal. As Krishna, I do not exist and that is the truth of the matter. George and Wedgwood have begun to deny this but fortunately there is great space and open fields of understanding. I am *not* going to convert anyone to my way of thinking but I am going to assert the fact, when it is necessary.

It is all rather curious.

My head has been and is very bad but there it is. I am not in the least concerned about it except that it is rather tiring. I am taking care *not* to be overworked.

I will see that you are kept in touch with all that I do, say and anything that's published will be sent to you hereafter. I am very sorry, if this has not been done before.

K told Lady Emily on May 9 that the press had asked him what he thought of the World Mother to which he had simply replied that he knew nothing about it and therefore could make no comments. "It's all so absurd," he wrote, "but for all foolish things there is happily a timely end. Vide Apostles!!!!"[1]

[1] The World Mother movement was short-lived. In 1936 Rukmini Arundale founded an Academy of Arts in Madras. She has also done a great deal for animal welfare in India. She stood for the Presidency of the T.S. in 1973 after the death of her brother, Sri Ram, who had been President for many years. She was defeated by only fifty votes by an Englishman, John Coats.

He mentioned in this letter that Raja and Helen were coming to Ojai for the first Star Camp. He said how glad he would be to see Raja again but made no comment on Helen at all, although this was his first mention of her in a letter since the beginning of 1925 when she had first gone to Sydney, nor does he mention her again in any of his letters to Lady Emily. He and Helen evidently drifted apart. In the early thirties she married the American author, Scott Nearing, and has lived a very happy and fulfilled life.

The Ojai Camp was a great success although only about a thousand people attended it. The organization was excellent and the food much better than at Ommen; the cafeteria system was used, whereas at Ommen helpers went round the tables serving the food from large metal buckets. The morning talks, to which the public were admitted, were held in a grove of live-oaks—the evergreen oaks of Southern California—and as the weather was perfect, all the meetings were held out of doors. The Oak Grove at Ojai was to become a sacred spot.

On May 30, two days after the Camp closed, K, Jadu and Rajagopal left for New York en route for Europe while Rosalind remained at Ojai. They arrived on June 14 in time to meet Mrs. Besant coming from India, and four days later went with her to Paris where, on the 23rd, K gave a talk in the largest concert hall, the Salle Pleyel. On the 27th he broadcast in French for fifteen minutes from the Eiffel Tower Radio Station to an estimated two million listeners. His subject was "The Search for Happiness."

On the last day of June a larger gathering than ever assembled at Castle Eerde for a month before the Ommen Camp. The other barn had now been partly converted so there was room for visitors from the outside world to come for a few days at a time. Sir Roderick Jones, the head of Reuter's, was there for a couple of days with his wife, Enid Bagnold, and Leopold Stokowski and his wife, who had met K at Adyar that winter, came on July 11 for a week.[1] Among K's old friends were Madame de Manziarly and her three daughters, Lady Emily, Mary, Jadu,

---

[1] A conversation between K and Stokowski at Eerde was published in the *International Star Bulletin*, May 1929, reprinted from *The World Today* (New York). They discussed inspiration and creativeness.

Rajagopal, Noomi Hagge and Ruth who, early in July,
had married John Tettemer, a bishop in the Liberal
Catholic Church whom she had met in Sydney. It was to
prove a very happy marriage. In the autumn the Tettemers
went to live in California where Ruth has lived ever since.
She is still a close friend of K's.

K was in bed again for the first week of the gathering
with the bronchitis that was almost becoming chronic. On
July 3 he wrote to Mrs. Besant in London:

> You have been in my mind so much and Amma,
> people have no understanding. I wish they would
> have more affection in their hearts. How angry some
> people are, specially those who ought to know better.
> But it is a strange world. People are building strong
> and foolish antagonism against what I am saying and
> I am sorry. I am not complaining, far from it but you
> ought to know, Mother. It is all rather amusing.
>
> I hear you will be free after the fifteenth of this
> month and how nice it would be if you can come
> here then. I do hope that you can come, Amma.
> They have built a special hut for you, to be used, if
> you wish, during the camp.[1] There is also a newly
> wall-papered room awaiting you here. Oh, Amma, I
> love you with all my heart and as long as we remain
> together, nothing matters. I am more certain than
> ever and I shall go on.

Shortly after this Mrs. Besant's magnificent health broke
down for the first time; she was obliged to cancel her remaining public engagements and was confined to bed in
Miss Bright's house at Wimbledon. It was said by some
Theosophists that the cause of her breakdown was shock
brought on by hearing that at Eerde K had declared more
vehemently than ever that the way to truth, happiness,
liberation, or whatever one cared to call it, could not be
found in any outward form or "shelters of comfort" but
only in oneself, and that he had even mentioned the possibility of dissolving the Order of the Star. He had said, "I
do not want to have followers. . . . I abhor the very idea of

---

[1] Several people had now built themselves permanent wooden huts,
costing about £100, on the Camp site. They had to be of a certain
approved design and were unobtrusively situated among the trees.
K himself had such a hut where he could rest between meetings.

anyone calling himself my disciple. Be rather the disciple of the understanding which is the fruit of ripe thought and great love, be the disciple of your own understanding." Mrs. Besant at Adyar the year before had called herself his "devoted disciple" and now he was saying that he abhorred the idea of disciples.

K himself, however, who was sent daily bulletins about Mrs. Besant by Miss Bright, took her illness at its face value—a severe feverish cold—and still hoped she would be able to come to the Camp, but on July 28 he heard that she was returning to India on August 9 without coming to Holland at all. On the 30th he went to England to see her although he could stay only one night because of the opening of the Camp. On his return he sent her a particularly loving letter saying how much it had meant to him to see her and how he would miss her at the Camp. He returned to the Castle just in time for Philip van Pallandt's wedding to a Dutch girl he had been engaged to for some time. After a civil marriage in Ommen, a wedding ceremony of the Liberal Catholic Church was performed in the drawing-room of the Castle by Ruth's husband, Bishop Tettemer. It was the first wedding ceremony K had ever attended and he pronounced "most of it bunk."

In spite of missing Mrs. Besant personally it must have been a relief to K not to have her at the Camp, for he was able to say just what he wanted without fear of wounding her. In a talk to the National Organizers before the Camp opened he said, "The truth I set before you is much too lovely to be rejected and much too great to be accepted without thought." He told them he would abolish the Order at once if it "claimed to be a vessel which holds the Truth and the only Truth."

At one of his talks during the Eerde gathering he explained what he meant by "the World Teacher":

I hold that there is an eternal Life which is the Source and the Goal, the beginning and the end and yet it is without end or beginning. In that Life alone is there fulfilment. And anyone who fulfills that Life has the key to the Truth without limitation. That Life is for all. Into that Life the Buddha, the Christ entered. From my point of view, I have attained, I have entered into that Life. That Life has no form as

Truth has no form, no limitation. And to that Life everyone must return.

At one of the Camp meetings he said, "The time has come when you must no longer subject yourself to anything. . . . I hope you will not listen to anyone, but will listen only to your own intuition, your own understanding, and give a public refusal to those who would be your interpreters." The interpreters were, of course, the leaders of the Theosophical society. He warned his listeners that they were to be shaken to their foundations.

During the meetings he was asked many questions such as, "Is it true that you do not want disciples?" "What do you think of rituals and ceremonials?" "Why do you tell us that there are no stages along the Path?" "As you tell us there is no God, no moral code and neither good nor evil, how does your teaching differ from ordinary materialism?" "Are you the Christ come back?" Some extracts from K's answers show how little those who asked the questions had understood him:

I say again that I have no disciples. Everyone of you is a disciple of the Truth if you understand the Truth and do not follow individuals. . . . The only manner of attaining Truth is to become disciples of the Truth itself without a mediator. . . . Truth does not give hope; it gives understanding. . . . There is no understanding in the worship of personalities. . . . I still maintain that all ceremonies are unnecessary for spiritual growth. . . . If you would seek the Truth you must go out, far away from the limitations of the human mind and heart and there discover it—and that Truth is within yourself. Is it not much simpler to make Life itself the goal—Life itself the guide, the Master and the God—than to have mediators, *gurus*, who must inevitably step down the Truth, and hence betray it? . . . I say that Liberation can be attained at any stage of evolution by a man who understands, and that to worship stages as you do, is not essential. . . . Do not quote me afterwards as an authority. I refuse to be your crutch. I am not going to be brought into a cage for your worship. When you bring the fresh air of the mountain and hold it in a small room, the freshness of that air disappears and

there is stagnation.... As I am free, as I have found
this Truth, which is limitless, without beginning or
end, I will not be conditioned by you. . . . I have
never said there is no God. I have said that there is
only God as manifested in you . . . but I am not going
to use the word God. . . . I prefer to call this Life. . . .
Of course there is neither good nor evil. Good is that
of which you are not afraid; evil is that of which you
are afraid. So, if you destroy fear, you are spiritually
fulfilled. . . . When you are in love with life, and you
place that love before all things, and judge by that
love, and not by your fear, then this stagnation which
you call morality will disappear.... I am not concerned with societies, with religions, with dogmas, but
I am concerned with life because I am Life. . . .
Friend, do not concern yourself with who I am; you
will never know. . . . If I say I am the Christ, you will
create another authority. If I say I am not, you will
also create another authority. Do you think Truth has
anything to do with what you think I am? You are
not concerned with the Truth but you are concerned
with the vessel that contains the Truth. You do
not want to drink the waters, but you want to find
out who fashioned the vessel which contains the
waters. . . . Drink the water if the water is clean: I
say to you that I have that clean water; I have that
balm which shall purify, that shall heal greatly; and
you ask me: Who are you? I am all things because I
am Life.

He closed the Convention with the words, "There have
been many thousand people at these Camps and what
could they not do in the world if they all understood!
They could change the face of the world tomorrow." He
told the Reuter's man who was covering the meetings that
neither Buddha nor Christ had claimed divinity or wished
to found a religion; it was their followers who had done so
after they were dead.

Lady Emily contributed an article about this Ommen
Camp to the *International Star Bulletin* for September
1928 which voiced the bewilderment of many of those
present that year and was also in fact expressing her own
inner turmoil:

How strange it seems that for seventeen years we have been expecting the World Teacher, and now when He speaks of what is beyond all forms, we are hurt or angry. He is making us do our own work, mentally and emotionally, and that is the last thing we expected of Him. Some people are returning home naked and alone, their foundations shattered, realizing the necessity of reorientating themselves in a world in which every value has changed. . . . If there can be tragedy associated with one who has attained ultimate liberation and eternal happiness, the tragic side of this Camp has been the way in which the dead past has arisen at every moment to confront the new ideas.

32

"Everyone will give me up"

Raja, who had been lecturing in America, arrived at the
Castle soon after the Camp closed, and K invited him to
go with him to St. Moritz on August 15 where he proposed to spend a few weeks resting. He and Raja had
many private talks together during this time in Switzerland, the result of which were to have a direct influence
on Mrs. Besant's future actions, Rajagopal, Lady Emily,
Mary and Jadu were also with K at St. Moritz in a chalet
overlooking the Lake of Silvaplana. K believed that Mary
at this time was having an affair with a married man
much older than herself, and she had some unhappy hours
before she was able to convince him that he was mistaken.
Nevertheless, he felt that her friendship with this man was
harmful from every point of view. K had just read a little
book, recently published—a narrative poem by Stephen
Phillips called *Marpessa*—which tells the story of the mortal girl, Marpessa, who, given the choice by Zeus between
the God Apollo and the mortal Idas, chooses Idas. K was
constantly telling Mary now not to be "a Marpessa." In
urging this he was not comparing himself with Apollo but
contrasting a life of thrilling spiritual adventure with the
mediocrity of a humdrum marriage.

From Switzerland K went to Paris where he gave more
sittings to Bourdelle for the bust begun the year before;
then back to Eerde and thence to Toulon from where he
and Jadu sailed for Colombo on October 20 while Rajagopal returned to Ojai. From Aden, on the 28th, K wrote to
Lady Emily:

I had a letter from Raja at Naples in which he enclosed a copy of a letter which he has sent to Amma
& C.W.L. He said to them (I am telling you this in
resumé) that he had been seeing me a great deal,
that I feel that they are not supporting me, that

L.C.C. [Liberal Catholic Church], Masonry, World mother etc., are from my point of view waste of time. That I maintain the "Direct Path" & everything [else] is a waste of time. That if they say I am only a part, how can then the part disagree with the whole. . . . That though he, (Raja), doesn't follow me entirely, he sees the absolute necessity for some action. That I am likely to change, as I am so one-pointed, & so they must do something about [it], alter the E.S. etc.

I am afraid Amma will be rather hurt, as she will think that I haven't talked to her as frankly as with Raja. I have talked to her frankly as you know, but somehow she doesn't see my point of view. . . . It's all to change my attitude for anybody, in this or in another world. They may deny that I am the World Teacher etc. but I am going on.

Life's a strange affair, but fortunately for me I have a strong sense of the ridiculous. . . . This boat is full of Austraelians, the scorning variety that laugh at you to your face. So that keeps me from being conceited!!!

He added, "I have written such a long letter to Mary, as I have been writing to her every day. She will read out to you interesting bits." He had been writing to Mary very frequently for the past two years but unfortunately she destroyed all his letters when she became engaged to be married in 1929.

He arrived at Colombo on November 5 and went straight on to Adyar from where he wrote to Lady Emily three days later:

Here I am at last & it's all curious. At Colombo the local papers, English and Indian, were full of Krishnamurti. Interviews, & I spoke there. Garlands at every station & devotion. . . .

Amma is in Delhi & will be back here the day after tomorrow morning. I had a letter from her & she has closed up the E.S. throughout the world, indefinitely. She says that as I am the Teacher, I ought to teach & no one else, & so the E.S. is closed. It's a good thing; it had to come & it has come in timely manner. Many will be relieved & many will dislike it & curse. But there it is. Here, at Adyar, many, I believe, are delighted and the thoughtless are becoming thoughtful. At last. It's all *very* serious & gives me an immense opportunity but I must be wise & full of patience. I am happy Amma has done this before I came, of her own accord.

Dwarkanath tells me that she is losing her memory. It's all tragic. Poor Amma. Life is painful, cruel, but it all has a purpose. . . . George and his wife left two days before I came to Adyar!!!! . . . Amma has done the biggest thing that anyone can do. To build up something & then to put it aside for something bigger is the greatest thing.

It was indeed a great step Mrs. Besant had taken. The Esoteric Section of the T.S. had been founded by Madame Blavatsky in 1889 and was at the very heart of the Society. It had been formed for the purpose of bringing its members into contact with the Masters, and therefore in closing it Mrs. Besant was virtually shutting off the Masters.

Three weeks later K wrote from Bombay to tell Lady Emily that he had spoken every day at Adyar. "Talking to people who have ceased to think is very exhausting. Some are at heart against [me] but respect has been drilled into them. They are all a bit nervous of me, as I am like a piece of glass that reflects—especially them, which they don't like." He had seen George and his wife, he went on, and they had had a long talk.

George says he doesn't believe I am etc. but doesn't want to say it outside on account of consideration (?) to Amma!!! He said, "You go your way & we will go ours. I have also something to teach etc." So there it is. It's all rather amusing but strangely tragic. Poor Amma, she's the only one that believes what she says. For the rest, they are mere words. They are not frank & direct about it all. They said they were both apostles of the Lord. . . . God, what a world!!! I want to be cynical but I won't.

On account of a very bad cold K had had to cancel a visit to Karachi and Lahore, so from Bombay he went to Benares for a winter gathering as at Eerde. Mrs. Besant came there for a night on her way to Allahabad.

She was awfully nice [he told Lady Emily on December 5], & said that whatever I wanted she would do. She said, pathetically, how she wants to give up her Presidentship of the T.S. & come with me wherever I went. But her Master told her to stand by her work, & there it was. She said she was disappointed. Poor Amma. . . . Presently there will be a clear-cut division which is much better than this pretense.

After speaking twice a day at the winter gathering the pain in his head and spine started up again very badly and no one could help, "not as before."

He had asked Lady Emily to send him any books that she and Mary had enjoyed. A parcel of them arrived at Benares, but what with his increasingly large correspondence, talks and interviews, he came to read less and less, and his reiterated desire to spend several months in quiet study was never to be fulfilled.

Mary was beginning to feel at this time, as no doubt many others felt too, that if everyone changed as he was urging them to do and became divine like him, without any personal desires, the world would come to a standstill. Lady Emily must have passed on these feelings of Mary's to K for he was writing from Benares in this same letter of December 5: "Please tell Mary I am not divine but the natural flower of the world. The way she means 'divine' is that I am a freak. Perfection is not freakishness. If all the world thought & lived like me it would be lovely & would not come to a standstill." He remembered Lady Emily's birthday (she would be fifty-four on December 26) and after wishing her many happy returns, added, "May our love for each other always increase."

He wrote to Raja on December 27, "I want to do something and I am going to do it and that is all. I am going to pursue that path which is the only path. No one can take away a particle from that which is eternal, which is in me. There is a lovely pure and open sky and people are quarreling about the small cloud that's driven by the blind wind."

While K was at Benares this time the Rishi Valley Trust managed to acquire from the military authorities some 300 acres of land which K had long wanted for a new school. This was at Rajghat, a lovely spot on the banks of the Ganges, just north of Kashi railway station. The pilgrims' path runs through the Rajghat estate, linking Kashi with Sarnath where the Buddha preached his first sermon after enlightenment. K told Lady Emily that all the capital of the Trust would be spent on this land but it could not be helped.[1]

Because of her political commitments Mrs. Besant was unable to attend the T.S. Convention at Benares that followed the winter gathering, and since Leadbeater and Raja were not there either that year it was left to K to preside over it. Mrs. Besant, entirely of her own volition, had given instructions that no ceremonials were to be held within the Theosophical Compound during the Convention, "for the life He pours out so richly will, when the hour comes, create its own forms in which His exquisite ideals will clothe themselves; but that time is not yet." George Arundale, however, asserted his right as a Bishop to hold services of the Liberal Catholic Church. He celebrated Mass, which was attended by hundreds of Star members as well as by Theosophists, just outside the Compound, thus obeying Mrs. Besant in the letter but defying her in spirit. Nevertheless, still doing everything in her power to try to reconcile K with the T.S., Mrs. Besant upheld George's action and quoted the *Bhagavad Gita*, when writing in the *Theosophist*, that all ways lead to the same spiritual goal, and Sri Krishna's dictum: "Mankind comes to Me along many roads."

Mrs. Besant was able to reconcile K's teaching with Theosophy in her own mind by emphasizing that only a fragment of the Lord's consciousness manifested itself through K. "Krishnamurti's physical consciousness does not share in the omniscience of the Lord Maitreya—that is the main point you have to remember," she wrote in the *Theosophist*. It was this which was causing "so much confusion." "I have heard Krishnamurti say over and over again: 'Throw away all forms,' but I do not do it. . . . I know this does not apply to me. . . . But if a person makes a form an end, then the sooner it is broken up the better." Leadbeater had confirmed this theory when writing to

[1] There is now a co-educational school at Rajghat, a women's college, an agricultural farm and a hospital giving practically free medical aid to the surrounding villages. Recently a teachers' training college was started there. Rama Rao was the first headmaster of the school. He died of tuberculosis at the age of forty-five.

Mrs. Besant before she left London, "Of course our Krishnaji has not the Omniscience of the Lord. No physical body of our stage could, I imagine, have that, I say so quite frankly."

Mrs. Besant's contradictory statements must have created more confusion among Theosophists than they cleared up. She was virtually saying, "The World Teacher is here but what He has to say is not necessarily valid for all of us." She was in fact trying to reconcile two irreconcilables.

After the Convention K returned to Adyar and then went to Bombay from where he and Jadu sailed for Europe on February 2, 1929. After brief visits to Paris, Eerde and London, they went on to New York at the end of the month. During the voyage K was writing to Mar de Manziarly, "I will never give up anyone, but everyone will give me up." He usually wrote to her in French but this sentence was in English.

This remark to Mar was no doubt called forth by his having heard from Mary in London that she was about to become engaged, for on the same day as he was writing to Mar (March 5) he also wrote to Lady Emily:

At first I was strangely upset about it all—you know what I mean—and I carefully thought about it while I was with you & it's alright now. One's innate poise returns, at least mine has. My ideas & my outlook must not interfere with Mary's growth. There will be very few who will go with me the whole way. I hope she will come out of it all a full blossomed flower.

Mary had made Marpessa's choice, yet it was with a sense of betrayal that she married her mortal; not betrayal of K, who, she knew, had no personal need of her or of any other individual, but betrayal of the view from the mountain top he had shown her. As her reaction against what she had found to be an impossible way of life was very strong, she married a very worldly young man. Not surprisingly this marriage ended in divorce.

It was not everyone who gave K up; a handful of old friends have never wavered in their loyalty to him, though certainly many have failed him in one way or another. Some left, their love for him turned to bitterness; some reacted against him only to return years later; some, though continuing to revere him, craved a positive religion; others, though striving to keep up with him, found themselves left far behind; some tried to possess him and when they failed to do so turned antagonistic. Yet always, when old friends dropped away, new one seemed to spring up.

K was back at Ojai by the middle of March. He wrote to Mrs. Besant on the 22nd to tell her how lovely the Happy Valley looked. The cottage where he was sleeping had been "fixed up" and a new bathroom added by an American lady, Mrs. Hastings, who had been at the Eerde gathering the year before.

> I am so surprised [he told Lady Emily] there is so much antagonism in this country about me, among the members ... but I suppose it has to be. It shows the leaven is working. I am feeling dead tired, though I am not doing much. Probably I am getting relaxation. I don't know when my head will begin. Rajagopal, Jadu & I have been talking, talking about everything, changing the belief in the Star, magazines, camps, and getting excited & quarrelling.

The pain in his head must have begun soon after this, for he was writing to tell Raja on May 13 that for the past six weeks not only had he been in pain but that he had been sick after every meal and was consequently very weak. Raja himself was evidently in a depressed state at this time and K's letter to him was very affectionate:

> I am so grieved at what you say. ... For heaven's sake, death won't solve anything. Loneliness is inevitable as long as——! You know what I think about that, so I won't bore you. I am so sorry Raja, my heart is with you. ... There are so many things I should like very much to talk over with you. ... Things are going to be very difficult, but tant mieux.

The press was now saying that there had been a rift between Mrs. Besant and K. "Those papers here are really absurd," he wrote to Mrs. Besant on the same day as he was writing to Raja. "They want us two to quarrel but as

we don't, they say we have. So that's settled for them. . . .
You are so much in my thoughts and in my heart."

Although the Ojai Camp was not to be until the end of
May, he had intended to speak every week-end from the
middle of April; then a new doctor in Hollywood, Dr.
Morris, whom he had been to see because he was feeling
so extraordinarily tired, shook him considerably by saying
that his frequent attacks of bronchitis had left his lung in
a weak condition and that if he went on as he was doing
he would have tuberculosis within two years. Dr. Strong
confirmed this, so he cancelled all his talks for the summer, including the three lectures he was to have given at
the Queen's Hall in London in July, and decided to attend
only the Ojai and Ommen Camps and the Eerde gathering. "Don't worry or tell anyone," he was writing to Lady
Emily on May 26. "I must be careful. It would never do if
anything happened to me." On Dr. Morris's recommendation he went to Pine Crest in the San Bernadino mountains for ten days with Rosalind and John Ingleman and
his wife. Although he put on a pound and a half while he
was away he still weighed less than eight stone on his
return.

He seemed by this time to have abandoned completely
his idea of becoming a *sanyasi*. He had not mentioned it
in any of his letters to Lady Emily since the one of December 8, 1927. He had come to realize that his work had
to be in the world—that he must go out and talk to the
many instead of waiting for the few to come to him.

The Ojai Camp, starting on May 27, had doubled its attendance that year and received very good press notices.
At one meeting K made a striking pronouncement: "I say
now, I say without conceit, with proper understanding,
with fullness of mind and heart, that I am that full flame
which is the glory of life, to which all human beings, individuals as well as the whole world, must come." There was
a rumor going round the Camp that he intended soon to
dissolve the Order of the Star.

Leaving from New York on the *Leviathan* on June 12
with Jadu and the Rajagopals, he reached London on the
18th. There he found Mrs. Besant who had arrived from
India on May 4. She was so busy with the Home Rule
League for India which she had started in England and
with her usual lectures that they hardly met but she

planned to attend the Camp at Ommen in August. K went with Jadu to Paris on June 24 and then to Montroc in the French Alps for a complete rest before the Eerde gathering.

"Truth is a Pathless Land"

The 1929 Ommen Camp opened on August 2 in an atmosphere of tension and expectancy, most of the people there realizing what was to happen. The next morning, in the presence of Mrs. Besant, more than three thousand Star members, and with many thousands of Dutch people listening on the radio, K made a speech dissolving the Order of the Star:

> We are going to discuss this morning the dissolution of the Order of the Star. Many will be delighted, and others will be rather sad. It is a question neither for rejoicing nor for sadness, because it is inevitable, as I am going to explain. . . .
>
> I maintain that Truth is a pathless land, and you cannot approach it by any path whatsoever, by any religion, by any sect. That is my point of view, and I adhere to that absolutely and unconditionally. Truth, being limitless, unconditioned, unapproachable by any path whatsoever, cannot be organized; nor should any organization be formed to lead or coerce people along any particular path. If you first understand that, then you will see how impossible it is to organize a belief. A belief is purely an individual matter, and you cannot and must not organize it. If you do, it becomes dead, crystallized; it becomes a creed, a sect, a religion, to be imposed on others.
>
> This is what everyone throughout the world is attempting to do. Truth is narrowed down and made a plaything for those who are weak, for those who are only momentarily discontented. Truth cannot be brought down, rather the individual must make the effort to ascend to it. You cannot bring the mountain-top to the valley. . . .
>
> So that is the first reason, from my point of view,

why the Order of the Star should be dissolved. In spite of this, you will probably form other Orders, you will continue to belong to other organizations searching for Truth. I do not want to belong to any organization of a spiritual kind; please understand this. . . .

If an organization be created for this purpose, it becomes a crutch, a weakness, a bondage, and must cripple the individual, and prevent him from growing, from establishing his uniqueness, which lies in the discovery for himself of that absolute, unconditioned Truth. So that is another reason why I have decided, as I happen to be the Head of the Order, to dissolve it.

This is no magnificent deed, because I do not want followers, and I mean this. The moment you follow someone you cease to follow Truth. I am not concerned whether you pay attention to what I say or not. I want to do a certain thing in the world and I am going to do it with unwavering concentration. I am concerning myself with only one essential thing: to set man free. I desire to free him from all cages, from all fears, and not to found religions, new sects, nor to establish new theories and new philosophies. Then you will naturally ask me why I go the world over, continually speaking. I will tell you for what reason I do this; not because I desire a following, nor because I desire a special group of special disciples. (How men love to be different from their fellow-men, however ridiculous, absurd and trivial their distinctions may be! I do not want to encourage that absurdity.) I have no disciples, no apostles, either on earth or in the realm of spirituality.

Nor is it the lure of money, nor the desire to live a comfortable life, which attracts me. If I wanted to lead a comfortable life I would not come to a Camp or live in a damp country! I am speaking frankly because I want this settled once and for all. I do not want these childish discussions year after year.

A newspaper reporter, who interviewed me, considered it a magnificent act to dissolve an organization in which there were thousands and thousands of members. To him it was a great act because he said: "What will you do afterwards, how will you live? You

will have no following, people will no longer listen to
you." If there are only five people who will listen,
who will live, who have their faces turned towards
eternity, it will be sufficient. Of what use is it to have
thousands who do not understand, who are fully em-
balmed in prejudice, who do not want the new, but
would rather translate the new to suit their own ster-
ile, stagnant selves? . . .

Because I am free, unconditioned, whole, not the
part, not the relative, but the whole Truth that is eternal, I desire those, who seek to understand me, to be
free, not to follow me, not to make out of me a cage
which will become a religion, a sect. Rather should
they be free from all fears—from the fear of religion,
from the fear of salvation, from the fear of spirituality, from the fear of love, from the fear of death,
from the fear of life itself. As an artist paints a picture because he takes delight in that painting, because
it is his self-expression, his glory, his well-being, so I
do this and not because I want any thing from anyone. You are accustomed to authority or to the atmosphere of authority which you think will lead you
to spirituality. You think and hope that another can
by his extraordinary powers—a miracle—transport
you to this realm of eternal freedom which is Happiness. Your whole outlook on life is based on that
authority.

You have listened to me for three years now without any change taking place except in the few. Now
analyze what I am saying, be critical, so that you
may understand thoroughly, fundamentally. . . .

For eighteen years you have been preparing for
this event, for the Coming of The World Teacher.
For eighteen years you have organized, you have
looked for someone who would give a new delight to
your hearts and minds, who would transform your
whole life, who would give you a new understanding;
for someone who would raise you to a new plane of
life, who would give you new encouragement, who
would set you free—and now look what is happening!
Consider, reason with yourselves, and discover in
what way that belief has made you different—not
with the superficial difference of the wearing of a
badge, which is trivial, absurd. In what manner has

such a belief swept away all unessential things of life? That is the only way to judge: in what way are you freer, greater, more dangerous to every society which is based on the false and the unessential? In what way have the members of this organization of the Star become different? . . .

You are all depending for your spirituality on someone else, for your happiness on someone else for your enlightenment on someone else . . . when I say look within yourselves for the enlightenment, for the glory, for the purification, and for the incorruptibility of the self, not one of you is willing to do it. There may be a few, but very, very few. So why have an organization? . . .

No man from outside can make you free; nor can organized worship, nor the immolation of yourselves for a cause, make you free; nor can forming yourselves into an organization, nor throwing yourselves into work, make you free. You use a typewriter to write letters, but you do not put it on an altar and worship it. But that is what you are doing when organizations become your chief concern. "How many members are there in it?" That is the first question I am asked by all newspaper reporters. "How many followers have you? By their number we shall judge whether what you say is true or false." I do not know how many there are. I am not concerned with that. If there were even one man who had been set free, that were enough. . . .

Again, you have the idea that only certain people hold the key to the Kingdom of Happiness. No one holds it. No one has the authority to hold that key. That key is your own self and in the development and the purification and in the incorruptibility of that self alone is the Kingdom of Eternity. . . .

You have been accustomed to being told how far you have advanced, what is your spiritual status. How childish! Who but yourself can tell you if you are incorruptible? . . .

But those who really desire to understand, who are looking to find that which is eternal, without a beginning and without an end, will walk together with greater intensity, will be a danger to everything that is unessential, to unrealities, to shadows. And they will concentrate, they will become the flame, because they understand. Such a body we must create, and that is my purpose. Because of that true friendship—which you do not seem to know—there will be real cooperation on the part of each one. And this not because of authority, not because of salvation, but because you really understand, and hence are capable of living in the eternal. This is a greater thing than all pleasure, than all sacrifice.

So those are some of the reasons why after careful consideration for two years, I have made this decision. It is not from a momentary impulse. I have not been persuaded to it by anyone—I am not persuaded in such things. For two years I have been thinking about this, slowly, carefully, patiently, and I have now decided to disband the Order, as I happen to be its Head. You can form other organizations and expect someone else. With that I am not concerned, nor with creating new cages, new decorations for those cages. My only concern is to set men absolutely, unconditionally free.

The Full Flower

After the dissolution of the Order, the Camps at Ommen and Ojai were open to the public. K, wanting to be free of all responsibilities, resigned from the various Trusts of which he had been a member. Castle Eerde and its estate, except for 400 acres on which the Camp stood, were returned to Philip van Pallandt who now had an heir. Philip was reluctant to take them back until K pressed him to do so; Philip refunded all the money that had been spent on conversions and improvements.[1]

Outwardly there was not much change in K's life after the dissolution, though inwardly he was changing continually as he has never ceased to do. As for money he still had the income settled on him for life by Miss Dodge—he has never personally had any other money—and he continued to live at Arya Vihara with Rosalind and Rajagopal when he was at Ojai.

In 1930 K resigned from the Theosophical Society. This became inevitable when barely two months after the dissolution of the Order Mrs. Besant reopened the Esoteric Section throughout the world. Nevertheless K had returned with her to India in October 1929. In Benares, on the way to Adyar, he had received a letter from Lady Emily telling him that she had seen Wedgwood in London who maintained that not only had "the Coming gone wrong" but that Mrs. Besant was "non compos," so that when she said that the consciousness of K and the Lord Maitreya were one she could not be relied upon.

I am really amazed at your account [K wrote to Lady Emily from Benares on December 12]. I sup-

---

1 Castle Eerde is now an international Quaker school. The Ommen Camp became a German concentration camp during the war and was never used by K afterwards. It now belongs to a Dutch business organization.

pose they will get together at Adyar & say my personality is in the way, limitations etc. I am interested to
see what C.W.L. does. They are out for my scalp & it
will be fun. In 1925 it was C.W.L. who was ga-ga &
now Amma... I am going to be definite & I don't
care what happens; they can ask me to get out.

At Adyar he found that Leadbeater, who had come from
Sydney for the Convention, had also turned against him
now. There were no more long talks; indeed they hardly
spoke to each other.

> The T.S. Convention is in full swing [he told Lady
> Emily on December 26], & I have to see so many
> people. There are extraordinary things going on and
> it will be impossible to write about them, as I shan't
> have time. I can only say that I am going to get out
> of it all. They are too hopeless. C.W.L. tells Mrs.
> Raja that the Coming has gone wrong & down he
> goes to the meeting & there "our Krishnaji" is in
> prominence. So the game goes on. Amma says to me
> & at meetings, that I am the World Teacher & says
> she will go on with ceremonies etc. etc!! I spoke very
> strongly last Sunday & she was rather upset about it.
> She treats the people like children & they remain chil-
> dren.

With Lady Emily's permission K had shown the account
of her meeting with Wedgwood to Mrs. Besant. "All she
said was 'I wish people were more kind, and strong belief
makes them harsh'," he reported in this same letter of December 26. "I didn't say a thing, it's no good. I am coming
to the conclusion that I must get out of all this rot."
  In the new year of 1930 he was wondering why Lady
Emily should be worried by the divergences of opinion between the T.S. leaders and himself. "Personally I am out
of their society," he wrote, "their quarrels & their politics.
There's something far more important. I want to be concerned entirely with what I am talking about and leave the
T.S. alone. I have said good bye to it. I am *not* writing
this to urge you to do the same thing as I have done."
Lady Emily did not resign from the T.S. until 1936.
  Mrs. Besant, although she was now so reverential to K
that she insisted on sitting on the ground with the rest of

the audience when he spoke instead of on the dais beside him, could not let go of her own guru, the Master Morya, nor understand that the question of whether the Masters existed or not was totally unimportant to K. As for Leadbeater, it was not difficult to explain his change of heart since 1927; then it had still been possible to fit K into the pattern designed for him; now there was no more room for Leadbeater in K's teaching. If the Masters were no longer recognized. Leadbeater, as their chief lieutenant, would lose all his power and prestige.

On leaving India in February 1930 K wrote to Mrs. Besant whom he still addressed as "My own beloved Mother":

> I know and it doesn't matter to me, that C.W.L. is against me and what I am saying but please don't be worried over it. All this is inevitable and in a way necessary. I can't change and I suppose they won't change and hence the conflict. It doesn't matter what a million people say or don't say, I am certain what I am and I am going on my way. So, please, dearest Amma, don't bother or worry about this. Only I hope you are carefully looking after yourself.

After all the years of proclaiming the Coming, of stressing over and over again the danger of rejecting the World Teacher when he came because he was bound to say something wholly new and unexpected, something contrary to most people's preconceived ideas and hopes, it is sad to see how the leaders of Theosophy, one after the other, fell into the trap against which they had so unremittingly warned others. They all published perfectly good reasons for remaining entrenched in their old dugouts. The "Great Ones" with whom Wedgwood was "privileged to have contact" saw the good in all things. Arundale was to declare that just as K was fulfilling his part of the work, so the others were fulfilling their part; he, Arundale, knew many of the Masters personally and had been face to face with the Lord Maitreya, and therefore he knew that he, Arundale, was giving to the world that Theosophy which the "Elder Brethren" would have him give; he would allow K a niche in the Theosophical Pantheon, but no more. Leadbeater was to say that K's teaching was for the average man and not for one "who has our special ad-

vantages," and that in spite of what K said, the Liberal
Catholic Church was an important part of the Teacher's
work because the Lord Maitreya himself had brought it
into being. In answer to the question, "Is Krishnaji the
only channel of the World Teacher?" Leadbeater would
reply, "The World Teacher is looking after all the religions
of the world, which He speaks of as 'My many faiths'. . . .
When He came last time, did the work of the old religions
stop? No." Raja wrote that it was a mystery why every
great religious teacher, even the Buddha, had always
maintained that *his* was the only way; the special value of
Theosophy was to show that all the separate and contradictory revelations were not really separate at all; K's
teaching was one more color in the spectrum, but lovely as
the separate colors were "some of us are seeking the White
Light also. That is to say we are Theosophists." Mrs.
Besant was to state that although K had said, in speaking
against ceremonials, that the man who wishes to be free of
all limitations must put aside all crutches, it was her
business to create crutches for the weak.

In fact they were all claiming to be exceptions, whereas
K had stated in answer to a question as to whether his
teaching was meant for the ordinary men and women of
the world: "Are you the specially chosen few? Then I am
sorry, for I will not speak to the chosen people. . . . What I
am saying is for everyone, including the unfortunate Theosophists."

The conflict for Mrs. Besant must have been very great,
but the twilight of old age was soon to close over her,
whereas for Lady Emily, and hundreds like her, there
were to be years of desolation ahead. They had been
prepared to leave their homes, forsake their husbands,
neglect their children and work themselves to breaking
point for the Lord, both before and after his Coming, and
now it seemed he had no need of them. Lecturing, writing
articles, travelling about as National Representative of the
Order, had given Lady Emily a sense of a valuable life lived
at tremendously high pressure; now she suddenly felt re-
dundant and utterly lost—thrown back on inner resources
that simply were not there. She was a natural devotee, a
follower, without any initiative.

K was back at Ojai in March 1930, and then at Ommen
in July for the first public Camp which attracted many
new people. He now stayed at a house, Henan, near the

Camp or in his hut in the Camp itself. Instead of return-ing to India for the winter, he fulfilled engagements to speak in Athens, Constantinople and Bucharest. He was invited to speak in many new parts of the world after his severance from Theosophy, including South America, and his audiences were to become, increasingly, of a different caliber, people interested in what he had to say, not in what they had been told he *was*.

Ojai again in the spring of 1931 and then back to Om-men for yet another Camp. In August the sad news reached him that Jadu, who had remained in America that year, had died of a stroke in Arizona. He was only thirty-five. "It's awful about Jadu," K wrote to Lady Emily. ". . . It's really too tragic. . . . We are thinning out alright. Nitya & Jadu. It's strange." Yes, the old friends were thinning out—dying or dropping away. But new friends quickly closed the ranks—new followers, new helpers—not of the old type who had accepted his authority and the authority of the Theosophical leaders, but people, with an ever-growing proportion of young, who longed for an entirely new way of living.

K did not go to India in 1931 either as he had been ill. Instead he returned to Ojai in October determined to have a complete rest. The Rajagopals now had a baby daughter, Radha, to whom K became very devoted. In December Rajagopal had to go to Hollywood to have his tonsils re-moved. Rosalind and the baby went with him. While they were away K was left quite alone. He wrote to Raja on December 11, "I am having a good thinking and 'meditat-ing'. In other words Samādi. . . . A reporter asked me if I was the Christ and I said, yes, in the true sense but not in the traditional, accepted sense of the word." On the same day he was writing to Lady Emily from his cottage:

> My being alone like this has given me something tremendous, & it's just what I need. Everything has come, so far in my life, just at the right time. My mind is so serene but concentrated and I am watch-ing it like a cat a mouse. I am really enjoying this solitude & I can't put into words what I am feeling. But I am not deceiving myself either. I go down to Arya Vihara to my meals [presumably he had a cook] & when Rajagopal & his family come, I shall have my food on a tray here. For the next three months, or as

long as I want to, I am going to do this. I can never
be finished but I want to finish with all the super-
ficialities which I have.

In that state of *samadhi* (see p. 168) K seemed to reach
the culmination of all those years of physical agony in the
attainment of an ecstasy that has never left him. It seems
to have been at about this time, when he had reached a
new stage of consciousness, that he lost his memory of the
past almost entirely. This was consistent with his teaching
that memory, except for practical purposes, was a dead-
weight that should not be carried over from one day to
another; death to each day was constant rebirth.

Lady Emily, however, and others like her felt that his
teaching had now become too abstract to be of any real
help to those who were obliged to live in a competitive
world with family responsibilities—that he was, in fact, escaping from life as it actually was. Many people who have
failed to understand him have felt, and still feel, this. He
tried to carry Lady Emily with him in some letters which
are as valid today as they were then:

> I am sorry you feel that way about what I say. The
> ecstasy that I feel is the outcome of this world. I
> wanted to understand, I wanted to conquer sorrow,
> this pain of detachment & attachment, death, continu-
> ity of life, everything that man goes through, every-
> day. I wanted to understand & conquer it. I have. So,
> my ecstasy is real & infinite not an escape. I know the
> way out of this incessant misery and I want to help
> people out of the bog of this sorrow. No, this is not
> an escape. [December 30, 1931.]
>
> It's not an escape when you see that certain things
> are unnecessary for you, not to plunge into them. I
> saw that family life with all its charms & entangle-
> ments was not needed for me, so I kept out of it. . . .
> I have deliberately chosen what to me is neither an
> escape nor an avoidance nor superstition nor fear but
> I saw through this blind complication what I wanted
> was not to be had. Knowing it was not there, why
> should I plunge into this blind rush, jealousies etc?
> [February 4, 1932.]
>
> I am trying to make it clear, trying to build a
> bridge for others to come over, not away from life

but to have more abundantly of life. I feel that, especially the last month, I have realized something that gives greater fullness to life. All this is so badly expressed and by constantly expressing & talking about it one hopes to make it clearer & clearer. I feel this—what I say—is the only help, the way out of all this chaos & misery. Not away but in life itself. Out of the few the mass is created but the few must make the supreme effort. I am trying to incite as many as I can to live rightly & by heaven, there are few alright!! It's all very strange. I can't lose my enthusiasm, on the contrary, it's intense & I want to go & shout & urge people to change & live happily. . . . The more I think of what I have 'realized,' the clearer I can put it & help to build a bridge but that takes time & continual change of phrases, so as to give true meaning. You have no idea how difficult it is to express the inexpressible & what's expressed is not truth. So it goes on! [March 26, 1932.]

These attempts to express the inexpressible in different words and phrases no doubt account for the repetitiveness that is so often criticized in K's talks. If one phrase does not strike home, another may do so, if one word does not convey his meaning, perhaps a synonym of it will. "I wish I could talk to you about what I am feeling. It's not an emptiness, a void, but what's light? Because there's void, emptiness, there's light, intense energy & vitality. So when one's wholly empty of all personal ideas & feelings, then there's the ecstasy of life." (April 6, 1932.)

Lady Emily was filled now with remorse, with a sense of having disappointed him. His response to this was immediate:

Mummy darling, I am not "disappointed" in you— what a thing to say & what a thing for you to write to me. I know what you are going through, but don't worry about it. . . . Only you have to transfer your emphasis. Look, one must have no beliefs or even ideas for they belong to all kinds of reactions & responses. . . . If you are alert, free from ideas, beliefs etc. in the present, then you perceive infinitely & this perception is joy, Truth, anything you like. . . . Knowledge is begotten from all this that you are going through. Now you can honestly say, beliefs are futile, to live in the future is not compatible with understanding & that one can't be a gramophone.... Wisdom is being born in you.... Wisdom has no direction. It is & all false things that come near it are burnt away. What more do you want? [May 31, 1932.]

Lady Emily was more confused than ever when she was told that she must have no beliefs or even ideas.

After the Ojai Camp in May 1932 K toured America. There was no Ommen Camp that year because he had intended to go to Australia until he discovered that Jadu in his absence had committed him to the American tour. Writing in the air between Buffalo and Cleveland he told Lady Emily on September 21,

I am full of something tremendous. I can't tell you in words what it is like, a bubbling joy, a living silence, an intense awareness like a living flame. These are words—in an airplane—but beyond the words there's something very real & profound.... I have been trying my hand at healing, two or three cases and asked them not to say anything about it & it has been pretty good. One lady who was going blind will I think be all right.

K has always been very reticent about his power of healing and has never considered it as more than a sideline to his main work. He does not want to become known as a healer or for people to come to him only for physical healing. In some cases he does not know even the names of the people who claim to have been cured by him. It is different with the clairvoyant powers he possessed at one time. He was so disgusted by Arundale's and Wedgwood's psychic revelations in 1925 that far from using these powers or developing them, he was determined from that time onwards to push them into the background if unable to suppress them altogether. His antipathy to clairvoyance is now even more positive; he regards it as an intrusion of privacy. When people come to him for help he does not want to know more about them than they are willing to reveal to him. As he says, most people come to him wearing a mask; he hopes they will remove the mask, but if not he would no more try to look behind it than to read their private letters.

In November 1932 K went with Rajagopal to India, via England. He had not seen Mrs. Besant since 1930, though he had continued to write her regular loving little notes saying nothing of importance. He was met in Bombay on December 5 by some old friends, including Madame de Manziarly. He denied firmly to reporters a rumor that had been circulating for some time that he and Mrs. Besant had quarrelled, and declared that he was going to Adyar only to see her. When the reporters asked him what he thought about the untouchables entering the temples he shocked them by the unexpected reply that there should be no temples. Mrs. Besant had in fact been ill on and off since a fall at Adyar in July 1931. Her memory was now failing; she had only nine months to live, but she had summoned up all her remaining energy for the annual T.S. Convention of 1932 which Leadbeater as well as K would be attending.

She was now confined to her room. As soon as K arrived at Adyar, having been met at Madras station by Leadbeater, Raja, the Arundales and Shiva Rao, he and Rajagopal went up to see her.

It was really tragic [he was writing to Lady Emily on December 8]. Her voice has changed like an old, old woman's, very thin. She recognized me. She said [to] me, "I am so glad to see you (two or three times she repeated) you look so well. I brought you up, didn't I? She recognized Rajagopal too & a few minutes later said to him "Aren't you glad to see Krishna?" It's really tragic and gave me such a shock to see her in such a state.

And a week later: "I had a long talk with Raja—they have all one phrase by heart—we know, you go your way & we by our way but we shall meet. You say there are no paths, we know there are. One repeats that ad nauseam & there it is. It's pretty hopeless. I believe they didn't want me to come here. There's distinct antagonism but one calls that tolerance, a creation of the intellect, a cursed thing by itself. It's amusing to watch and I am not even emotionally fluttered, as I am completely out of it all—their illusions, fights for power & their so called occultism. Adyar is

lovely but the people are *dead*. I walk every evening along
the beach, an hour. Adyar is not the same. The beauty of
moonlit nights, the palm leaf shadows and the stillness of
the evenings but something has gone out of Adyar." It was
he who had gone out of Adyar.

K saw Mrs. Besant for the last time at the beginning of
May 1933. He had had chicken-pox very badly in April,
caught from the schoolchildren at Benares, and had not
been able to shave because of the sores on his face. He
still had a beard when he went to Adyar to say good-bye
to her before sailing for Europe.

"She recognized me," he wrote: "she said how beautiful
I was with my beard, that I must drink grape juice to get
strong, that I must write to her & tell her how I was, if it
was not too much of a bother, that I must get painted by
a great artist, had I enough money? She was more coher-
ent & very affectionate. Dear Amma, it is tragic to see her
like this. It's all so sad for them all."

Sad, yes, for those left behind on the treadmill of their
traditions, but for K, who had shed the burden of the past,
each day was to be a fresh discovery of joy as with the
passionate energy of freedom he continued on his way as
a teacher of the world.

Postscript

Mrs. Besant died peacefully on September 20, 1933. Leadbeater did not survive her six months. Summoned to Adyar when it was known she was dying, he was present at her deathbed. On his way back to Sydney he died in Perth on March 1. By chance Krishnamurti happened to be in Sydney at the time on a lecture tour and was able to attend his cremation which took place there.

George Arundale succeeded Mrs. Besant as President of the Theosophical Society. He himself died in 1945 after a long illness. Jinarajadasa then became President, a position he held until a year before his death in 1953. As for Wedgwood, he became mentally deranged in 1931 and lived thereafter at the Theosophical Estate, Teckels Park, Camberley, Surrey. He was quite lucid at times but had to be restrained from going out since his madness took the form of taking off his clothes in public. He died in 1951.

After Lady De La Warr's early death in 1930, Miss Dodge moved to Hove; she and Krishnamurti remained devoted to each other until her death five years later. Madame de Manziarly gradually drifted away from Krishnamurti when, a few years before her death in 1956, she became interested in the Ecumenical Church movement.

Lady Emily lived on until 1964, her ninetieth year. She had made up her mind in the thirties that she could no longer understand Krishnamurti's teaching; nevertheless, she never stopped loving and revering him and described him in her autobiography as "the purest and most beautiful being" she had ever come across—"the perfect flower of humanity." He continued to write to her and to see her whenever he came to London. Even after she lost her memory and conversation became impossible he would sit with her for an hour or more on end, holding her hand and chanting to her, which never failed to give her delight.

Mrs. Besant's death severed Krishnamurti's last tie with

Theosophy. From that time onwards he has gone his own way, free from every form of spiritual organization. There are now three Krishnamurti Foundations, one in England, one in India and one in America, but they are of a purely administrative nature; they make arrangements for his talks and for the publication of his books, and help to run the schools he has inspired. There is nothing in the least esoteric about them or about his present teaching.

At eighty, he continues with as much vigor as ever and in far better health to travel between Europe, India and America every year. For the past fourteen years he has held an international summer gathering at Saanen in Switzerland where he gives seven public talks in the course of a fortnight and holds daily discussions with all who wish to take part in them. For the past six years he has also held an autumn gathering at Brockwood Park, a beautiful estate in Hampshire, acquired by the English Foundation. All these talks are freely open to the public. At Saanen those wishing to attend the gathering make their own arrangements for staying in the village, whereas the Brockwood Park talks are attended for the most part by day visitors, but in both places there are ample facilities for camping, so that young people, who form a large proportion of his audience, are put to the minimum of expense.

Recently a great deal of interest in Krishnamurti's teaching has been aroused in the scientific world and for the first time, in October 1974, a group of distinguished physicists and psychologists stayed for ten days at Brockwood Park and held daily discussions with him, the theme of the meeting being "What place has knowledge in the transformation of man and society?"

Education has always been closer to Krishnamurti's heart than anything else. He now has four co-educational schools in India, two of them international, as well as an international co-educational school at Brockwood Park. Ten per cent of the places in all the schools are reserved for non-paying pupils. Krishnamurti visits them all every year for discussions with students and teachers. Although the ordinary academic curriculum is followed in these schools, his main object in starting them is to give children a chance to grow up without any of the national, racial, religious, class and cultural prejudices that build barriers between one human being and another and give rise to so much violence. He himself feels that he belongs everywhere and nowhere in particular.

The chief difficulty about these schools is to find teachers who are themselves free from all prejudice and yet possess the necessary scholastic qualifications. Krishnamurti never loses heart, however. He hopes very soon to start a school near Vancouver, a new school at Ojai, California (he has not been associated with the Happy Valley School there for several years), and he also has plans for more schools in India where education is so desperately needed. He has always been able to fire people with his own enthusiasm and gently overrules the cautious and prudent. Wise friends·tell him regretfully that such and such a school is an impossible dream; there is just not the money for it. He smiles and agrees; yet before long the money has miraculously materialized, a property has been acquired, staff and pupils have been magnetically drawn there and the school is a going concern.

Krishnamurti's teaching has naturally changed considerably in all these years and continues to change as he seeks in new words to express a truth that is so clear to him as his own hand but which it is so difficult to make clear to others. Basically, though, his sole concern is still the same as it was when he dissolved the Order of the Star—to set men psychologically free. He maintains that this freedom can come about only through a complete transformation of the human spirit and that every individual has it in his power to change himself radically, not at some future date but instantaneously. Krishnamurti has never lost the joy that came to him in the early thirties and it is this joy that he longs to share. He knows he has found the cure for sorrow and like a good doctor he would give it to the world.

Chronology

Here, and in the Source Notes, the following initials are used in place of full names:

AB	Annie Besant
CWL	C. W. Leadbeater
EL	Emily Lutyens
GA	George Arundale
K	Krishnamurti
N	Nitya
OSE	Order of the Star in the East
TS	Theosophical Society

1831
August 11 — Birth of H. P. Blavatsky (née von Hahn)

1832
August 2 — Birth of H. S. Olcott

1847
February 17 — Birth of CWL
October 1 — Birth of AB

1875
November 17 — TS inaugurated in America

1882
December — TS headquarters moved to Adyar, Madras

1883
December 16 — CWL joins TS

1884 — CWL meets Mme. Blavatsky and

	travels with her to India, arriving Adyar December 21
1888	
March 15	AB meets Mme Blavatsky
1889	
May 21	AB joins TS
December	CWL returns to England with Raja to become tutor to Mr. Sinnett's son and to GA
1890	AB and CWL meet
1891	
May 8	Death of Mme. Blavatsky
1893	
November	AB first goes to India
1895	
May 11	Birth of K
1897	K nearly dies of malaria
1898	AB founds Central Hindu College, Benares
May 30	Birth of Nitya
1901	K's *Upanyanam*
1905	
January 7	K's mother dies
1906	
May 16	Enquiry in London into accusations of immorality against CWL. CWL resigns from TS
1907	
February 17	Death of H.S. Olcott at Adyar
June	AB elected President of TS

1908
November   CWL reinstated in TS

1909
January 23   Narianiah and family arrive Adyar
February 10   CWL arrives Adyar
April 22   AB leaves Adyar on seven months' tour of Europe and America
August 1   K and N put on probation by Master Kuthumi
November 27   AB arrives back at Adyar and meets K for first time
December 31   K accepted by Master Kuthumi

1910
January 11   K's first Initiation. N accepted
March 6   Document signed by Narianiah transferring guardianship of boys to AB
April   Narianiah complains of CWL's behavior to K
May 29   K meets GA at Adyar for first time
Late October   K starts teaching group at Benares
December   *At the Feet of the Master* published

1911
January 11   Order of the Rising Sun founded by GA which afterwards becomes the International OSE
March 22   Boys leave Adyar with AB en route for Europe
April 22   Boys sail from Bombay with AB and GA
May 5   Party arrive in London. EL meets K for first time
May 28   K makes first speech in London
June 12   Boys with AB in Paris where she speaks at Sorbonne. K sees Master the Count

| October 7 | AB and boys back at Adyar |
| December 28 | People fall at K's feet at Benares while he hands out certificates of membership in OSE. December 28 sacred day thereafter in OSE |

1912

January 1	Quarterly magazine, the *Herald of the Star*, founded in India
January 19	Narianiah signs document at Adyar stating he has no objection to AB taking boys to England to be educated
February 16	AB and boys arrive in England
March 26	Boys at Taormina with CWL, GA and Raja
May 1	K's second Initiation at Taormina
May	AB joins party at Taormina
Late July	Boys back in England with GA and Raja. CWL returns to India after visit to Genoa
August	AB returns to India to fight lawsuit, leaving boys guarded in England for fear of kidnapping
October 24	Narianiah files suit against AB in District Court of Chingleput, later transferred to High Court of Madras
November–April 1913	Boys and Guardians at Old Lodge, Ashdown Forest

1913

March 20	Trial opens after various delays
April 11	AB loses guardianship, but charge of immorality against CWL and K is dismissed
April 15	Judgement delivered. AB ordered to hand over boys on or before May 26 but awarded all costs
April 25	AB granted stay of execution pending appeal

May 17	AB leaves India for England
June 28	Boys to Varengeville, Normandy, with GA, Raja and EL
July 5	AB arrives back at Adyar
Late September	Varengeville party return to London
October	Miss Dodge settles £500 a year on K
October 29	Judgement given on appeal upholding decision of lower court and reversing order as to costs
October 31	Important letter from K to CWL, asking to be relieved of Raja's tutorage
December 1	AB lodges petition to appeal to Judicial Committee of Privy Council in London

1914
January 1	Enlarged international *Herald of the Star* appears as a monthly
Early January	Boys taken secretly to Taormina by GA
January 23	Party back to England
January 27	Stay of execution pending appeal granted by Privy Council in presence of boys
February 20	CWL leaves Adyar for Australia which thereafter becomes his home
March	Boys to Shanklin, Isle of Wight, with GA and Wodehouse
May 5	AB wins her appeal in the Privy Council and is awarded costs
June–June 1915	Boys in Cornwall with GA studying to get into Oxford
August 4	Outbreak of war with Germany

1915
February 18	K writes long letter to CWL in Sydney explaining all his difficulties
Late March	Nitya joins Red Cross in France as dispatch rider

April	K hopes to get to France. Orders uniform
May	K's hopes dashed
June	K leaves Cornwall and works with EL at Endsleigh Palace Hotel, Bloomsbury, which is to be turned into hospital. N returns from France
October	K gives up idea of war work at AB's request. Both boys settle in London to study again for Oxford. Baillie-Weaver becomes important influence in their lives
Early November	GA appointed General Secretary of TS for England and Wales. Thereafter sees little of K
Late November	Boys return to Cornwall with Wodehouse as tutor
1916	
January–February	Difficulties of getting into Oxford
June	Boys to Mr. Sanger, a crammer near Rochester, Kent
July 15	CWL in Sydney consecrated Bishop in Liberal Catholic Church
November 11	Raja's marriage in London to Dorothy Graham
1917	
March	Hope gone of getting into Oxford; decide to try for Cambridge
June	No hope of Cambridge; decide to try for London University
June 21	AB and GA interned at Ootacamund
September 21	AB and GA unconditionally released
November	K tries to cure N's eyes
December	Boys move to flat in London
1918	
January 14	Boys sit for matriculation

March	K hears he has failed; N passed with honors. Both boys return to Sanger's
May 24	Boys leave Sanger's to live in Wimbledon. K attends lectures at London University
June	N's name entered at Lincoln's Inn
September 9	K sits second time for matriculation
October 1	K hears he has failed again. Continues attending lectures at London University
December	Boys leave London to recuperate after influenza
1919	
February	Boys return to London. K attends lectures again at L.U. N reads for the Bar
June 6	AB arrives in London after more than four and a half years
June 14	K presides over OSE meeting, his first work for the Star since AB left England in 1914
July	K plays golf in Scotland and becomes scratch player
October	K and N to Paris with AB. On return to London take flat in St. James's
1920	
January 13	N passes exam. in Constitutional Law and Legal History
January 24	K goes to Paris and stays with Blechs while N remains in London
January	K makes friends with de Manziarlys and Isabelle Mallet, and renews friendship with Ruspoli
February 8	K feels unseen presence. K and Ruspoli unhappy in the same way

February 12	K goes to South of France with Max Wardall
February 28	K returns to Paris to flat on his own
March 24	N prevented by AB from going to India
April	GA marries Rukmini Devi in India
May 6	K has continual thought all day of Lord Buddha, and meditates
July 20	K joins de Manziarlys at Amphion near Geneva
July 25	K's interest reawakened in TS and OSE. He hears Raja has come to London with Rajagopal
July 31	K declares his belief in the Masters but rebels against certain things he finds "monstrously unwholesome" in TS
September 30	K and N return to London and stay in new flat
October	K meets Rajagopal
October 5	N passes exam. in Criminal Law
December 8	K returns to Paris to hotel in Rue de Ponthieu
December 28	K speaks voluntarily at TS meeting

1921	
January 1	K's editorial notes appear again in the *Herald*
Middle of May	N has first hemorrhage
May 22	K doing slight meditation. He decides he must have a philosophy of life
May 29	N goes to Paris to be under Dr. Carton
July 23–26	AB and K attend first World Congress of TS in Paris
July 27–28	First World Congress of OSE. K takes everything into his own hands and astonishes even AB
August 1	K and N go to Boissy-St. Leger

September 4	K and N go to Switzerland with Rajagopal
September 15	K goes to Holland, sees Castle Eerde for first time; meets Helen Knothe and falls in love
October 20	K to London, then to Amsterdam for TS and OSE Conventions
November 19	K and N (believed cured) leave Marseilles for India
December 3	K and N met by AB in Bombay
December 5	The party arrive Adyar
December 14	Honorary doctorate conferred on AB at Benares
December 17	EL arrives Bombay, met by K and N
Late December	K gives one of four Convention lectures at Benares

1922

January 11	K speaks well at Adyar meeting of OSE
Mid January	K and N meet their father
March 22	K and N sail from Colombo with Raja for TS Convention in Sydney
April 12	They arrive Sydney and are met by CWL whom they have not seen since July 1912
April 19	Trouble starts at Convention between CWL and Martyn faction
April 29	Nitya ill again. He and K go to Katoomba
May 9	AB arrives in Sydney
May–June	Uproar in the newspapers
May 15	K, N, Raja and others go voluntarily to Police Department to refute charges of immorality against CWL
Late May	Decision made to return to Europe via San Francisco and stay summer in Ojai Valley
June 1?	Message from Master Kuthumi given to K

July 3	K and N arrive San Francisco
July 6	They arrive Ojai
Middle of July	Nitya very ill again. Rosalind Williams comes to nurse him
August 5	K starts to meditate on Master's message
August 17–20	K undergoes experience that completely changes his life. CWL maintains it is his third Initiation
Late August	K's strange "process" begins

1923

January	K starts writing a monthly message for Self Preparation Groups as well as editorial notes. His first poem published in *Herald*
February	K begins working for OSE, speaking and collecting money
Middle of February	They buy their cottage and six acres with larger house on it
May	K tours America lecturing. AB and CWL unable to account for K's "process"
June 11	K and N arrive in England
July 18-29	TS and OSE Congresses in Vienna; AB unable to be present so K presides over Ose
July 30–September 22	K and N with party of friends at Ehrwald in Austrian Tyrol. K's "process" very painful
Late September	K and party visit Castle Eerde which, with a 5,000-acre estate, is offered to K by Baron van Pallandt
October 22	K and N return to America with Rajagopal
November 8	They reach Ojai and live in the larger house which they name Arya Vihara
November 20	K's "process" starts again and continues until April 11, 1924

1924	
February	K's "process" reaches climax but still continues
April	Dr. Rocke arrives, sent from Sydney by CWL to make sure K's body is not overstrained
April 11	Described by N as a marvellous night for them all. Dr. Rocke present
April 15	AB arrives in England
June 15	K, N and Rajagopal arrive in England
July	AB, K and N go to Paris. First time in an airplane
August 9–15	TS and OSE Conventions at Arnhem, Holland, followed by first Star Camp at Ommen
August 18	K and N with party of friends go to Pergine near Trento
August 21	K's "process" starts again
August 31	K begins talking to party
September 24	"Process" stops
September 28	All leave Pergine
November 2	K and N sail from Venice for Bombay with EL
November 18	Arrival in Bombay where AB meets them
November 24	Arrival at Adyar
1925	
Early January	K goes to Madanapalle to look for suitable site for university. Finds land in the Tettu (afterwards renamed Rishi) Valley which is acquired in 1926
January 26	N, very ill again, goes to Ootacamund with Mme de Manziarly
April 3	K, N, Raja, Rama Rao and EL arrive Sydney, met by CWL
April 7	Specialist sees N and orders him to the mountains
April 10	OSE Convention opens

April 19	K, N, Rosalind, Mrs. Roberts and Rama Rao move up to cottage at Leura
May 8	Many occult advancements at Wesak Festival
May 25	K speaks at The Manor
June 1	Announced in *Herald* that K will not be able to attend Camp at Ommen in August because of N's health
June 2	CWL tells EL that K's "process" is the forcing of the spirillae in each atom
June 24	K, N, Rosalind and Rama Rao leave Sydney for San Francisco
July 15	They arrive Ojai after fearful voyage. N very ill
July 18	AB, EL and Shiva Rao arrive in England
July 24	AB postpones Queen's Hall lectures and goes to Huizen
August 7	GA maintains that K and others have passed fourth Initiation
August 10	GA "brings through" names of ten of the twelve Apostles
August 11	AB announces at Ommen Camp the names of seven of the Apostles
August 14	K and others said by GA to have taken final Initiation. EL returns to London to find letter from K full of unhappy skepticism
August 24	Rajagopal arrives in Ojai, sent by AB to help look after N
September 16	K tactfully declines to confirm Initiations "brought through" at Huizen
October 23	K, Rajagopal and Rosalind arrive in England, leaving Mme. de Manziarly and Rama Rao to look after N. K very unhappy

	and skeptical about Initiations and Apostles
November 2	AB and K address meeting in London without mentioning Apostles
November 8	AB, K, EL, Rajagopal, Rosalind, Shiva Rao, Wedgwood, GA and Rukmini sail from Naples for Colombo
November 13	N dies Ojai 10:37 a.m.
November 14	K hears news of N's death. Ten days of grief follow after which K pulls himself together and writes article about N
November 25	Party arrive Adyar. Rajagopal becomes General Secretary of OSE in N's place
December 3	CWL and party arrive Adyar from Sydney. Soon afterwards AB makes final attempt to get K to acknowledge Apostles
December 21	K officiates for first time at reformed Hindu ritual
December 24–27	TS Convention
December 28	OSE Convention opens. Lord speaks through K at morning meeting
1926	
January	CWL and party return to Sydney
February 6	K goes to Benares to talk to children at TS school
March 25–April 19	K at Ootacamund recovering from food poisoning
May	Many reporters in Bombay from where AB and K sail for England
July 3–19	First gathering at Castle Eerde with 35 people invited by K
July 7	K begins speaking every morning
July 19	All present believe that the Lord has spoken through K for an hour at morning talk

July 24–29	Ommen Camp. Convention opened in presence of AB and Wedgwood
July 27	Lord speaks through K at Camp fire in evening. Wedgwood tells AB it is famous Black Magician speaking through K. AB tells K who declares he will never again speak in public if she believes this. AB very upset
August 19	AB, K, Rosalind and Rajagopal sail for America. Sudden decision of AB's to go with him
August 26	Party arrive New York. Reporters swarm on board
August 27	K interviewed alone by 40 reporters. Makes good impression. Much publicity in Chicago also where they go for Convention after New York
October 3	K takes AB to Ojai for first time
Middle of October	Because of painful swelling in breast K advised by doctors not to go to India as planned. AB decides to stay the winter with him at Ojai
November	AB acquires land in Ojai Valley for K's work
1927	
January	K's "process" starts again with intense pain. He writes poems every day
January 14	AB issues statement to Associated Press of America declaring, "The World Teacher is here"
April 19	AB, K, Rosalind and Rajagopal arrive England
May 25	K goes to Paris where he says at an E.S. meeting that the Masters are only "incidents."

	Shocks and disturbs many people
June 19	A larger gathering assembles at Castle Eerde. After first talk K in bed for ten days with bronchitis
June 24	GA states at meeting in London that he does not agree with AB that K's consciousness is blended with that of the Lord
June 28	EL and Rajagopal draw up new objects for the OSE. The name is changed to Order of the Star, and the *Herald* to the *Star Review*. An *International Star Bulletin* is also proposed
June 30	K resumes his talks. He longs to become a *sanyasi*
July 22	Raja comes from Huizen and depresses gathering
July 23	K speaks in morning reproving Raja
July 24	Raja declares that the gathering has been a failure
July 29	K talks to Star Council, saying he is now certain of his mission
August 2	K gives his first answer to vital question as to whether or not he believes in Masters
August 7–12	Star Camp at Ommen with AB and Raja present. K speaks of his union with the Beloved
August 15	K speaks at Service Camp after AB's departure. Report of talk greatly upsets her
End of August	K goes to Switzerland for some weeks
September 21	K goes to Paris and sits for eight days for the sculptor Antoine Bourdelle
September 30	K flies to London to celebrate with AB her eightieth birthday on October 1

October 3	Rosalind and Rajagopal married in London
October 13	AB and K leave Marseilles for India
October 27	AB and K land in Bombay to face crowd of reporters. AB "bears witness" that a fragment of K's consciousness is now blended with that of the Lord
November	K at Adyar. He gives public lecture in Madras
December 4	CWL arrives Adyar for TS Convention; very reverential towards K. AB and CWL make it clear during Convention that K is the Teacher. AB declares herself "his devoted disciple"

1928

January 11 (Star Day)	GA "in a state" about K, not believing he is the Teacher. First Star Camp at Guindy
January	The Rishi Valley Trust founded
February 1–6	First Camp at Benares
February	K tours India
February 29	K, exhausted, sails with Jadu for Europe. For the first time he gives talks on board at passengers' request
March 31	K gives first public lecture in London at Friends Meeting House
April 3	K sails for New York after visits to Paris, Eerde and London
April	K rests at Ojai
May	K annoyed at being dragged into World Mother movement
May 15	K gives first public talk in America to 16,000 at the Hollywood Bowl
May 21-28	First Star Camp at Ojai on Happy Valley Foundation land

June 14	K with Rajagopal and Jadu arrive in England
June 18	K lectures at Kingsway Hall
June 23	K lectures at Salle Pleyel, Paris
June 27	K broadcasts from Eiffel Tower
June 30	Larger gathering than ever assembles at Eerde. Not so harmonious in consequence
July 8	K's first talk at gathering after a week's illness. AB very ill in London
July 30	K goes to London for night to see AB
August 2–10	Ommen Camp
August 9	AB returns to India
August–September	K at St. Moritz with Raja
October 20	K sails with Jadu for Colombo
Late October	AB closes E.S. throughout the world
November 6	K arrives Adyar
December 7–14	Winter gathering at Benares on lines of Eerde gatherings
December	AB tells K she would like to give up Presidentship of TS to follow him wherever he goes, but her Master will not allow it
December	Land at Rajghat, Benares, acquired for school
December 23–28	TS Convention at Benares. K presides in AB's absence. AB gives instructions no ceremonies to be held during Convention. GA celebrates Mass outside TS Compound
1929	
January	K back at Adyar
January 16	Star Headquarters opened at Adyar
February	K sails for Europe with Jadu
March	K returns to America with Jadu. On the 5th, on board, K writes to Mar de Manziarly, "I will

	never give up anyone but everyone will give me up"
March 19	K at Ojai surprised to find antagonism against him among Star members
May	K at Ojai feels ill and weak. New doctor says he must be careful as constant bronchitis has left his lung weak. Consequently cancels Queen's Hall lectures in London scheduled for July. Newspapers say there is a rift between K and AB which K declares absurd
May 27–June 4	Ojai Camp. K says at a meeting, "I am that full flame which is the glory of life"
June 18	K with Jadu and the Rajagopals arrive London
June 25	K goes to French Alps with Jadu for rest
July 10–August 1	Gathering at Eerde
August 3	K dissolves Order of the Star at Ommen Camp
October 1	E.S. reopened
October 11	K returns to India with AB
October 23	They arrive Bombay and stay few days during which K speaks three times
November 10–17	Camp at Benares
Late November	K tours northern India
December 23–27	TS Convention at Adyar. CWL, who has come from Sydney, turns against K and maintains that "the Coming has gone wrong"
December 26	K writes to EL saying he is going to resign from TS
December 28–January 3	K's Camp at Guindy
1930	
February 1	K leaves Bombay with Jadu for England en route for America
March 21	They arrive Ojai

May 27–June 1	First Camp at Ojai open to the public
June	K tours America
June 26	K sails from New York for England with Rajagopal
July 16–25	Eerde gathering
July 26–August 7	First Ommen Camp open to the public
October 15–November 5	K in France and Switzerland. He has bad bronchitis and cancels Italian tour
November 6–30	K at Taormina, recuperating
December 9–14	K speaks in Athens.
December 17–23	K in Bucharest having come here by boat via Constantinople. He has police guard night and day as his life has been threatened by nationalist Catholic students

1931

January 5–8	K in Jugoslavia
January 10–February	K in Hungary where he falls ill
February 6–10	Last Gathering at Castle Eerde
March 7 and 9	K gives public talks in London at Friends Meeting House
March–May	K tours northern Europe
March 26	Deed of transfer signed returning Eerde to Baron van Pallandt
July 28–August 6	Ommen Camp
August 19	Death of Jadu in Arizona while on a lecture tour
October	K returns to Ojai
December	K in *samadhi* at Ojai

1932

January–April	K speaks every Sunday at the Oak Grove at Ojai
June 2–8	Ojai Camp
July 13–November 6	K tours U.S.A. and Canada
December 7	K and Rajagopal arrive Adyar via England. K sees AB who has lost her memory
December 28–January 4	K's Camp at Guindy following

TS Convention. K does not
speak at Convention

1933

January 7–17	K at Benares where he gives six public talks
January 21–February 27	K tours northern India
March	K ill with chicken-pox in Benares
April	K recuperates near Darjeeling
May 2	K says good-bye to AB at Adyar
May	K sails from Bombay with Rajagopal
September 20	Death of AB

1934

March 1	Death of CWL

Notes and Sources

The same abbreviations are used here as in the Chronology,
with the following additions:

AA	Adyar Archives
Lutyens	*Candles in the Sun* by Lady Emily Lutyens (Hart-Davis, 1957)
M. Lutyens	*To Be Young* by Mary Lutyens (Hart-Davis, 1959)
MLCK	Personal communications from K
MLP	Papers in my possession
Nethercote II	*The Last Four Lives of Annie Besant* by A. N. Nethercote (Hart-Davis, 1961)
SPT	Star Publishing Trust, Ommen
TPH	Theosophical Publishing House, Adyar

General Sources

K's letters to EL: MLP; his other letters: AA
AB's letters to EL: MLP; her other letters: AA
CWL's letters to EL: MLP; his other letters, unless otherwise
    stated: AA
N's letters: AA

Mlle Marcelle de Manziarly has most kindly copied out for
me dates from her diaries and extracts from K's and N's letters
to her, and lent me N's letters to her mother. A *Bibliography
of the Life and Teachings of Jiddu Krishnamurti* by Susanaga
Weeraperuma was published in 1975 by E. L. Brill of Leiden,
Holland. I am greatly indebted to Mr Weeraperuma for giving
me a copy of this work before publication, and also to Mr
Yajnasvara Sastry for the loan of a four-volume dossier he has
compiled consisting of references to the Coming of the World
Teacher in the various Theosophical and Star publications from

1909 to 1934. I wish also to express my thanks to Mrs Radha Burnier for the research she has done at Adyar on my behalf. Above all my thanks are due to Mr Sri Ram, the late President of the Theosophical Society, for permission to use material from the archives at Adyar.

page

1   K's father spelled his name Giddu or Geddu. The name is taken from the village from which the family originally came, though no such village has been traced. It is not invariable to put the family name first among Hindus.

2   Before K's horoscope was found, the date of his birth was variously given as May 4, 11 and 25 (the 25th being the day most often adopted), and although the month never varied, the year for a long time was thought to be 1896 or 1897. These contradictory dates were given by Narianiah. The horoscope was first published by C. Jinarajadasa in the *Theosophist,* April 1932. Copies in Sanskrit and English of the original had been given by Narianiah to the astrologer, S. E. Sutcliffe, who passed them on to Jinarajadasa. The latter presumed that the original, which was in Sanskrit, had been written on palm-leaf as was his own.

4   Narianiah's account of K's childhood was taken down from his dictation in 1911 by Mrs Katherine Taylor, an English Theosophist living at Adyar. The account was signed by Narianiah in the presence of two witnesses, Johann van Manen and Mrs Georgia Gagarin: AA.

5–6 K's memoir. In 1913, at Varengeville in Normandy, K was set to write an essay on "Fifty Years of My Life." He decided to make it autobiographical, intending to add to it year by year. All that was actually written was some 3,500 words giving a sketch of his life up till 1911: AA.

7   K's and N's entrance into Madanapalle High School: a letter dated December 14, 1914, from the headmaster, Retini Rau, in answer to a request from CWL for information as to the date of K's birth. The headmaster was not able to give the correct date but volunteered the information that K had attended the primary school at Madanapalle from September 1902 until the end of the year during one of his father's brief transfers: AA

7   K in his mother's *puja* room: Varengeville memoir.

8   Narianiah's request to be allowed to live at Adyar: letter from him to AB from Madanapalle, dated

page

May 10, 1908, beginning, "Respected and dear Mother." A note on this letter in AB's writing reads: "No, no school. Family of boys inconvenient": AA.

11 Descriptions of the Masters: *The Masters and the Path* by C. W. Leadbeater (TPH, 1925).

13 CWL joining the TS and meeting Mme Blavatsky: *How Theosophy Came to Me* by C. W. Leadbeater (TPH, 1928).

13 CWL carrying a chamber pot: related by N at Pergine in 1924.

16 For a full account of the Leadbeater scandal of 1906 see Nethercote II, pp. 92–8.

17–18 CWL's letters to AB of 1906: *The Evolution of Mrs Besant* by the editor of *Justice*, pp. 144–5 (Madras, 1918). See p. 66n.

19 Olcott's letters to CWL: ibid, pp. 192–4.

22 Wood's account of K's "discovery": *Clairvoyant Investigations by C. W. Leadbeater and 'The Lives of Alcyone'*, some facts described by Ernest Wood; with notes by C. Jinarajadasa (privately printed Adyar, 1947). See also *Theosophical Journal* (England) January–February 1965.

23 K's description of going to CWL's room: Varengeville memoir.

23 K being called stupid at school: MLP.

24 CWL's letters to AB in this chapter were published by Jinarajadasa in the *Theosophist*, June 1932.

25 In 1924 further "Lives of Alcyone" appeared in the *Theosophist*, ranging from 70,000 to 30,275 B.C. In 1935 the complete set of "Lives" was published in two volumes (TPH).

25–26 Shiva Rao on CWL's investigations: MLP.

26 Clarke's account of the early days at Adyar: *The Childhood of Krishnaji* by Captain R. Balfour Clarke (*Australian Theosophist*, August, September, October, December, 1928). An MS by Clarke, entitled "Impressions," gives further details of K's boyhood: AA.

27–28 CWL's method of eliminating fear in K: Lutyens, p. 26.

28 CWL striking K: MLCK.

29 Clarke's statement about *At the Feet of the Master*: *Australian Theosophist*, August 1928, and "Impressions."

29 Mrs Russak's statement about *At the Feet*: *Adyar Bulletin*, November 1912.

30–31 K's meeting with AB: Varengeville memoir.

32–33 K on CWL playing tennis: ibid.

page

34 The Master's instructions were relayed in CWL's letters to AB.

36 Clarke's account of K's Initiation: *Australian Theosophist*, September 1928, and "Impressions."

43 Lakshman's evidence of seeing CWL and K in a compromising position was given in Court (see p. 68). It then came out that it was the nakedness, contrary to caste rules, that had so shocked him; he did not think CWL was "doing anything wrong."

44 A plan of the Headquarters building, published in an album of photographs of Adyar taken by K in 1911, shows the position of CWL's and K's rooms. The parallel bars for K's exercises were in CWL's room. Album: TPH, 1911.

44 K on routine at Adyar: Varengeville memoir.

46 GA's first meeting with K was on May 29, 1910, on AB's veranda at Adyar. GA wrote about it: ". . . never had I looked upon such a face as his— it was the face of the Boy Christ in incarnation before me: *Alcyone and Mizar*, pamphlet by George Arundale, 1912.

46–47 CWL on arranging K's notes for *At the Feet of the Master*: *The Masters and the Path*, pp. 65–6 (TPH, 1925).

48–49 Wodehouse on K: *The Man and His Message* by Lilly Heber, p. 49 (Allen & Unwin, 1931).

50 AB's defence for heralding World Teacher: *Adyar Bulletin*, June 1912.

52 EL's descriptions of K in this chapter: Lutyens, pp. 30–5.

53–54 Account of K's activities in England: his and AB's letters to CWL.

56 Enid Bagnold on AB: *Autobiography* (Heinemann, 1961).

56 K's first speech at Round Table: *Adyar Bulletin*, July 1911.

56–57 Miss Bright on N: *Old Memories and Letters of Mrs. Besant* by Esther Bright (TPH, London, 1936).

58–59 CWL's letters to Ruspoli: *Australian Theosophist*, October 1928.

61 Story given out by Narianiah's supporters: *Occult Investigations* by C. Jinarajadasa (TPH, 1938).

62 EL's recollections in this chapter: Lutyens, pp. 38–9.

63 CWL's account of K's second Initiation: *The Masters and the Path*, pp. 198–209.

63 Message from the Master after K's second Initiation: *Theosophist*, November 1932.

page
63 *Education as Service* (TPH, London, October 1912).
      This little book is based on many of K's own
      experiences at school.
65 EL's description of CWL: MLP.
75 *The Times* of May 8, 1913, p. 7, gave a whole column
      to the case, reporting inaccurately that "Mr Lead-
      beater was certainly a most immoral person."
77 EL's descriptions of Varengeville: Lutyens, pp. 56–60.
87 EL's recollections in this chapter: Lutyens, pp. 63–70.
87 The Master's instructions: summary published in
      Theosophist, November 1932. Part of these instruc-
      tions were that Alcyone and his brother should not
      reside in London, though short visits might be paid
      there when the work required it; wherever possible
      they should combine the hills with the sea as at
      Taormina; if they must be in the British Isles, the
      Channel Islands or the Isle of Wight were preferable,
      though there were many places in Devonshire and
      Cornwall which would do.
88 AB gives K and EL her blessing: EL's diary, May 2,
      1914.
88 The Privy Council case was reported in *The Times*,
      May 5 and 6, 1914. The judgement on May 25 (*The
      Times*, May 26) laid down for the first time for
      India what was the law in England, that when
      minors are of the age of discretion they must be
      represented in all matters vitally affecting them.
89 AB's objection to K eating meat: Lutyens, p. 69.
90–91 Letter from GA to EL: MLP.
91 CWL's pronouncement about the blessing of being
      killed in the War: *Theosophist*, January 1915.
92 Warnings about rejecting the Teacher when he came,
      or failing to recognize him, had appeared as early
      as May 1909 and were reiterated frequently up till
      1930.
92–97 Birthday telegram to CWL: AA.
98 Pronouncement on K's hospital work: *Theosophist in
      Australia*, October 1915.
98 K's efforts to get war work: letter to CWL, January
      11, 1916.
107–8 K's letter to AB about power of healing: January 20,
      1918.
108 K fails exam: EL's diary.
108 Sanger's opinion of K: *Occult Investigations* by C.
      Jinarajadasa (TPH, 1938).
113 Jamnadas on K cleaning his shoes: MLP.
113–14 Mary's description of K and N: M. Lutyens, pp. 43–4.

page
114–15   Jamnadas and N at race meeting: MLP.
121   K going to woman's bedroom: MLCK.
121–22   Details of N's life in this chapter come from his 1920 diary: MLP.
131   CWL on Lord choosing one person from each country: *Theosophy in Australia*, April 1919.
135   N's first haemorrhage: Lutyens, p. 89.
136   N's letter to CWL: August 22, 1921; part of a long joint letter from K, N and Ruspoli. N wrote that K had not seen this part of the letter praising him.
142   EL's impressions of K and N in Indian dress: Lutyens, p. 92.
142   K's lecture at Benares on December 28: *Herald*, September 1922.
142   EL on K's speaking: Lutyens, p. 95.
143   K's talk at Adyar on January 11: *Herald*, June 1922.
144   N's suggestion that he and K should meet their father: letter to AB, October 12, 1921.
144   Narianiah washing his feet: MLCK.
149   N's letter to Ruspoli: from SS *Ventura* en route to San Francisco, July 2, 1922.
150–51   CWL's letter to AB on becoming a bishop: *Extracts from Letters from C. W. Leadbeater to Annie Besant 1916–1923*, compiled by C. Jinarajadasa (TPH, 1952).
152–53   K on uproar at Convention: letter to EL of April 22, 1922.
153   For a full account of the accusations against Wedgwood and CWL see Nethercote II, pp. 317–29.
153   Wedgwood's resignation from TS: official letter to AB, March 7, 1922, ibid., p. 323.
158   K on Berkeley University: letter from Ojai, July 9, 1922.
160   *Abrams' Method of Diagnosis and Treatment*, edited by Sir James Barr (Heinemann, 1925).
160   *The Book of Life, Mind and Body* by Upton Sinclair (New York, 1923–4).
161   K and N sent in their blood to be tested soon after August 12; N had completed the treatment and his blood had been tested again and found free from disease by September 17: K's letters to EL.
162   K's and N's accounts of K's experience: MLP.
172   Mr Warrington's statement: MLP.
175   EL's letter to Ruspoli: October 12, 1922, MLP.
180   For a full description of the force centres in the human body see *The Chakras* by C. W. Leadbeater, illustrated (TPH, 1927).

page
183 K wrote a piece about the spirit of a Red Wood tree: *Herald*, August 1923.

186 EL's recollections of K fainting: Lutyens, p. 103.

186 EL's letter to AB: AA.

187 Two of K's speeches at Vienna Congress: *Herald*, September 1923.

187–88 EL's letters to AB from Ehrwald: AA.

193–94 Message from Master Kuthumi: AA.

202 N's letters to AB about "third eye": March 11, 1924.

203–4 Message to K from Lord Maitreya and Master Kuthumi: AA.

204 K's letter to EL about Dr Rocke's visit: April 26, 1924.

206 Information for this chapter: MLP

208 K's talks at Pergine: *Towards Discipleship* (TPH, 1925).

209 Betty's feeling about K: *A Goldfish Bowl* by Elisabeth Lutyens (Cassell, 1972).

211 The Master's message: Lutyens, p. 112, and K's editorial notes, *Herald*, January 1925.

213 N's love for Mary and recurrence of his illness: M. Lutyens, pp. 125–9.

219 Information for this chapter: MLP.

223 For CWL on spirillae: EL's diary June 2, 1925, and Clarke's "Impressions."

227 Information for this chapter: MLP.

230–31 AB's public announcement of names of apostles: *Herald*, September 1925.

231 GA's speech about World University: ibid.

236 Information for this chapter: MLP.

237 Conditions laid down by GA and Wedgwood for saving N's life: MLCK.

238 Shiva Rao on K's agony after N's death: MLP.

238–39 K's article on N: Editorial Notes, *Herald*, January 1926. At the end of the article K quoted Shelley's *Adonais*. The original MS in pencil: MLP.

239 CWL's remark to K about being an Arhat: Lutyens, p. 140.

241 AB asking K whether he would accept disciples: MLCK.

242 K's talk of December 28, 1925: *Herald*, February 1926.

242 AB also wrote in *Theosophist*, January 1926: "There was no excitement, no flurry, even on the 28th of December when, as our Brother Krishnaji was concluding his 'speech', his sentence was broken into

page

261   Information about Eerde gathering 1927: MLP.

264   The first number of the *Star Review* appeared in January 1928. In America and India it was called the *Star*. Other countries had their own names for it, the best known being the French *Cahiers de l'Etoile*, edited by Mme de Manziarly and Carlo Suarès. EL edited the English version and Mrs Russak Hotchener the American. These magazines stopped publication at the end of 1929. The *International Star Bulletin*, edited by EL and Rajagopal, started publication in November 1927. In 1930 the title was simplified to the *Star Bulletin*. It stopped publication at the end of August 1933.

265   EL's letter to husband: MLP.

265–66   K's rebuke to Raja—"There is a person called Krishnamurti . . .": MLP.

267   *Who Brings the Truth* (SPT, 1928).

269   K's Camp Fire talks at Ommen 1927: *By What Authority* (SPT, 1928).

269   Peter Freedman on Service Camp talk: Nethercote II, p. 397.

271   AB's concern at increasing division between K and TS: EL's diary, October 11, 1927.

271   Bourdelle on K: interview with Antoine Bourdelle in *L'Intransigéant*, March 18, 1928, quoted in English translation in *International Star Bulletin*, April 1928. See also *Une Lettre d'Antoine Bourdelle du Août, 1927: Cahiers de l'Etoile*, January–February 1928.

273   GA's article disagreeing with AB: *Theosophy in India*, October 1927.

274   CWL's tribute to AB on her eightieth birthday: *Theosophy in Australia*, October 1927.

274   AB declares herself K's devoted disciple: Presidential address, *Theosophist*, January 1928.

277   For an account of the World Mother movement and Rukmini Arundale's comments on it see Nethercote II, p. 404.

278   K's talks at Eerde gathering 1928: *Life the Goal* (SPT, 1928).

280   K's opinion of marriage ceremony: *Life at Eerde*, MS by Edmund Kiernan, 1928.

281–82   Questions and answers at the camp meeting on August 6: *Let Understanding Be the Law* (SPT, 1928). K's answers to these questions were considered so important that by a stupendous effort the booklet was published and on sale before the Camp closed on August 10.

page

286   AB had written in her "Watch-Tower Notes" (*Theosophist*, December 1928) that she had wanted to resign the Presidency in order to follow K but that her *"Guru"* had not permitted it.

288   ". . . for the life he pours out so richly . . .": ibid. This quotation begins, "I have placed in his [K's] strong hands the sole management of everything at Benares and all who love me will serve me best by serving him. There will be no ceremonies during the T.S. Convention days . . ."

288   AB upholds GA: *Theosophist*, February 1929.

289   AB on fragment of Lord's consciousness: ibid.

291   K's pronouncement at Ojai Camp: *International Star Bulletin*, July 1929.

293–97   K's speech dissolving the Order of the Star: ibid.: September 1929.

300   Wedgwood's statement about "the Great Ones": Supplement to *Theosophist*, December 1929.

300   GA's pronouncement on "Elder Brethren" and TS Parthenon: *Theososphist*, June 1931 and March 1934.

300   CWL's pronouncements: ibid., December 1931.

301   Raja's pronouncements: *Theosophy in India*, 1931, p. 273, and 1932, p. 328. Raja was also to write in the *Theosophist* for November 1932: "The past cannot be brushed aside as non-existent; thousands in the past sacrificed at our call time, devotion and money for Krishnaji and to help prepare for Krishnaji's later work . . . . The two parts of the work are not separate, *though they seem to be*. What does appearance matter? What is important is that the world should be helped."

301   AB's statement about "crutches": *Theosophy in India*, 1931, p. 273.

305   K's attitude to healing and clairvoyance: MLCK.

307   K's description of his last meeting with AB: letter to EL from the Red Sea, May 17, 1933.

Index

Besant, *Cont.*

GA becoming priest, 228; at Huizen, 228–32; half starved, 229; publicly announces names of apostles, 230–31; goes on journey to Count's castle, 232; presses K to confirm announcements, 235; and N's death, 237, 239–40; and GA, 236, 240; tries to reconcile factions, 241; declares "The Coming has begun," 242; to Europe with K, 246; and "black magician" incident, 253; wants to give up Presidency, 254 , 287; in America with K, 254; buys land at Ojai, 258–59; makes statement "The World Teacher is here," 259; returns to England, 260–61; upset by K, 271, 299–300; feels people are hostile to her, 265, 271; 80th birthday, 262, 271–74; difficulty reconciling K's teaching with Theosophy, 279–80, 288–89; makes statement about K to press, 273; declares herself K's disciple, 274, 280; sponsors World Mother, 276; in Paris with K, 278; health breaks, 278–80; closes Esoteric Section, 285–86; memory fails, 285, 306; instructs no ceremonial to be held at Benares, 288; upholds GA in defying her, 288; rumors on rift with K, 290–91, 306; in England again, 291; reopens Esoteric Section, 298; reverential towards K, 299–300; her business to "create crutches," 301; last illness, 306–7; death, 308

Articles: 112, 136–37, 242, 288–89

Comments on K: 41, 46, 77

Lectures: in America, 12, 254–55; in England, 55–56, 88, 232, 254, 261; at Ommen, 230, 271; in Paris, 55; in Stockholm, 76

Besant, *Cont.*

Letters: to CWL, about Hubert, 26, 44; about K, 26, 34–35, 41, 46–48, 56, 62; about K and N, 77; about Narianiah, 64; to EL, 67, 86; to K, 90–91

Proclaims World Teacher, 12, 55, 89, 92, 242, 254, 259, 261, 269, 273; on the Lord's manifestations, 242; on the blending of K's consciousness with the Lord's, 259, 273–74

Work for India, 7, 14–15, 92, 106, 112, 201

Besant, Sir Walter, 13
Bibby, Joseph, 134
Bible, The, 159
Bindley, Mrs Jean, 112
Black Forces, The, 232, 236, 253
Blavatsky, Mme P. H., 10–13, 21, 33, 35n, 50, 150–51, 154, 284
Blech, Charles, 76, 116, 119, 132, 186, 224
Blech, Mme Zelma, 116–17, 119, 132, 175, 224
Bodhisattva, *see* Maitreya
Boissy-St Leger, 136, 138
Bombay, 51, 61, 141, 213–14, 246, 273, 275–76, 286, 306
Bourdelle, Antoine, 271, 284
Bradlaugh, Charles, 14
Brahmins and Brahminism, 1–3, 7, 33, 59, 185, 214, 241
Bright, Esther, 52, 56, 62, 64, 80, 83, 100, 279; on N, 57; moves to Wimbledon, 110; at Huizen, 228–32; asked to join party to Count's castle, 232
Bright, Mrs Jacob, 52, 57, 62, 64, 83; death, 97
Bruno, Giordano, 55
Buddha, 11, 39, 54, 87, 204, 288, 301; his presence felt, 125, 167–68; 171; K sees, 85; K speaks about, 267, 281; film about, 255; *Buddha's Way of Virtue*, 126; *The Gospel According to Buddha*, 208
Buddhic plane, the, 40, 169
Bude, 89–98, 101–3

Knothe, *Cont.*

nation, of Mrs Meuleman, 172, 177; able to help K, 187–94, 207, 210; put on probation, 191; miserable at separation, 195; CWL on, 177, 199; returns to Europe, 206; in India, 212; in Sydney, 214, 216, 219, 222. 224, 245; accepted, 224; at Adyar, 214, 239; rumour of engagement to K, 255; marriage, 278

Köllerström family, 149

Köllerström, Oscar, 227–33

KRISHNAMURTI, JIDDU; appearance, 22, 27, 44–45, 52, 54, 55, 62, 67, 85, 113–14, 136, 188–89, 191, 222, 224, 225, 241, 252, 307; dress, 45, 51, 52, 113, 114, 124, 141–42, 155, 189, 191, 222, 224, 225, 241, 250, 307; pierced ears, 51; with beard, 246, 307; aura, 22, 52; birthdate and horoscope, 2, 25, 62, 63, 76, 77; chanting, 167, 187, 189, 207, 208, 250, 308; manners, 46–49, 77, 141

Characteristics: accused of being easily influenced, 101–2; affectionate, 48–49, 121; always standing, 62, 114; appears stupid, 22, 23–24, 28; critical and stern, 188, 209–10, 251, 258; dreamy, 4, 62, 77, 125; empty minded, 102; generous, 4, 33; gentle, 33, 107; honest, 90, 176; innocent, 83, 121; lacking conceit, 7, 48–49, 124, 126, 146, 181, 285, 291; lacking confidence, 181; love of children, 83, 245; love of fun, 99, 100, 107, 118, 238; love of machinery, 4, 51, 90; love of nature, 4, 118, 126, 144, 257; mother fixation, 32, 86–87; power of observation, 4; preference for female society, 65, 121; self-effacing, 49, 141; self-possessed, 59; self-reliant, 77; sensitive, 111, 205; shrinking from publici-

KRISHNAMURTI, *Cont.*

ty, 90, 146, 147, 155, 246; shy and timid, 23–24, 31, 54, 55, 147; unaggressive, 101; unambitious, 90; uncompetitive, 112; unselfish, 22, 35, 48, 181

Comments on: antagonism towards him, 279, 290, 306–7; "apostles," 246, 277, 286; authority, 281–82; badges, 224; being a democrat, 111; being a freak, 117, 147, 287; being in love, 124–25, 140, 154, 171–72, 207; beliefs, 304–5; the body, 256, 260; his brain, 92, 103; ceremonial, 136; changing oneself, 209, 303–4; colour prejudice, 147, 157–58; death, 145, 238–39, 303; his destiny, 259; disciples, 279–81; his duty, 81–82, 93; his education, 82, 98–99, 106–7, 129, 133; expressing the inexpressible, 303–4; family life, 200, 203; his father, 41, 144; fear, 27–28; 282; freedom, 262–63; God, 281–82; good and evil, 282; gossip, 94, 143, 154; happiness, 117, 239, 251–52; himself, 98–99, 134–35, 181, a home, 117; horse racing, 115; jealousy, 218, 303; karma, 263; Initiations, 63, 233, 246; internationalism, 107, 110; interpreters, 281; Liberal Catholic Church, 151, 285; liberation, 281–82; life, 280–82, 303–5; living dangerously, 209; loneliness, 200, 290; love, 99, 124–25, 135, 209, 251–52, 282; marriage, 103, 124, 182, 209, 272, 280, 289; mediocrity, 195, 209; his mental condition, 128, 155, 172; his mother, 5–7, 179; mountains, 125, 138, 255, 270; personality, 109, 127, 281–82; possessiveness, 258; his role, 128–29, 146–47; separation, 104; sex, 121; sorrow, 117, 145, 303–4; speaking, 132, 143, 147; suf-

Lutyens, *Cont.*
218; meets CWL, 65; put on probation, 78; incurs CWL's and AB's displeasure, 86; tries to be self-reliant and unselfish, 90, 94, 97; receives reproving letters from AB, 86, 97; edits *Herald*, 87, 89, 110; feels a failure, 109; moves house, 113; and jealousy, 125; accepted, 172, 177, 181; changed, 175; corrects K's MSS, 200–1; on "great adventure," 212; reads aloud, 214, 262; first Initiation, 224; consecrated abbess, 229, 276; second Initiation, 231; sceptical, 236, 240; belief in manifestations, 243–44, 249–50; writes about Ommen Camp, 282–83; resigns from TS, 299; feels desolation, 301; feels K is escaping from life, 303; urged by K to have no beliefs, 304–5; death, 308

Letters: to AB, 186, 187–94; to husband, 65, 257, 265; to Jinarajadasa, 249–50; to Ruspoli, 175

Diary entries, 87, 91, 104, 209, 225, 229, 269–70

Love for K, 80, 88, 97; recollections of K, 52, 54–55, 62, 77–78, 86–87, 90, 141–42, 186

Lutyens, Mary, 78, 137, 206; recollections of K, 113–14, 208, 221–22, 239, 149; love for N, 122, 213, 239; diary entries, 209, 225, 239, 249; private talks with K, 209, 225, 239, 249; voyage to India, 213; unhappiness, 213–14, 218, 222, 225; voyage to Sydney, 217; on CWL, 219–21; put on probation, 224; meets Rosalind, 225; says good-bye to N, 226; feels K and N are one, 239, 249; belief in manifestations, 244, 249, 250; "mothers" K, 257–58; taught to drive by K, 258; rumour of engagement to K, 265;

Lutyens, *Cont.*
told not to be "Marpessa," 284; destroys K's letters, 285; feels K's teaching is unrealistic, 287; marriage, 289

Lutyens, Robert, 54, 65, 83, 85, 92, 95, 181; liked by K, 56, 77, 78, 95; reaction against TS, 96n; edits *Herald*, 134

Lutyens, Ursula, 212, 225, 228

Mackay, John, 149, 153, 215, 219, 221

Madanapalle, 1, 7, 216

Mahachohan, The, 39, 217, 229, 231, 237, 240

Maitreya, Lord (the Bodhisattva, the Christ, the Lord, "Surya," the World Teacher); appearance, 11; house, 11, 36–40; the "vehicle" for, 12, 22, 37n, 41, 60, 63; 230, 241–44, 274; gives K into AB's and CWL's charge, 34–35; decides to take K's body, 41, 60; kind to K, 41; approves *At the Feet of the Master*, 47; his Coming proclaimed, 12, 49–50, 55, 57, 89, 92, 254, 259, 261, 269; dangers of rejecting him, 92, 137, 269, 300–1; and *Herald*, 79, 109–10; may work through several "vehicles," 131–32; and Liberal Catholic Church, 150, 301; and Order for Women, 229, 276; his presence felt, 167–68, 210–11; K's wish to serve, 169, 173–74; K sees, 171, 202; AB on, 34; CWL on, 47, 274, 301; GA on, 273–74, 301; K on, 109, 110, -173, 174, 216–17, 243; K explains, 267–68; N on, 167–69

Messages from brought through: by CWL, 34–35, 47, 109, 110; by GA, 79; by K, 90, 203–4, 210–11

Manifests through K: at Adyar, 241–43; at Benares, 60; at Eerde, 249; at Ommen, 250–53

Index

353

Oxford, 53–55, 89, 90, 91, 96, 98–101, 103, 105–6

Pallandt, Baron Philip van, 138, 194, 207, 261, 272, 280, 298
Paris; K visits, 55, 114, 125, 206, 260, 271, 278, 284, 289, 292; K lives in, 116–25, 131–38; AB visits, 55, 114, 206; N in, 55, 97, 121–23, 125, 206; Sorbonne, 55, 129
Path of Discipleship, *see* Discipleship
Patwardhan, Mr and Mrs V., 187, 207, 213, 245, 246, 248, 261
Pergine, 207–11, 213, 222, 248
Physical elemental, the, 170, 190–92
Prince of Wales (Duke of Windsor), 142
Privy Council, the, 81, 83, 86, 88
Purple Order, the, 48, 63, 165

Race: root-race, 12, 223, 229; sub-race, 12, 91
Raja, *see* Jinarajadasa
Rajagopal, D., 87; character, 196, 247; charm, 247; chants with K, 187, 207; possible rival to K, 127–29, 131; at Boissy and Montesano, 137–38; at Cambridge, 139, 212; types K's MS, 175; at Eerde, 194, 248, 253, 279; an Initiate, 195; at Ojai, 195, 201; 228, 234, 257; returns to Europe, 206; at Pergine, 207, 210; second Initiation, 228; made deacon, 228; as apostle, 230; travels with K, 235–38, 246, 260, 270, 278, 284, 291, 306; draws close to Rosalind Williams, 239–40; celebrates *puja*, 241; appointed Organising Secretary of OSE, 245; in love with Rosalind, 261; draws up new objects for OSE, 264; marriage, 271–72; makes home at Ojai, 276, 284, 298, 302; K talks everything over with, 290; daughter, 302

Rajagopal, Mrs D., *see* Williams
Rajghat, 287–88
Rama Rao, N. S., 207, 208, 213, 216, 217, 220, 226; an Initiate, 224; at Ojai, 233, 235; death, 288*n*
Ratansi, D. M., 122, 123, 125, 141, 213
Riddell, Lord, 265
Rishi Valley Trust, 216*n*, 287
Roberts, Mrs Percy, 220, 261
Roberts, Ruth; appearance, 154, 187; in Sydney, 153, 214–15, 220, 222, 224, 245; at Ehrwald, 187, 188, 191, 205; at Pergine, 207; to India, 212; first Initiation, 224; at Adyar, 239; at Eerde, 261; marriage, 279
Rocke, Dr Mary, 66, 77, 79; at Taormina, 85; in Sydney, 153, 208, 219; and amphitheatre, 218; consecrated abbess, 229, 276; present during "process," 202–3, 204–5; at Eerde, 260–62; death, 272
Rollier, Dr, 139, 140, 153
Ruspoli, Don Fabrizio, 27, 30, 36, 58, 67, 149, 154, 156; in Paris with K, 117, 132, 135; in Geneva, 138; receives copy of K's experience, 175; first Initiation, 224
Russak, Mrs Marie, 19, 27, 29, 32, 36, 141, 144

Sadanand, Jiddu, 8, 22, 144*n*–145*n*
St John, Theodore, 219, 220, 222, 224, 239, 240
Sanat Kumara, *see* King of the World
Sandow, Eugene, 53, 56
Sanger, Rev. John, 103, 106, 108, 109
Sanjeevamma, Jiddu, 1–7, 25; anniversary of her death, 34
Sempill, the Master of, 122
Shakespeare, William, 44, 53, 77, 190
Shamballa, 35, 39, 41
Shanklin, 87
Shaw, G. B., 14
Shelley, P. B., 87

Shiva Rao, Benegal; on CWL's clairvoyance, 25–26; at Bude, 89; first Initiation, 224; travels with AB, 227; at Huizen, 228–33; second Initiation, 231; commended by AB, 233; on N's death, 237–38; mentioned, 99, 213, 214, 237, 306

Sivakamu, Dr, 207

Sinclair, Upton, 160

Sinnett, Alfred Percy, 12–13, 15

Sivaram, Jiddu, 8, 83, 144*n*–145*n*

Sri Krishna, 1, 207, 209, 230, 288; on, 267–68

Star, *see* Order of the Star in the East

Steiner, Rudolph, 50

Stokowski, Mr and Mrs Leopold, 278

Strong, Dr, 160–61, 180, 181, 256, 291

Subrahmanyam, *see* Aiyar

Sutcliffe, G. E., 34

Sydney; CWL in, 149 *et passim*; K in, 149–57, 219–25, 308; scandal in, 154–56; AB in, 154–56; amphitheatre, 218; The Manor, 176; as occult forcing house, 208, 224; life at The Manor, 219–25; spiritual snobbery at, 223

Taormina, 62, 85–86, 120, 167, 181

Telang, Dwarkanath, 144, 201, 286

Telang, P, K., 58–59

Tettemer, Bishop John, 279, 280

Theosophical Society, 7, 9, 10; objects of, 10; Lodges, 50, 52, 152; and finance, 57, 69, 80; membership, 50, 250*n*; rifts in, 17, 50, 128*n*, 151–52; under attack, 65–67; London Headquarters, 52, 56, 57; ceremonial in, 127–28; K resigns from, 298; EL resigns from, 299
Conventions: at Adyar, 8, 19–20, 31*n*, 215, 225, 235, 239 (Jubilee), 241–42, 274, 299, 306; in Amsterdam, 139; at Arnhem, 206; at Benares, 31,

Theosophical Society, *Cont.* 34, 58, 142, 256, 288; in Bombay, 214; in Chicago, 183–84, 255; in London, 206; in Paris, 136; in Sydney, 146, 152, 215, 220; in Vienna, 183, 184, 186
Esoteric Section of, 10, 60, 71, 128*n*, 151–52; K speaks at E.S. meetings, 183, 186, 260; growing division between E.S. and OSE, 263–64, 271, 285–86; AB closes, 285–86; AB reopens, 298

Theosophist, The, 21, 25; AB's articles in, 112, 136–37, 141, 242, 288

Third eye, the, 202

Times, The, 75

Varengeville, 77, 94, 96*n*, 104, 143*n*, 181

Vienna, 183, 186–87

Villiers, Barbara, 143–45, 213

Walton, Bishop, 163, 166

Wardall, Captain Max, 119–21

Warrington, Albert P., 156–60, 177, 261; present during K's experience, 163–67, 171, 172, 174

Wedgwood, J. I., 149–50, 154, 157, 266, 277; accused of immorality, 151–53; and Initiations, 151, 227, 228, 246; at Huizen, 227–32; clairvoyance, 227, 233, 305; at Ommen, 230–31, 250, 251, 253; as apostle, 230–31, 237, 241; and Count's castle, 229, 232; at Adyar, 239–44; and "black magician" incident, 253; declares AB *non compos*, 298–99; in touch with "Great Ones," 300; madness and death, 308

Wesak Festival, the, 203, 206, 223–24

West Side House, 105, 110, 113, 186, 236, 247

Williams, Rosalind; appearance, 159; looks after N, 159, 217, 219, 220, 225–26, 233; present at K's experience, 163–